Lyn Robison

D1476318

SAMS

Teach Yourself

Database
Programming
with Visual C++® 6

in 21 Days

SAMS

A Division of Macmillan Computer Publishing
201 West 103rd St., Indianapolis, Indiana, 46290 USA

Sams Teach Yourself Database Programming with Visual C++® 6 in 21 Days

Copyright © 1999 by Sams Publishing

International Standard Book Number: 0-672-31350-2

Library of Congress Catalog Card Number: 98-85225

Printed in the United States of America

First Printing: November 1998

00   99   98   4   3   2   1

Trademarks

Warning and Disclaimer

EXECUTIVE EDITOR
Bradley L. Jones

ACQUISITIONS EDITORS
Kelly Marshall
Chris Webb

DEVELOPMENT EDITOR
Matt Purcell

MANAGING EDITOR
Jodi Jensen

SENIOR EDITOR
Susan Ross Moore

COPY EDITORS
Kate O. Givens
Kate Talbot

INDEXER
Rebecca Hornyak

PROOFREADER
Eddie Lushbaugh

TECHNICAL EDITOR
Mickey Williams

SOFTWARE DEVELOPMENT SPECIALIST
Dan Scherf

TEAM COORDINATOR
Carol Ackerman

INTERIOR DESIGN
Gary Adair

COVER DESIGN
Aren Howell

LAYOUT TECHNICIAN
Marcia Deboy

Overview

Contents

WEEK 2 IN REVIEW   305

WEEK 3 AT A GLANCE   307

DAY 15 THE ODBC API AND THE MFC ODBC CLASSES   309

DAY 16 THE ULTIMATE DATABASE API: OLE DB   329

About the Authors

Lyn Robison is a career software developer who specializes in database, COM, C++, and Java development on the Windows platform. In addition to software development, Lyn enjoys writing, speaking, and teaching new technologies to technical and nontechnical audiences.

Lyn works as a developer at Webridge Inc., in Portland, Oregon. Webridge is a small software company poised on the edge of greatness.

When he is not working, Lyn enjoys watching college football and playing basketball. He lacks just 12 inches in his vertical leap from being able to slam-dunk the basketball.

You can reach Lyn via email at `LynRobison@aol.com`.

K. David White is a software developer with over 10 years' experience developing control, database, and user interface applications. He has been developing Windows NT applications for the last five years. Dave can be reached at `kdwhite@donet.com`.

Acknowledgments

Writing a book is something that I've always wanted to do. I am very pleased that I have had the opportunity to do so. There are many people who made it possible for me to complete this work and who deserve my thanks.

Many friends and colleagues gave me much needed encouragement. I appreciate their helpful feedback, which kept my motivation from sinking at critical times.

My wife and my three young sons made many sacrifices to give me the time I needed to write. My sons endured the long hours of my absence from them with selflessness and maturity. My wife, Capri, carried the burden of being virtually a single parent while I was holed up in the office, pouring my best efforts into these pages. In addition, Capri produced the line drawings for this book and did some initial editing as well. Without a doubt, her help was instrumental in my completing it.

Tell Us What You Think!

As the reader of this book, *you* are our most important critic and commentator. We value your opinion and want to know what we're doing right, what we could do better, what areas you'd like to see us publish in, and any other words of wisdom you're willing to pass our way.

As the Executive Editor for the Advanced Programming team at Macmillan Computer Publishing, I welcome your comments. You can fax, email, or write me directly to let me know what you did or didn't like about this book—as well as what we can do to make our books stronger.

Please note that I cannot help you with technical problems related to the topic of this book, and that due to the high volume of mail I receive, I might not be able to reply to every message.

When you write, please be sure to include this book's title and author as well as your name and phone or fax number. I will carefully review your comments and share them with the author and editors who worked on the book.

Fax: 317-817-7070

Email: adv_prog@mcp.com

Mail: Bradley L. Jones
          Executive Editor
          Advanced Programming
          Macmillan Computer Publishing
          201 West 103rd Street
          Indianapolis, IN 46290 USA

Introduction

Welcome to *Sams Teach Yourself Database Programming with Visual C++ in 21 Days*. The 21 lessons presented in this book provide C++ developers with a much needed treatise on databases from a C++ programmer's perspective.

C++ Windows developers already possess valuable knowledge of object-oriented programming in the Windows environment. However, many C++ programmers lack knowledge of database technology. Knowledge of database technologies is crucial for building software for business applications, as well as for many scientific applications.

A Windows application that is written in C++ and has a powerful database as its foundation can perform amazing feats. With the advent of multitier architectures, C++ takes on a major role as an excellent language for building server and middle-tier software components. Writing multitier software components frequently involves using C++ with database technology. Having knowledge of C++ alone is often not enough for these modern applications. You need knowledge of C++ database programming if your skills are to be at the forefront of Windows software development.

This book builds on your knowledge of C++ Windows programming by teaching database expertise in a way that you, as a C++ developer, can really take advantage of it.

Here is a brief rundown of what you will learn:

- How to choose the most appropriate database technology for each of your applications
- Evaluations of direct file access, simple record managers, ISAM databases, relational database servers, and object databases
- Database APIs, including ADO, OLEDB, ODBC, and DAO, and how to use them in C++ applications
- Relational database design principles and techniques
- Relational database programming and SQL
- COM programming for building and using software components
- Multitier application development, including Web-based development, and how to build and use Microsoft Transaction Server (MTS) software components in C++
- How to take full advantage of relational database servers, such as SQL Server and Oracle
- How to meld relational databases with object-oriented programming

Who Should Read This Book

This book is designed to teach database programming to intermediate-level C++ Windows developers. If you already know something about C++ Windows programming and want to expand your skills to include database programming, this is your book.

What You Will Need to Use This Book

Most of the programming examples in this book use Visual Studio 6 Enterprise Edition. The Enterprise Edition has built-in tools for relational databases; these tools are very helpful for database programming. You can get by with the Professional Edition of Visual Studio if the Enterprise Edition is not available to you. This book also teaches programming for Microsoft Transaction Server (MTS), Internet Information Server (IIS), and Internet Explorer version 4 (IE4), so you will need these software packages as well. You can use Microsoft's Personal Web Server (PWS) in place of IIS if you like. In terms of operating systems, Windows NT 4.0 makes an excellent platform running MTS and IIS. You probably could make do with Windows 98 instead of Windows NT as long as your machine has sufficient memory to run Visual Studio, MTS, IIS (or PWS), and IE4 simultaneously.

WEEK 1

At a Glance

This week, you learn essential database application programming in Visual C++. You learn the database tools that are included in Visual Studio 6. You write database applications and do some relational database programming. You wrap up the week by learning how to design a good relation database.

- Day 1   You examine the various database technologies at your disposal.
- Day 2   You learn about the relational database tools built into Visual Studio.
- Day 3   You learn about SQL and write some SQL queries to retrieve data from a database.
- Day 4   You write your first database application, using ADO—a C++ database programming API.
- Day 5   You write SQL and C++ code to add, modify, and delete data in relational databases.
- Day 6   You learn client/server programming techniques and the power of relational database servers.
- Day 7   You learn to design your own relational databases.

DAY 1

Choosing the Right
Database Technology

The storing of data is an essential part of most software applications. Virtually all C++ applications have the need to *persist*, or store, data of some kind.

Many applications also need to retrieve data efficiently. These applications typically need to search through data that has been stored in order to retrieve specific information. This need to search for and retrieve data means that an application must use a database.

A variety of database technologies are available to C++ programmers. Today you will explore these database technologies and gain the knowledge you need to choose the appropriate technologies for your applications.

Today you will learn

- How to choose the appropriate database technology for your Visual C++ applications
- The difficulties of trying to invent your own database system

- The different database technologies, including OLE structured storage, record managers (such as Btrieve), desktop databases (such as FoxPro and Access), object databases, and relational database servers (such as Oracle and SQL Server)
- How to take advantage of existing database technology to make your development efforts more productive and successful

In addition to covering these topics, you will see how to write the code for implementing each of the various database technologies available to C++ programmers.

Deciding the Appropriate Database Technology for Your Visual C++ Applications

Choosing the right database technology means finding a technology that fills the requirements of your application.

Without knowing the capabilities of the various database technologies, you can easily choose the wrong one for your particular application. In the following sections, you will learn the capabilities of each database technology.

When choosing a database technology, you need to carefully consider the importance of your application's data. It would be easy to think that the data needs to be used only by your application. However, if you write your application with that thought in mind, you will end up creating an application that has a closed, proprietary database that no one else can use or make sense of.

You might think a closed, proprietary database is okay for your application because your application is the only one that needs access to the data. Don't underestimate the value of the data and the need to access the data through more than just your application.

 Note   If your data is important to you, it's probably important to someone else, who will want access to the data through more than just your application.

Even if you are certain that others will never want to access your data except through your application, what about future implementations of your application? What if your application is Windows executable, and you need to produce a new version of it that runs behind a Web server and provides information to users with Web browsers? Because of the nature of Web development tools, an open, nonproprietary database can enable you to perform this conversion in much less time than a closed, proprietary database.

1

In the end, if you do decide to write an application that has a closed database, you will ultimately shorten the life expectancy of your own application. An application that has an open, accessible database and can interoperate with other databases and applications will sooner or later replace yours.

Now you will go through the process of choosing a database technology for an imaginary application. You will examine each database technology and see what each one has to offer. Through this process, you will learn the capabilities (and limitations) of each database technology and how to choose the most appropriate technology for your applications.

The best way to learn to choose a database is by using an example and applying it to each technology. Let's say that your job is to write an application for a company that sells products through television advertising. The company advertises products such as a vegetable slicing machine, a bamboo steamer, 8-track love songs of the 70s, and so on, and offers them for the low, low price of $19.95. Each time the TV commercial airs, the company's 800 line is flooded with calls from buyers.

The salespeople who take these calls have your application running on their computers. They use your application to enter each order so that the product can be shipped and the buyer's money can be collected.

This sounds easy enough. Your application needs to present a window into which the salesperson can enter the order, and then your application must write the information for the order to a data file. This being said, you might decide it would be easier to create your own database.

Building Your Own Database in C++

A C++ programmer is usually confident of his ability to write software. After all, if you can master a language as complex and powerful as C++, you can no doubt write any software tool you need, including your own database system.

However, because of the maturity of existing database technology, writing your own database is rarely a productive effort. Although an electrical engineer can perhaps build her own cell phone, doing so makes little practical sense. Existing cell phones are plentiful and inexpensive and adhere to standards that enable them to interoperate with cellular networks and other cell phones.

Likewise, a C++ programmer can build his own database system, but doing so makes little practical sense. Existing databases are plentiful and inexpensive and adhere to standards that enable them to interoperate with computer networks and other applications. You should concentrate on building your application, not on building its database.

Listing 1.1 shows what is required to store structured data in a file on disk to create a rudimentary database. To create this application, run Visual C++ and create a new project as a Win32 console application. You can call the new project anything you want. Calling it something like CPPDb would be appropriate. Create a source file in the project, perhaps called main.cpp, and enter the following code into it.

LISTING 1.1. C++ CODE TO WRITE DATA TO A FILE

```
 1:   #include <fstream.h>
 2:
 3:   struct Date
 4:   {
 5:       int iMonth, iDay, iYear;
 6:   };
 7:
 8:   struct Product
 9:   {
10:       int iPartNumber;
11:       char szName[80];
12:       double dPrice;
13:   };
14:
15:   struct Customer
16:   {
17:       int iID;
18:       char szName[50];
19:       char szAddress[50];
20:       char szCity[20];
21:       char szState[20];
22:       char szZip[9];
23:   };
24:
25:   void main()
26:   {
27:       Date dt = { 6, 10, 92 };
28:       Product prod = {122, "Vegamatic", 19.95};
29:       Customer cust = {15, "Seymore Hoskins", "300 Oak St",
                           "Boring", "Oregon", "97203"};
30:       ofstream datafile( "data.dat" , ios::binary );
31:       datafile.write( (char *) &dt, sizeof dt );
32:       datafile.write( (char *) &prod, sizeof prod );
33:       datafile.write( (char *) &cust, sizeof cust );
34:   }
```

Notice a couple of things about this code. First, you can see that data structures are defined in lines 3–23. The structures are used to write data to the file in a predictable way (lines 31–33), in a pattern. Other routines in the application can also use these structures to read the data from the file and make sense of it.

Build the application. You should receive no errors or warnings. When you run the application, it creates a file called data.dat in your application's directory and writes the data to the file. If you open data.dat with a hex file viewer, or even with Notepad.exe, you will see the data in the file.

Defining Metadata

NEW TERM The structures used in Listing 1.1 are a kind of *metadata*, or data about data. This metadata must be defined somewhere, or the data in the file will be unorganized and totally inaccessible.

When building your own C++ database, you define the metadata within your source code. Unfortunately, your C++ source code isn't the best place for the metadata to reside. Anyone who wants to use this data must have access to your source code. This is one of the many limitations to building your own database in C++.

This metadata should, ideally, reside with the data. That way, the data file can be self-describing, and other routines can have easier access to it.

Note Metadata is what makes a database a database. A true database contains a description of its own structure. A database contains both data and metadata.

A C++ Base Class to Handle the Database Work

The other thing to note is that the source code in Listing 1.1 is not very object-oriented.

Using C++, you can write a base class that handles the reading and writing of object data to files on disk. You can call this base class the Persistent class. In the sample application, you can derive an Orders class from the Persistent class, thereby making instances of the Orders class automatically capable of persisting (or saving) themselves to disk.

Sounds great, doesn't it? Unfortunately, C++ has a few limitations that make this Persistent base class approach unworkable. The Persistent base class can't know at runtime how big an object of a derived class is, so it can't persist an object of a derived class to disk. There also can be data members in an object of a derived class that deal with runtime context or contain pointers. It would be very difficult for a Persistent base class to have the intelligence to handle these data members properly.

These problems ultimately mean that you can't write a C++ base class to handle all database work. Some code for persisting data from a class must be contained in the class itself.

Problems with Building Your Own Database

When building your own database in C++, you typically embed the metadata in your source code and must build some code to store and retrieve objects into each and every class that needs persistence.

I haven't talked about how to handle multiple threads and multiple applications accessing the same data file simultaneously. One application can be reading while another is writing, or two can write at the same time and produce garbage in the file. Certainly this would be a common occurrence in our sample application, with multiple salespeople receiving a flood of calls each time a TV commercial airs. Believe me, the source code you need to write to handle the file locking and retrying is not trivial.

For our sample application, building your own database by using C++ and data files on disk forces you to write a lot of code, and no one could make sense of the data.

OLE Structured Storage

Within Microsoft's OLE technology is a technology called *OLE structured storage* (the newer documentation from Microsoft refers to it simply as *structured storage*). OLE structured storage promises to give other applications the potential of exploring the internal structure of your files. OLE structured storage is a storage architecture that enables a file on disk (as well as other storage mediums) to be divided into a hierarchy of storages and streams. Storages are analogous to operating-system directories or subdirectories. Streams are analogous to files in the operating system. These storages and streams can all exist within a single disk file.

Listing 1.2 shows how to create an OLE structured storage file, create a stream within it at the root storage, and write your order information into the stream. The code in Listing 1.2 doesn't check return values for errors to ensure code clarity and brevity.

To create this sample, run Visual C++ and create a new project as a Win32 console application. You can call the new project anything you want. Calling it OLESS might be appropriate. Create a source file in the project, perhaps called main.cpp, and enter the following code into it.

LISTING 1.2.   OLE STRUCTURED STORAGE

```
 1:  #include <windows.h>
 2:  #include <ole2.h>
 3:  struct Date
 4:  {
 5:      int iMonth, iDay, iYear;
 6:  };
 7:
 8:  struct Product
 9:  {
10:      int iPartNumber;
11:      char szName[80];
12:      double dPrice;
13:  };
14:
15:  struct Customer
16:  {
17:      int iID;
18:      char szName[50];
19:      char szAddress[50];
20:      char szCity[20];
21:      char szState[20];
22:      char szZip[9];
23:  };
24:
25:  void main()
26:  {
27:      Date dt = { 6, 10, 92 };
28:      Product prod = {122, "Vegamatic", 19.95};
29:      Customer cust = {15, "Seymore Hoskins", "300 Oak St",
                            "Boring", "Oregon", "97203"};
30:
31:      IStorage * pRootStorage;
32:      IStream * pOrderInfo;
33:
34:      CoInitialize(NULL);
35:
36:      StgCreateDocfile(L"data.dat",
          STGM_CREATE | STGM_READWRITE | STGM_SHARE_EXCLUSIVE,
          0, &pRootStorage);
37:
38:      pRootStorage->CreateStream(L"Order Information",
          STGM_CREATE | STGM_WRITE | STGM_SHARE_EXCLUSIVE,
          0, 0, &pOrderInfo);
39:
40:      pOrderInfo->Write(&dt, sizeof(dt), NULL);
41:      pOrderInfo->Write(&prod, sizeof(prod), NULL);
42:      pOrderInfo->Write(&cust, sizeof(cust), NULL);
43:
44:      pOrderInfo->Release();
```

```
45:        pRootStorage->Release();
46:
47:        CoUninitialize();
48: }
```

Within a single data file, you create a hierarchy of streams and storages (or files and directories). Lines 31 and 32 define pointers to two OLE interfaces (IStorage and IStream). Line 34 calls CoInitialize to initialize the COM libraries. Line 36 calls an API function, StgCreateDocFile, to create the OLE structured storage file. This call creates an instance of IStorage and returns a pointer to it in the last parameter, pRootStorage. Line 38 calls the CreateStream function of the IStorage class through the pRootStorage pointer to create a stream in the root storage. The CreateStream function returns an IStream class and returns a pointer to it in the last parameter, pOrderInfo. Lines 40–42 call the Istream's Write function to write our order data into the stream. Lines 44 and 45 call Release to delete the pOrderInfo and pRootStorage instances. Line 47 uninitializes the COM libraries.

Build the application. You should receive no errors or warnings. When you run the application, it creates an OLE structured storage file called data.dat in your application's directory and writes the data to the file.

You still had to define the metadata for your order information. The metadata for the sample application is too complex for OLE structured storage to represent. You need to be able to specify that an order includes an order date (with month, day, and year), a product (with product number, name, and price), and a customer (with name, address, and so on). Also, you need to be able to specify the data types and lengths. That level of detail cannot be represented using only a hierarchy of streams and storages.

If you use OLE structured storage, another routine or application that wants to open your data file and see the structure of the data won't be able to do so. The only thing it will see is a hierarchy of storages and streams. Other routines and applications still would need access to your source code in order to make sense of your data. Also, OLE structured storage has no inherent file-locking or record-locking capability, so it wouldn't reduce the amount of locking code you would have to write.

OLE structured storage is primarily used by document-centric applications, such as Microsoft Word and Excel, to create data files for documents. Word and Excel files are not self-describing. Any application that wants to access the data in an OLE structured storage file containing Excel data must have knowledge of how the data inside the streams is organized.

If you used OLE structured storage for the sample application, you would still have to write a lot of code and no one else would be able to make sense of your data. This would not be ideal for the database in the sample application.

Record Managers (Btrieve)

Record managers on the market can simplify the data storage piece of the sample application. Let's take a look at a popular record manager, Btrieve, to see what it does.

Btrieve provides a layer of insulation between your application and its data files. In other words, your application doesn't directly talk to the data files. The application talks to Btrieve, and Btrieve talks to the data files.

Btrieve provides an API (application programming interface) for record-based data access from your application. This API enables your application to insert, edit, and delete records from data files. Btrieve also enables your application to search the data files for a certain record, such as an order placed by John Smith on June 1. Your application can tell Btrieve to position its record pointer at this record and read, edit, or delete it.

Listing 1.3 shows the code to open a data file in Btrieve, find a certain record, and display it. This is a code snippet only and will not compile as shown.

LISTING 1.3. BTRIEVE EXAMPLE

```
 1: #define FILE1_NAME "c:\\data.btr"
 2: typedef struct
 3: {
 4:   BTI_LONG  ID;
 5:   BTI_CHAR  FirstName[16];
 6:   BTI_CHAR  LastName[26];
 7:   BTI_CHAR  Street[31];
 8:   BTI_CHAR  City[31];
 9:   BTI_CHAR  State[3];
10:   BTI_CHAR  Zip[11];
11:   BTI_CHAR  Country[21];
12:   BTI_CHAR  Phone[14];
13: } PERSON_STRUCT;
14:
15: typedef struct
16: {
17:   BTI_CHAR networkAndNode[12];
18:   BTI_CHAR applicationID[2];
19:   BTI_WORD threadID;
20: } CLIENT_ID;
21:
```

continues

LISTING 1.3. CONTINUED

```
22:   CLIENT_ID       clientID;
23:   PERSON_STRUCT   personRecord;
24:
25:   strcpy((BTI_CHAR *)keyBuf1, FILE1_NAME);
25:
27:   keyNum  = 0;
28:   dataLen = 0;
29:
30:   status = BTRVID(
            B_OPEN,
            posBlock1,
            dataBuf,
            &dataLen,
            keyBuf1,
            keyNum,
            (BTI_BUFFER_PTR)&clientID);
31:
32:   printf("Btrieve B_OPEN status (c:\\data.btr) = %d\n", status);
33:
34:   /* get the record with key 0 = 263512477 using B_GET_EQUAL */
35:   if (status == B_NO_ERROR)
36:   {
37:     file1Open = TRUE;
38:     memset(&personRecord, 0, sizeof(personRecord));
39:     dataLen = sizeof(personRecord);
40:     personID = 263512477;     /* this is really a social security
                                 ➥number */
41:     *(BTI_LONG BTI_FAR *)&keyBuf1[0] = personID;
42:     keyNum = 0;
43:
44:     status = BTRVID(
            B_GET_EQUAL,
            posBlock1,
            &personRecord,
            &dataLen,
            keyBuf1,
            keyNum,
            (BTI_BUFFER_PTR)&clientID);
45:
46:     printf("Btrieve B_GET_EQUAL status = %d\n", status);
47:     if (status == B_NO_ERROR)
48:     {
49:       printf("\n");
50:       printf("The retrieved record is:\n");
51:       printf("ID:     %ld\n", personRecord.ID);
52:       printf("Name:   %s %s\n", personRecord.FirstName,
                  personRecord.LastName);
53:       printf("Street: %s\n", personRecord.Street);
54:       printf("City:   %s\n", personRecord.City);
```

```
55:          printf("State:   %s\n", personRecord.State);
56:          printf("Zip:     %s\n", personRecord.Zip);
57:          printf("Country: %s\n", personRecord.Country);
58:          printf("Phone:   %s\n", personRecord.Phone);
59:          printf("\n");
60:     }
61: }
```

In Listing 1.3, line 1 defines the data filename. Lines 2–23 define two structures and declare an instance of each. The PERSON_STRUCT structure is the definition of the metadata for a data record. The CLIENT_ID structure is used internally by Btrieve to identify the application. Line 25 copies the filename into a variable. Lines 27 and 28 initialize a couple of variables, and then line 30 uses those variables in a call to the Btrieve record manager API to open the data file.

If there are no problems opening the data file, lines 37–42 initialize some variables to use in searching for a particular record in the data file. Line 44 calls the Btrieve record manager API to find the record. Line 47 tests to see whether the record was found in the data file. If it was, lines 49–59 display the data contained in the record.

Btrieve uses a form of data storage known as the Indexed Sequential Access Method (ISAM). Btrieve ISAM files are a highly advanced version of the data files created in Listing 1.1.

Btrieve can index the data in the data files to enable very fast record searches. Btrieve can also handle record locking, so multiple threads and applications can simultaneously access the data files.

Using a record manager is much easier than writing all that code from scratch. In fact, many commercial software packages use the Btrieve record manager. It provides excellent performance (compared to what you can probably write yourself) and is easy to distribute with a commercial application.

However, record managers such as Btrieve do have limitations and can leave some important database work undone. As you see in Listing 1.3, the metadata is defined in your source code. Btrieve doesn't store the metadata within the ISAM files. A Btrieve data file isn't self-describing. No one else can make sense of a Btrieve data file without some outside knowledge of its structure.

Note

Btrieve provides a way to store metadata in separate files named DDF files. This isn't ideal because the files can be changed or deleted independent of each other. No mechanism ensures that the metadata is accurate or in sync with the actual data.

The Btrieve record manager never makes use of metadata. Btrieve interprets a record in a data file only as a collection of bytes and doesn't recognize discrete pieces of information within a record. To Btrieve, a product number, name, and price don't exist inside a record. The record is simply a collection of bytes. Because Btrieve doesn't use the metadata, the application must handle all information about the format and type of data in a Btrieve data file. Btrieve does nothing to ensure the integrity of the data within a record. Your application must do all the work of validating the data before it's stored in the data file.

Another limitation of a record manager is a lack of set-based operations on the data. The application must touch each and every record that is involved in any given operation. For example, in the sample application, to discover the total sales volume in dollars, the application needs to iterate through the records of all the orders, adding up the sales amount of each one.

Set-based operations, however, like those found in true databases (as opposed to record managers), can enable the application to issue a single command to ask the database for the total sales volume in dollars. You will learn more about set-based operations in the sections "Desktop Databases" and "Relational Database Servers."

Note

Btrieve has produced an open database connectivity (ODBC) driver and database engine that sit on top of the Btrieve record manager and provide set-based operations through an ODBC API. Applications can use this ODBC API to access Btrieve data files. However, the Btrieve ODBC API doesn't provide the same level of performance that the Btrieve record manager API provides.

Using a record manager for the sample application would be easier than creating your own C++ database and easier than using OLE structured storage. The location of the metadata still isn't ideal, however. The lack of integrated metadata can limit the capability of other applications to read the data file. For instance, this might prevent the manager from being able to analyze sales data from the database in a spreadsheet. You need to consider these questions regarding this technology and the sample application: Will the record manager provide sufficient open access to the data for other applications? Will the data file become too large for the record manager to handle? Will the performance of the record manager be fast enough, especially with multiple users over a network?

Desktop Databases (FoxPro and Access)

Desktop databases is a class of database software, sometimes called *ISAM databases* because they use ISAM files. Several desktop databases are on the market. These include Microsoft Access, Microsoft FoxPro, and Borland Paradox. These database products differ from each other in many ways, but they all have certain features and characteristics in common.

Desktop databases store the metadata within their ISAM data files. The data files are self-describing. This enables a variety of applications to readily access the data in desktop databases. Desktop databases have their own languages and data types and include an interpreter to run programs written in their language. You can use the language of a desktop database to build database applications. (These interpreted database languages typically aren't used to build complete commercial applications because of their many limitations.)

The desktop databases are designed to provide standard DBMS (database management system) functionality such as data definition, data manipulation, querying, security, and maintenance. The desktop databases are built specifically to run on personal computers.

C++ programs can use the ODBC (open database connectivity) API to talk to desktop databases. For instance, a C++ program can call ODBC API functions to store and retrieve data in a Microsoft Access database file. You can even use ODBC to send language statements to the Access interpreter (also called the *Jet database engine*) and then retrieve any data that Access (Jet) might return as a result of that operation.

Listing 1.4 shows some ODBC API function calls. This is a code snippet only and will not compile as shown.

LISTING 1.4.   ODBC API FUNCTION CALLS

```
 1:  long        lResult;
 2:  SDWORD      cbResult;
 3:  HSTMT       hstmt;
 4:  CDatabase   mfcdb;
 5:
 6:  mfcdb.OpenEx("DSN=MyDataSource;UID=MyUserLogin;PWD=MyPassword;");
 7:
 8:  AFX_SQL_SYNC(::SQLAllocStmt(mfcdb.m_hdbc,&hstmt));
 9:
10:  AFX_ODBC_CALL(::SQLExecDirect(hstmt, (UCHAR FAR*)
                    "SELECT * FROM Orders",SQL_NTS));
11:
12:  while (::SQLFetch(hstmt) != SQL_NO_DATA_FOUND)
```

continues

LISTING 1.4.   CONTINUED

```
13:  {
14:      ::SQLGetData(hstmt, 1, SQL_C_LONG, &lResult, 0, &cbResult);
15:  }
16:
17:  AFX_SQL_SYNC(::SQLFreeStmt(hstmt,SQL_CLOSE));
18:
19:  mfcdb.Close();
```

Line 4 declares an instance of the MFC CDatabase class. CDatabase encapsulates and simplifies the code for connecting to ODBC databases. Line 6 calls the Cdatabase's OpenEx function to connect to (or open) a database. Line 8 allocates a statement handle, which enables SQL language statements to be sent to the database to be interpreted. Line 10 calls SQLExecDirect to send a SQL statement, "SELECT * FROM Orders", to the database to be interpreted and executed. Lines 12–15 retrieve the information that the database returns as a result of the SQL statement in line 10. Line 14 places the value of the first field in each record that was returned into the lResult variable. Line 17 frees the statement that was allocated in line 8. Line 19 closes the database connection that was opened in line 6.

Desktop databases index the data and use ISAM for fast record searches. Desktop databases can also handle record locking, so multiple threads and applications can access the data files simultaneously.

 Note

A key difference between the ISAM files used by Btrieve and the ISAM files used by desktop databases is that desktop databases store metadata inside the ISAM files with the data. This means other programs can make sense of the data without having to obtain your source code.

Desktop databases provide type checking of the data within the records. Whenever an application sends data to a desktop database, the database checks the values and data types to make sure they are appropriate. Thus, the database itself can help ensure the integrity of the data.

Desktop databases provide set-based operations in their programming model. With a single command, an application can perform operations that affect potentially thousands of records. For example, in the sample application, to discover the total sales volume in dollars, the application need issue only a single command to the database—for example,

SELECT SUM(price) FROM Orders

Desktop databases do have some limitations. The raw performance of desktop databases is generally not as good as the performance of straight record managers such as Btrieve.

Note The Btrieve record manager is lean and fast but doesn't provide the programming functionality and data openness that the desktop databases provide. In choosing between a record manager such as Btrieve or a desktop database, you have to balance your need for execution speed, which a record manager can provide, with your need for speedy development time and data openness, which a desktop database can provide).

Accessing ISAM Data over a LAN

ISAM data files from a desktop database can be accessed from a remote machine over a local area network (LAN). (The machine running the application is usually called the *client* machine, and the machine where the data file resides is usually called the *server* machine.) However, the capacity and efficiency of accessing ISAM files over a LAN is limited.

When an ISAM data file is accessed over a LAN, the data is processed on the client machine. All the data and indexes must travel from the server machine over the network to the client machine to be processed. This is because all the logic for processing the records exists in the application running on the client machine.

Because all the data and indexes must travel over the network, desktop databases can't be used to build high-capacity client/server applications. I talk more about client/server architectures in the section "Relational Database Servers."

Desktop databases are designed to run on personal computers, so their capacity and throughput is limited. The client/server limitations of ISAM files hinder the capacity of desktop databases. The documentation for desktop databases typically specifies that they are limited to a dozen or so concurrent users and to data files of 100MB or so in size.

Using a desktop database for the sample application provides many advantages over creating your own database, using OLE structured storage, or using Btrieve. The programming model for desktop databases is more advanced and requires less code. Desktop databases store the metadata in the data file, so the data can more easily be queried by other applications, such as spreadsheets. However, you need to consider these questions regarding this technology and the sample application: If the application uses a desktop database, will the database run fast enough, especially over a network with multiple users? Will the data file become too large for the desktop database to handle?

For raw speed, a rich programming model, data openness, and client/server capability, you need to use a relational database server. I'll explain more about relational database servers after I talk about object databases.

Object Databases

Primitive database technologies store only raw data (bits and bytes) with no metadata in the data file. Desktop and relational databases store data and metadata together to make the data files self-describing. Object databases go one step further. Object databases store data, and the code to act on that data, in the data file. Several object databases on the market provide a broad range of features and capabilities.

Object databases are typically tied to a particular programming language. C++ object databases directly support the type system of the C++ language. In other words, you can use a C++ object database to store instances of C++ classes right in the database.

Listing 1.5 shows how to use a C++ object database to store product information. This is a code snippet only and will not compile as shown.

LISTING 1.5. AN OBJECT DATABASE

```
 1:  #include <string.h>
 2:
 3:  // Header file for the Object Database
 4:  // Management Group (ODMG) object model.
 5:  #include <odmg.h>
 6:
 7:  // Derive our Product class from d_Object
 8:  // so Product can persist itself in the database.
 9:  class Product : public d_Object
10:  {
11:  public:
12:      int iPartNumber;
13:      char szName[80];
14:      double dPrice;
15:  private:
16:      d_Ref<Product> next;   // For iterating instances of Product
17:                             // in the database.
18:  };
19:
20:  d_Database db;             // Global instance of the object database.
21:  const char * const db_name[] = "Products";
22:
23:  void main()
24:  {
25:      db.Open(db_name);   // Opens the Products database.
```

```
26:     d_Transaction tx;    // Create and begin a transaction.
27:     tx.begin();
28:
29:     // Create a new product instance in the database.
30:     Product *prod = new(&db, "Product") Product;
31:     prod->iPartNumber = 122;
32:     strcpy(prod->szName, "Vegamatic");
33:     prod->dPrice = 19.95;
34:
35:     tx.commit();         // Commit the additions to the db.
36:     db.close();          // Close the db.
37:   }
```

In Listing 1.5, line 5 assumes that the object database vendor has provided a header file called odmg.h, which contains the declarations for the d_Object class. The d_Object class is a C++ base class that enables instances of derived classes to be persisted to the object database. Line 9 derives the Product class from the d_Object class, which enables instances of Product to be persisted. The Product class has a d_Ref<Product> member (line 16). d_Ref<> is a smart pointer class provided by the object database vendor that enables references (or pointers) to objects to be stored in the database.

The new operator in line 30 has been overloaded in d_Object to take a pointer to a d_Database instance as a parameter. The call to new in line 30 creates a persistent instance of Product in the database. Lines 31–33 change the values of the data members in this instance of Product (in the database). Line 35 commits the changes to the database, and line 36 closes the database. As you can see, using an object database, you get database functionality for your C++ objects with very little extra code.

This tight integration with the C++ programming language provides great power for designing and building applications that have complex information models. You can use the full power of C++ with encapsulation, inheritance, and polymorphism to reduce complexity.

If you use an Object DBMS, your application has a database that can handle great complexity. C++ classes enable you to model elaborate data entities and their relationships, and an Object DBMS enables you to store instances of those elaborate C++ classes right in the database. However, object databases have limitations, too. Because object databases are so tightly integrated with the programming language of the application, the data tends not to be open or accessible to other applications.

> **Note**
>
> Some Object DBMS vendors pledge that their object databases support (or will support in the future) open technologies such as COM, CORBA, XML, and ODBC/OLEDB. Support for these technologies will make object databases more open and accessible. However, support for these open technologies is neither universal nor uniform among Object DBMS vendors. So *caveat emptor* (let the buyer beware).

Also, with a C++ object database in a client/server environment, the object functionality executes primarily in the client application. Like desktop databases, C++ object databases will do most of their processing on the client machine. This varies between object database implementations, but object databases tend to be client-centric and do not fully take advantage of the server machine in client/server applications.

Relational database servers, however, tend to be better able to take advantage of client/server architectures. The next section talks about relational database servers in more detail.

Using an object database for the sample application could be easier than using your own database, OLE structured storage, Btrieve record manager, or a desktop database. However, consider these questions regarding this technology and the sample application: Would an object database be overkill for the application? Is the data model sufficiently complex and intricate to require a direct mapping of C++ classes into the database? Would this capability justify the added time you would have to spend researching the capabilities of the various object databases? Would the database be open to other applications? Would the performance with multiple users over a network be sufficient? Would performance degrade significantly as the amount of data in the database increases?

Relational Database Servers (Oracle and SQL Server)

Relational database servers are in some ways similar to desktop databases. Relational database servers have their own programming languages, interpreters, and data types. They integrate data and metadata. C++ programs can talk to them through ODBC. The code in Listing 1.4 operates with a relational database server as well as a desktop database.

> **Note**
>
> C++ applications that use the ODBC API can interoperate with desktop database as well as with relational database servers.

Relational database servers provide the rich functionality and data openness of desktop databases while far exceeding desktop databases and record managers in capacity and throughput. Relational database servers can capitalize on client/server architectures much more than desktop servers, record managers, and object databases. They provide true set-based operations.

Note

With set-based operations, a relational database can process thousands, even millions, of records at the server machine and then send only a small result set to the client computer. Set-based operations are a powerful tool to make your applications highly scalable. Set-based operations at the server enable relational database servers to do the heavy lifting in large client/server applications.

Relational database servers are also built to take advantage of server hardware, such as large amounts of RAM and high-performance disk subsystems. If you put a record manager on a RAID disk system, the record manager probably wouldn't know what to do with it. However, if you put a relational database server on a RAID system, it takes advantage of the RAID drives to provide phenomenal throughput and reliability.

Relational database servers have their downside, too. They tend to be more expensive than record managers and desktop databases. (Of course, some relational database servers are more expensive than others.) Relational database servers also are more difficult to integrate with commercial applications. They might have stringent hardware requirements and complex installation processes. Relational database servers also require the periodic attention of a database administrator to tune and maintain them. This also varies between database servers.

Also, compared to object databases, relational database servers are limited in the complexity of the data model they can support. For an application with a highly complex data model, the process of converting from C++ to the relational database server's type system and language interpreter can be very difficult.

Using a relational database server for the sample application would be easier than using your own database, OLE structured storage, or the Btrieve record manager. However, consider the following questions regarding this technology and the sample application: Would the fact that the relational database might be more time-consuming to implement than other technologies be a problem? Is a relational database overkill for the application? Does the application require the capacity and throughput a relational database server provides? Would the cost of the licensing fees for the database server be prohibitive?

How Do the Database Technologies Compare?

Table 1.1 illustrates the relative strengths and weaknesses of the various database technologies. In Table 1.1, a plus sign (+) indicates a strength of the technology, a minus sign (–) indicates a weakness, a blank indicates no particular strength or weakness, and a question mark (?) indicates that it varies between vendors or implementations of the technology.

- *Openness of the Data* refers to the capability of other routines or applications to make sense of the data file without access to your source code.
- *Complex Data Models* refers to the technology's capability to handle applications that have complex data entities and relationships.
- *Multiuser* refers to the capability of multiple threads, applications, and users to access the data simultaneously.
- *Performance* refers to the speed with which data can be read from and written to the database.
- *Scalability and Capacity* refers to the database's capability to sustain good performance as the amount of data increases.
- *Set-based Operations in Code* indicates whether the technology offers set-based operations in its programming model.
- *Set-based Operations at the Server* refers to the capability of the technology to process data at the server without having to send it all to the client machine to be processed.
- *Embeddable with Your Application* indicates how easy or difficult it would be to ship this technology with a commercial application.
- *Data Validation/Integrity* refers to the database's capability to validate the data to ensure the integrity of the data.
- *Code-to-Functionality Ratio* refers to how much code you have to write compared to the database functionality you get from that code.

TABLE 1.1. HOW DO THE DATABASE TECHNOLOGIES COMPARE?

	C++	OLE SS	Record Mgr	Desktop Db	Object Db	RDBMS Server
Openness of the Data	–	–		+	–?	+

	C++	OLE SS	Record Mgr	Desktop Db	Object Db	RDBMS Server
Complex Data Models	–	–	–		+	
Multiuser	–	–			+?	+
Performance	–	–	+		+?	+
Scalability and Capacity	–	–			+?	+
Set-based Operations in Code	–	–	–	+	+	+
Set-based Operations at the Server	–	–	–	–	–?	+
Embeddable with Your Application	+	+			?	–
Data Validation/ Integrity	–	–	–	+	+	+
Code-to-Functionality Ratio	–	–	–	+	++	+

As you can see from the table, the appropriateness of each of these technologies depends on the requirements of the application. If you need your commercial application to write a small amount of simple data to a temporary file, your own C++ database would probably work fine. If, however, you need to store moderately complex data to a file with multiple threads or multiple applications using it, consider one of the more advanced database technologies.

Summary

Today's database technology offers a broad spectrum of functionality. Choosing the right database technology means finding one that fills the requirements of your application.

In choosing a database technology, don't underestimate the importance of the data. Consider carefully which database technology is the best steward of the data. A database should ensure the data's integrity and provide appropriate open access to the data for other routines and applications, now and in the future.

Q&A

Q **It looks like I will have to learn so much before I can even start using databases. Shouldn't I just write a database myself so that I can get up and running more quickly?**

A For all but the very simplest applications, it doesn't make sense to invent your own database. You must realize that the time you spend writing your database is time spent not writing your application. It's best to learn once how to use real databases and then apply this valuable knowledge over and over.

Q **If I decide to use a desktop database for my application, which one of the desktop databases (Access, Paradox, FoxPro, and so on) should I use?**

A Which desktop database you should use depends on the requirements of your application. Microsoft Access offers one advantage over the other desktop databases, however. Access does the best job of mimicking the functionality of a relational database server: It uses a version of Structured Query Language (SQL), it can have multiple tables per file, and it can store predefined queries.

Q **Doesn't ODBC provide a single API that can be used with all ODBC databases? If my application uses ODBC, why should I care which database is used underneath?**

A The capabilities of the various database technologies differ fundamentally from each other, and these differences are reflected in the way that the technologies implement the ODBC API. Some databases support a superset of the ODBC API, whereas other databases support only a subset of it. Also, some technologies provide excellent performance through ODBC, whereas others provide very poor performance with ODBC. You need to select the database for your application based on the database's capabilities. If you plan to use ODBC, you need to consider how well the database you want to use supports it.

Q **Object databases look like they provide excellent power and flexibility. Why would I use relational database servers when object databases seem to integrate so well with C++?**

A Relational database servers and object databases each have their own strengths and weaknesses. Be aware that object databases are not yet fully mature, and the capabilities of the different object databases vary greatly. Also remember that relational database servers provide open and accessible databases, whereas object databases generally do not. The need for open access to the data shouldn't be underestimated and might outweigh the other areas in which object databases can be superior.

Workshop

The Workshop quiz questions test your understanding of today's material. (The answers appear in Appendix F, "Answers.") The exercises encourage you to apply the information you learned today to real-life situations.

Quiz

1. What are the primary benefits of using a record manager (such as Btrieve) rather than invent your own database routines?

2. What do the desktop databases provide that record managers do not?

3. What are the benefits of using a database technology that provides open, accessible data stores?

4. Which database technologies provide open, accessible data stores?

5. What is the significance of server-side processing of set-based operations in a client/server architecture?

Exercises

1. The code in Listing 1.1 creates a data file that contains order information. Write a program that reads the order data from that file.

2. Decide which database technology would be most appropriate for the sample application described earlier. Create a list of capabilities that the database for this application needs to provide. Justify your decision by comparing the database requirements with the capabilities of the database technology that you have chosen.

DAY **2**

Tools for Database Development in Visual C++ Developer Studio

Today you will learn how to create and manage database applications by using the Visual C++ Professional and Enterprise Editions. With the Visual C++ Professional or Enterprise Editions, you can retrieve data and modify the contents of databases. With the Enterprise Edition, you can also create and modify the structure of the database (the database's metadata).

Today you will

- Learn how to build a perfect database.
- Explore the relational database model inside the Visual C++ Developer Studio.
- Work with the components of a relational database.

How to Build a Perfect Database Every Time

Building a good database is not rocket science. It is, however, computer science. If you can learn C++, you already possess enough computer science savvy to learn the science of building good databases. A good database has a flexible design, speedy performance, and efficient capacity and is adaptable to meet today's, and future, requirements.

Your first design decision is to choose which database model to use for your application. There are several database models to choose from, including flat file, object, and relational.

 Caution   Neglecting to make a definite choice of a database model for your application means that you are choosing to invent your own. Inventing a database model is harder than it looks. If you try to invent your own database model, you will severely handicap your database.

One particular database model offers a unique combination of power, flexibility, and universal acceptance. That model is the relational model.

The relational model enables you to build databases that can be implemented on all popular computing platforms, including mainframes, servers, PCs, and even some handheld machines. Most popular programming languages can communicate with databases that adhere to the relational model.

The relational model also provides enough abstraction to enable you to add elements and features to the database without having to recompile and redistribute the code for the applications that use it. This level of abstraction also enables you and your customers to retrieve combinations of data from the database that you hadn't anticipated needing at the time that the database was created.

Support for the Relational Database Model in the Visual C++ Developer Studio

E.F. Codd, a computer scientist from IBM, first formulated relational theory in 1970. The first commercially available relational database system (RDBMS) was Oracle. Many relational database systems have become commercially available since then. It is interesting to note that the relational database systems commercially available do not fully implement Codd's relational theory.

The relational model is based on *relational calculus,* a complex mathematics, but some fundamental principles of the model make it easy to use. You can get up and running right away with the basics of the relational model and learn the advanced portions of it later as the need arises.

The Visual C++ Professional and Enterprise Editions provide built-in support for the relational database model. You can view and modify the contents of relational databases inside the Visual C++ Developer Studio.

Installing the Database Components for Visual C++

First, you need to make sure that you have installed the necessary Visual C++ database components. These components consist of ODBC drivers and OLE DB providers. To install these (or to verify that they're already installed), run the Visual Studio 6 setup program. Your first screen will look like Figure 2.1.

FIGURE 2.1.

The Visual Studio 6 Setup dialog. Click the Add/Remove button.

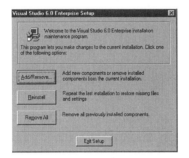

Click the Add/Remove button. You will be presented with the Maintenance setup dialog, shown in Figure 2.2.

FIGURE 2.2.

The Visual Studio 6 Maintenance setup dialog.

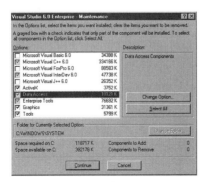

Select Data Access from the list and click the Change Option button.

Select OLEDB Components from the list shown in Figure 2.3 and click the Change Option button.

FIGURE 2.3.

*The Visual Studio 6
Data Access dialog.*

Check the boxes for the OLE DB providers, shown in Figure 2.4, that you will need. If
you are unsure which providers you will need, you can install all of them except those
that you're certain you will not use. You need to install the Microsoft OLEDB Jet
Provider for the examples in this book, so make sure it's checked. Click the OK button to
return to the Data Access dialog shown in Figure 2.5.

FIGURE 2.4.

*The Visual Studio 6
OLEDB Components
dialog.*

FIGURE 2.5.

*The Visual Studio 6
Data Access dialog.*

Select Microsoft ODBC Drivers from the list and click the Change Option button. Your
screen will look like Figure 2.6.

Check the boxes for the ODBC drivers you need. If you're unsure which drivers you
need, install all of them except those that you're certain you will not use. For the examples in this book, you need to install the Microsoft Access ODBC Driver; make sure it's
checked. Click the OK button to return to the Data Access dialog.

FIGURE 2.6.

The Visual Studio 6 Microsoft ODBC Drivers dialog.

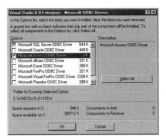

Click the OK button on the Data Access dialog to return to the Maintenance setup dialog. The bottom right of the dialog shows the number of components you are adding. If that number is zero, the database components you need for this book are already installed. You can click the Cancel button and exit the setup program.

If the number of components to add isn't zero, click the Continue button. The setup program will install the OLE DB providers and ODBC drivers you need for this book.

After the OLE DB providers and ODBC drivers are installed, you need to install the author's examples from the CD-ROM included with this book. The examples include a Microsoft Access database file, VCDb.mdb, which is used in examples throughout this book. Follow the installation instructions for the CD in order to install the author's examples.

Setting Up an ODBC Data Source for the Sample Database

You need to set up the sample database VCDb.mdb as an ODBC data source on your machine. This is done with the 32-bit ODBC applet in the Control Panel.

Run the 32-bit ODBC applet, which will display a dialog that enables you to create, edit, and delete ODBC data sources (see Figure 2.7). An ODBC data source is also called a *Data Source Name (DSN)*.

FIGURE 2.7.

The System DSN tab in the 32-bit ODBC Administrator applet.

The first three tabs along the top of the dialog enable you to create DSNs. A User DSN is accessible only on this local machine and only by the current user. A System DSN is accessible on this local machine by any user. A File DSN is a file-based data source that is accessible on a local or remote machine by any user.

Now you will create a System DSN for the sample database. Select the System DSN tab and then click the Add button (see Figures 2.8 and 2.9).

FIGURE 2.8.

Specifying an ODBC driver for a new System DSN. Select the Microsoft Access driver and click the Finish button.

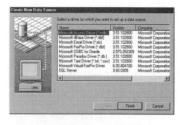

FIGURE 2.9.

The DSN setup for the Microsoft Access database.

Type in a name for the data source (such as OrdersDb). You can also type in a description for the data source. (This description is not used programmatically.)

Click the Select button to specify the path and name of the database file. Make sure to specify the VCDb.mdb file on your hard disk instead of the one on the CD-ROM. The one on the CD is read-only and won't work for the examples in the book.

Click the OK button to create the ODBC data source. To open the VCDb.mdb database inside Visual Studio, you need to create a database project. Run Visual C++ and select the File...New menu. Click the Projects tab (see Figure 2.10) and select Database Project. Specify a directory and a project name and click OK.

FIGURE 2.10.

The New Projects dialog.

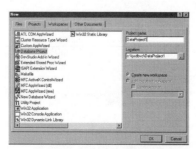

On the Machine Data Source page, you will be prompted to select the data source for this database project, as shown in Figure 2.11.

FIGURE 2.11.

Selecting the ODBC data source for a database project.

Select the ODBC data source you created earlier and click OK. Now click the Data View tab at the bottom left of the Developer Studio main window.

Components of a Relational Database

The Data View in Developer Studio shows the components contained in the database. In the Data View, you can double-click the elements (or click the plus sign [+]) to expand the tree view to display the components of the database. As you can see in Figure 2.12, a relational database can consist of many components and has considerable structure (or metadata).

FIGURE 2.12.

The Visual C++ Data View.

The structure of a relational database might seem like too much overhead, but this structure provides amazing benefits.

As an illustration, you can liken the raw data and complex structure of a relational database to those of a human body. A human body is more than raw chemical elements. A human body contains complex structures such as proteins and enzymes. The abundance of structures is what enables the chemical elements to provide us much more value than they would if they were less highly structured.

A relational database is more than a data file containing raw bits and bytes. A relational database contains a complex structure. As in the human body, the abundance of structure in a relational database is what enables the data to provide so much more value than it would if it were less highly structured.

The structure is where the value lies. The raw elements (and the raw data) provide the building blocks, but the structure is what makes it all valuable.

This is one reason why I advise developers not to attempt building their own database models. The structure of a homemade database model can never be as good as the structure of a relational database. A database that uses a homemade model is far less valuable than it would be if it used the relational model.

Tables in a Relational Database

The Microsoft Access database VCDb.mdb contains four tables and two views. Expand the Data View so that it shows the tables in the database. Double-click the `Products` table in the Data View to see the data inside the table, shown in Figure 2.13.

FIGURE 2.13.

Opening a database table inside Visual C++.

The data in relational databases is arranged in tables. (In relational database parlance, tables are called *relations*. I will refer to them as *tables* throughout this book.) These tables contain rows of like information. The tables can be compared to arrays of structures in C++. The columns in the database table are like the data members of the structure. The rows in the table are like the elements of the array.

It's important to note that database tables are not like arrays of unions in C++. As you might know, a *union* is a user-defined data type that can hold data of different types at different times. In an array of unions, the number of data members, their types, and their lengths can vary from one element of the array to the next. A database table isn't like that. The number of columns, their type, and their length do not vary from row to row.

In relational database parlance, the process of creating tables of like information is called *normalization.*

Good table design is fundamental to a good database. If you don't properly design your tables, your database will not be as functional as it could be. I will explain the rules of thumb for good table design on Day 8, "Utilizing the Capabilities of Database Servers."

Fields in a Relational Database Table

The columns in a database table are called *fields.* (In relational database parlance, fields are called *attributes.*)

A field is the smallest element in a database. Each field in a table has a data type and a length. In the Data View, click the plus sign by the Products table name to see the fields in the table, as in Figure 2.14.

FIGURE 2.14.

Fields in a database table.

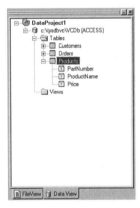

Each field should contain one data element. For instance, rather than have a single field to hold both the first and last name of a customer, a table should have one field for the customer's first name and another field for the last name. This enables easier searching and editing of the database.

Think carefully about the granularity of the data in the fields. Make each field as granular or precise as possible. The usefulness of the database depends on the integrity of its smallest element—the field.

Data Types in Relational Database Systems

As I described on Day 1, "Choosing the Right Database Technology," relational databases have their own type systems. This means that the data types in C++ aren't the same as the data types in relational databases.

In the Data View, click the plus sign by a table name to display the fields in the table. Right-click a field name and select Properties from the Context menu (see Figure 2.15). The properties of each field are name, data type, length, and precision. Look at the data types for several fields and note that they're similar to but not the same as C++ data types.

FIGURE 2.15.

The Column Properties window.

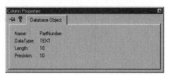

The ODBC API and the OLE DB API (explained on Day 15, "The ODBC API and the MFC ODBC Classes," and Day 16, "The Ultimate Database API: OLE DB") provide a translation facility between C++ data types and database data types.

Many C++ data types readily translate to and from database data types. However, some types do not. When designing your database applications, you need to carefully read the appropriate documentation.

An interesting data value that fields can hold is NULL. In relational databases, NULL does not mean zero. Zero is a value, whereas NULL is undefined.

The use of NULL values is best illustrated with an example. Let's say you have a table that lists men and the color of their hair. The hair color field would contain values such as Brown, Black, Red, and so on. What about men who are bald? Well, that would be an ideal place to use NULL. A bald man's hair color is undefined because he doesn't have hair.

Records in a Relational Database Table

The rows in a database table are called *records*. (In relational database parlance, records are called *tuples*.)

Records can be likened in C++ to elements of an array of structures. When interfacing a C++ program to a relational database, you use records to store instances of C++ classes. The topic of mapping C++ objects to relational databases is discussed in more detail on Day 14, "Legacy Database APIs." For now, the basic idea is that the class definition corresponds to a table, the data members in the class correspond to the fields, and each instance of the class that is created at runtime can be persisted as a record in the table.

The important thing about records in a database is that each record must be unique. It makes no sense to have several records containing the same data. For example, if you had a table that listed your customers, you would not want duplicates. Each customer would be listed once, and only once, in the customer table. If there were duplicate customer records and you needed to change a customer's address, you would not know which record to change.

The requirement that each record be unique can be fulfilled with good database design. Database design is discussed further on Day 8.

Primary Keys in a Relational Database Table

Creating unique records raises the necessity of discussing keys. A *key* is a field, or combination of fields, with which you can uniquely identify a record.

It's easier to identify unique records by using a single field instead of a combination of several fields. That's why you frequently see things such as account numbers, customer numbers, part numbers, and so on.

As you can see in the sample database (and in Figure 2.14), there is a part number field in the Products table. This part number field uniquely identifies each product and is the key field in the Products table.

A good real-life example of a key is a Social Security number. If you know a person's Social Security number, you can identify that person. A Social Security number is a key attribute.

When you design a database, try to think carefully about what field or fields would constitute the key for each table.

Relationships Between Records in Different Tables

A benefit of having a *primary key*, which uniquely identifies each record, is that keys can be used to relate records to each other.

In the sample database, you have one table that lists your customers and another table that lists their orders (see Figure 2.16). The Orders table consists of an order number, the date of purchase, the customer, the product purchased, and the price and payment information.

In the Orders table, you don't need to store all the customer data with every order. That would be redundant. You simply store the customer number with each order. In C++ parlance, think of it as storing a pointer to the customer with each order. That way you can easily tell which customer bought what when, and the database will have no duplicate data.

FIGURE 2.16.

Fields in the sample database.

The customer number is the primary key in your Customers table because it uniquely identifies the customer. The customer number in the Orders table is a foreign key (see Figure 2.17). A *foreign key* is a primary key from another table. Again, in C++ you would think of a foreign key as a pointer to an object.

FIGURE 2.17.

The Orders table with primary and foreign keys.

OrderNumber	OrderDate	CustomerNumber	PartNumber	Price	Shipping	Payment Method
1	11/1/98	4	8TRACK-002	19.95	4	Visa 1921-3893-29!
3	11/20/98	4	8TRACK-001	19.95	4	Visa 1921-3893-29!
2	11/16/98	5	GRAPF-45	19.95	4	COD

The same customer number could appear in the Orders table several times. That's okay. Foreign keys can repeat within a table, but primary keys cannot. The customer number must appear only once in the Customers table but can appear in several records in the Orders table. There is a one-to-many relationship between the customer numbers in the Customers table and the customer numbers in the Orders table.

The process of using primary keys and foreign keys is how the relationships between the data are defined in a relational database. I will go into greater detail on this subject in the next few days.

Summary

The most widely used and accepted database model is the relational model. The relational model provides great openness and flexibility. Applications in addition to a database's original application can access the data. The database is sufficiently abstracted from the application so that the database and the application can be independently updated.

A relational database consists of tables, which are arranged in columns and rows. Each column is called a *field*. Each row is called a *record* and is unique, based on some key field or fields. The records in the tables in a relational database are related to each other, based on key fields that are called *primary* and *foreign keys*.

2

Q&A

Q Does Visual Studio provide support for other database models or technologies in the same way that it supports relational databases?

A No. The database integration that you find inside Visual Studio is based on ODBC. ODBC is designed to work with relational databases only. Therefore, Visual Studio 6 provides direct support of and integration with only relational database technology.

Q What's the difference between Microsoft Access and Jet?

A Jet is the name of the database engine portion of Microsoft Access. You can think of Microsoft Access as a user interface (UI) to the Jet database engine. The Jet database engine is also used in the Access ODBC driver. When you write a C++ application that stores data in an Access MDB file, your application makes calls to the Access ODBC driver, which calls the Jet engine, which talks to the MDB file.

Q Can't I build a relational database by using a record manager such as Btrieve or a desktop database such as FoxPro?

A You can build a set of tables that use primary and foreign keys to relate records to each other, using Btrieve or FoxPro. However, with Btrieve and FoxPro, each table is stored in a separate file. Also, Btrieve and FoxPro make no effort to help you enforce relational rules inside your database as a relational database server (and, to a certain extent, Microsoft Access) does. With Btrieve and FoxPro, you will likely end up with a database that is partly relational and partly your own model, which will be a handicap in the future when you try to add new features or capabilities to your database.

Q **Can't I use a spreadsheet such as Microsoft Excel as a database?**

A Some spreadsheet applications do provide support for database-type functionality. However, this functionality merely consists of storing rows and columns of data in a manner akin to a single table in a relational database. Spreadsheets provide no relational capabilities. Some spreadsheets, such as Microsoft Excel, do enable users to obtain data from relational databases and analyze that data inside the spreadsheet. The data must be formatted as a single table of data, however.

Q **With all the overhead of a relational database, isn't a relational database going to be slow when compared to a lean and mean database that I create myself in C++ or compared to a record manager?**

A A desktop database such as Microsoft Access will probably perform much faster than any database you can write yourself. A relational database server, with its capability to take full advantage of multiprocessor servers and modern disk subsystems, will outperform record managers in handling large quantities of data.

Workshop

The Workshop quiz questions test your understanding of today's material. (The answers appear in Appendix F, "Answers.") The exercises encourage you to apply the information you learned today to real-life situations.

Quiz

1. Which editions of Visual C++ enable viewing and editing data from relational databases inside Visual Studio?

2. What is a DSN?

3. What gives a database its value and why?

4. What is the fundamental requirement for records in a relational database?

5. What mechanism is used to relate records in different tables to one another?

Exercises

1. Open the Orders table in the database project you created today. Note the foreign keys that appear in the table. Open the Customers and Products tables and see primary keys for customers and products. Try to change one of the foreign key values, such as a customer number, to a number that doesn't exist as a primary key. What happens? Does the database help enforce the integrity of the data?

2. Open the Orders table in the database project you created today. Try to change one of the order numbers in the table by typing in letters for the contents of the field.

When you move the cursor off that record, what happens? Does the database validate the data type you tried to enter? (You can press Esc to abort the edit.)

2

DAY 3

Retrieving Data Through Structured Query Language (SQL)

Today you will learn how to capture data from relational databases by using Structured Query Language (SQL). SQL is a powerful language designed specifically for manipulating data.

When you complete this lesson, you will be able to use SQL to transform a relational database's raw data into a rich harvest of useful information. You will appreciate how SQL queries and a properly designed relational database enable you to fulfill requests for information that were unanticipated at the time that the database was first created.

Today you will

- Learn about the Structured Query Language.
- Understand and use the SQL SELECT statement.
- Work with SQL Joins.

- Explore SQL subqueries.
- Use resultsets and cursors.

Structured Query Language

In Day 1, "Choosing the Right Database Technology," you learned that relational databases have their own language interpreter. This language interpreter enables a relational database to interpret and execute commands sent to the database. These commands are written in Structured Query Language, a language specifically designed to work with data that resides in relational databases. The name for the original version of this database language was Sequel. However, that name has been changed to SQL.

Note

> When referring to the SQL language, the word SQL should be pronounced *ess-que-ell* instead of *sequel*. The *sequel* pronunciation is sometimes used when referring to Microsoft SQL Server and Sybase SQL Server. However, when talking about the SQL language, use *ess-que-ell*.

Just as there is a standard for the C++ language, there is a standard for SQL. The most recent version of the SQL standard is SQL-92 (ANSI Document Number X3.135-1992). Relational databases use SQL. Each database vendor implements the SQL standard in its database but then adds its own extensions. For instance, the ANSI SQL used in Microsoft SQL Server is essentially the same as the ANSI SQL used in Oracle. However, SQL Server and Oracle each add their own custom extensions to the language.

SQL is not a procedural language. It's not like C++ or BASIC. In fact, SQL is probably unlike any programming language you have ever seen. SQL is built to deal with sets of records. These records can come from a table or from multiple tables inside a relational database.

With SQL, the whole idea is to collect a set of records that match the criteria you specify and then to perform some operation on these records. SQL has an almost English-like syntax (but with no accent). SQL statements typically have a verb, which indicates the action to be taken—a command such as SELECT, UPDATE, DELETE, or INSERT. The most common operation is to retrieve (or SELECT) records.

The SQL SELECT Statement

The SQL SELECT statement enables you to retrieve information from the database. The SELECT statement begins with the SELECT command and is followed by the noun(s) indicating which field(s) you want to SELECT. You can use an asterisk to indicate that you want all the fields. You have to tell the database which table you are talking about, so you include a FROM clause that indicates the table. The basic syntax looks like this:

```
SELECT which fields FROM which table
```

An SQL query selects a set of records that match the criteria you specify. The preceding SELECT statement would select all the records from the table. You can see a SELECT statement like this in action right inside Visual C++.

Open the database project you created in yesterday's lesson (Day 2, "Tools for Database Development in Visual C++ Developer Studio"). Select the Data View tab on the Workspace pane. As you know, this database relates to the sample application mentioned in Day 1—software for taking orders for products advertised on TV commercials. Double-click the Customers table (see Figure 3.1) to open it and view all the records, shown in Figure 3.2.

FIGURE 3.1.

The Visual C++ Data View.

FIGURE 3.2.

The Customers table.

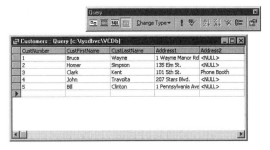

Click the SQL button on the Query toolbar (the third button from the right), and you will see an SQL SELECT statement in the splitter window above the records in the table.

FIGURE 3.3.

The Customers *table with a* SELECT *statement.*

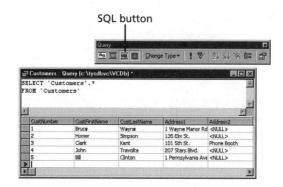

The SELECT statement shown in the window retrieved those records from the database. The SQL statement looks like this:

```
SELECT 'Customers'.*
FROM 'Customers'
```

Visual C++ sent this statement to the database (in this case, the Access ODBC driver and Jet database engine). The database interpreted the SQL statement, read the data from the MDB file, and returned the set of records to Visual C++. Visual C++ displays those records in the window.

You can see that the SQL statement follows the basic syntax for the SELECT statement described earlier. However, this statement uses *tablename.fieldname* syntax to indicate which fields should be selected. The statement says SELECT 'Customers'.* to select all the fields in the Customers table. It places single quotes around the table name in case the table name contains spaces. The statement then says FROM 'Customers' to indicate from which table to select the records.

Because the statement says FROM 'Customers', the 'Customers'.* syntax might seem redundant. (The table name is specified twice in the same statement.) However, the *tablename.fieldname* syntax comes in handy when you have two tables in your FROM clause and the same field name exists in both tables. The *tablename.fieldname* syntax enables you to indicate from which table you want the field.

This SELECT statement selects all the fields from all the records in the table. Try editing the SELECT statement so that you don't get all the fields. Change the 'Customers'.* to 'Customers'.custlastname. Figure 3.4 shows the results.

Press the SQL Check button on the Query toolbar to verify the SQL syntax. This ensures that the syntax of your SQL statement is correct. It sends your SQL statement to the database's SQL interpreter—in this case, the Jet database engine—to see whether it can properly run the statement. If you haven't edited something you should have (or vice versa), you will receive the message that appears in Figure 3.5.

FIGURE 3.4.

Editing the SELECT *statement.*

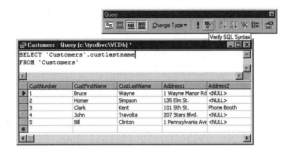

FIGURE 3.5.

The SQL Syntax Verified message box.

Run the SQL statement by pressing the ! (run) button on the Query toolbar. When you run your SELECT statement, you will see only the custlastname field of every record in the Customers table, as in Figure 3.6.

Run button

FIGURE 3.6.

The Last Name field from the Customers *table.*

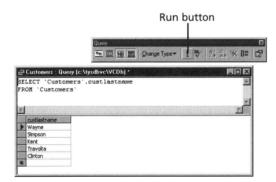

It's disappointing to note that if you misspell the field name, the Jet syntax checker will not catch it. When you run the query, you receive a rather unhelpful error message (see Figure 3.7). Some databases do a better job than others of verifying the syntax.

With certain SQL syntax errors, you receive a more descriptive error message, such as the one in Figure 3.8. However, if you ever need to track down some mysterious bug in your SQL statement, you might feel that this error message isn't descriptive enough either.

FIGURE 3.7.

*The error message
from the Jet/Access
ODBC driver.*

FIGURE 3.8.

*The error message
from the Jet/Access
ODBC driver.*

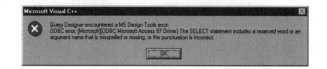

Change the SELECT statement back so that it selects all the fields and run the query again
to see the whole table.

```
SELECT *
FROM Customers
```

The ORDER BY Clause

Wouldn't it be nice to see the customers in alphabetical order? That's very easy to do
with SQL. All you have to do is add an ORDER BY clause to the SELECT statement, like
this:

```
SELECT *
FROM Customers
ORDER BY custlastname
```

When you run this query, you will see all the customer records, ordered by the
CustLastName field (see Figure 3.9).

FIGURE 3.9.

*Customer names in
order by last name.*

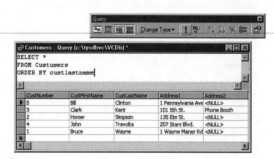

You can select the customers in reverse alphabetical order by adding DESC to the end of
the ORDER BY clause. Observe the results in Figure 3.10.

Figure 3.10.

Customer names descending in order by last name.

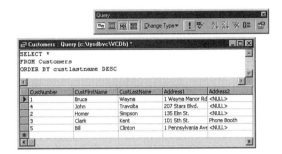

The WHERE Clause

With SQL SELECT statements, you can collect a set of records that fit specific criteria. The SELECT statements you have used so far select all the records. That's pretty broad criteria. To narrow that down, you add a predicate to the SQL statement. The predicate takes the form of a WHERE clause that indicates which records to select. Edit the SELECT statement to include a WHERE clause, like this:

```
SELECT 'Customers'.*
FROM 'Customers'
WHERE custnumber = 2
```

You can type a lowercase WHERE. When you click the button to check the SQL syntax, this will convert the WHERE to uppercase, as in Figure 3.11. Uppercase letters for SQL keywords are a standard convention.

Figure 3.11.

The customers WHERE CustNumber = 2.

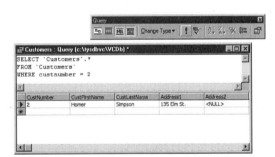

Now change the WHERE clause to find all customers with a last name of Travolta. Use single quotes around Travolta to indicate to the database that it's a string data type. Case sensitivity varies between different relational databases. Don't worry too much about it now. Nothing that you do with this database is case sensitive.

```
SELECT *
FROM Customers
WHERE custlastname = 'travolta'
```

Execute the statement and you will see that there really is only one John Travolta (see Figure 3.12).

FIGURE 3.12.

The customers WHERE
CustLastName =
'Travolta'.

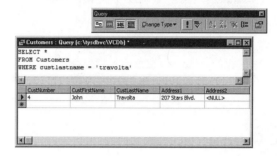

SQL Joins

Wouldn't it be interesting to see what products John Travolta buys from TV advertising? SQL lets us find that information quite easily from our relational database. The first thing to do is look at John's orders. Double-click the Orders table to see all the orders, as shown in Figure 3.13.

FIGURE 3.13.

The Orders *table.*

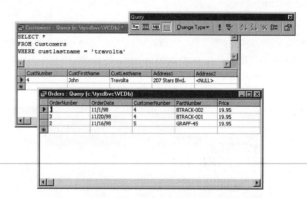

You can see in the Customers table that John Travolta's customer number is 4. You can see a CustomerNumber field in the Orders table. A couple of records in the Orders table contain 4 in the CustomerNumber field. You can rightly assume that those were orders placed by Mr. Travolta.

What you're doing is looking at the primary key in the Customers table, which is the CustNumber field, and comparing it to a foreign key field in the Orders table, which is the `CustomerNumber` field. Is there some way to put this information together without having to eyeball it? Yep, there is. It's called an *SQL join*.

First, you change the SQL query so that you find only the fields you are interested in. Edit and run the query so that you obtain only the first and last name fields of records in which the last name equals Travolta (see Figure 3.14).

FIGURE 3.14.

The first and last name fields for Travolta.

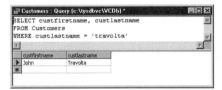

You want to retrieve the part number from the `Orders` table, so add `partnumber` to the list of fields to select. You need to pull information from the `Orders` table, so add the `Orders` table to the `FROM` clause.

```
SELECT custfirstname, custlastname, partnumber
FROM Customers, orders
WHERE custlastname = 'travolta'
```

Here's the nifty part. You want only the records from the `Orders` table that have John Travolta's customer number. You specify this in the `WHERE` clause. You want records in which the `CustomerNumber` field (in the `Orders` table) equals the `CustNumber` field (in the `Customers` table). You still want only records from the `Customers` table that have a last name of Travolta. To do this, you add an `AND` to the `WHERE` clause, like this:

```
WHERE custlastname = 'travolta'
AND customers.custnumber = orders.customernumber
```

Run the query, and the results will look like Figure 3.15.

FIGURE 3.15.

The part numbers purchased by John Travolta.

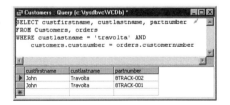

You performed a two-table join to discover the part numbers of the products that John Travolta purchased. However, having part numbers isn't sufficient. You want to know the names of the products he purchased. That means you need information from the Products table, too. Double-click the Products table to open it and view all the products, as in Figure 3.16.

FIGURE 3.16.

The Products *table.*

You know that you want the product name instead of the part number, so change the SELECT statement to select the ProductName field instead of the PartNumber field. You also know that the ProductName field comes from the Products table, so add the Products table to the FROM clause.

You want only product names that have the same part number as the ones you found in the Orders table for John Travolta. You specify this by adding another AND condition to the WHERE clause. Your SELECT statement will look like this:

```
SELECT custfirstname, custlastname, productname
FROM Customers, orders, products
WHERE custlastname = 'travolta' AND
    customers.custnumber = orders.customernumber AND
    orders.partnumber = products.partnumber
```

When you run the query, you can see in Figure 3.17 that Mr. Travolta has a particular penchant for 8-track music from the 70s.

FIGURE 3.17.

The product names purchased by John Travolta.

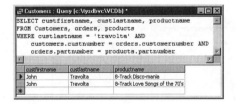

Now that you have the information you need, you can close the query windows. When you close the Customers Query window, you will be prompted to save the query. Because you could probably re-create this query in a heartbeat if necessary, you don't need to save it.

SQL Subqueries

SQL syntax can be elegant and powerful. SQL queries can be nested to perform operations requiring lengthy code in a procedural language. Nested queries are called *subqueries*.

A subquery enables you, with very little code, to find all the customers who have placed orders since a certain date, such as November 11, 1998.

Open a query window for the Orders table by double-clicking the Orders table in the Data View. Click the SQL button to view the SELECT statement that retrieved the records (see Figure 3.18).

FIGURE 3.18.

The Orders *table.*

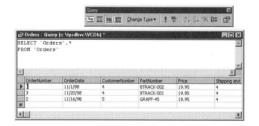

You need to find the customers who have ordered since November 11, 1998. The first step is to find the orders placed since then. Modify the query so that the window contains only order records after that date. You do this by adding a WHERE clause like this:

```
SELECT 'Orders'.*
FROM 'Orders'
WHERE OrderDate > { d '1998-11-11' }
```

The ANSI SQL convention is to use braces and the d, with single quotes around the date to indicate to the database that this is a date, as opposed to a text string or numeric type. When you run the query, you will find only the orders placed since that date, as shown in Figure 3.19.

FIGURE 3.19.

The orders since November 11, 1998.

Now that you have the orders since that date, you are going to find the customers who placed those orders, by retrieving the customer numbers from the orders. You need to change the query so that you obtain only the customer numbers, as shown in Figure 3.20.

FIGURE 3.20.

The customer numbers from orders since November 11, 1998.

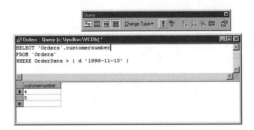

Now you can use these customer numbers to find the customer information. Build a `SELECT` statement that retrieves the customer records from the `Customers` table in which the customer number is among the numbers retrieved in the orders query. To do this, you can embed the orders query into the `WHERE` clause of a new query, like this:

```
SELECT 'Customers'.*
FROM 'Customers'
WHERE custnumber IN
      (SELECT 'Orders'.customernumber
      FROM 'Orders'
      WHERE OrderDate > { d '1998-11-11' })
```

The easiest way to create this new query is to open a new query window to the `Customers` table. Press the SQL button on the Query toolbar so that you can see the customers query. Add the `WHERE` clause so the query looks like the following:

```
SELECT 'Customers'.*
FROM 'Customers'
WHERE custnumber IN ()
```

Then select the text of the orders query, copy it to the Clipboard, and paste it inside the parentheses at the end of the `WHERE` clause in the customers query, like this:

```
SELECT 'Customers'.*
FROM 'Customers'
WHERE custnumber IN (SELECT 'Orders'.customernumber
FROM 'Orders'
WHERE OrderDate > { d '1998-11-11' })
```

When you run the query, you can see in Figure 3.21 that two customers have placed orders since November 11, 1998.

The code you would have to write in C++ to retrieve this same information from a binary data file, or even from a record manager, is considerably more complex. SQL is made to work with data, and that is where it excels.

FIGURE 3.21.

The customers with orders since November 11, 1998.

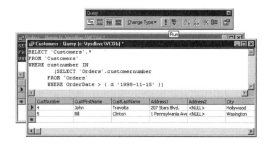

Another helpful query to learn is which order in the database is the most recent order. One way to find this is to select all the orders and include an ORDER BY OrderDate DESC clause.

```
SELECT 'Orders'.*
FROM 'Orders'
ORDER BY orderdate DESC
```

The first record is the most recent order.

Another way to find the most recent order is to ask the database for the order in which the date is equal to the maximum date in the table. Asking for the maximum date in the table is easy. You do it like this:

```
SELECT MAX(orderdate)
FROM Orders
```

MAX is an aggregate function, meaning that it operates on multiple records but returns a single value. You can embed this SQL statement as a subquery in another SELECT statement to find the most recent order (see Figure 3.22).

FIGURE 3.22.

The most recent order.

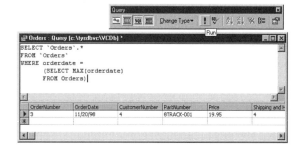

You can also perform a join with the Customers table to find the customer who placed the most recent order.

3

Resultsets and Cursors

When an application issues an SQL SELECT statement to a database, the database interprets it and returns a set of records. As you know, this is what happens in Visual C++
when you double-click a table in the Data View. Visual C++ sends a SELECT * statement
to the database and the database returns the records. Visual C++ then displays those
records in a query window.

NEW TERM   The set of records that a relational database returns as the result of a query is
            called the *resultset*.

SQL doesn't care whether that resultset contains one record or one million records. SQL
cares only about giving you a set of records that fit the criteria you specified. Most relational databases provide a simple model for the application to retrieve data after a submitting query. Records are returned to the application one at a time in the order specified
by the query, until the end of the set is reached. SQL has no provision for moving back
to a previous record.

Applications often require the capability to move back and forth through a resultset, one
record at a time, and possibly edit or delete a particular record in the set. SQL was not
originally designed to provide that capability. This is where cursors come in.

NEW TERM   A *cursor* is a mechanism that enables the individual records of a resultset to be
            processed one record at a time. The mechanism is called a *cursor* because it indi-
cates the current position in a resultset. This is similar to the cursor on a computer
screen, which indicates the current position of the input pointer in, for example, a document.

NEW TERM   A cursor that provides the ability to move only forward within a resultset is
            called a *forward-only cursor.*

NEW TERM   A cursor that provides the ability to move forward and backward within a result-
            set is called a *scrollable cursor*.

NEW TERM   A cursor that enables a user to change or delete data in addition to scrolling is
            referred to as a *scrollable, updatable cursor.*

You can see that Visual C++ uses scrollable, updatable cursors when you open a query
window. You can move back and forth through the records and edit the information in the
records.

Summary

Today you learned that SQL is a language that excels at manipulating data. You learned how to issue SELECT queries to retrieve records from a single table in a relational database. You learned how to perform joins to retrieve records from multiple tables. You learned how to use subqueries in SQL to obtain information that requires a large quantity of procedural code to retrieve. Last, you learned that cursors are a mechanism that enables record-at-a-time navigation through a resultset.

Q&A

Q Is it possible to write complete applications, using SQL?

A It's not possible to write applications by using ANSI SQL as the only programming language. ANSI SQL has no control of flow constructs, such as conditional loops and if statements. No user interface mechanisms or input/output routines (other than SELECT, which provides output) are available. However, some relational database servers, such as Microsoft SQL Server, do provide some control of flow extensions in their SQL implementations.

Q Is SQL always interpreted? Wouldn't SQL run faster if there were a way to compile the SQL statements?

A SQL is often interpreted, but there are ways to compile SQL statements to make them run faster. Relational database servers have the capability to store SQL statements in the database with the data. The database server interprets, optimizes, compiles, and saves the SQL statements in their compiled form for speedy execution. These prepared SQL statements are called *stored procedures*.

Workshop

The Workshop quiz questions test your understanding of today's material. The answers appear in Appendix F, "Answers." The exercises encourage you to apply the information you learned today to real-life situations.

Quiz

1. What is SQL?

2. What is an SQL join?

3. What is wrong with this SQL query?

```
SELECT customers.*
WHERE customers.custnumber = 3
```

4. What is an aggregate function?

5. What does a cursor make possible?

Exercises

1. Discover what happens when you add a table name to the FROM clause without mentioning that table in the WHERE class of an SQL SELECT statement, like this:

```
SELECT customers.*
FROM customer, orders
WHERE customers.custnumber = 3
```

2. Add a join to the SQL query shown in Figure 3.22 to retrieve the name of the customer who placed the most recent order.

DAY 4

Retrieving SQL Data Through a C++ API

Today you will learn how to retrieve data from relational databases by using an API for C++ programs. Using a database API in your C++ programs enables you to combine the strengths of C++ and SQL. When you complete today's work, you will know how to build applications in C++ that have the data-handling power and elegance of SQL.

Today you will

- Retrieve data, using relational database APIs for C++.
- Work with Microsoft Universal Data Access.
- Understand ActiveX Data Objects (ADO).

Relational Database APIs

On Day 1, "Choosing the Right Database Technology," you learned that relational databases have their own language interpreters and type systems. On Day 3, "Retrieving Data Through Structured Query Language (SQL)," you learned that relational databases use a language called *SQL*. You also learned that SQL is fundamentally different from C++ (SQL is interpreted, deals only with relational data, has no procedural constructs, and so on).

C++ compilers don't know SQL, and SQL interpreters don't know C++. Therefore, you have to use a relational database API to act as a translator for them.

Relational database APIs provide an interface between C++ and SQL. They offer a way for C++ programs to communicate with relational databases. Database APIs provide a bridge between C++ and SQL by translating between the type system of the database and the type system of C++. They provide a way to pass SQL code to the database to be run by the database interpreter and retrieve the resultset into C++ program variables.

Some database APIs are database specific and are built to work only with a particular database from a particular vendor. Other database APIs try to provide an open interface to multiple databases. ODBC is a database API that tries to provide an API to all relational databases.

OLE DB is supplanting the venerable ODBC. OLE DB is newer, more modern, and more feature-rich. OLE DB encapsulates ODBC functionality for relational databases and also provides access to nonrelational data sources, such as data from spreadsheets, VSAM data (from mainframes), email systems, directory services, and so on.

Microsoft Universal Data Access

OLE DB is the foundation of Microsoft Universal Data Access. With Microsoft Universal Data Access, you can access data through one API, regardless of where the data resides. Your application speaks to a common set of interfaces that generalize the concept of data. Microsoft examined what all types of data have in common and produced an API that can represent data from a variety of sources.

The Microsoft Universal Data Access strategy is based on OLE DB, a low-level C/C++ API designed to enable an individual data store to easily expose its native functionality without necessarily having to make its data look like relational data. The vendor for that particular data store needs simply to provide an OLE DB driver for it. OLE DB drivers are actually called *OLE DB providers*. As a C++ programmer, you can use the OLE DB API to gain access to any data source for which there is an OLE DB provider.

ActiveX Data Objects (ADO)

ActiveX Data Objects (ADO) is a high-level database API that sits on top of OLE DB. Compared to OLE DB, ADO programming is much simpler. ADO is suitable for scripting languages such as VBScript and JavaScript and for programming languages such as Visual Basic (VB) and Java. You can also call ADO from C++ programs.

ADO provides a *dual interface*. This dual interface makes it possible to use ADO from scripting languages, such as VBScript and JavaScript, as well as from C++. ADO actually provides two APIs (hence the term *dual*). One API is provided through OLE Automation for languages that don't use pointers, such as scripting languages. The other API is provided through a `vtable` interface for C++ programming. You will learn more about COM on Day 10, "Database Client Technologies and the Secrets of ADO," and Day 11, "Multitier Architectures." Now you will jump right into learning ADO.

The programming model in ADO typically consists of a sequence of actions. ADO provides a set of classes that simplifies the process of building this sequence in C++ code.

- Connect to a data source.
- Specify a query of the data source.
- Execute the query.
- Retrieve the data from the query in an object that you can easily access in C++ code.
- If appropriate, update the data source to reflect the edits made to the data.
- Provide a general means to detect errors.

NEW TERM   A *recordset* is a resultset coupled with a cursor. ADO returns the data from a query in a recordset object. A recordset object encapsulates the data that was retrieved from the database (which is the resultset) as well as functions for moving or navigating through records one at a time (which is the cursor).

Typically, you will employ all the preceding steps in the ADO programming model. However, ADO is flexible enough that you can use just part of the model if you need to. For example, you could create a new recordset object and populate it from your code, without making a connection to a data source or executing any queries. You could even pass that recordset object to other routines or applications.

The first step in accessing a data source with ADO is opening (or connecting to) the data source. With ADO, you can open a data source through its OLE DB provider or through its ODBC driver. You installed the Jet OLE DB Provider on Day 2, "Tools for Database Development in Visual C++ Developer Studio." You will use the Jet OLE DB Provider for the examples in this book.

With ADO, you can connect to ODBC data sources by using the OLE DB provider called *MSDASQL*. In the Visual C++ setup program, it's called the *Microsoft OLEDB*

ODBC Provider. You can use it with ADO for those data sources that have no OLE DB provider but do have an ODBC driver.

In ADO, you make a connection to a data source by using the ADO Connection object. The ADO Connection object has data members for the OLE DB provider name, data source name, username, password, and so on. The idea is to set the Connection object's data members and call the Open member function to establish and the Close member function to terminate the connection. You use the Connection object to handle transactions, which are often crucial in database applications. You will learn about transactions in Day 6, "Harnessing the Power of Relational Database Servers." You can also use the ADO Connection object's Execute function to send SQL queries to and receive resultsets from the data source.

An alternative to sending queries with the Connection's Execute function is to create an ADO Command object and use its Execute function. The Command object enables more complex queries and commands to be run against the data source. For instance, you could use a Command object to call a stored procedure with parameters in SQL Server. You will learn more about stored procedures on Day 6. A Command can create its own connection to the database or use a reference to an existing Connection object for greater efficiency.

Techniques for Using ADO in C++ Applications

There are a couple of ways to use ADO in your C++ code. You can use the ADO header files and import library from the OLE DB SDK. You include the ADO header files (adoid.h and adoint.h) in your source and add the ADO import library adoid.lib to your linker input. This enables you to create instances of the ADO objects and access their member functions. Using this method, the code to connect to a data source and create a Command object could look something like Listing 4.1. The code in Listing 4.1 doesn't check return values for the sake of code brevity. This is a code snippet only and will not compile as shown.

LISTING 4.1. USING ADO VIA THE OLE DB SDK

```
1:  ADOConnection* piConnection;
2:  ADOCommand* piCommand;
3:
4:  CoCreateInstance(CLSID_CADOConnection, NULL,CLSCTX_INPROC_SERVER,
    ➥IID_IADOConnection, (LPVOID *)&piConnection);
5:
6:  CoCreateInstance(CLSID_CADOCommand, NULL,CLSCTX_INPROC_SERVER,
    ➥IID_IADOCommand, (LPVOID*)&piCommand);
7:
```

```
 8:  piConnection->Open(L"MyDSN", L"sa", L"bodacious");
 9:
10:  piCommand->putref_ActiveConnection(piConnection);
```

Lines 1 and 2 declare pointers to two ADO COM interfaces. Lines 4 and 6 call `CoCreateInstance` to create instances of the ADO interfaces and assign the pointers to them. (You will learn more about `CoCreateInstance` and COM interfaces on Day 9, "Understanding COM.") Line 8 uses the `Open` function of the ADO Connection object to open a connection with an ODBC data source called `MyDSN`. It uses a username of `sa` (system administrator) and a password of `bodacious`. Line 10 calls the ADO Command object's `putref_ActiveConnection` function to tell it to use the connection that was opened in line 8. Later in your program you will need to call the `Release` function on `piConnection` and `piCommand` to free those objects.

The other way to use ADO in a C++ application is to use the Visual C++ `#import` directive. Using the `#import` directive with the ADO library enables you to write less verbose code to accomplish the same tasks with ADO. For instance, with `#import`, the preceding code can be abbreviated to the code in Listing 4.2. This code doesn't check return values for the sake of code brevity. This is a code snippet only and will not compile as shown.

LISTING 4.2.   USING ADO VIA #IMPORT

```
1:  _ConnectionPtr pConnection;
2:  _CommandPtr pCommand;
3:
4:  pConnection.CreateInstance(__uuidof( Connection ));
5:  pCommand.CreateInstance(__uuidof( Command ));
6:
7:  pConnection->Open(L"MyDSN", L"sa", L"bodacious");
8:
9:  pCommand->ActiveConnection = pConnection;
```

In Listing 4.2, lines 1 and 2 define instances of two ADO smart pointer classes. Lines 4 and 5 call the `CreateInstance` function of those smart pointer classes to create instances of the ADO classes. Line 7 uses the `Open` function of the ADO Connection object to open a connection with an ODBC data source called `MyDSN`. It uses a username of `sa` and a password of `bodacious`. Line 9 sets the ADO Command object's `ActiveConnection` data member so that it uses the connection opened in line 7.

Later in your program, you should not call the `Release` function on `pConnection` and `pCommand` to free those objects. `pConnection` and `pCommand` are smart pointers, so when they go out of scope, `Release` will be automatically called. Also, using the `#import` directive means that you don't need to include the ADO header files (adoid.h and adoint.h) in your source, nor do you need to link with the ADO import library adoid.lib. Article Q169496 in the Microsoft Knowledge Base (KB) provides additional information on using the #import directive with ADO. You can obtain KB articles from the MSDN subscription CDs. Also, you can send email to the KB email server at mshelp@microsoft.com.

As you can see from the code listings, using the #import directive enables you to write code that is less verbose than OLE DB SDK code. Article Q174565 in the Microsoft Knowledge Base compares the processes of using ADO via the OLE DB SDK, via the #import directive, and via the OLE DB SDK, using the MFC OLE classes. That Knowledge Base article recommends using ADO via the #import directive. Based on my personal experience in writing ADO applications, I have found that the #import directive hides some of the complexity of using ADO. Therefore, the ADO examples in this book use ADO via the #import directive.

Article Q174565 in the Microsoft Knowledge Base compares the process of using ADO via the OLE DB SDK, via the #import directive, and via the OLE DB SDK using the MFC OLE classes. That Knowledge Base article also recommends using ADO via the #import directive.

If you are interested in exploring the process of using ADO via the OLE DB SDK, there is a sample application, ADOSDK, on the CD-ROM. It's an MFC application that gives you some idea of what code you need to write in order to use ADO via the OLE DB SDK.

Note

ADO is a COM DLL. To call ADO functions from your C++ programs, the ADO DLL must be registered, which means that the location of the ADO DLL must be recorded in your machine's registry. When you install the Visual C++ data access components, ADO is automatically installed and registered for you. If you ever need to register ADO manually, at the command line you can run the following:

```
RegSvr32 msado15.dll
```

You run RegSvr32 from the directory containing msado15.dll; this directory typically is

```
\program files\common files\system\ado
```

Building C++ Applications That Use ADO

The best way to learn ADO is to build an application with it. Your application needn't be an MFC application in order to use ADO—MFC is not required for ADO. However, the ADO examples in this book use MFC because MFC provides an application framework that you don't have to build from scratch. Using MFC for the ADO examples enables you to concentrate on learning ADO, not on building an application framework. It's also interesting to see how the ADO objects can map to the objects in the MFC document/view architecture.

The first step is to create a new MFC AppWizard (exe) project in Visual C++: Name it ADOMFC1.

FIGURE 4.1.

A new AppWizard exe.

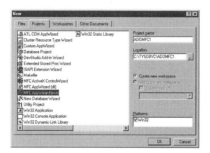

Specify that the application should be a multiple document application, as in Figure 4.2.

FIGURE 4.2.

Choose Multiple Documents in Step 1.

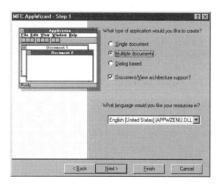

Specify that AppWizard include no database or OLE support in the application. You will add that code yourself. Specify whatever you like on the AppWizard options for toolbars, status bars, and so on. In AppWizard's last step (step 6 of 6, shown in Figure 4.3), make sure that the View class derives from CListView instead of CView.

Let AppWizard generate the project and the source code. Run the application to make sure it builds successfully with no errors or warnings.

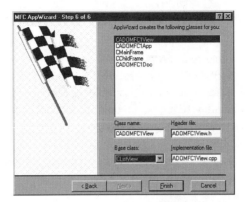

FIGURE 4.3.

Derive the View *class from* CListView.

As mentioned earlier, the ADO library is a COM DLL. This means applications that use it must initialize the OLE/COM libraries before making any ADO calls. In your MFC application, the call to initialize the OLE/COM libraries is best done in the InitInstance function of the application class.

LISTING 4.3.   INITIALIZING THE OLE/COM LIBRARIES

```
1:  BOOL CADOMFC1App::InitInstance()
2:  {
3:      // Add this function to initialize the OLE/COM libraries
4:      AfxOleInit();
```

Add the code shown in line 4 to initialize the OLE/COM libraries every time the application is loaded. Listing 4.4 shows some additions to StdAfx.h for ADO.

LISTING 4.4.   CHANGES TO STDAFX.H

```
1:  #include <comdef.h>
2:
3:  #import "C:\program files\common files\system\ado\msado15.dll" \
4:          no_namespace \
5:          rename( "EOF", "adoEOF" )
```

The code in Listing 4.4 can be added to the end of the StdAfx.h file. The most important thing is to not place the code inside the brackets in StdAfx.h that mark the autogenerated code. Line 1 includes a header file that enables your application to use some special COM support classes in Visual C++. These classes make it easier to work with OLE

Automation data types, which are the data types ADO uses. Lines 3, 4, and 5 use the #import directive to import the ADO library class declarations into your application.

As mentioned earlier, ADO is a COM DLL and provides dual interfaces. The declarations of the ADO classes are stored as a resource in the ADO DLL (msado15.dll) inside what is called a Type Library. The Type Library describes the automation interface as well as the COM vtable interface for use with C++. When you use the #import directive, at runtime Visual C++ reads the Type Library from the DLL and creates a set of C++ header files from it. These header files have .tli and .tlh extensions and are stored in the build directory. The ADO classes that you call from your C++ code are declared in these files.

Line 4 in Listing 4.4 specifies that no namespace is to be used for the ADO objects. In some applications, it might be necessary to use a namespace because of a naming collision between objects in the application and objects in ADO. You can specify a namespace by changing line 4 to look like the following:

```
rename_namespace("AdoNS")
```

Specifying a namespace for ADO enables you to scope the ADO objects using the namespace, like this:

```
AdoNS::ADO_Object_Name
```

Line 5 renames EOF (end of file) in ADO to adoEOF so that it won't conflict with other libraries that define their own EOF. Microsoft Knowledge Base article Q169496 provides further information on this topic, if you need it.

Run your application to make sure it builds successfully with no errors or warnings. After the build, you should see the TLI and TLH files in the build directory. They are the header files that the compiler created from the Type Library in msado15.dll. Feel free to have a look at them. They declare the ADO classes you can call from your code.

As mentioned earlier, the typical ADO programming sequence starts with making a connection to the database. A single ADO Connection object is normally shared and reused by multiple instances of other ADO objects.

This is very similar to the way an MFC Document class is used in an MFC application. Therefore, it makes sense to place an ADO Connection object in the Document class of an MFC application. When a document is opened in OnNewDocument, you can call the ADO Connection object's Open function to connect to the data source. In OnCloseDocument, you can call the Connection object's Close function to close the connection to the data source.

4

In an MFC application, the Document object is easy to access from the other objects (particularly the MFC View objects). By placing the ADO Connection object within that Document object, you create a connection to the data source, which you can share and reuse and which automatically opens and closes as the document(s) opens and closes.

Declare a pointer to an ADO Connection object in your Document class's header file as a public member of the Document class. You also need to add a data member that you will use to indicate whether the connection is open.

LISTING 4.5. CHANGES TO THE DOCUMENT HEADER FILE

```
1:  class CADOMFC1Doc : public CDocument
2:  {
3:  // Attributes
4:  public:
5:      BOOL m_IsConnectionOpen;
6:      _ConnectionPtr m_pConnection;
```

After making the additions shown in lines 5 and 6, your application should still build with no errors or warnings. In your Document class constructor, initialize the m_IsConnectionOpen member to FALSE, like this:

m_IsConnectionOpen = FALSE;

Open the connection to the data source in the Document class OnNewDocument function.

LISTING 4.6. ONNEWDOCUMENT

```
1:   BOOL CADOMFC1Doc::OnNewDocument()
2:   {
3:     if (!CDocument::OnNewDocument())
4:       return FALSE;
5:
6:     HRESULT hr;
7:     hr = m_pConnection.CreateInstance( __uuidof( Connection ) );
8:     if (SUCCEEDED(hr))
9:     {
10:      hr = m_pConnection->Open(
11:      _bstr_t(L"Provider=Microsoft.Jet.OLEDB.3.51;
                   ➥Data Source=c:\\tysdbvc\\vcdb.mdb;"),
12:      _bstr_t(L""),
13:      _bstr_t(L""),
14:      adModeUnknown);
15:      if (SUCCEEDED(hr))
16:      {
17:        m_IsConnectionOpen = TRUE;
```

```
18:       }
19:     }
20:
21:     return TRUE;
22:  }
```

Line 6 defines an HRESULT variable, hr. ADO functions (and COM functions, in general) return HRESULTs. Macros help you decode the meaning of an HRESULT. The SUCCEEDED macro on line 8 is a good example. Line 7 calls the _ConnectionPtr class CreateInstance function to create an instance of an ADO Connection object. If that succeeds, lines 10–14 call the Open function to actually make a connection to a data source. Line 11 is location specific, so you need to verify that it matches the location of the file on your machine. If it succeeds, line 17 sets m_IsConnectionOpen to TRUE.

Lines 11–13 create (temporary) instances of the _bstr_t class, which are passed as parameters to the Open function. As you know, _bstr_t(L"") calls the _bstr_t class constructor to create a temporary instance of _bstr_t. The L in front of the quote marks makes the string that is passed to the _bstr_t constructor a wide-character string.

The _bstr_t class is one of the COM support classes included with Visual C++. It is declared in comdef.h, which you included in StdAfx.h (see Listing 4.4, line 1). _bstr_t encapsulates the BSTR data type, which COM and ADO use to pass strings in function calls. You will learn more about COM, _bstr_t, and BSTR later. For now, know that _bstr_t makes it easier to use BSTR from C++ (using BSTR in C++ without the _bstr_t class is somewhat involved). You can pass instances of _bstr_t as arguments to ADO functions that require BSTR.

Line 11 is where you tell ADO which OLE DB provider to use and how to find the database file. The Provider= portion of the string specifies that you want to use the Jet OLE DB Provider. The Data Source= portion of the string specifies the location of the file.

Line 12 specifies the username for logging on to the database. The sample database vcdb.mdb has no users defined, so it can be an empty string. Line 13 specifies the password for logging on to the database. Again, it can be empty because none are defined in vcdb.mdb.

Now that you have the code to open a connection to the database when the document opens, you need to add the code to close the connection when the document closes in the Document class OnCloseDocument function. You can run ClassWizard to do the work of adding the function to the class (see Figure 4.4).

4

FIGURE 4.4.

Using ClassWizard
to override
`OnCloseDocument`.

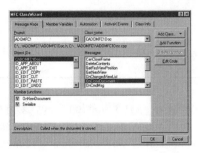

Specify the `Document` class, highlight the `OnCloseDocument` function, and press the Add Function button. Then highlight the `OnCloseDocument` function in the Member Functions list box and press the Edit Code button.

LISTING 4.7. ONCLOSEDOCUMENT

```
 1:  void CADOMFC1Doc::OnCloseDocument()
 2:  {
 3:    if (m_IsConnectionOpen)
 4:    {
 5:      m_IsConnectionOpen = FALSE;
 6:      m_pConnection->Close();
 7:    }
 8:
 9:    CDocument::OnCloseDocument();
10:  }
```

Add the code so that your `OnCloseDocument` function looks like Listing 4.7. Line 3 looks at `m_IsConnectionOpen` to see whether the connection is open. If it is, line 5 sets the flag to `FALSE` and line 6 closes the connection. After you add this code, your application will build without any errors or warnings.

Before running your application, however, you add some error handling code. One of the peculiarities of using ADO with `#import` is that, rather than return errors from functions, ADO throws exceptions . This means that you must add exception-handling code where you use ADO, or your application will die an ugly death every time ADO encounters an error condition at runtime and throws an exception.

Exception Handling for ADO

The exception-handling code for ADO is easy to add to your code. Add `try...catch` blocks where your code calls ADO functions, as in Listing 4.8.

LISTING 4.8. ONNEWDOCUMENT WITH EXCEPTION HANDLING

```
 1:  BOOL CADOMFC1Doc::OnNewDocument()
 2:  {
```

```
3:    if (!CDocument::OnNewDocument())
4:      return FALSE;
5:
6:    HRESULT hr;
7:
8:    try
9:    {
10:     hr = m_pConnection.CreateInstance( __uuidof( Connection ) );
11:     if (SUCCEEDED(hr))
12:     {
13:       hr = m_pConnection->Open(
14:       _bstr_t(L"Provider=Microsoft.Jet.OLEDB.3.51;
                    ➥Data Source=c:\\tysdbvc\\vcdb.mdb;"),
15:       _bstr_t(L""),
16:       _bstr_t(L""),
17:       adModeUnknown);
18:       if (SUCCEEDED(hr))
19:       {
20:         m_IsConnectionOpen = TRUE;
21:       }
22:     }
23:    }
24:    catch( _com_error &e )
25:    {
26:      // Get info from _com_error
27:      _bstr_t bstrSource(e.Source());
28:      _bstr_t bstrDescription(e.Description());
29:      TRACE( "Exception thrown for classes generated by #import" );
30:      TRACE( "\tCode = %08lx\n", e.Error());
31:      TRACE( "\tCode meaning = %s\n", e.ErrorMessage());
32:      TRACE( "\tSource = %s\n", (LPCTSTR) bstrSource);
33:      TRACE( "\tDescription = %s\n", (LPCTSTR) bstrDescription);
34:    }
35:    catch(...)
36:    {
37:      TRACE( "*** Unhandled Exception ***" );
38:    }
39:
40:    return TRUE;
41:  }
```

4

Add the try and the open brace in lines 8 and 9. Add the close brace and the catch blocks in lines 23–38. The catch in line 24 catches _com_error exceptions, which is the type that ADO throws. _com_error is another of the COM support classes declared in comdef.h.

If an error occurs at runtime—for example, if the mdb database file doesn't exist at the location specified in the Open function, the Jet OLE DB Provider will create the

_com_error object and fill its members with information describing the error. The ADO
Open function will throw the _com_error object. Lines 27–33 catch the _com_error
object, retrieve that error information, and display it in TRACE output to the debug window in Visual C++. Without catching this exception and displaying the error information,
tracking down the error would be nearly impossible. With this code to catch the exception, you can track down errors quite easily. Add a similar try...catch block to the
OnCloseDocument function as well.

Make sure your application builds with no errors or warnings; then run the application in
debug mode to see whether you can successfully connect to the database. You can do this
by setting three breakpoints. Set one breakpoint on the CreateInstance call in
OnNewDocument. Set another on a line inside the catch block in OnNewDocument. Set the
third in OnCloseDocument on the if statement that tests whether m_IsConnectionOpen is
TRUE. When you reach a break point, single step to see what the code does. You should
create an instance of an ADO connection and open the connection when the application
loads. When you close the application, the ADO connection will close as well. If there
are errors, you should see some indications of what caused the errors in your TRACE
statements in the debug window in Visual Studio.

Displaying Records in a List Control

When your application can connect to the database, the next step is to display records in
a list control in your application. One easy way to create a list control is to use the
ClistCtrlEx class that is included with the DAOVIEW example in Visual C++. To use
the ClistCtrlEx class, copy three files—CtrlExt.cpp, CtrlExt.h, and CtrlExt.Inl—from
the DAOVIEW example into the source code directory for your application. Add
CtrlExt.cpp to the list of source code files and add CtrlExt.h and CtrlExt.Inl to the list of
header files in your project. Make the additions to StdAfx.h shown in Listing 4.9.

LISTING 4.9. MORE CHANGES TO STDAFX.H

```
1:  #include <comdef.h>
2:
3:  #import "C:\program files\common files\system\ado\msado15.dll" \
4:          no_namespace \
5:          rename( "EOF", "adoEOF" )
6:  #include <afxcmn.h>  // if not already included
7:  #include <afxcview.h>
8:  #include "ctrlext.h"
```

Lines 1–5 show the code you added previously. Add the include files shown in lines 6–8.
Line 6 (afxcmn.h) might already be included, depending on the options you chose in

AppWizard. These include files are required for the `CListCtrlEx` class. After adding this code, your application should build without any errors or warnings.

Use ClassWizard to override the `OnCreate` function in your application's `View` class.

FIGURE 4.5.

Using ClassWizard to override `OnCreate`.

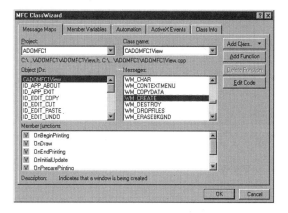

Specify the `View` class, highlight the `WM_CREATE` message, and press the Add Function button. Then highlight the `OnCreate` function in the Member Functions list box and press the Edit Code button.

LISTING 4.10. OVERRIDING THE VIEW'S ONCREATE

```
1:  int CADOMFC1View::OnCreate(LPCREATESTRUCT lpCreateStruct)
2:  {
3:    lpCreateStruct->style |= LVS_REPORT;
4:    if (CListView::OnCreate(lpCreateStruct) == -1)
5:      return -1;
6:
7:    return 0;
8:  }
```

Listing 4.10 shows how the `OnCreate` function should look. The only code you need to add is line 3. All the other code is already there. Line 3 gives the list control a `LVS_REPORT` style, which means that the list control will display its columns.

Add some code to the `OnInitialUpdate` function of the `View` class. The `OnInitialUpdate` function already exists in your code; AppWizard put it there when you specified that the `View` class should derive from `CListView`. Add code like that shown in Listing 4.11.

Listing 4.11. ONINITIALUPDATE

```
 1:  void CADOMFC1View::OnInitialUpdate()
 2:  {
 3:  CListView::OnInitialUpdate();
 4:
 5:  CListCtrlEx& ctlList = (CListCtrlEx&) GetListCtrl();
 6:
 7:  ctlList.AddColumn(" First Test Column  ",0);
 8:  ctlList.AddColumn(" Second Test Column ",1);
 9:  ctlList.AddColumn(" Third Test Column ",3);
10:
11:  ctlList.AddItem(0,0,"First Test Row");
12:  ctlList.AddItem(1,0,"Second Test Row");
13:  }
```

Lines 7–12 use the AddColumn and AddItem functions from the ClistCtrlEx class declared in CtrlExt.h. The AddColumn and AddItem functions in the ClistCtrlEx class make it very easy to add columns and rows to a list control.

Your application should build successfully without any errors or warnings. When you run the application, it will look like Figure 4.6.

FIGURE 4.6.

The application with a list control.

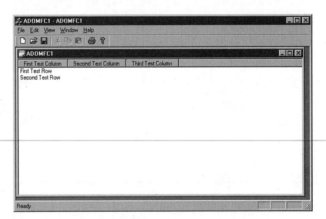

Querying Records from the Database

You will now add code to execute a query and display the results in the list control every time you right-click the View.

Use ClassWizard to override the WM_RBUTTONDOWN message. In the OnRButtonDown function, add the code shown in Listing 4.12.

LISTING 4.12. ONRBUTTONDOWN

```
 1:  void CADOMFC1View::OnRButtonDown(UINT nFlags, CPoint point)
 2:  {
 3:    _RecordsetPtr pRecordSet;
 4:    CADOMFC1Doc * pDoc;
 5:    pDoc = GetDocument();
 6:
 7:    _bstr_t bstrQuery("SELECT * FROM Customers");
 8:    _variant_t vRecsAffected(0L);
 9:
10:    try
11:    {
12:      pRecordSet = pDoc->m_pConnection->Execute(bstrQuery,
                                             ➥&vRecsAffected,
13:                                          adOptionUnspecified);
14:      if (!pRecordSet->GetadoEOF())
15:      {
16:        CListCtrlEx& ctlList = (CListCtrlEx&) GetListCtrl();
17:        ctlList.DeleteAllItems();
18:        while(ctlList.DeleteColumn(0));
19:
20:        ctlList.AddColumn("  First Name  ",0);
21:        ctlList.AddColumn("  Last Name   ",1);
22:
23:        int i = 0;
24:        _variant_t vFirstName;
25:        _variant_t vLastName;
26:        while (!pRecordSet->GetadoEOF())
27:        {
28:          vFirstName = pRecordSet->GetCollect(L"CustFirstName");
29:          ctlList.AddItem(i,0,(_bstr_t) vFirstName);
30:          vLastName = pRecordSet->GetCollect(L"CustLastName");
31:          ctlList.AddItem(i,1,(_bstr_t) vLastName);
32:          i++;
33:          pRecordSet->MoveNext();
34:        }
35:      }
36:
37:      pRecordSet->Close();
38:    }
39:    catch( _com_error &e )
40:    {
41:      // Get info from _com_error
42:      _bstr_t bstrSource(e.Source());
43:      _bstr_t bstrDescription(e.Description());
44:      TRACE( "Exception thrown for classes generated by #import" );
45:      TRACE( "\tCode = %08lx\n", e.Error());
46:      TRACE( "\tCode meaning = %s\n", e.ErrorMessage());
47:      TRACE( "\tSource = %s\n", (LPCTSTR) bstrSource);
```

continues

LISTING 4.12. CONTINUED

```
48:        TRACE( "\tDescription = %s\n", (LPCTSTR) bstrDescription);
49:    }
50:    catch(...)
51:    {
52:      TRACE( "*** Unhandled Exception ***" );
53:    }
54:
55:    CListView::OnRButtonDown(nFlags, point);
56: }
```

Line 3 defines a smart pointer to a Recordset class. Lines 4 and 5 define and initialize a pointer to the MFC Document. Line 6 constructs a _bstr_t that contains the SQL query string to select records from the Customers table. Line 7 constructs a _variant_t that is passed as a parameter to the Connection's Execute function in line 12. This variable is used to show how many records were affected. The Jet OLE DB Provider apparently does not use this variable. Other OLE DB providers might use it. In any case, you are required to pass the address of the variable as a parameter to the Execute function.

The _variant_t class is another of the COM helper classes declared in comdef.h. The _variant_t class encapsulates the OLE Automation VARIANT data type. Using the _variant_t class is much easier than trying to use the VARIANT data type directly in C++. See the explanation of lines 28–31 for examples of using the _variant_t class.

Line 12 (and line 13) calls the Connection object's Execute function through the MFC Document object. The Execute function returns a Recordset object that contains the resultset from the query and a cursor pointing to the first record. Line 14 tests for an EOF file condition of the cursor in the Recordset. An EOF condition immediately after the Recordset object is created indicates that the query returned no records. If the query did return some records, the cursor would be positioned at the first record in the Recordset.

If the query returned records, lines 17–21 delete the existing rows and columns from the list control and add a last name column and a first name column.

Line 26 starts a while loop that tests for the EOF condition in the cursor of the Recordset. Line 33 calls the MoveNext function in the Recordset to scroll the cursor forward one record at a time. The loop executes until the cursor moves beyond the last record in the Recordset.

Lines 24 and 25 create two instances of _variant_t, for the customer first name and last name. Lines 28 and 30 call the GetCollect function from the Recordset class. The field name from the table in the database is passed as a parameter to the GetCollect function.

The GetCollect function returns a VARIANT containing the contents of the field in the current record.

The *current* record is the record on which the cursor is currently positioned.

Lines 28 and 30 store the VARIANT data from the field in the instances of _variant_t that were created in lines 24 and 25. Lines 29 and 31 cast these _variant_ts as _bstr_ts and pass them to the list control's AddItem function to display their contents in the window.

The _variant_t class is very handy for dealing with data from fields in a database. You can simply cast the contents of a _variant_t, whether it is numeric or string or date/time data, to C++ and COM data types. See the Visual C++ documentation under "_variant_t Extractors" for further information.

There you have it. Your application is now capable of displaying data from the database in a list control. Run the application and right-click the View window. The list control will display the contents of first and last name fields in the Customers table.

Summary

To access a database that has a different type system from C++ and has its own language interpreter, it's necessary to use a database API. Several database APIs are available to C++ developers.

The future of all data access in Microsoft Windows is OLE DB. The easiest way to use OLE DB is to use ADO. ADO provides an object model that encapsulates the process of communicating with databases from within C++ programs as well as from other programming languages.

Q&A

Q What is the best database API to use for my application?

A The database API you choose depends on the particular database you have chosen for your application. If you are using a popular relational database, the most modern and robust APIs are OLE DB and ADO.

Q I've heard that ODBC and OLE DB are slow. Shouldn't I use my database's native API?

A The speed of the drivers for ODBC or OLE DB depends largely on the quality of the vendor's implementation. For at least a couple of the popular databases, namely SQL Server and Access, ODBC and OLE DB are highly optimized.

Q **Where do I find an OLE DB provider for my database?**

A You should check with your database vendor. If the vendor doesn't offer an OLE DB provider, it might know of a third party that does. You can also check the Microsoft Web site for a list of available OLE DB providers.

Q **Using these _variant_ts and _bstr_ts looks a little weird. Isn't there an API that lets me use C++ data types?**

A Databases typically don't use C++ data types. It's the job of the database API to translate between these data types. The _variant_t and _bstr_t classes provide great functionality for translating between database types and C++ types, so don't be afraid of them.

Workshop

The Workshop quiz questions test your understanding of today's material. (The answers appear in Appendix F, "Answers.") The exercises encourage you to apply the information you learned today to real-life situations.

Quiz

1. What does a database API do?
2. What database APIs work with nonrelational data sources?
3. What does an ADO Connection object do?
4. What does the *current* record mean?

Exercises

1. Change the code in Listing 4.12 so that the customers are sorted by last name.
2. Change the code in Listing 4.12 to display the customer number as well as the customer first and last name.

DAY **5**

Adding, Modifying, and Deleting Data

One reason for the existence of database applications is to modify data in databases. You will learn how to modify data in relational databases by using ADO functions, as well as SQL statements, in your C++ programs. When you complete today's work, you will know how to create applications that alter the data in relational databases.

Today you will

- Learn about cursor types in ADO Recordsets.
- Use the ADO AddNew, Update, and Delete functions.
- Use SQL INSERT, UPDATE, DELETE statements.

Cursor Types in ADO Recordsets

As you know, an ADO Recordset object encapsulates a resultset, which contains records from a query, and a cursor, which enables you to move through those records. There are four different types of cursor in ADO—dynamic, keyset, static, and forward-only—each with unique capabilities and attributes.

A dynamic cursor enables you to view additions, changes, and deletions made by other users while the recordset is open. A dynamic cursor also enables all types of movement through the Recordset, including the ability to move *n* number of records forward or backward, move to the first record, and move to the last record.

A keyset cursor enables you to see changes made by other users. However, you can't see records that other users add, nor can you access records that other users delete. It enables all types of movement through the Recordset.

A static cursor provides a static copy (or snapshot) of a set of records and enables all types of movement through the Recordset. Additions, changes, or deletions by other users are not visible.

A forward-only cursor enables you to see changes made by other users and to scroll only forward through records. This improves performance when you need to make only a single pass through a Recordset.

The type of cursor you choose depends on your requirements. However, bear in mind that queries execute much faster if you use a forward-only cursor. In database applications, performance is always an issue. Therefore, you should typically use forward-only cursors and save dynamic, keyset, or static cursors for when you need the features they offer.

You specify the cursor type in ADO before opening the Recordset, or you pass a CursorType argument with the Recordset Open function. Some providers don't support all cursor types. Check the provider's documentation. If you don't specify a cursor type, ADO opens a forward-only cursor by default.

The ADO AddNew, Update, and Delete Functions

One way to add, change, and delete records in a database is to create a Recordset object and call its member functions to add, change, and delete the records in the Recordset. The changes made to the Recordset are applied to the database. In other words, if you change the records in the Recordset, you change records in the database.

The ADO Recordset class has three member functions that enable you to modify the records in the Recordset. These functions are AddNew, Update, and Delete.

Create a new `Recordset` menu with three items for `AddNew`, `Update`, and `Delete`, as shown in Figure 5.1.

FIGURE 5.1.

The new `Recordset` *menu.*

To view the changes you will make to the database today, it would be handy to add a database project to your current project. Select the Project Add to Project New… menu. Select the Project tab and specify a database project, as shown in Figure 5.2.

FIGURE 5.2.

Add a database project.

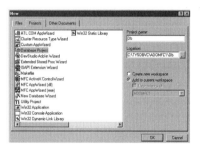

When you click the OK button, you are presented with a dialog window where you specify the ODBC DSN for the database project, as you did in Day 2, "Tools for Database Development in Visual C++ Developer Studio" (refer to Figures 2.11 and 2.12). After you specify the DSN, the database project will be added to your current project. You need to select the Project Set Active Project menu to specify that your current project should be the active one, not the database project. (Otherwise, you will not be able to build or debug your application.)

The `AddNew` Function

The process of adding records by using the `AddNew` function involves creating two arrays and passing them as parameters to the `AddNew` function. The first array is an array that contains the names of the fields that will contain the data in the new record. The second array is an array of values to assign to each field.

The tricky part of using `AddNew` is that the two arrays you pass as parameters must be `VARIANT` arrays. The code to produce and manipulate `VARIANT` arrays in C++ can be involved. Because you are using MFC for the sample applications in this book, your code can be simplified by using the MFC `ColeSafeArray` class.

Listing 5.1 shows the code for adding a new record by using the AddNew function. Use ClassWizard to add a handler function to the View class for the AddNew menu choice. In the AddNew handler function for that menu item, add the code in Listing 5.1.

LISTING 5.1. USING THE ADO ADDNEW FUNCTION

```
 1:  void CADOMFC1View::OnRecordsetAddnew()
 2:  {
 3:    _RecordsetPtr pRecordSet;
 4:    CADOMFC1Doc * pDoc;
 5:    pDoc = GetDocument();
 6:
 7:    HRESULT hr;
 8:    _bstr_t bstrQuery("SELECT * FROM Products WHERE PartNumber IS
                        ➡NULL");
 9:    _variant_t vNull;
10:    vNull.vt = VT_ERROR;
11:    vNull.scode = DISP_E_PARAMNOTFOUND;
12:
13:    try
14:    {
15:      hr = pRecordSet.CreateInstance(__uuidof(Recordset));
16:      if (SUCCEEDED(hr))
17:      {
18:        pRecordSet->PutRefActiveConnection(pDoc->m_pConnection);
19:        hr = pRecordSet->Open(_variant_t(bstrQuery), vNull,
20:          adOpenForwardOnly, adLockOptimistic, adCmdText);
21:        if (SUCCEEDED(hr))
22:        {
23:          // Create an array for the list of fields in
24:          // the Products table.
25:          COleSafeArray vaFieldlist;
26:          vaFieldlist.CreateOneDim(VT_VARIANT,3);
27:          // Fill in the field names now.
28:          long lArrayIndex[1];
29:          lArrayIndex[0] = 0;
30:          vaFieldlist.PutElement(lArrayIndex,
31:            &(_variant_t("PartNumber")));
32:          lArrayIndex[0] = 1;
33:          vaFieldlist.PutElement(lArrayIndex,
34:            &(_variant_t("ProductName")));
35:          lArrayIndex[0] = 2;
36:          vaFieldlist.PutElement(lArrayIndex,
37:            &(_variant_t("Price")));
38:
39:          // Create an array for the list of values to go in
40:          // the Products table.
41:          COleSafeArray vaValuelist;
42:          vaValuelist.CreateOneDim(VT_VARIANT,3);
```

```
43:            // Fill in the values for each field.
44:            lArrayIndex[0] = 0;
45:            vaValuelist.PutElement(lArrayIndex,
46:              &(_variant_t("8TRACK-003")));
47:            lArrayIndex[0] = 1;
48:            vaValuelist.PutElement(lArrayIndex,
49:              &(_variant_t("Bell Bottom Hits")));
50:            lArrayIndex[0] = 2;
51:            vaValuelist.PutElement(lArrayIndex,
52:              &(_variant_t((float)19.95)));
53:
54:            pRecordSet->AddNew(vaFieldlist, vaValuelist);
55:            pRecordSet->Close();
56:        }
57:    }
58:    }
59:    catch( _com_error &e )
60:    {
61:    TRACE( "Error:%08lx.\n", e.Error());
62:    TRACE( "ErrorMessage:%s.\n", e.ErrorMessage());
63:    TRACE( "Source:%s.\n", (LPCTSTR) _bstr_t(e.Source()));
64:    TRACE( "Description:%s.\n", (LPCTSTR) _bstr_t(e.Description()));
65:    }
66:    catch(...)
67:    {
68:      TRACE( "\n*** Unhandled Exception ***\n" );
69:    }
70: }
```

In Listing 5.1, line 3 defines a smart pointer to a Recordset. Lines 4 and 5 obtain a pointer to the MFC document, which will enable you to get to the ADO Connection object that was opened with the document.

Line 8 defines a _bstr_t object that contains a SQL SELECT statement. This SQL statement will be passed to the Recordset Open function and will open a recordset that contains no records. The WHERE clause specifies records where the PartNumber IS NULL. PartNumber is the primary key in the Products table and will never be NULL. You want to use this Recordset only for adding new records to the database, so you don't need the Recordset to contain any records. In other words, you want an empty Recordset.

Lines 9–11 define a _variant_t object named vNull and set two of its data members. vNull will be passed as the second parameter to the Recordset Open function. This parameter can contain a string for connecting to the database during the Open call. Rather than pass a connect string, you pass vNull and (in line 18) specify that the Recordset should use the connection already opened in the MFC document.

Line 15 calls the `_RecordsetPtr CreateInstance` function to instantiate the `Recordset` object. If that succeeds, lines 18–20 set the connection and open the `Recordset`. The `Open` function specifies a forward-only cursor (`adOpenForwardOnly`) with optimistic record locking (`adLockOptimistic`).

Optimistic locking means that just before the record is added, it is locked so that no other users can muck with it while you're trying to write it to the database. Another option for locking is *pessimistic locking*, which holds the lock for a longer time in the database. You will learn more about optimistic and pessimistic locking later today in the section on the `Update` function.

In line 20, the last parameter for the `Open` call is `adCmdText`, which tells the database that you are passing the text of a SQL statement, which it needs to interpret.

Lines 23–37 create an array of `VARIANT`s, called `vaFieldlist`, which contains the field names of the new record. Lines 39–52 create another array of `VARIANT`s, called `vaValuelist`, that contains the actual data values you will place in the fields of the new record. If you were adding multiple records, you would probably define these arrays once and simply change the values of the `vaValuelist` array before calling `AddNew` to add each record.

Line 54 passes these two arrays in the `AddNew` call to add the record to the database. Line 55 closes the `Recordset` object. The rest of the code does exception handling.

You should be able to build the application with no errors or warnings. When you run the application, set a breakpoint on line 5 or so and another breakpoint in the exception-handling code, such as line 61. When you run the application and take the `AddNew` menu choice, you will receive no exceptions, and it will add the new record to the `Products` table. If you try to add the same record twice, you will receive an exception from the database, telling you that the changes were not successful because they would create duplicate values in the index or primary key. This is an example of the database ensuring the integrity of the data.

This might seem like a large amount of code for adding merely one record to the database. It is. However, you must realize that the `Insert` performance (the speed with which you can add records to a database) is often a critical factor in database applications. The ADO `AddNew` function is highly optimized so that it executes very efficiently (when used with an empty, forward-only `Recordset`, as in Listing 5.1). To reduce the amount of code you must write, you could encapsulate the code in Listing 5.1 into a function that builds the `VARIANT` arrays and takes the values of the data for the new records as parameters.

The Update Function

The ADO Update function enables you to edit an existing record. The idea is to open a Recordset that contains the record you want to edit. Position the cursor at the appropriate record (if it is not there already). Change the data in the field(s) you want to edit. Then call Update to commit the changes to the database. (An alternative to calling Update is to move the cursor off the record. This has the effect of implicitly calling Update.)

Use ClassWizard to add a handler function to the View class for the Recordset Update menu; then add the code in Listing 5.2.

LISTING 5.2.   USING THE ADO UPDATE FUNCTION

```
 1:   void CADOMFC1View::OnRecordsetUpdate()
 2:   {
 3:      RecordsetPtr pRecordSet;
 4:     CADOMFC1Doc * pDoc;
 5:     pDoc = GetDocument();
 6:
 7:     HRESULT hr;
 8:      bstr_t bstrQuery(
 9:       "SELECT * FROM Products WHERE PartNumber = '8TRACK-003'");
10:      variant_t vNull;
11:     vNull.vt = VT_ERROR;
12:     vNull.scode = DISP_E_PARAMNOTFOUND;
13:
14:     try
15:     {
16:       hr = pRecordSet.CreateInstance(_uuidof(Recordset));
17:       if (SUCCEEDED(hr))
18:       {
19:         pRecordSet->PutRefActiveConnection(pDoc->m_pConnection);
20:         hr = pRecordSet->Open(_variant_t(bstrQuery), vNull,
21:           adOpenForwardOnly, adLockOptimistic, adCmdText);
22:         if (!pRecordSet->GetadoEOF())
23:         {
24:           pRecordSet->PutCollect(L"ProductName",
25:             L"Bell Bottoms and Bass Guitars");
26:           pRecordSet->Update(vNull, vNull);
27:           pRecordSet->Close();
28:         }
29:       }
30:     }
31:     catch( _com_error &e )
32:     {
33:       TRACE( "Error:%08lx.\n", e.Error());
34:       TRACE( "ErrorMessage:%s.\n", e.ErrorMessage());
35:       TRACE( "Source:%s.\n", (LPCTSTR) _bstr_t(e.Source()));
```

continues

LISTING 5.2. CONTINUED

```
36:        TRACE( "Description:%s.\n", (LPCTSTR) _bstr_t(e.Description())));
37:    }
38:    catch(...)
39:    {
40:      TRACE( "\n*** Unhandled Exception ***\n" );
41:    }
42:  }
```

Lines 3–7 are identical to the code in Listing 5.1 and merely initialize some variables you will need. Line 8 defines an instance of _bstr_t that contains a SQL SELECT statement that selects the record you added in Listing 5.1. Lines 10–19 are the same as Listing 5.1. Line 20 opens the Recordset. Line 22 tests whether the EOF file condition is true. If it isn't, that means you have the record you are looking for.

Lines 24 and 25 call the Recordset PutCollect function to change the product name for this record to *Bell Bottoms and Bass Guitars*, which is obviously a much groovier title than *Bell Bottom Hits*. As an alternative to calling PutCollect, you could pass an array of field names and an array of values to the Update function. Line 26 calls Update to commit the change, and line 27 closes the Recordset.

This code will build with no errors or warnings. It will run with no exceptions or errors and will update the product name in the database. To ensure that this code runs properly, set some breakpoints when you execute this function. After you run it, you can open the Products table in Developer Studio and see whether the ProductName field for that record changed, as it should.

I mentioned locking earlier. The difference between optimistic and pessimistic locking consists primarily in the length of time the lock is held in the database. With pessimistic locking, the lock is initiated as soon as you modify the contents of a field in the record (in this case, by calling PutCollect). The lock is held until after you call Update or move the cursor off the record to commit the change.

With optimistic locking, the lock is initiated and held only when the change is committed to the database during the Update call. This means the lock is held for a very short time. However, if another user modifies the record during the time between your PutCollect call and your Update call, your Update call will fail (the database will reject your change to the record). If that happens, you need to retry to make the change.

Optimistic locking generally supports larger numbers of concurrent users than pessimistic locking. However, with optimistic locking, the users might have to try to commit their changes more than once.

The `Delete` Function

The ADO `Delete` function enables you to delete an existing record from the database. The idea is to open a `Recordset` that contains the record you want to edit. Position the cursor at the appropriate record (if it isn't already there). Then call the `Delete` function to remove the records from the database.

Use ClassWizard to add a handler function to the `View` class for the Recordset Delete menu; then add the code in Listing 5.3.

LISTING 5.3. USING THE ADO DELETE FUNCTION

```
 1:  void CADOMFC1View::OnRecordsetDelete()
 2:  {
 3:    RecordsetPtr pRecordSet;
 4:    CADOMFC1Doc * pDoc;
 5:    pDoc = GetDocument();
 6:
 7:    HRESULT hr;
 8:    bstr_t bstrQuery(
 9:     "SELECT * FROM Products WHERE PartNumber = '8TRACK-003'");
10:    variant_t vNull;
11:    vNull.vt = VT_ERROR;
12:    vNull.scode = DISP_E_PARAMNOTFOUND;
13:
14:    try
15:    {
16:      hr = pRecordSet.CreateInstance(__uuidof(Recordset));
17:      if (SUCCEEDED(hr))
18:      {
19:        pRecordSet->PutRefActiveConnection(pDoc->m_pConnection);
20:        hr = pRecordSet->Open(_variant_t(bstrQuery), vNull,
21:          adOpenForwardOnly, adLockOptimistic, adCmdText);
22:        if (!pRecordSet->GetadoEOF())
23:        {
24:          pRecordSet->Delete(adAffectCurrent);
25:          pRecordSet->Close();
26:        }
27:      }
28:    }
29:    catch( _com_error &e )
30:    {
31:      TRACE( "Error:%08lx.\n", e.Error());
```

5

continues

LISTING 5.3.   CONTINUED

```
32:        TRACE( "ErrorMessage:%s.\n", e.ErrorMessage());
33:        TRACE( "Source:%s.\n", (LPCTSTR) _bstr_t(e.Source()));
34:        TRACE( "Description:%s.\n", (LPCTSTR) _bstr_t(e.Description()));
35:      }
36:    catch(...)
37:      {
38:        TRACE( "\n*** Unhandled Exception ***\n" );
39:      }
40:  }
```

In Listing 5.3, lines 3–23 are identical to the code in Listing 5.2. You are opening a `Recordset` that contains the record that you added to the database in Listing 5.1. If the record is there, line 24 calls `Delete` and passes `adAffectCurrent` as a parameter so that only the current record is deleted from the database.

The code will build with no errors or warnings and run with no exceptions. It will delete the record that you added in the `AddNew` section earlier today.

The SQL INSERT, UPDATE, and DELETE Statements

So far, you have used the ADO `Recordset` to make changes to records in the database. You can also use SQL statements to make changes to records.

You've already learned about the SQL `SELECT` statement for retrieving data from the database. Now you will learn about three SQL statements that enable you to modify the data in a database. You could use the `Execute` statement in the ADO Connection object to send these statements to the database, but the easiest way to learn these statements is to use Developer Studio. You will now learn how to send these statements to the database by using Developer Studio.

The SQL INSERT Statement

The SQL `INSERT` statement enables you to add records to the database. The basic syntax looks like this:

```
INSERT INTO which table( list of columns ) VALUES( list of values )
```

Now you will use the `INSERT` statement to add a record to your database. Switch to the Data View and double-click the `Products` table to open it. Click the SQL button on the Query toolbar so that you can view and edit the SQL query. Change the query so that it looks like the one in Figure 5.3.

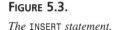

FIGURE 5.3.

The INSERT statement.

Visual Studio can help you by building the basic structure of the INSERT statement. If you click the Change Type button on the Query toolbar and then select Insert Values from the drop-down list, Visual Studio will create a basic INSERT statement for you. All you need to do is fill in the field names and their values.

Note

> In SQL statements, text field values are bounded by single quotes (') and numeric values are not. This enables the database engine to properly interpret these data types.

Press the SQL Check button on the Query toolbar to verify the SQL syntax. The syntax should verify okay. Press the Run (!) button on the Query toolbar to execute the statement and insert the record.

After you run the query, a message box will appear, telling you that one record was affected. Also, the area below the SQL INSERT statement in the query window will become empty. As you know, the query window displays the records that the database returned as a result of the SQL statement. The window is empty because the SQL INSERT statement doesn't return data. To view the contents of the table, you must change the query back to a SQL SELECT statement (which does return data).

Edit the SQL query so that it looks like this:

```
SELECT Products.* FROM Products
```

Visual Studio can help you easily create the SELECT statement. If you click the Change Type button on the Query toolbar and then select Select from the drop-down list, Visual Studio will create most of a SELECT statement for you. All you need to do is add the table name and an asterisk after SELECT.

When you run the query, you should see all the records, including the one you just added to the table with your INSERT statement.

5

You can use an incomplete field list in an INSERT statement to add data to only some of the fields in the new record. For example, in the Products table, you could use a statement such as the one below to add a record without specifying the price.

```
INSERT INTO Products (partnumber, productname) VALUES('xxx', 'yyy')
```

You can perform more advanced operations by using the SQL INSERT statement, such as inserting multiple records that were retrieved from other tables with a SELECT statement. You will learn more about advanced INSERT operations tomorrow on Day 6, "Harnessing the Power of Relational Database Servers."

The SQL UPDATE Statement

The SQL UPDATE statement enables you to modify the data in existing records in the database. The basic syntax looks like this:

```
UPDATE which table SET which field = new value, which field = new value, ...
WHERE condition
```

Now you will use the UPDATE statement to modify the record you inserted into your database. Change the query in the query window so that it looks like the one in Figure 5.4.

FIGURE 5.4.

The UPDATE statement.

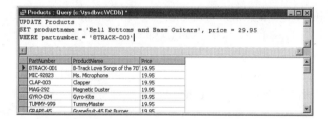

Visual Studio can help you by building the basic structure of the UPDATE statement. If you click the Change Type button on the Query toolbar and then select Update from the drop-down list, Visual Studio will create a partial UPDATE statement for you. All you need to do is fill in the field names and their values and add a WHERE clause.

 Caution   Make sure to include a WHERE clause in your UPDATE statement! An UPDATE statement that does not contain a WHERE clause will modify every record in the table.

Press the SQL Check button on the Query toolbar to verify the SQL syntax. The syntax should verify okay. Press the Run (!) button on the Query toolbar to execute the statement and update the record.

A message box will appear, telling you that one record was affected. The portion of the query window that displays the data will be empty because the UPDATE statement doesn't return any data. Change the SQL statement to a SELECT statement so that you can view the records, including the one you just modified. The record should reflect the changes you specified in your UPDATE statement.

As you can see from Figure 5.4, you can use an incomplete field list in an UPDATE statement to modify only some of the fields in the record. You can also do more advanced operations with the UPDATE statement, such as replacing numeric data with the results of a mathematical operation. Also, you can use a SELECT statement in the WHERE clause to modify records that match very complex criteria. Tomorrow you will learn more about advanced operations with the UPDATE statement.

The SQL DELETE Statement

The SQL DELETE statement enables you to delete existing records in the database. The basic syntax looks like this:

```
DELETE FROM which table WHERE condition
```

Because you are deleting an entire record, the DELETE statement doesn't require you to specify a list of fields. You tell it which table you want to delete a record from and the criteria for the record.

Now you will use the DELETE statement to remove the record you inserted into your database. Change the query so that it looks like the one in Figure 5.5.

FIGURE 5.5.

The DELETE *statement.*

5

Visual Studio can help you by building the basic structure of the DELETE statement. If you click the Change Type button on the Query toolbar and then select Delete from the drop-down list, Visual Studio will create a DELETE statement for you. In fact, Visual Studio will remember the WHERE clause from the UPDATE statement and use that for your DELETE statement.

> **Caution**
>
> Make sure to include a WHERE clause in your DELETE statement! A DELETE statement that doesn't contain a WHERE clause will delete every record in the table.

Press the SQL Check button on the Query toolbar to verify the SQL syntax. The syntax should verify okay. Press the Run (!) button on the Query toolbar to execute the statement and delete the record.

A message box will appear, telling you that one record was affected. The portion of the query window that displays the data will be empty because the DELETE statement doesn't return any data. Change the SQL statement to a SELECT statement so that you can view the records. The record you added should no longer exist in the Products table.

Summary

Today you learned two methods for manipulating records in a database. You learned how to manipulate records from C++ code by using the ADO Recordset member functions to insert, update, and delete records. You also learned how to manipulate records from SQL, using the INSERT, UPDATE, and DELETE statements.

Q&A

Q Is it possible to present a UI that lets users edit the contents of records in the database?

A Of course. It would be a matter of positioning the cursor on the appropriate record and calling the ADO Recordset GetCollect function to read the values of the data from the record's fields. You could place those data values in edit controls for the users to change if they want. Then, if users specify that they want to commit the changes to the database, your code could call the PutCollect and Update functions to make the changes in the database.

Q I need to optimize the query performance of my database. What is the fastest cursor type for queries?

A As I mentioned, forward-only cursors are the fastest for query processing. For even greater speed, you could specify a read-only, forward-only cursor. You make a cursor read-only by specifying adLockReadOnly as the lock type in the ADO Recordset Open function. You cannot insert, update, or delete records in a read-only cursor, but select performance will be optimal and significantly faster than other cursor types.

Q When should I use the ADO Recordset AddNew, Update, and Delete functions, and when should I use the SQL INSERT, UPDATE, and DELETE statements?

A If you need to modify data from within a C++ program, you could use the ADO Recordset functions. You could also execute a SQL INSERT, UPDATE, or DELETE statement from within a C++ program by using the ADO Connection `Execute` function. Typically, you would use the ADO Connection to execute a SQL statement only when you need to build the SQL statement dynamically at runtime and submit it to database for processing. If you know at design time what the operations on the database will be, you should use the ADO `Recordset` functions because they generally give better performance.

Workshop

The Workshop quiz questions test your understanding of today's material. (The answers appear in Appendix F, "Answers.") The exercises encourage you to apply the information you learned today to real-life situations.

Quiz

1. What is a forward-only cursor?
2. What function do you use to place a value in a field of the current record in an ADO `Recordset`?
3. What is wrong with this SQL statement?
   ```
   DELETE FROM customers
   ```
4. What are the two arguments that you must pass to the ADO `Recordset` `AddNew` function?
5. What happens if you specify only one field/value pair in the `SET` clause of the SQL `UPDATE` function?

Exercises

1. Discover what happens in the `Price` field when you specify only the `PartNumber` and `ProductName` fields in a SQL `INSERT` statement for the `Products` table, like this:
   ```
   INSERT INTO Products(PartNumber, ProductName)
   VALUES ('xxx', 'yyy')
   ```
2. Modify the code in Listing 5.1 so that it doesn't specify a price for the new record.

DAY 6

Harnessing the Power of Relational Database Servers

Database servers have the capacity to process huge amounts of data at the server while requiring very little processing from client applications. This enables you to use database servers as backend data-processing engines for large client/server applications and for database-driven Web sites.

When you complete today's work, you will understand how to use relational database servers as backend data-processing engines.

Today you will

- Learn about multitier applications.
- Discover how to process data at the server.
- Create SQL statements that process data at the server.
- Use C++ tools for processing data at the server.

Multitier Applications

In a conventional C++ application, all the logic for the application is implemented in C++ code, and at runtime a single process executes the code. If the database for the application is merely a file on disk, the database is basically inert. The database has no life of its own because all the logic and processing are done inside the application's C++ code.

This is a classic single-tier system. The application consists of one process that does all the work. (As you know, a process in Win32 is one instance of a running program.)

In a multitier system, the application consists of more than one process. These processes run simultaneously and cooperate with each other to accomplish the work of the application. The processes can be running on different machines. Each process typically has certain tasks that it is optimized to perform. The different processes in the application are organized into tiers, based on the type of tasks they perform and the machine on which they are running.

A relational database server is a process that is optimized to handle large amounts of data and can do this without any help from the other processes in the application.

Keep in mind that in a multitier application, the database server is not inert. The database itself has logic and processing power. You can write code that is executed by the database. The trick is to build your database code so that the database fulfills the task of handling large amounts of data without burdening the other processes in the application.

To avoid burdening other processes in the application, the database server code must do all the heavy lifting when it comes to processing records from the database. The database code must reduce records from the database into information, information that has been processed and summarized into bite-size pieces that the other processes in the application can easily swallow. To accomplish this, you must learn how to process data at the server.

How to Process Data at the Server

The programs you have thus far created for this book have processed records one at a time. Relational database servers are capable of processing many records at a time. In fact, they are built to do just that. Using a relational database to process one record at a time is like using a dump truck to haul one shovelful of dirt at a time. You can do it, but it's wasteful.

You need to know how to do two things to create multitier applications that take advantage of relational database servers. You need to learn how to use SQL statements that process more than one record at a time and how to call those SQL statements from within a C++ program in such a way that the database server (instead of your C++ program) does the heavy lifting of the data.

SQL Statements for Processing Data at the Server

Yesterday you learned how to use the SQL INSERT, UPDATE, and DELETE statements. The SQL statements you worked with yesterday added, modified, and deleted single records.

In your work yesterday, the SQL INSERT, UPDATE, and DELETE statements were underutilized. A single INSERT, UPDATE, or DELETE statement needn't be limited to one record. The statement can affect literally millions of records in the database, and the database will execute these statements without any need for help or intervention from other processes.

The SQL INSERT Statement

As you will recall, the SQL INSERT statement enables you to add records to the database. The basic syntax to add a single record looks like this:

```
INSERT INTO which table( list of columns ) VALUES( list of values )
```

However, you can extend this syntax to add multiple records by using one INSERT statement. You can add multiple records to a table by replacing the VALUES clause with a SELECT statement that selects multiple records, like this:

```
INSERT INTO which table( list of columns ) SELECT * FROM which table
```

You can use this technique yourself in the VCDb.mdb database. Open your ADOMFC1 project, select the Data View, and open a Query window on the Orders table. You will see that three orders are recorded in the table. Let's say a customer named Bill Clinton wants to order all the 8-track tapes the company sells. (Remember that in the sample application from Day 1, "Choosing the Right Database Technology," you are writing a C++ program that salespeople use to record these orders.)

As you know, the products are listed in the Products table. Open a Query window on the Products table, and you will see that the company sells two 8-track tapes. You added a third 8-track yesterday when you learned about the SQL INSERT statement. You also removed it when you learned about the DELETE statement. To make this exercise more interesting, again add the third 8-track into the Products table by using the following INSERT statement:

```
INSERT INTO Products (partnumber, productname, price)
 VALUES('8TRACK-003', 'Bell Bottoms and Bass Guitars', 29.95)
```

Mr. Clinton wants to order all the 8-tracks the company sells. That means that to record the order, you need to insert three records into the Orders table. You could issue three INSERT statements, one for each record. The first INSERT statement would look like Listing 6.1.

LISTING 6.1. THE INSERT STATEMENT TO ADD A SINGLE ORDER RECORD

```
1:  INSERT INTO Orders (ordernumber, orderdate,
2:                       customernumber, partnumber, price,
3:                       shippingandhandling, paymentmethod)
4:  VALUES      (4, { d '1998-11-16' }, 5, '8TRACK-001',
5:              19.95, 4, 'MC 1223 9873 2028 8374 9/99')
```

You would need to issue two more INSERT statements, one for each additional 8-track. Issuing these INSERT statements from your C++ program (using ADO) would mean three calls from your program into the database. If your C++ program and the database were running on different machines, it would require three network round trips between machines just to add one order.

For your application to be efficient, the database needs to do the bulk of the work with the data. There needs to be some way to add an order for all the 8-tracks by using just one call from your C++ program: You use a single INSERT statement to add multiple records. To do this, you must replace the VALUES clause of the INSERT statement with a SELECT statement.

First, you need to create a SELECT statement that produces output that can be inserted into the Orders table. The output from the SELECT must produce data that matches the fields in the Orders table. The SELECT statement in Listing 6.2 does this.

LISTING 6.2. THE SELECT STATEMENT THAT MATCHES ORDER RECORDS

```
1: SELECT 4, { d '1998-11-16' }, 5, PartNumber, Price, 4,
2:   'MC 1223 9873 2028 8374 9/99'
3:  FROM Products
4:  WHERE (PartNumber LIKE '8TRACK%')
```

In the Data View, click the plus sign next to the Orders table so that you can see its fields and can compare them with the SELECT statement in Listing 6.2. The SELECT statement begins in line 1 by selecting 4, which will be the order number for this order. The 4 is hard-coded into the SELECT statement, so every record that the SELECT produces will begin with a numeric 4. The next value the SELECT produces is a date of November 16, 1998. This is followed by a 5, which is Mr. Clinton's customer number. Then it selects the PartNumber and Price fields (you can see in the FROM clause in line 3 that these fields come from the Products table). Last, the SELECT statement produces another numeric 4 (for the ShippingAndHandling field in Orders) and a credit card number (for the PaymentMethod field in Orders).

The WHERE clause in line 4 uses the LIKE keyword and the % wildcard character to find all product records that have a part number that begins with "8TRACK". Issue this SELECT statement against the Products table, and it will return three records.

You now have a SELECT statement that produces output that can be inserted into the Orders table. You can use this SELECT statement inside an INSERT statement to add an order for all the 8-tracks the company sells, as in Listing 6.3.

LISTING 6.3. THE INSERT STATEMENT WITH SELECT FOR ADDING MULTIPLE RECORDS

```
1:  INSERT INTO Orders (ordernumber, orderdate, customernumber,
                        ↪partnumber,
2:                      price, shippingandhandling, paymentmethod)
3:  SELECT 4, { d '1998-11-16' }, 5, PartNumber, Price, 4,
4:    'MC 1223 9873 2028 8374 9/99'
5:  FROM Products
6:  WHERE (PartNumber LIKE '8TRACK%')
```

Issue this statement from a Query window; then open the Orders table and see that it added three records.

Now you have a single SQL statement that adds multiple records. Your C++ program no longer needs to issue three INSERT statements to the database to add this order. Your C++ program can send this single INSERT statement to add all three records. The database is handling all the processing of the data, with only one call from the client application.

This is the essence of multitier database application development. The idea is to take advantage of the power of the relational database servers to reduce the number of round trips between the client and server processes.

6

The SQL UPDATE Statement

The SQL UPDATE statements you wrote yesterday updated only one record. As you might have guessed, though, the UPDATE statement can update multiple records in a single call. The syntax for doing this is straightforward. As you recall, the syntax for UPDATE is

```
UPDATE which table SET which field = new value, which field = new value ...
WHERE condition
```

Suppose you need to change the price of all the 8-tracks in the database. Despite sales to Mr. Travolta and Mr. Clinton, the company is not selling enough 8-track tapes. To spur demand, management has decided to reduce the price of each 8-track by $10.

As you know, there are three 8-track records in the Products table. You could issue three UPDATE statements, or you could issue a statement like the following:

```
UPDATE products SET price = (price - 10) WHERE (PartNumber LIKE '8TRACK%')
```

This statement will update every record where the PartNumber field starts with "8TRACK", replacing the Price field with $10 less than the current price listed in that record. Execute this statement to make sure it works the way you would expect.

The SQL DELETE Statement

Now suppose, even after the price decrease, that sales of the 8-tracks still aren't sufficient. Therefore, the company has decided to discontinue selling 8-tracks.

You must delete the three 8-track records from the Products table. Should you issue three DELETE statements? I think not. You should issue a single DELETE statement with the WHERE clause written so that it affects all the 8-track records, like this:

```
DELETE FROM Products WHERE (PartNumber LIKE '8TRACK%')
```

However, if you try to issue this command, you will receive an error from the database (provided the Access database is set up to enforce referential integrity, like the database on the CD-ROM). The DELETE statement is correct, but what you are trying to do will cause orphaned data in the Orders table. You can't delete these records from the Products table because their part numbers are included in orders recorded in the Orders table. If you delete these product records, you would not be able to obtain complete information on past orders that include these products. The orders would show a part number only. You would not be able to look up the name of the product because that information would no longer exist in the Products table. In relational database parlance, deleting these records would violate the referential integrity of the data.

A less-than-relational database would let you make the mistake of deleting these product records. Relational database servers such as SQL Server and Oracle prevent this type of mistake and help you preserve the referential integrity of your data. Microsoft Access, which does the best job of applying the relational model in desktop databases, also prevents this mistake. When using other database technologies, *caveat developer* (let the developer beware).

Rather than delete these records, a better approach might be to add a field to the Products table to indicate whether the product is currently for sale. You will learn more about relational database design in the next few days.

SQL Stored Procedures

I mentioned earlier today that a database server is not inert. The database itself has logic and processing power. As you know, client programs can send text strings containing SQL statements to the database, and the database will interpret the statements and return any data that they produce. It is possible for relational database servers to save SQL statements in a compiled form.

NEW TERM *Stored procedures* are compiled SQL statements, which are stored inside a relational database. Each stored procedure is given a unique name so that client programs can call it.

Stored procedures provide two important benefits. They enable SQL code to run in compiled instead of interpreted form. The benefit of compiled SQL code is faster execution. In addition, stored procedures execute at the server and require no resources from a client program. The second benefit derives from stored procedures providing a layer of abstraction that can hide the details of the database design. The benefit of this abstraction is that client programs need not know the details of how the various tables and fields in database are constructed. The client code can be simpler, and the database design can be modified without breaking the client code.

A stored procedure may be a straight SQL statement that simply executes as it is written, or it may accept parameters from the calling program for more dynamic execution, as you will see later today.

Relational database servers (such as Oracle and SQL Server) are the only databases that provide true stored procedures. Microsoft Access provides something similar to stored procedures, called Queries. These Queries in Access are in some ways similar to stored procedures: They can be called by name from client programs, they can accept parameters, and they can abstract the details of the database.

However, Queries in Access are not compiled like stored procedures in relational database servers. Queries also do not execute at the server (because Access applications are file based, as described in Day 1). Another difference is that Visual Studio treats Access Queries as Views in the Data View window. This is unfortunate because, as you will see later, it prevents you from executing Queries that take parameters from inside Visual Studio. By contrast, SQL Server stored procedures appear in a folder titled Stored Procedures in the Data View window. If you execute a SQL Server stored procedure that takes parameters from inside Visual Studio, you will be prompted to enter the parameters, and the stored procedure will execute properly.

Despite their shortcomings, Queries in Access do provide a place to begin your exploration of stored procedures. In fact, two Queries are included in VCDb.mdb. The first

6

Query is called `CustomerWithMostRecentOrder` and consists of a simple `SELECT` statement. The text of the `SELECT` statement is shown in Listing 6.4.

LISTING 6.4. THE CustomerWithMostRecentOrder SQL STATEMENT

```
 1:  SELECT 'Customers'.*
 2:  FROM Customers
 3:  WHERE custnumber IN
 4:  (
 5:        SELECT 'Orders'.customernumber
 6:        FROM 'Orders'
 7:        WHERE orderdate =
 8:        (
 9:                SELECT MAX(orderdate)
10:                FROM Orders
11:        )
12:  );
```

This is the same query you saw in Day 3, "Retrieving Data Through Structured Query Language (SQL)," that returns the customer who placed the most recent order. Because it's now stored as a Query in the Access database, you can run it without having to send all the SQL code to the database from a client program. A client program can simply call the Query. One way to call Queries in Access (and stored procedures in a relational database) is to use an ADO Command object. You will learn about ADO Command objects later today. You can execute this Query in Visual Studio by double-clicking it in the Data View.

The second Query is called `CustomersWithOrdersSinceDate` and consists of a `SELECT` statement that takes a date as a parameter. The text of the Query is shown in Listing 6.5.

LISTING 6.5. THE CustomersWithOrdersSinceDate SQL STATEMENT

```
 1:  SELECT 'Customers'.*
 2:  FROM Customers
 3:  WHERE custnumber IN
 4:  (
 5:    SELECT 'Orders'.customernumber
 6:    FROM 'Orders'
 7:    WHERE OrderDate > [param1]
 8:  );
```

The `CustomersWithOrdersSinceDate` query shown in Listing 6.5 selects the customers who have ordered after a certain date. What date? Well, the database lets the client application (or the human user) specify that date at runtime. Unfortunately, if you try to run this query from inside Visual Studio, you will receive an error message indicating that it was expecting one parameter. However, you will be able to execute this query from C++ code that you will write in the next section of today's work.

If this were a stored procedure in a relational database server, the SQL code would look like Listing 6.6.

LISTING 6.6. THE CustomersWithOrdersSinceDate STORED PROCEDURE

```
1:  CREATE PROCEDURE CustomersWithOrdersSinceDate @param1 datetime AS
2:  SELECT Customers.*
3:  FROM Customers
4:  WHERE custnumber IN
5:  (
6:    SELECT Orders.customernumber
7:    FROM Orders
8:    WHERE OrderDate > @param1
9:  )
```

Line 1 in Listing 6.6 uses the SQL CREATE PROCEDURE statement to cause the stored procedure to be compiled and saved in the database. Line 1 also specifies the parameter name (prefixed by an @) and type immediately after the stored procedure name. You execute this SQL code to create and store the stored procedure in the database. When the stored procedure is stored in the database, client applications can call CustomersWithOrdersSinceDate and pass it a date as a parameter to obtain a resultset of customers who have made purchases since that date. A client program can do this, using an ADO Command object.

Note that a client program that uses CustomersWithOrdersSinceDate doesn't try to obtain all the orders and all the customers and then process all that data to find the customer records. Rather, the client program makes a single request to the database and retrieves only the data that is relevant.

As you'll see in the next section, the programming models are identical, whether the client program is using Access or a relational database server. You can use an ADO Command object to call Access Queries as well as SQL Server stored procedures. The difference between Access and SQL Server is that, with Access, all the records are brought into the client process. This happens behind the scenes, so you don't deal with it in your code. It happens because Access applications are file based (as described in Day 1) and because the Jet database engine is a DLL that runs inside the client program's address space. With SQL Server, only the data that the client program requested is brought into the client process (because the server processes all the records and returns only the resultset).

6

C++ Tools for Processing Data at the Server

Yesterday, you created ADO Recordsets and used the AddNew, Update, and Delete functions. These functions work well when you are dealing with single records or when the number of records in the resultset is very small.

However, there will likely be occasions when you need to perform an operation that affects thousands or millions of records. The following is a programming sequence you should *not* follow in your client program when you need to perform an operation on a large number of records:

- Create a Recordset that contains all the records that will be affected.
- Pull all the records into the client process by starting at the first record in the Recordset and calling the MoveNext function to scroll to the last record.
- Process each record singly (by evaluating the contents of the fields in each record or by calling Update or Delete on each record).

Using a programming sequence like this to deal with a large number of records would be slow and could hog the network's bandwidth and consume the client computer's memory. The solution in cases where you have a large number of records to process is to write a stored procedure so that all those records can be processed at the server. You call the stored procedure by using an ADO Command object.

Open your ADOMFC1 project and add a menu for Commands with two choices, as shown in Figure 6.1.

FIGURE 6.1.

Menus for ADO Commands.

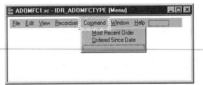

Calling Stored Procedures with ADO Command Objects

Use ClassWizard to create a handler function for the Most Recent Order menu choice. In the handler function, add the code shown in Listing 6.7.

```
 1: void CADOMFC1View::OnCommandMostrecentorder()
 2: {
 3:   _CommandPtr pCommand;
 4:
 5:   pCommand.CreateInstance(__uuidof( Command ));
 6:
 7:   CADOMFC1Doc * pDoc;
 8:   pDoc = GetDocument();
 9:
10:   try
11:   {
12:     pCommand->ActiveConnection = pDoc->m_pConnection;
13:
14:     pCommand->CommandType = adCmdStoredProc;
15:
16:     pCommand->CommandText = _bstr_t("CustomerWithMostRecentOrder");
17:
18:     _variant_t vNull;
19:     vNull.vt = VT_ERROR;
20:     vNull.scode = DISP_E_PARAMNOTFOUND;
21:
22:     _RecordsetPtr pRS;
23:
24:     pRS = pCommand->Execute( &vNull, &vNull, adCmdUnknown );
25:
26:     if (!pRS->GetadoEOF())
27:     {
28:       CListCtrlEx& ctlList = (CListCtrlEx&) GetListCtrl();
29:       ctlList.DeleteAllItems();
30:       while(ctlList.DeleteColumn(0));
31:
32:       ctlList.AddColumn("  Customer Number  ",0);
33:       ctlList.AddColumn("  First Name  ",1);
34:       ctlList.AddColumn("  Last Name   ",2);
35:
36:       int i = 0;
37:       _variant_t vCustName;
38:       _variant_t vFirstName;
39:       _variant_t vLastName;
40:       while (!pRS->GetadoEOF())
41:       {
42:         vCustName = pRS->GetCollect(L"CustNumber");
43:         ctlList.AddItem(i,0,(_bstr_t) vCustName);
44:         vFirstName = pRS->GetCollect(L"CustFirstName");
45:         ctlList.AddItem(i,1,(_bstr_t) vFirstName);
46:         vLastName = pRS->GetCollect(L"CustLastName");
47:         ctlList.AddItem(i,2,(_bstr_t) vLastName);
48:         i++;
```

continues

6

LISTING 6.7.   CONTINUED

```
49:            pRS->MoveNext();
50:          }
51:        }
52:
53:        pRS->Close();
54:    }
55:    catch( _com_error &e )
56:    {
57:      TRACE( "Error:%08lx.\n", e.Error());
58:      TRACE( "ErrorMessage:%s.\n", e.ErrorMessage());
59:      TRACE( "Source:%s.\n", (LPCTSTR) _bstr_t(e.Source()));
60:      TRACE( "Description:%s.\n", (LPCTSTR) _bstr_t(e.Description()));
61:    }
62:    catch(...)
63:    {
64:      TRACE( "\n*** Unhandled Exception ***\n" );
65:    }
66:  }
```

Lines 3 and 5 of Listing 6.7 create an ADO Command object. Line 12 tells the Command object to use the existing database connection stored in the MFC Document. Lines 14 and 16 tell the Command object that you are going to call a stored procedure; also, lines 14 and 16 tell the Command object the name of the stored procedure. Line 22 creates a Recordset pointer, and line 24 calls the Command object's Execute function to execute the stored procedure and place any resulting data in a Recordset object (which is pointed to by the Recordset pointer). Lines 26–51 display the contents of the Recordset in the list control in the View. (The code in lines 40–50 uses a while loop, which is probably unnecessary because this stored procedure returns only one record.)

Note that the C++ code in Listing 6.7 does not retrieve a Recordset containing all orders, find the most recent order by looking at every record, and then finally retrieve the customer for that order. This code issues a single call to the database, enables the database to process the records, and retrieves only the customer information it's looking for.

This approach is elegant and harnesses the power of a relational database server. It could handle millions of records without hogging network bandwidth or consuming memory in client process space.

In this example, Microsoft Access appears to be processing the records at the server, just like a relational database server. However, with Access, all the records are brought into the client program address space to be evaluated by the Jet database engine (which resides in a DLL mapped into the client program address space). The programming model is identical to a relational database server, but the actual execution model doesn't utilize true client/server capabilities.

Calling Stored Procedures That Take Parameters

Use ClassWizard to create a handler function for the Ordered Since Date menu choice. In the handler function, add the code shown in Listing 6.8.

LISTING 6.8. THE ADO COMMAND OBJECT TO CALL ORDEREDSINCEDATE

```
 1:  void CADOMFC1View::OnCommandOrderedsincedate()
 2:  {
 3:    _CommandPtr pCommand;
 4:
 5:    pCommand.CreateInstance( __uuidof( Command ) );
 6:
 7:    CADOMFC1Doc * pDoc;
 8:    pDoc = GetDocument();
 9:
10:    try
11:    {
12:      pCommand->ActiveConnection = pDoc->m_pConnection;
13:
14:      pCommand->CommandType = adCmdStoredProc;
15:
16:      pCommand->CommandText = _bstr_t("CustomersWithOrdersSinceDate");
17:
18:      pCommand->Parameters->Append
19:      (
20:        pCommand->CreateParameter
21:        (
22:          _bstr_t("ParamDate"),
23:          adDBTimeStamp,
24:          adParamInput,
25:          0,
26:          _variant_t(COleDateTime(1998, 10, 1, 0, 0, 0))
27:        )
28:      );
29:
30:      _variant_t vNull;
31:      vNull.vt = VT_ERROR;
32:      vNull.scode = DISP_E_PARAMNOTFOUND;
33:
34:      _RecordsetPtr pRS;
35:
36:      pRS = pCommand->Execute( &vNull, &vNull, adCmdUnknown );
37:
38:      if (!pRS->GetadoEOF())
39:      {
40:        CListCtrlEx& ctlList = (CListCtrlEx&) GetListCtrl();
41:        ctlList.DeleteAllItems();
```

continues

6

LISTING 6.8.   CONTINUED

```
42:            while(ctlList.DeleteColumn(0));
43:
44:            ctlList.AddColumn("  Customer Number  ",0);
45:            ctlList.AddColumn("  First Name  ",1);
46:            ctlList.AddColumn("  Last Name  ",2);
47:
48:            int i = 0;
49:            _variant_t vCustName;
50:            _variant_t vFirstName;
51:            _variant_t vLastName;
52:            while (!pRS->GetadoEOF())
53:            {
54:              vCustName = pRS->GetCollect(L"CustNumber");
55:              ctlList.AddItem(i,0,(_bstr_t) vCustName);
56:              vFirstName = pRS->GetCollect(L"CustFirstName");
57:              ctlList.AddItem(i,1,(_bstr_t) vFirstName);
58:              vLastName = pRS->GetCollect(L"CustLastName");
59:              ctlList.AddItem(i,2,(_bstr_t) vLastName);
60:              i++;
61:              pRS->MoveNext();
62:            }
63:        }
64:
65:        pRS->Close();
66:    }
67:    catch( _com_error &e )
68:    {
69:      TRACE( "Error:%08lx.\n", e.Error());
70:      TRACE( "ErrorMessage:%s.\n", e.ErrorMessage());
71:      TRACE( "Source:%s.\n", (LPCTSTR) _bstr_t(e.Source()));
72:      TRACE( "Description:%s.\n", (LPCTSTR) _bstr_t(e.Description()));
73:    }
74:    catch(...)
75:    {
76:      TRACE( "\n*** Unhandled Exception ***\n" );
77:    }
78: }
```

The code in Listing 6.8 is nearly identical to Listing 6.7. One crucial difference is in line 16 where the name of the stored procedure is specified. Another important difference is in lines 18–28. The ADO Command object contains a Parameters collection, which stores the parameters that will be passed to the stored procedure when Execute is called. The pCommand->Parameters->Append call in line 18 appends a new parameter to the Parameters collection for this Command object. The argument passed to the Append function is the result of the pCommand->CreateParameter call in lines 20–27.

Line 22 names the parameter (so you can access it to change its value later if you want). Line 23 specifies the data type for this parameter, which is adDBTimeStamp. The available data types are declared in the DataTypeEnum in msado15.tlh, which is one of the files created when you use #import on the ADO type library. Line 24 specifies that this is an *input parameter*, meaning that this client program is giving this parameter to the database. The parameter directions (input, output, or both) are declared in the ParameterDirectionEnum in msado15.tlh. An *output parameter* would be one where the value of the parameter is changed by the stored procedure and then read by the client program after executing the stored procedure. Line 25 specifies the length of the parameter data. This is not used for adDBTimeStamp types but is used for numeric and string types. Line 26 is a _variant_t containing the data value for the parameter that will be passed to the stored procedure. In this case, a COleDateTime is used because it encapsulates the VARIANT date/time stuff and makes it easier to use. You need to pass data of the appropriate type to the _variant_t constructor in line 26, based on the data type you specify in line 23.

That's it. When you run the application and take this menu choice, you will see displayed in the list control the customers who have made purchases since the date specified. The parameter value needn't be hard-coded. You could, of course, expand this code to let the user enter a date, and then you could pass that date to the stored procedure.

Note

If you specify a COleDateTime of 11/1/1998 0:0:00, you will see that the stored procedure returns customers who made purchases on 11/1/1998. This might seem strange because the SQL code specifies OrderDates that are *greater* than the parameter value. However, you must realize that this a date/time data type. It will take the time into account, as well as the date. If you specified a COleDateTime of 11/1/1998 23:59:59 instead, you probably wouldn't see any customers who placed orders on 11/1/1998.

Summary

6

Today you learned how to harness the power of relational database servers. You saw how the SQL INSERT, UPDATE, AND DELETE statements can be used to process many records at a time. You also learned about stored procedures and how to call them by using ADO Command objects.

You wrote code that illustrated methods for processing data at the server. Your ability to write code that processes data at the server will enable you to create applications that can handle huge amounts of data and work efficiently over a LAN, a WAN, or the Internet.

Q&A

Q **What's the difference between client/server applications and multitier applications?**

A Client/server applications typically consist of client machine(s) running a Windows application, connected over a LAN to a relational database server on a network server machine. This is a two-tier system (client and server). Multitier applications typically consist of more than two tiers. The client tier consists of machine(s) running some kind of a thin client program, such as a Web browser or a simple application. There is often a middle tier, consisting of machine(s) running a Web server, such as Internet Information Server (IIS) and/or an Object Request Broker (ORB) such as Microsoft Transaction Server (MTS). The server tier typically consists of a server running a relational database. Client tier programs typically communicate with programs on the middle tier, which then communicate with the database at the server tier. The clients do not communicate with the database directly, only through the middle tier programs.

Q **When should I use the ADO Recordset `AddNew`, `Update`, and `Delete` functions instead of stored procedures?**

A For inserting records, the ADO Recordset `AddNew` function can be faster than calling a stored procedure to insert records. For summarizing, updating, and/or deleting records, it depends on the number of records you need to work with. If the number of records is small, you can get by with pulling the records into a Recordset at the client to process them. If, however, the number of records isn't small, you should consider using a stored procedure called from an ADO Command object. The only caveat for ADO Command objects seems to be that the process of changing parameter values in the Parameters collection can be CPU intensive at the client. Your mileage might vary, so write some test code and benchmark the performance for your own applications.

Q **Can I create Access Queries from within Visual Studio?**

A No, the only way to create new Queries in an Access database (.mdb file) is to run Microsoft Access and create the new Queries through the Access UI.

Workshop

The Workshop quiz questions test your understanding of today's material. (The answers appear in Appendix F, "Answers.") The exercises encourage you to apply the information you learned today to real-life situations.

Quiz

1. What is a single-tier application?

2. How do you make the SQL INSERT statement insert multiple records?

3. What databases help you preserve the referential integrity of your data?

4. How is a stored procedure in a relational database different from a Query in Microsoft Access?

5. Where can you find the data types available for use in ADO Parameter objects?

Exercises

1. Modify the SELECT statement in Listing 6.2 so that the customer number is not hard-coded. Make it so that the customer number is retrieved based on the customer's last name.

2. Add code to the OrderedSinceDate handler shown in Listing 6.8 to change the value of the parameter after it has been appended to the command but before the Command has been executed.

6

DAY 7

Database Design

A good database design pays big dividends. A database that is properly designed is easy to write code for, provides good performance, and furnishes useful information that you had not anticipated needing at the time the database was first designed.

Today you will learn

- How to normalize a database to ensure ready access to the data
- SQL Data Definition Language (DDL) for creating and altering the structure of databases
- How to use constraints and indexes in a relational database to manage relationships and improve performance
- Tools and techniques for managing relationships among the tables in your database

Designing a good database is harder than it looks. It is also more important than many developers realize. In other words, designing a database takes time and effort, but it is time and effort well spent.

Database Normalization

Even though designing a database can be difficult, a few rules of thumb simplify the process. In addition, there are some sound scientific principles for designing relational databases. These scientific principles of database design are called the *normal forms* of relational databases.

NEW TERM *Normal forms* are database design rules that specify levels of conformance to the relational model. There are six levels of conformance, beginning at the first normal form (1NF), progressing through the fifth (5NF), and concluding with the highest level of conformance, which is the domain/key normal form (DKNF).

NEW TERM *Database normalization* is the process of designing the tables in a database so that they conform to the *normal forms* of the relational database model.

The normal forms are essentially a measure of how well the tables in your database conform to the relational model. The normal forms are nested. If a table in your database conforms to the 3NF, it automatically conforms to the 2NF and the 1NF as well.

Building a database that conforms to the normal forms of the relational model takes effort, but it is a worthwhile effort. If your database conforms to the relational model, everyone who uses your database (now and in the future) will be assured of having access to the data in a way that makes the database open and therefore valuable.

Rules of Thumb for Relational Database Design

Before delving into the normal forms, I will explain the rules of thumb that simplify the process of database design. There are three of them, and I call them *Robison's Rules of Database Design*, or *R2D2* for short.

Tip

R2D2 #1 (the first rule): The number of records in your database should mirror the number of objects in real life.

If one instance of an object exists in real life (IRL), one and only one record (one row in a table) should exist in your database. If exactly twenty instances exist IRL, exactly twenty records should exist in your database.

For example, if your database stores information about customers, the database should have one, and only one, record for each customer. The database should not hold more than one customer per record, nor should it split a customer across multiple records.

R2D2 #1 is fundamental to designing a relational database and will make your application more valuable because it helps ensure that your database is open and accessible. I worked on a commercial application that, to optimize performance, stored more than one IRL object per record in the database. The result was a marginal gain in the performance of the database. However, because of its lack of conformance to the relational model, the database could not be accessed outside the application. This limitation proved to be a detriment to the application's commercial success.

Tip

R2D2 #2: The fields in each record should represent the attributes of the objects in real life.

If you use R2D2 #1 and make each record represent an object IRL, you can use R2D2 #2 to figure out what fields those records should contain. You can also deduce what the data types of those attributes should be.

Tip

R2D2 #3: The relationships between objects in real life should be mirrored in the relationships between records in the database.

If a customer can place more than one order, this is a one-to-many relationship. The database must be built to store more than one order record for each customer record, thus mirroring the one-to-many relationship between customers and orders IRL. The other types of relationships are one to one and many to many.

NEW TERM The relationships between records in various tables in a relational database are called the *entity relationships*.

There are tools and techniques for implementing one-to-one, one-to-many, and many-to-many relationships in relational database. You will learn about these tools and techniques later today.

Normal Forms of the Relational Database Model

In addition to Robison's Rules for Database Design are the normal forms of the relational model. Based on sound scientific principles and ensure that your database will be accessible and valuable, now and in the future.

The First Normal Form

The *first normal form* (1NF) requires that, in a given table, the data type of each field must not change from record to record. In C++ parlance, a database table must be like an array of structures; the data structure does not vary from element to element in the array. A database table must not be like an array of unions, in which the data structure can vary from element to element.

7

Each column must have a unique name. Each field in each record must contain a single value, meaning it must describe a single attribute and cannot contain a compound data type that holds more than one attribute.

There can be no repeating fields. A record cannot contain any repeating data, such as multiple fields in the record that contain the same type of attribute. (This would be a one-to-many relationship and should be represented in two tables.)

Each record must be unique; there can be no duplicate records in the table. Creating a primary key for the table (such as a Social Security number for people, a part number for products, and so on) usually ensures the uniqueness of records in a table. The primary key cannot contain a NULL in any records.

Sometimes it's necessary to create a composite key, which is made up of two or more fields in the record.

NEW TERM   A *composite key* is a key that consists of two or more fields in a database table.

For example, you might have a table that records the dates that products were shipped. You might specify the part number field and the ship date field as the primary key. The fields are separate fields, but the combination of the two fields constitutes a composite key.

In a nutshell, 1NF requires that your tables be simple two-dimensional tables with no repeating fields and with the fields containing no compound data types.

The Second Normal Form

The *second normal form* (2NF) requires that all the fields in the database contain data that depends on the entire primary key. If a table uses a single field as its key and is in 1NF, it is automatically in 2NF.

If you were to apply 2NF to a table with a composite key of the part number field and the ship date field, you couldn't have any fields in the table that apply only to the ship date field or only to the part number field. For instance, in this table you wouldn't want a field for the total number of all products shipped that day, such as the Quantity field shown in Figure 7.1. In this example, three products were actually shipped on 11/16/98 (one each of the three 8-tracks).

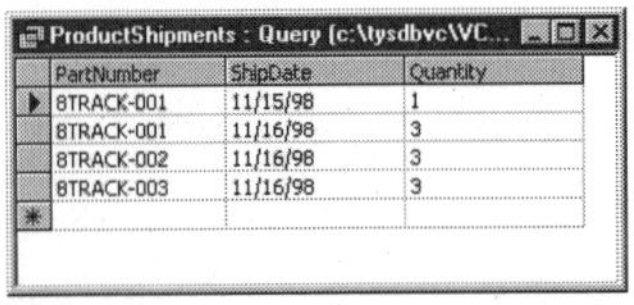

FIGURE 7.1.

A table showing the quantity of all products shipped daily.

PartNumber	ShipDate	Quantity
8TRACK-001	11/15/98	1
8TRACK-001	11/16/98	3
8TRACK-002	11/16/98	3
8TRACK-003	11/16/98	3

The Quantity field contains the total of all products shipped that day. Supposedly, you could select any record that has a ship date you are looking for and use the Quantity field from that record to discover the total number of products shipped that day. However, the `Quantity` field violates the 2NF. The `Quantity` field applies only to the ship date field, not to the part number field. This results in duplicate data (multiple records with 3 for the quantity for 11/16/98).

All the non-key fields in the record must apply to the unique combination of ship date and part number. Therefore, you could have a field in the table that contains the total number of each particular product that was shipped that day. This field would depend on both the part number and the ship date, as the `Quantity` field now does in Figure 7.2.

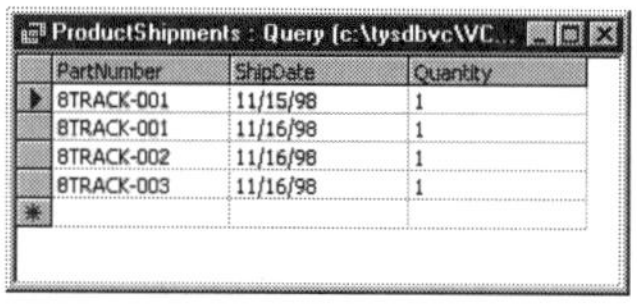

PartNumber	ShipDate	Quantity
8TRACK-001	11/15/98	1
8TRACK-001	11/16/98	1
8TRACK-002	11/16/98	1
8TRACK-003	11/16/98	1

FIGURE 7.2.
A table showing the quantity of each product shipped daily.

The `Quantity` field shown in Figure 7.2 applies to both the part number field and the ship date field. The part number field and the ship date field make up the entire key, so the table is in 2NF. One way to discover the total number of products shipped on a given day is to use an aggregate function to add up the quantity field of all the records for that date. You will learn more about aggregate functions in the next few days.

The Third Normal Form

The *third normal form* (3NF) requires that there be no transitive dependencies, in which one field depends on another field, which in turn depends on another field. When a table violates 3NF, lack of records in one table can result in loss of information.

For example, look at the following table with the `PartNo` as the key:

PartNo	*Description*	*Artist*	*Gender*
000001	8-TrackTape	Hendrix	Male

The `Gender` field depends on a field (`Artist`) rather than the `PartNo` key.

Technically, if you have the zip code, city, and state in an address record, it probably isn't in 3NF, because an argument can be made that the city and state depend on the zip code.

Lack of normalization does not necessarily ruin the design, however. The higher levels of normalization (4NF, 5NF, and DKNF) prevent any loss of information. As you progress to higher levels of normalization, you end up creating more and more specialized tables. However, conforming to the higher levels of normalization can have a negative effect on performance because of the increasing number of tables and the complexity of the SQL joins you have to write.

You should design your tables to conform to the highest normal form as is practical. Violating the normal forms should be the exception rather than the rule in your database designs. The optimum database design is often slightly denormalized (but only slightly).

SQL Data Definition Language

Open your ADOMFC1 project, select the Data View, and open a Query window on the Customers table. You will see that the Customers table does conform to R2D2 #1; there is one customer per record. Does it conform to the normal forms? Well, almost. There are two address fields. Strictly speaking, this is a violation of 1NF because the records have repeating fields. However, you could make the case that the two address fields are not repeating data but are two distinct elements that make up a street address. With this possible exception, the Customers table conforms to the 1NF, 2NF, and 3NF.

Open the Products table. You will see that it conforms to the R2D2s and the 3NF as well.

Open the Orders table. You will see that it does not conform to R2D2 #1.

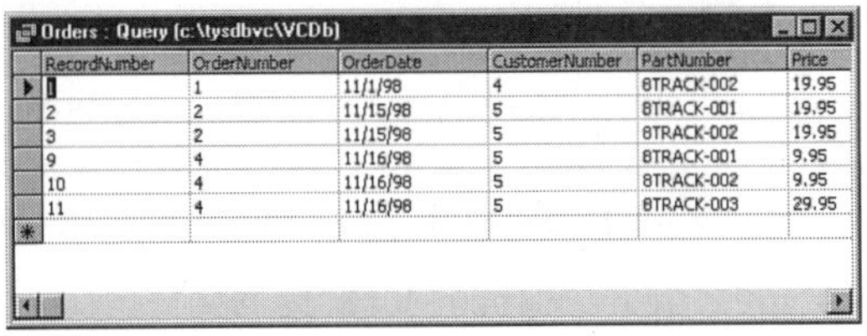

FIGURE 7.3.

The Orders *table.*

RecordNumber	OrderNumber	OrderDate	CustomerNumber	PartNumber	Price
1	1	11/1/98	4	8TRACK-002	19.95
2	2	11/15/98	5	8TRACK-001	19.95
3	2	11/15/98	5	8TRACK-002	19.95
9	4	11/16/98	5	8TRACK-001	9.95
10	4	11/16/98	5	8TRACK-002	9.95
11	4	11/16/98	5	8TRACK-003	29.95

This table is supposed to store orders, but as you can see in Figure 7.3, there are multiple records in this table for single orders IRL. Notice that there are two records for order number 2 and three records for order number 4.

The primary key for the Orders table is the RecordNumber field. This field has no real relevance to an order; a record number is not an attribute of an order. This Orders table does not conform to the normal forms.

To bring the database into conformance with the relational model, you need to create an Orders table that contains orders as single records.

You need to identify the single attributes of an order. These single attributes would include an order number, an order date, the payment method, and the customer number for the customer who placed the order. You might want to store the shipping address as well. You might be able to obtain the shipping address from the customer's address field(s) in the Customers table. However, the address to which each order was shipped is actually an attribute of the order and could be different than the customer's address.

Multiple products can be purchased in a single order. That means the products for the orders need to be moved to a separate table.

The new table that contains products for orders could be called the ProductsPurchased table. Each product purchased would have a single record in this table. The attributes of each product purchased would be the product number, the order number under which this product was purchased, the price that the product sold for, the quantity of the product purchased, and the shipping charge for that product.

You could make a case for not including the price in the ProductsPurchased table. You might be able to obtain the price by using the product number and looking up the price in the Products table. However, the price in the ProductsPurchased table could change. This would cause the price the product sold for on past orders to be lost. Therefore, it's best to treat the price that the product sold for as an attribute of the products purchased and make it a field in the ProductsPurchased table.

The question of which table should contain the shipping charge field depends on how the company assesses shipping charges. If a shipping charge is dependent on each product shipped, the shipping charge should be a field in the ProductsPurchased table. If the shipping charge is a flat fee for each order, it should be a field in the Orders table. In the sample application, the shipping charge is assessed for each product purchased. Therefore it is a field in the ProductsPurchased table.

One place the shipping charge should not be stored is in your application source code. You might assume that the shipping charge is a fee that's always added to each product. You might hard-code the shipping charge into your application source code and not store it in the database. That would be a bad idea because the shipping charge might change. The logic to add the shipping charges to the price of the order should be written into your application source code. However, the amount of the shipping charge should be stored in the database because it could change over time.

Tip

Keep the business formulas separate from the business variables. In your application source code, place the formulas you use to make calculations. Place the variables for those formulas in your database.

7

Perhaps a more precise name for the ProductsPurchased table would be the
OrderLineItems table because each product purchased IRL doesn't necessarily have its
own single record in this table (as specified in R2D2 #1). If a customer purchased three
of a particular item in one order, only one record would be in the table, and that record
would contain a quantity of three. However, I prefer to call the table ProductsPurchased
because that name denotes that you can use it to obtain information on what products
were purchased and when.

Click the SQL button with the Orders table open. Change the SQL statement so that it
looks like the code in Listing 7.1.

LISTING 7.1. THE CREATE TABLE STATEMENT FOR THE PRODUCTSPURCHASED TABLE

```
1:  CREATE TABLE ProductsPurchased(OrderNumber INTEGER,
2:  PartNumber varchar(10), Price CURRENCY,
3:  Quantity INTEGER, ShippingAndHandling CURRENCY)
```

NEW TERM *Data Definition Language* (DDL) consists of those SQL statements that create
or alter the structure of a database. This structure consists of database tables,
indexes, constraints, and so on.

NEW TERM The structure of the entire database is called the *schema* of the database.

The DDL code in Listing 7.1 is a statement that will create a table called
ProductsPurchased. Notice that the fields are listed in the CREATE TABLE statement, followed by their data type. Microsoft Access supports the CURRENCY data type. Other databases might not have this data type but will have other type(s) that can store decimal
numbers such as monetary values. Consult your database documentation for information
on the specific data types that it supports.

Run this statement against your database by clicking the Run (!) button. Click the minus
sign by Tables in the Data View to contract the list of tables. Click the plus sign to
expand the list of tables, and you will see your new table in the Data View.

Now you need to move the data from the Orders table into your new
ProductsPurchased table. Close the Orders table and open it again so that you get a
SELECT statement for the Orders table. Modify the SELECT statement so that it looks like
Listing 7.2.

LISTING 7.2. THE INSERT INTO STATEMENT FOR THE PRODUCTSPURCHASED TABLE

```
1:  INSERT INTO productspurchased
2:      (ordernumber, partnumber, price, quantity,
3:      shippingandhandling)
4:  SELECT ordernumber, partnumber, price, 1,
5:      shippingandhandling
6:  FROM Orders
```

Execute the statement in Listing 7.2. It should insert the six records from the Orders table into the ProductsPurchased table. Open the ProductsPurchased table to make sure.

Now you need to normalize the Orders table. SQL makes it easy to add new columns to a table. However, most relational databases do not enable you to delete columns. The surest course is to create a new table. You could call the new table NewOrders. Enter the DDL code shown in Listing 7.3 into a Query window and execute it to build the NewOrders table.

LISTING 7.3. THE CREATE TABLE STATEMENT FOR THE NEWORDERS TABLE

```
1:  CREATE TABLE NewOrders(OrderNumber INTEGER,
2:  OrderDate DATETIME, CustomerNumber INTEGER,
3:  PaymentMethod VARCHAR(50))
```

Your next task is to move the appropriate records from the Orders table into the NewOrders table. You can do this by using an INSERT INTO, and SELECT, statement, as shown in Listing 7.4.

LISTING 7.4. THE INSERT INTO STATEMENT FOR THE NEWORDERS TABLE

```
1:  INSERT INTO NewOrders
2:      (ordernumber, orderdate, customernumber,
3:      paymentmethod)
4:  SELECT DISTINCT
5:      ordernumber, orderdate, customernumber,
6:      paymentmethod
7:  FROM orders
```

Line 4 of Listing 7.4 uses the DISTINCT modifier with the SELECT statement. This causes only unique records to be returned by the SELECT statement. In other words, no duplicate records will be returned by the SELECT statement. Without the DISTINCT modifier, all the records in the Orders table (six records) would be inserted into the NewOrders table.

7

Using the DISTINCT modifier, only three records are inserted, which is the actual number of orders IRL. Figure 7.4 shows the records inserted into the NewOrders table.

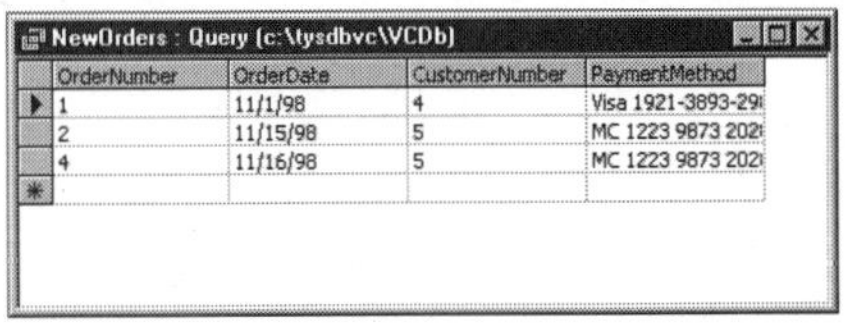

FIGURE 7.4.

The NewOrders *table.*

OrderNumber	OrderDate	CustomerNumber	PaymentMethod
1	11/1/98	4	Visa 1921-3893-29(
2	11/15/98	5	MC 1223 9873 202(
4	11/16/98	5	MC 1223 9873 202(

You can see in Figure 7.4 that there were actually three orders IRL: order numbers 1, 2, and 4. The NewOrders table conforms to R2D2 #1 and to the 3NF.

Now that you have split the data from the Orders table into two normalized tables, you can get rid of the Orders table. This is done with the following DROP TABLE statement:

```
DROP TABLE Orders
```

Open a Query window and execute this statement to delete the Orders table. In the Data View, contract and expand the list of tables or right-click the data source and select the Refresh menu to see that the Orders table is now just a memory.

Using Constraints and Indexes in a Relational Database

Relational databases have built-in mechanisms to ensure the integrity of the data in the database. One of these mechanisms is called a *constraint*.

NEW TERM   *Constraints* are rules for valid data that the database enforces for you.

You can place different kinds of constraints on the database. For instance, you can place a primary key constraint on a field to enforce the primary key. The constraint makes sure that the data in the primary key field(s) is unique. In other words, it prevents duplicate records in the table by not allowing new records to have the same data in the key field as other records.

You need to specify primary keys in the new tables you added to the database. Add a primary key to the NewOrders table by issuing the SQL statement shown in Listing 7.5.

LISTING 7.5. THE PRIMARY KEY CONSTRAINT FOR THE NEWORDERS TABLE

```
1:  ALTER TABLE NewOrders
2:  ADD CONSTRAINT OrderNumberIndex
3:  PRIMARY KEY (ordernumber)
```

Line 1 in Listing 7.5 uses the ALTER TABLE statement and specifies the NewOrders table. Line 2 tells the database to add a constraint called OrderNumberIndex. Line 3 specifies this is a primary key constraint on the OrderNumber field. This makes the OrderNumber field the primary key in the NewOrders table. The constraint will enforce the uniqueness of the OrderNumber field.

Add a primary key to the ProductsPurchased table by issuing the SQL statement shown in Listing 7.6.

LISTING 7.6. THE PRIMARY KEY CONSTRAINT FOR THE PRODUCTSPURCHASED TABLE

```
1:  ALTER TABLE ProductsPurchased
2:  ADD CONSTRAINT ProductsPurchasedIndex
3:  PRIMARY KEY (ordernumber, partnumber)
```

The code in Listing 7.6 adds a primary key constraint to the ProductsPurchased table. The primary key is a composite key consisting of the OrderNumber field and the PartNumber field. The constraint will prevent duplicate OrderNumber/PartNumber combinations among the records in the table.

Relational databases use indexes to optimize the performance of data access operations. If you merely create tables and do not use indexes, the database will be forced to perform table scans. The database will start at the beginning of the table and sequentially look at every record until it finds the record(s) it needs. If, on the other hand, you create indexes for your tables, the database can look up the value it is searching for in the index and move directly to the appropriate record(s).

The primary key is indexed. When you specify a primary key on a table, the database creates an index for the table using the primary key.

If you will frequently use other fields in queries, such as in the WHERE clause or the ORDER BY clause of SELECT statements, you will probably want to create indexes for those fields as well. You can create as many indexes as you need for each table (within practical limits). The following is the syntax for creating an index:

```
CREATE INDEX myIndex ON myTable (myField)
```

7

You should use indexes only where they are needed. They will reduce insert, update, and delete performance because every time you change an indexed field in a record, the database has to update the index as well.

Tools and Techniques for Managing Relationships in a Relational Database

You learned earlier today that you should carefully identify the one-to-one, one-to-many, and many-to-many relationships in your database designs (see R2D2 #3).

To model a one-to-one relationship in your database, use primary keys and foreign keys as you learned in Day 2, "Tools for Database Development in Visual C++ Developer Studio," and Day 3, "Retrieving Data Through Structured Query Language (SQL)." For every instance of the primary key in one table, you will have no more than one instance of the foreign key in the foreign table.

To model a one-to-many relationship, use primary keys and foreign keys as you learned in Day 2 and Day 3. For every instance of the primary key in one table, you can have any number of instances of the foreign key in the foreign table.

Modeling many-to-many relationships requires that you create a third table. The two tables that you want to relate will contain their primary keys (as you would expect). The third table, called the *link table*, will contain the foreign keys from both primary tables. This is best understood through an example.

You will recall that the design of the original Orders table contained the product number and the customer number as foreign keys (see Figure 7.5).

The original Orders table was a link table that facilitated a many-to-many relationship between customers and products. You could perform a join between these three tables and find out which customers bought which products. This is an excellent example of a many-to-many relationship because a single customer could buy many products and many customers could buy a single product.

Figure 7.5 is a simple entity relationship diagram (ER diagram) that shows the relationship between these three tables. The Customers table and the Products table contain the primary keys. The Orders table contains the foreign keys, so it is the link table.

You can see that lines run between the primary and foreign key fields. A *1* is next to the primary keys and an infinity sign next to the foreign key fields. This is due to the one-to-many relationship between the primary keys in the Customers and Products tables and the foreign keys in the link (Orders) table. When the one-to-many relationships are combined in the link table, it produces a many-to-many relationship between the Customers and Products tables.

FIGURE 7.5.

Many-to-many relationships.

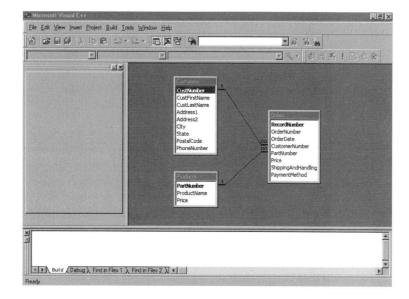

Using Constraints to Enforce Relationships

You can place constraints on the database that enforce the relationships. These constraints prevent a user from deleting a record whose primary key constitutes a foreign key in another table.

NEW TERM   *Referential integrity constraints* are constraints that ensure that the data in one table is consistent with data in other tables in the database.

A referential integrity constraint will prevent you from deleting a product from the Products table that is listed in the ProductsPurchased table. You will recall that you encountered a constraint like this in Day 6, "Harnessing the Power of Relational Database Servers," when you tried to delete all the 8-track products from the Products table. This is because that delete operation would have left orphaned records in the Orders table.

To create a referential integrity constraint, you can use the ALTER TABLE statement with the ADD CONSTRAINT clause, as shown in Listing 7.7.

7

LISTING 7.7. THE FOREIGN KEY CONSTRAINT BETWEEN THE PRODUCTSPURCHASED AND PRODUCTS TABLES

```
1:   ALTER TABLE ProductsPurchased
2:   ADD CONSTRAINT fk_partnumber
3:   FOREIGN KEY (PartNumber)
4:   REFERENCES Products (PartNumber)
```

Listing 7.7 creates a constraint to enforce the referential integrity between the ProductsPurchased table and the PartNumber table. Line 2 in Listing 7.7 names the constraint (in case you want to drop it later). Line 3 specifies that the PartNumber field in the ProductsPurchased table is a foreign key. Line 4 tells the database where the primary key is that matches this foreign key.

Listing 7.8 creates a constraint to enforce the referential integrity between the ProductsPurchased table and the NewOrders table.

LISTING 7.8. THE FOREIGN KEY CONSTRAINT BETWEEN THE PRODUCTSPURCHASED AND NEWORDERS TABLES

```
1:   ALTER TABLE ProductsPurchased
2:   ADD CONSTRAINT fk_ordernumber
3:   FOREIGN KEY (OrderNumber)
4:   REFERENCES NewOrders (OrderNumber)
```

Listing 7.9 creates a constraint to enforce the referential integrity between the NewOrders table and the Customers table.

LISTING 7.9. THE FOREIGN KEY CONSTRAINT BETWEEN THE NEWORDERS AND CUSTOMERS TABLES

```
1:   ALTER TABLE NewOrders
2:   ADD CONSTRAINT fk_custnumber
3:   FOREIGN KEY (CustomerNumber)
4:   REFERENCES Customers (CustNumber)
```

Open a Query window in Visual Studio and issue these SQL statements to add the constraints. With these constraints in place, users of the database will not be able to make modifications to the data that would cause the data in one table to be out of sync with the data in the other tables.

Summary

Designing your database to conform to the relational model is important and can be difficult. The process of designing a relational database is made easier by using the intuition-based R2D2s and the science-based normal forms. The process of normalizing your database typically involves separating tables in your database into more specialized tables.

Use SQL Data Definition Language (DDL) to build the schema of your database, which includes tables, indexes, and constraints. Indexes enable better query performance. Constraints help ensure the integrity of the data inside the database.

Q&A

Q If I know my database stores data in 2KB pages, wouldn't it make sense to structure my database tables so that each record is 2KB, also?

A That approach would certainly optimize your database for speed. However, it would be impossible to make such a database conform to the relational model. Your database might be marginally faster, but it would be incompatible with all the other database software and data access tools in the Universe. Your database would be a closed, proprietary system with no value outside your application. This ultimately would lessen the value of your application.

Q Is there a typical level of conformance to the relational model?

A No. However, if your database conforms to the 3NF, you can be well assured of its usability and its compatibility with relational data access tools.

Q Do all relational database systems support the same DDL statements?

A Support for DDL statements varies among relational database vendors. Check your database software documentation for specifics.

Q Is it necessary to add constraints to my database?

A Primary key constraints are necessary for a relational database to function reliably. Other constraints might not be necessary but are a great help to you in maintaining your database's value and usefulness. Rather than look for ways to avoid constraints, you should look for places to use constraints wherever possible. They will protect the integrity and validity of the information stored in your database.

7

Workshop

The Workshop quiz questions test your understanding of today's material. (The answers appear in Appendix F, "Answers.") The exercises encourage you to apply the information you learned today to real-life situations.

Quiz

1. What is the highest normal form in the relational database model?

2. What are entity relationships?

3. How can you guarantee that a table conforms to the second normal form?

4. What is the proper term for the structure (the tables, indexes, constraints, and so on) of a relational database?

5. What does a referential integrity constraint do?

Exercises

1. Write a SELECT statement that shows all the products purchased on each order. Hint: The SELECT statement should perform a join between the NewOrders, ProductsPurchased, and Products tables.

2. Write a SELECT statement showing the products purchased by each customer.

Week 1

In Review

The first day's lesson examines the different database technologies, including OLE structured storage, record managers (such as Btrieve), desktop databases (such as FoxPro and Access), object databases, and relational database servers (such as Oracle and SQL Server).

The lesson on Day 2 explains that the most widely used and accepted database model is the relational model. A relational database consists of tables, which are arranged in columns and rows. Each column is called a *field*. Each row is called a *record* and is unique, based on some key field or fields. The records in the tables in a relational database are related to each other, based on key fields that are called *primary* and *foreign keys*.

In Day 3's lesson, you learned that SQL is a language that excels at manipulating data. You learned how to issue SELECT queries to retrieve records from a single table in a relational database. You learned how to perform joins to retrieve records from multiple tables. You learned how to use subqueries in SQL to obtain information that requires a large quantity of procedural code to retrieve. Last, you learned that cursors are a mechanism that enables record-at-a-time navigation through a result set.

On Day 4, you learned that to access a database from C++, it's necessary to use a database API. Several database APIs are available to C++ developers. The future of all data access in Microsoft Windows is OLE DB. The easiest way to use OLE DB is to use ADO. ADO provides an object model that encapsulates the process of communicating with databases from within C++ programs, as well as from other programming languages.

On Day 5, you learned two methods for manipulating records in a database. You learned how to manipulate records from C++ code by using the ADO Recordset member functions to insert, update, and delete records. You also learned how to manipulate records from SQL, using the INSERT, UPDATE, and DELETE statements.

On Day 6, you learned how to harness the power of relational database servers. You saw how the SQL INSERT, UPDATE, and DELETE statements can be used to process many records at a time. You also learned about stored procedures and how to call them, using ADO Command objects.

You wrapped up your first week of study by learning how the process of designing a relational database can be made easier by using the intuition-based R2D2s and the science-based normal forms. The process of normalizing your database typically involves separating tables in your database into more specialized tables. Use SQL Data Definition Language (DDL) to build the schema of your database, which includes tables, indexes, and constraints. Indexes can enable better query performance. Constraints can help ensure the integrity of the data inside the database.

WEEK 2

At a Glance

This week, you learn how to build real-world database applications. You explore multitier architectures and Microsoft Transaction Server. You acquire a deeper understanding of relational database servers, COM, and Microsoft's database client APIs.

- Day 8   You discover the powerful innovations of relational database servers.

- Day 9   You acquire an understanding of the Component Object Model (COM) and write some COM software.

- Day 10   You learn Microsoft's database client technologies and learn how ADO uses COM.

- Day 11   You learn the tools to build multitier applications.

- Day 12   You explore Microsoft Transaction Server (MTS) and learn to build and use MTS components.

- Day 13   You learn to combine object-oriented programming with relational databases.

- Day 14   You learn the ODBC, DAO, and RDO database APIs.

8

9

10

11

12

13

14

DAY **8**

Utilizing the Capabilities of Database Servers

Relational database servers include tools that provide incredible power for processing and presenting information. These tools can be highly valuable and productive for you in writing database applications. However, the value—or even the existence—of these tools is often not readily apparent from database documentation. Today you will discover these relational database server power tools.

Today you will

- Use transactions to ensure that complex operations execute reliably.
- Create triggers that will automatically execute SQL code when data is inserted, updated, or deleted.
- Learn about the SQL aggregate functions and the power of the GROUP BY clause.
- Build SQL views to provide users with the particular information that interests them.

> **Note**
>
> Today's work deals specifically with relational database servers, such as SQL Server and Oracle. Some of the functionality described today is not available in the Access/Jet engine. The tools that are not available in Access/Jet are noted for you. If you have use of a relational database server, you will be able to try all the database tools described today. If not, you will have to learn some of these tools without being able to try them yourself.

Database Transactions

As you learned yesterday, when you normalize a database, you create a large number of specialized tables. One side effect of normalization is that operations on the database typically involve several tables. For instance, in the sample application, when a customer places an order, you must add records to two tables in the database: the NewOrders table and the ProductsPurchased table.

When you add records to two different tables, you need to be assured that the two tables remain in sync before, during, and after that operation. You don't want a database failure of some kind to cause a record to be added to one table without the corresponding record also being added to the other table. If that happened, the usefulness of your database would be reduced because some of its information would not be reliable.

NEW TERM   A *transaction* in a relational database is a series of operations that must happen together. A transaction is a single unit of work that must be done completely or not at all.

In database parlance, a transaction must have atomicity, consistency, isolation, and durability. These are called the *ACID properties* of database transactions:

- Atomicity—Either all of the operations are performed on the database, or none of the operations are performed.
- Consistency—All the related changes that occur as a result of the operations in the transaction must occur successfully. The state of the database must be consistent after the transaction. For example, the transaction cannot result in any orphaned records because that would mean the database is in an invalid or inconsistent state.
- Isolation—The transaction must be isolated from the operations of other transactions that have not yet completed. Transactions must be (or appear internally to be) serialized.
- Durability—When the transaction completes, its changes will be present in the database, even if system failures occur.

8

Relational databases use a variety of mechanisms to ensure the ACID properties of trans-actions. These mechanisms include locking (which you learned a little about in Day 5, "Adding, Modifying, and Deleting Data"), referential integrity constraints (which you learned about in Day 7, "Database Design"), SQL transaction statements (which you will learn next), and triggers (which you will learn later today).

SQL Transaction Statements

The syntax for SQL transaction statements varies somewhat among relational databases. The basic idea is that you initiate a transaction, execute a series of SQL statements, and then either commit or rollback the transaction.

In Microsoft SQL Server, the code to execute SQL statements inside a transaction could look something like Listing 8.1.

 Note   The code in Listings 8.1 and 8.2 isn't compatible with the Access/Jet engine. You cannot run this code from a Query window in Visual Studio that is con-nected to an Access/Jet database.

INPUT   **LISTING 8.1.** TRANSACTION CODE IN MICROSOFT SQL SERVER

```
1:  BEGIN TRANSACTION
2:    INSERT INTO neworders(ordernumber, customernumber)
3:      VALUES (5, 3)
4:    INSERT INTO productspurchased(ordernumber, partnumber)
5:      VALUES (5, 'CLAP-003')
6:    INSERT INTO productspurchased(ordernumber, partnumber)
7:      VALUES (5, 'MAG-292')
8:  COMMIT TRANSACTION
```

Line 1 in Listing 8.1 initiates the transaction. Lines 2–7 perform a series of INSERT state-ments to record an order in the database. If some kind of a database failure occurred while, say, line 6 was being executed, the records inserted in lines 2–5 would be auto-matically removed (rolled back) by the database. Therefore, the process of adding these three records is an all-or-nothing proposition.

All three inserts in Listing 8.1 will occur in the database, or none of them will. If the execution goes as expected, line 8 commits the transaction. When line 8 executes, you can be assured that all three records have been written to the database and will be persis-tent despite any database failures.

In Oracle, the code to do the same transaction would be somewhat different, as in Listing 8.2.

INPUT   **LISTING 8.2.** TRANSACTION CODE IN ORACLE

```
1:  INSERT INTO neworders(ordernumber, customernumber)
2:     VALUES (5, 3)
3:  INSERT INTO productspurchased(ordernumber, partnumber)
4:     VALUES (5, 'CLAP-003')
5:  INSERT INTO productspurchased(ordernumber, partnumber)
6:     VALUES (5, 'MAG-292')
7:  COMMIT
```

In Oracle, the transaction begins implicitly with the first INSERT statement. Therefore, line 1 in Listing 8.2 begins the transaction. If the commit in line 7 isn't performed, all the changes in lines 1–6 are rolled back.

Like Oracle, SQL Server can be made to begin transactions by implicitly using the SET IMPLICIT_TRANSACTIONS ON statement. When this option is turned on, and if there are no outstanding transactions already, every SQL statement automatically starts a transaction.

You can see that the syntax can be different between SQL Server and Oracle. However, the principles of database transactions are the same in both databases.

Code like that shown in Listings 8.1 and 8.2 ensures the transactions' atomicity and consistency. The transactions' isolation is controlled through locking and the isolation level of the transaction.

A key function of a relational database server is its capability to ensure that multiple users can read consistent sets of records and make modifications without inadvertently overwriting each other's changes. The isolation level tells the database how zealous to be in protecting a user's work from interaction with the work of other concurrent users.

Oracle and SQL Server perform the task of isolating concurrent users by using very different locking and isolation strategies. Consult your database server documentation for information on transaction isolation levels.

The basic thing to understand is that higher degrees of transaction isolation typically result in more locks being placed on the data for longer periods of time. This can cause the database performance to bog down.

To enable the database to provide transaction isolation without too much burdensome locking, it's necessary to keep transactions as brief as possible. If possible, a transaction should not span multiple round trips to the server. Transactions also should not remain open during the wait for user input.

8

Setting the appropriate level of isolation for the transactions and keeping transactions as brief as possible enable the database to provide isolation between multiple transactions that execute concurrently.

 A *distributed transaction* is a transaction that involves making changes to the data in more than one database server.

Distributed transactions enable transactions to cover changes to data in two or more networked database servers. SQL Server and Oracle both support distributed transactions. The implementation of distributed transactions varies between database vendors, so consult your database documentation for details on distributed transactions.

> **Tip**
>
> You need to use transactions only for those operations that modify (INSERT, UPDATE, or DELETE) data in the database. You should not use transactions when performing SELECT queries.

Transactions are a vital tool for effective database applications. Transactions ensure that complex operations on the database are performed reliably. As you can see from Listings 8.1 and 8.2, transactions don't require you to write much extra code. The database server automatically handles the commit or rollback of transactions.

Triggers to Execute SQL Code Automatically

Triggers are SQL statements that are executed, or triggered, when certain operations are performed in the database. Triggers provide the capability to easily perform the following:

- Audit trails to track modifications to particular tables or records
- Cascading updates and deletes of records, for those cases when you want a change in one record to result in an automatic change in other records
- Updates on period-to-date fields to keep, for instance, year-to-date sales figures always current
- Data replication, in which data is automatically copied to another table or another database server

> **Note**
>
> SQL Server and Oracle both have replication capabilities built in to their database engines, so with those databases, triggers might not be the optimum way to perform replication.

Listing 8.3 shows the code for creating a trigger in SQL Server.

 Note The code in Listing 8.3 isn't compatible with the Access/Jet engine. You can't run the code from a Query window in Visual Studio that is connected to an Access/Jet database.

INPUT **LISTING 8.3.** CODE TO CREATE A TRIGGER IN MICROSOFT SQL SERVER

```
1:   CREATE TRIGGER SaveDelOrders
2:   ON neworders
3:   FOR DELETE
4:   AS
5:   INSERT DeletedOrders
6:     SELECT * FROM deleted
```

Line 1 in Listing 8.3 creates a trigger named SaveDelOrders. Line 2 indicates that this trigger is attached to the NewOrders table. Line 3 specifies that this trigger should fire whenever record(s) are deleted from the NewOrders table. Lines 5 and 6 insert the deleted record(s) into the DeletedOrders table.

You will notice the FROM deleted statement in line 6. SQL Server triggers can use two tables called inserted and deleted, which are temporary holding tables for records being inserted, deleted, or updated (an update causes both a record to be deleted and a new record to be inserted).

The inserted and deleted tables can be accessed only by code inside triggers. Oracle has temporary holding tables similar to inserted and deleted; these are called new and old.

When a record is deleted from the NewOrders table, it is removed from the NewOrders table and placed in the deleted table. A trigger attached to the NewOrders table, such as the one in Listing 8.3, can access that record while it's in the deleted table.

The trigger in Listing 8.3 reads the record from deleted and inserts it into another table. This trigger provides a backup copy of all records deleted from the NewOrders table.

With SQL Server, you can also create triggers that fire when records are inserted into a table and when records are updated in a table. Line 3 of Listing 8.3 indicates that it's a delete trigger. For an insert trigger, line 3 would say

```
FOR INSERT
```

For an update trigger, line 3 would say

```
FOR UPDATE
```

For a trigger that fires on insert, update, and delete operations, line 3 would say

```
FOR INSERT, UPDATE, DELETE
```

Oracle uses a slightly different syntax for triggers. Oracle triggers also offer some capabilities not found in SQL Server triggers. Consult the documentation of the relational database server you are using for details on its implementation of triggers.

SQL Aggregate Functions

You've learned that relational databases have the capability to process thousands, or even millions, of records at the server and then send only the relevant resultset to the client application. You saw some examples of server-side processing in Day 6, "Harnessing the Power of Relational Database Servers."

Today you will learn more about the server-based processing power of relational databases. You will explore server code that can summarize mountains of raw data and return small polished gems of information to client applications. This power comes in the form of SQL aggregate functions.

NEW TERM   *Aggregate functions* process multiple records and return a single value. They are also called *set functions* because they operate on sets of records. They calculate summary values from a particular field in a set of records. For each set of records they process, they return a single value.

At times, the information you want to retrieve from a database table isn't stored in an individual record but rather in a set of records. For instance, you might want to count the number of records that meet a certain criteria or to know the maximum or minimum value of the data in a particular field in a set of records. You might need to calculate the average or sum of a field in a set. Cases like these are where aggregate functions come in very handy.

The following define five aggregate functions and give an example of each:

- The COUNT function returns the number of records that match the criteria you specify in the WHERE clause.
  ```
  SELECT COUNT(*) FROM productspurchased
  WHERE ordernumber = 4
  ```

- The MAX function returns the maximum value that occurs in the field you specify, in records that match the criteria you specify in the WHERE clause.

```
SELECT MAX(quantity) FROM productspurchased
WHERE ordernumber = 4
```

- The MIN function returns the minimum value that occurs in the field you specify, in records that match the criteria you specify in the WHERE clause.

```
SELECT MIN(quantity) FROM productspurchased
WHERE ordernumber = 4
```

- The SUM function adds up the values that occur in the field you specify, in records that match the criteria you specify in the WHERE clause.

```
SELECT SUM(price) FROM productspurchased
WHERE ordernumber = 4
```

- The AVG function returns the average of the values that occur in the field you specify, in records that match the criteria you specify in the WHERE clause.

```
SELECT AVG(price) FROM productspurchased
WHERE ordernumber = 4
```

COUNT

The COUNT function returns the number of records that match a criterion. You can substitute COUNT(*) for the field list in a SELECT statement to see how many records it will return. Open a Query window and enter the query shown in Listing 8.4. As you can see, the COUNT function is not restricted to working with records from a single table.

INPUT　**LISTING 8.4.**　USING COUNT(*) TO COUNT THE ROWS RETURNED BY A SELECT STATEMENT

```
1:  SELECT COUNT(*)
2:  FROM customers, neworders, productspurchased, products
3:  WHERE custlastname = 'clinton' AND
4:  customers.custnumber = neworders.customernumber AND
5:  neworders.ordernumber = productspurchased.ordernumber AND
6:  productspurchased.partnumber = products.partnumber
```

Listing 8.4 performs a join of four tables. Selecting COUNT(*) returns the number of rows that are selected.

If you use COUNT(*fieldname*) instead of COUNT(*), the function will not count records that have a NULL value in the specified field. You could use this to count how many records have non-NULL entries in a field. You can also use COUNT(DISTINCT *fieldname*) to determine how many distinct values exist in a field.

MAX, MIN, SUM, and AVG

These functions take a single field name or a numeric expression as a parameter. For example, Listing 8.5 will return the sum of the `Price` and `ShippingAndHandling` fields for all records that have an `OrderNumber` of 4.

INPUT **LISTING 8.5.** USING THE SUM FUNCTION TO CALCULATE THE TOTAL PRICE OF AN ORDER

```
1:   SELECT SUM(Price + shippingandhandling) FROM ProductsPurchased
2:   WHERE ordernumber = 4
```

The `MIN`, `MAX`, and `AVG` functions work similarly. You will notice that you didn't need to write a loop that reads every record into a client application and then adds the appropriate fields to a variable. The programming model used by the aggregate functions makes the code for performing calculations on sets of records very straightforward.

The aggregate functions can be helpful to you not only because they reduce your code complexity but also because they execute at the server. The database server can process all the records in the database and then return only a single value to the client application that requested the information.

This means that a LAN would not be burdened by huge amounts of network traffic between client and server. It also means that the client application could be a browser accessing the database over the Internet. If you were not using a relational database server, which is capable of processing data at the server, there is no way that a thin client (such as a browser) could effectively access your database over a low-bandwidth, high-latency connection such as the Internet.

Aggregate Functions and the GROUP BY Clause

Aggregate functions enable you to obtain sums, averages, and so on, from the database. However, at times you need to obtain *sets* of sums or *sets* of averages. For instance, you might need to calculate the total sales revenue for each month during the past year or to discover the average number of products purchased each week for the past six months. These are the cases where you need to use the aggregate functions with the GROUP BY clause.

To try the GROUP BY clause, you first need to select a set of records. Try the query shown in Listing 8.6.

LISTING 8.6. USING THE SELECT STATEMENT TO RETRIEVE ALL PRODUCTS PURCHASED, THE ORDER NUMBER, AND THE DATE

```
1:  SELECT neworders.ordernumber, neworders.orderdate,
2:    productspurchased.*
3:  FROM neworders, productspurchased
4:  WHERE neworders.ordernumber =
5:    productspurchased.ordernumber
```

The query shown in Listing 8.6 will return all the products that have been sold, the order number each was sold under, and the date of the order. The results are shown in Figure 8.1.

FIGURE 8.1.

All products purchased, the order number, and the date.

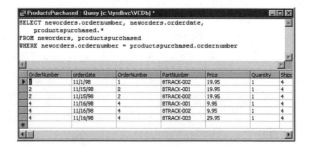

It would be interesting to see the total price of each order. This means that you need to add up the Price and the ShippingAndHandling fields for every record on each order. You saw in Listing 8.5 how to obtain the total of a single order. How do you find the total of every order? Listing 8.7 shows you how.

LISTING 8.7. USING THE SUM FUNCTION WITH THE GROUP BY CLAUSE TO CALCULATE THE TOTALS OF EACH ORDER

```
1:  SELECT neworders.ordernumber,
2:    SUM(price + shippingandhandling)
3:  FROM neworders, productspurchased
4:  WHERE neworders.ordernumber = productspurchased.ordernumber
5:  GROUP BY neworders.ordernumber
```

Line 1 of Listing 8.7 selects the order number (so you have the context for the totals). Line 2 selects the sum of the Price and ShippingAndHandling fields. Lines 3 and 4 specify the tables and the join. (Actually, a join with the NewOrders table isn't necessary in this query because all the fields you need are in the ProductsPurchased table. Having the NewOrders table in this query doesn't hurt anything, so just leave it in because the next query will require the OrderDate field from NewOrders.)

Line 5 specifies that you want the sum of the Price and ShippingAndHandling fields grouped by OrderNumber. Figure 8.2 shows the output of this query.

FIGURE 8.2.

The total price of each order.

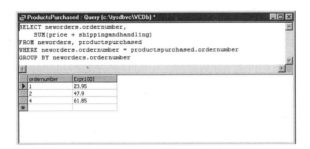

If you look at Figure 8.1 and add up the numbers yourself, you will see that the totals in Figure 8.2 are correct. With the small amount of data in this example, you could probably perform these calculations inside the client application (or even in your head). However, imagine the amount of work required to process thousands of orders or tens of thousands of product sales. If you retrieved all those records and did the calculations at the client, the application would bog down. The GROUP BY clause lets you perform all the work at the server and then return only the small resultset to the client. Is that cool, or what?

It would be interesting to see the total sales volume per week. To do this, you must group by the order date. More specifically, you must group by the week of the order date. Even more specifically, you must group by the year and the week, in case you have orders that span more than one year. The GROUP BY clause lets you group by multiple fields and multiple expressions. Listing 8.8 shows how to retrieve the total sales volume per week.

LISTING 8.8. USING THE SUM FUNCTION WITH THE GROUP BY CLAUSE TO SHOW THE TOTAL SALES VOLUME PER WEEK

INPUT

```
 1:  SELECT DATEPART ('yyyy', neworders.orderdate) AS Year,
 2:    DATEPART ('ww', neworders.orderdate) AS Week,
 3:    SUM(price + shippingandhandling) AS Total
 4:  FROM neworders, productspurchased
 5:  WHERE neworders.ordernumber = productspurchased.ordernumber
 6:  GROUP BY DATEPART ('yyyy', neworders.orderdate),
 7:    DATEPART ('ww', neworders.orderdate)
```

Line 1 of Listing 8.8 uses the DATEPART function to retrieve the year. The AS Year modifier on the end makes it so that the first field in the resultset has a name of Year. Specifying a name for a field that contains an expression is handy because it gives you an easy way to access the field in ADO with the GetCollect function. (You learned about the GetCollect function on Day 4, "Retrieving SQL Data Through a C++ API," in Listing 4.12.)

Line 2 uses the DATEPART function to retrieve the week of the year for the OrderDate. It names this field Week. Line 3 selects (and calculates) the sum of the Price and ShippingAndHandling fields in the group. This field is named Total. Lines 4 and 5 are identical to Listing 8.6. Lines 6 and 7 group the results of the SUM function by both the year and the week of the order date.

In Figure 8.3, you see the results of the query in Listing 8.8. There are two records, one for the 45th week and one for the 47th week of the year. No other weeks of the year had any sales, so they don't appear in the resultset.

FIGURE 8.3.

The total sales volume per week.

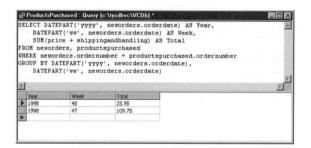

The code in Listing 8.8 works with Access/Jet. However, the code to break down the date (the DATEPART function) and modifiers to specify the field names for expressions will vary slightly in SQL Server and Oracle. Check your database server documentation for details.

Note

In a client/server application, the Access/Jet database engine will process the GROUP BY query shown in Listing 8.8 at the client machine (rather than at the server machine). Running a similar query on a relational database server, such as Oracle or SQL Server, will cause all the records to be processed at the server machine and only the small resultset to be sent to the client. This is one of the fundamental differences between relational database servers and databases, such as Access/Jet, that use ISAM files.

SQL Server provides the CUBE and ROLLUP operators as optional switches in the GROUP BY clause. These operators produce superaggregate rows, where the rows generated by the GROUP BY clause are aggregated. The CUBE and ROLLUP operators are typically used in data warehouse applications. Oracle also provides extensions to the GROUP BY clause that are useful in data warehouse applications. See your database server documentation for more information on extensions to the GROUP BY clause.

As you can see, aggregate functions enable relational database servers to process and summarize vast quantities of information and make it available to thin clients across thin network connections. The ability to place intelligence at every tier in an application, and to use each tier where its strengths are, enables you to build highly advanced client/server and multitier systems.

SQL Views

NEW TERM   A *view* is a virtual table whose contents are defined by a query (a SELECT statement).

A view looks like a normal table. However, a view doesn't actually exist as a table in the database. Instead, the view is materialized whenever it is opened. A view can consist of fields and records from several tables.

NEW TERM   A view's *base query* is the SELECT statement that defines the view.

NEW TERM   A view's *base tables* are the tables from which the view gets its data.

The SELECT statement that defines the view (its base query) is stored in the database. The view doesn't store any data. In other words, no records are stored in the view. The records that appear in a view are actually stored in the view's base tables. Every time a view is opened, the database reads the records into the view from its base tables by executing the view's base query.

Views enable users to work with the particular data that interests them. For instance, in the sample application, the company manager might want to be able to see the weekly sales totals on demand. Listing 8.9 shows the code to create a view that the manager could use to find that information.

INPUT **LISTING 8.9.** CODE TO CREATE A VIEW THAT SHOWS THE TOTAL SALES VOLUME
PER WEEK

```
1:  CREATE VIEW WeeklySales AS
2:  SELECT DATEPART ('yyyy', neworders.orderdate) AS Year,
3:    DATEPART ('ww', neworders.orderdate) AS Week,
4:    SUM(price + shippingandhandling) AS Total
5:  FROM neworders, productspurchased
6:  WHERE neworders.ordernumber = productspurchased.ordernumber
7:  GROUP BY DATEPART ('yyyy', neworders.orderdate),
8:    DATEPART ('ww', neworders.orderdate)
```

Line 1 in Listing 8.9 issues the SQL CREATE VIEW statement to create a view called
WeeklySales. The SELECT statement in lines 2–8 is the same as the one in Listing 8.8.
This SELECT statement defines the WeeklySales view; it is the WeeklySales view's base
query.

Execute the code in Listing 8.9 against the sample Access database. When you do, the
view will be created in the database. It will appear as a view in the Data View of Visual
Studio (you will need to right-click the data source and select the Refresh menu to see it
the first time).

When you double-click the WeeklySales view in the Data View, it will open just like a
table. In fact, you can even use WeeklySales like a table name in a query. Click the SQL
button on the Query toolbar, and you will see that the SELECT statement queried the view
as if it were a table. As you can see, a view looks and acts like a table.

Change the SELECT statement in the Query window so that it looks like the one shown in
Listing 8.10. This will cause only the record that applies to week 45 to appear in the
Query window.

INPUT **LISTING 8.10.** THE SELECT STATEMENT THAT USES A VIEW

```
1:  SELECT *
2:  FROM WeeklySales
3:  WHERE week = 45
```

When making a query against a view like this, two queries are actually executed. First,
the base query for the view is executed to populate the view with records. Second, the
query you are making against the view (as in Listing 8.10) is executed.

Caution	When you run a SELECT statement against a view, it might execute more slowly than you expect. Before anything else happens, the database has to populate the view with records by executing the view's base query. Then, after the view is completely populated, the database can execute the SELECT statement you are running against it. This process of populating the view before running your SELECT statement, combined with your inability to build indexes on views, can make SELECT statements that run against views take longer than you might expect.

Views can be updateable or read-only. If the view is updateable, users can insert, update, and delete records in it just as they can from a table. Bear in mind that when users insert, update, and delete records in a view, they are actually inserting, updating, and deleting records in the view's base table(s).

For a view to be updateable, the particular field(s) and record(s) in the view must correspond directly to field(s) and record(s) in its base table(s). The database must be able to discern which field/record to update in the base table. In the view created in Listing 8.10, no direct correspondence exists between the records in the view and the records in the base tables. The records in the view in Listing 8.10 are aggregates of several records in the base tables. There is no way that the database can figure out how to map records in the view to records in the base tables, so the WeeklySales view is read-only.

Note	In Day 6, "Harnessing the Power of Relational Database Servers," you learned that Visual Studio treats stored queries in Access as views rather than as stored procedures. In Day 6 you also worked with two Access stored queries called CustomerWithMostRecentOrder and CustomersWithOrdersSinceDate. In Day 7, "Database Design," you normalized the database and dropped the Orders table. These two Access stored queries that you worked with on Day 6 will no longer run properly. They accessed the Orders table, which no longer exists in the database.

Views can provide a layer of abstraction for users of your database. Views enable users to concentrate on the data they are interested in without needing to know the details of the database schema underneath the view.

Summary

Today you learned some powerful tools that relational database servers have to offer. You learned about transactions, triggers, aggregate functions, and views.

These tools can enable you to build highly advanced database applications. Transactions enable reliable changes to the data. Triggers make the database react automatically to changes in the data. Aggregate functions cause the bulk of the data processing to happen at the server. Finally, views enable you to customize the way people see your database.

Q&A

Q How do relational database servers ensure that transactions will be durable even when there is some kind of database failure?

A Relational database servers typically log all the changes to the data. The database writes to the log file first and then commits the changes to the database. Every time the database is started, it checks the log for uncommitted changes and uncompleted transactions. At this point, the database will automatically complete the transactions or roll them back.

Q If I have an insert trigger that inserts another record into the table, won't the insert trigger fire again and put the database into an endless loop?

A Typically, relational database servers are written so that a trigger won't cause itself to fire again. Consult your relational database server documentation for clarification of this.

Q Why can't I create an index on a view?

A A view is a virtual table. No records are stored in it. It is populated with records every time it's opened. These records are released from the view when it's closed. The *virtual-ness* of the records in a view prevents you from being able to create a (nonvirtual) index on the records in the view.

Workshop

The Workshop quiz questions test your understanding of today's material. (The answers appear in Appendix F, "Answers.") The exercises encourage you to apply the information you learned today to real-life situations.

Quiz

1. What are the ACID properties of a transaction?
2. What is the isolation level of a transaction?
3. How does the GROUP BY clause interact with the SQL aggregate functions?
4. How many triggers can be attached to a table in Microsoft SQL Server?
5. Does a view on a large table occupy much room in the database? Why or why not?

Exercises

1. Modify the SELECT statement in Listing 8.7 so that the resultset is sorted by the total sales volume, from the highest volume to the least.
2. Modify the SELECT statement in Listing 8.7 so that the query returns the average product price, from the highest to the least.

DAY 9

Understanding COM

The Component Object Model (COM) is the basis for much of the next generation of software on the Microsoft Windows platforms. An understanding of COM is a prerequisite for developing advanced applications with Microsoft technology.

COM is a huge topic. Those who learn it all must conquer a vast technical landscape. Fortunately, you don't need to learn all of COM. You can learn the fundamentals of COM and use that knowledge to be quite productive, particularly when it comes to database applications. Knowledge of the COM fundamentals will serve you well and is sufficient for building advanced database software.

Today you will learn

- The limitations of traditional Windows DLLs
- Component software and C++ abstract base classes
- COM components, class factories, and registry entries
- `IUnknown`, `QueryInterface`, `AddRef`, and `Release`
- Interface definition language
- Automation (formerly called OLE Automation)
- COM type libraries

COM is used extensively in Microsoft's latest database client technologies. In fact, you used COM in Day 4, "Retrieving SQL Data Through a C++ API," Day 5, "Adding, Modifying, and Deleting Data," and Day 6, "Harnessing the Power of Relational Database Servers," when you used ADO. ADO sports a COM interface.

The first step in learning COM is understanding what problems COM solves. This gives you the context for COM technologies. You will learn what problems COM solves in the next section, which explains the limitations of Windows DLLs (dynamic link libraries).

After you understand the problems COM solves, you can study its technical foundation. Today, you will examine COM from the bottom up. A bottom-up approach to learning COM is a good approach for C++ programmers for at least three reasons.

First, COM is narrower at the bottom than at the top. There is less to learn at the foundation than at the top, where COM technology is applied in myriad different ways.

Another reason for the bottom-up approach is that you, being a C++ programmer, are capable of understanding COM's foundation. As you will see, COM's foundation rests on a few particular C++ techniques, with which you might already be familiar.

Last, if you understand the foundation of COM technology, it will be much easier for you to grasp the higher levels of COM. In COM, technologies are built on other technologies. If you learn the foundation, you are in a much better position to understand the rest of COM.

The Limitations of Traditional Windows DLLs

Windows DLLs do one thing really well. They enable code to be shared among applications at runtime in a very efficient manner.

However, there are some things that DLLs don't do very well. To understand the limitations of traditional Win32 DLLs, you must first understand what Win32 DLLs are and how they actually work. (When I say *traditional* DLLs, I am talking about DLLs that don't use COM.)

What Win32 DLLs Are and How They Work

The best way to think of a Win32 DLL is to picture it as a chunk of code sitting in memory. That chunk of code can be mapped into your application's address space, which is what happens when your application loads the DLL. When the DLL is mapped into your application's address space, your application can execute the code in the DLL by calling the functions that it exports.

A DLL in Win32 does not have a life of its own. A DLL doesn't have its own process. A DLL has no Windows message loop. Any objects created by code in the DLL are owned by the calling application. A DLL never owns anything. Remember that DLLs are just code—code that is inert until it is loaded into an application's address space and executed as part of that application's code.

An application can load a Win32 DLL into its address space in the following two ways:

- Implicit load-time linking
- Explicit runtime linking

With implicit load-time linking, the application statically links with the DLL's import library (a LIB file). The import library contains the list of functions that the DLL exports for applications to call. The import library also stores the addresses of the exported functions in the DLL file image. When the import library for the DLL is linked with an application, the information from the import library becomes part of the EXE file image.

When the application is executed, the operating system (the OS) loads the EXE file, and the OS looks in the EXE file image to see which DLLs are required for the application. The operating system loads these DLLs when it loads the application's EXE file.

With explicit runtime linking, the DLL is loaded by the application, not by the OS. The DLL is loaded at application runtime, not at application load-time. The application loads the DLL whenever it needs it, by calling the LoadLibrary Windows API function, like this:

```
HINSTANCE LoadLibrary(LPCTSTR lpszDLLFileName);
```

Also, the application can use the LoadLibraryEx function to load DLLs. The LoadLibraryEx function enables the application to specify some options in how the DLL is loaded. The LoadLibraryEx function is

```
HINSTANCE LoadLibraryEx(LPCTSTR lpszDLLFileName,
  HANDLE hFile, DWORD dwFlags);
```

When the operating system loads the DLL, it uses a search procedure to find the DLL file. The search procedure is the same whether the DLL is loaded when the application is loaded through implicit linking or whether the DLL is explicitly loaded by the application code with LoadLibrary. The OS looks in the following series of locations to find the DLL file:

- The directory containing the application EXE file
- The application's current directory

- The Windows system directory
- The Windows directory
- The directories listed in the PATH environment variable

With implicit load-time linking, if the OS cannot find the DLL file in any of these locations, it will present the user with a message box containing an error message. The message will state that it was unable to load the DLL. The application then will not load or run.

If the application is loading the DLL at runtime with explicit runtime linking, and the DLL file is not present, the LoadLibrary function will fail. It's up to the application to check for errors returned by LoadLibrary and act accordingly.

After the application loads the DLL, it must get the addresses of the DLL function(s). If the application uses implicit load-time linking (through the DLL's import library), the function addresses are already linked into the application's EXE file image.

If the application calls LoadLibrary to load the DLL at runtime, the application must call GetProcAddress to get the address of the function(s) in the DLL. The GetProcAddress function is

```
FARPROC GetProcAddress(HINSTANCE hinstanceDLL, LPCSTR lpszProc);
```

Note   Developers might be accustomed to exporting DLL functions by assigning each function an ordinal value. However, Microsoft wants you to link by using the function's name instead of an ordinal value. If you use ordinals to export your DLL functions, you are not guaranteed that your DLL will run on all Win32 platforms and versions.

I mentioned that DLLs enable code to be shared among applications in a very efficient manner. When multiple applications load the same DLL, the OS doesn't load multiple instances of the DLL. Rather, when the first application loads the DLL, it's loaded into memory and mapped into the application's address space. Figure 9.1 illustrates this.

When subsequent applications load the DLL, the OS simply maps the already loaded DLL into those applications' address space. This is illustrated in Figure 9.2.

FIGURE 9.1

A DLL image mapped into an application's address space.

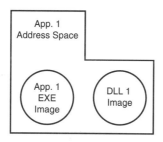

FIGURE 9.2

A DLL image mapped into two applications' address spaces.

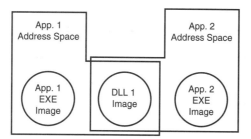

DLL code in memory can be shared by multiple applications. This is what DLLs do really, really well. They reduce code size at runtime by letting the code be shared among applications. The DLLs that contain the Win32 API functions are a perfect example of this. The Windows system DLLs are loaded once and are shared by and mapped into the address space of every Win32 application that runs on the machine.

> You should use DLLs for sharing common code among concurrently running applications. DLLs do this very well.

The Limits of Using Win32 DLLs for Building Software Components

DLLs enable efficient code sharing among concurrently running applications. However, because of some limitations of DLLs, it's difficult to build truly modular, component-based software using traditional Win32 DLLs.

You need to understand what I mean when I talk about component-based software. A true software component would be a piece of software that does the following:

• Plugs into other software systems in a modular, object-oriented fashion

• Can be updated independently of the other software in the system

- Can be used by software systems with which the component author is not intimately familiar
- Consists of a small or manageable number of files that can be distributed on disk or electronically to component users/customers

In essence, a *software component* is a piece of software that you can give (or sell) to other people to use with their software. You can also update your component, and your users can begin using the updated version without breaking their existing software.

Traditional Win32 DLLs, by themselves, do not enable component-based software. The limitations of using DLLs to build software components include

- The requirement to export your DLL functions by name
- Incompatibilities of C++ function decorating
- Hard-coded DLL names in application EXE files
- Build-time dependencies between DLLs and EXEs

DLL Functions Must Be Exported by Name

I noted previously today that Microsoft wants functions exported from DLLs by their name, not by an ordinal value. When an application uses a DLL, the application must use absolutely unique names to identify the DLL function(s) it wants to call.

If you are going to distribute your DLL for use in other systems (systems with which you are unfamiliar), you need to make sure the function names in your DLL don't duplicate any function names from other DLLs that the system might use. With traditional DLLs, there is no easy way to do that. Your DLL could contain a function that has the same name as a function in another DLL.

Incompatible C++ Function Name Decorating

The need to export your DLL functions by name also causes a problem with C++ function decorating. (Function decorating is also called function *name mangling*, but *decorating* is a nicer word.)

As you know, C++ functions can be overloaded. *Overloaded functions* are functions that have the same name and differ only in their parameter list. The compiler and linker, however, must give each function a unique symbol name.

Visual C++ gives each function a unique symbol name by decorating the function's name with additional alphanumeric characters based on the function's parameters. These alphanumeric characters are derived from the function parameters and their types and enable the compiler and linker to differentiate between the overloaded functions.

With Visual C++ name decorating, the function

```
void Foo(int i)
```

becomes

```
?Foo@@YAXH@Z
```

You can witness C++ function name decorating in the following example. Open your
ADOMFC1 project. Click the File View tab and add a header file called
DbComponent.h. Put the code shown in Listing 9.1 in DbComponent.h.

INPUT   **LISTING 9.1.**   THE DbCOMPONENT CLASS DECLARATION

```
1:  class DbComponent
2:  {
3:  public:
4:    DbComponent();
5:    int BeepIfDbIsOk();
6:  };
```

Next, include the DbComponent.h file in the CADOMFC1Doc.cpp file, like this:

INPUT
```
#include "DbComponent.h"
```

Then add the code in Listing 9.2 to the CADOMFC1Doc::OnNewDocument function. (You
should, of course, leave the existing code in OnNewDocument and merely add this code to
it, perhaps near the beginning of the function.)

INPUT   **LISTING 9.2.**   CALLING THE DbCOMPONENT BEEPIFDBISOK FUNCTION

```
1:  DbComponent * pDb = new DbComponent();
2:  pDb->BeepIfDbIsOk();
3:  delete pDb;
```

Now try to build the ADOMFC1 application. You should receive two linker errors for
unresolved external symbols. You will notice that one symbol, which corresponds to the
BeepIfDbIsOk function, looks like this:

```
?BeepIfDbIsOk@DbComponent@@QAEHXZ
```

The other symbol, which corresponds to the constructor for DbComponent class, looks
like this:

```
??0DbComponent@@QAE@XZ
```

You are seeing C++ function name decorating in action. When the Visual C++ compiler builds ADOMFC1Doc.obj, it decorates the names of the DbComponent constructor and the BeepIfDbIsOk function. The linker then tries to find the code for those functions, but it cannot, and it generates the unresolved external symbol errors.

If a DLL existed with the DbComponent code in it, the DbComponent constructor and the BeepIfDbIsOk function would need to exist in the DLL with the decorated names that the Visual C++ linker expects. Otherwise, the linker would not find them and would still generate unresolved external symbol errors.

Unfortunately, function decorating is not uniform among C++ compilers. C++ functions exported from a DLL built with Visual C++ cannot be called in an application built with Borland C++. A Visual C++ DLL and a Borland C++ EXE are incompatible, at least in terms of C++ function calls.

Therefore, if you put your C++ component in a traditional Win32 DLL, it can be used only in software built with the same compiler that you used.

Note

> You can disable C++ name decorating for functions that you export from a DLL, by placing the DLL within external "C" { } blocks. This causes the exported functions to have the signature of a standard C language function. This will enable your DLL functions to be called from EXEs built with other compilers but will cost you the C++ features and the object-oriented nature of your component.

Hard-Coded DLL Names

Whether an application uses implicit load-time linking or explicit runtime linking to call functions in a DLL, the DLL's name is hard-coded into the application's EXE file. This results in a few limitations from a component software standpoint.

The DLL file must exist somewhere that the OS can find it. One place is the application directory. However, if the DLL file existed in the application directory, no other application on the machine would be able to find it.

Another place to put the DLL might be the Windows System directory. If the DLL exists in the Windows System directory, it runs the risk of being overwritten by, or at least conflicting with, another DLL that happens to have the same name.

A true software component needs to be safely installable on any machine and accessible to all the appropriate applications on that machine. Hard-coded DLL names in the application EXE files are detrimental to this.

Build-Time Dependencies Between the DLL and the EXEs That Use It

The most common way for applications to use a DLL is to link with its import library (implicit load-time linking). The other method—explicit runtime linking with the `LoadLibrary` and `GetProcAddress` functions—is not used nearly as often. Using `LoadLibrary` and `GetProcAddress` isn't as convenient for the application developer as simply linking to the DLL's import library and having the OS automatically load the DLL.

However, a problem occurs when it comes time to update the DLL. A true software component can be updated independently of the rest of the system. In other words, you can install and use a new version of a component without breaking the existing system.

With traditional Win32 DLLs, when you modify the code and rebuild the DLL, the information in the import library can change. You will recall that the import library contains the function names exported from the DLL. The import library also contains import records for those functions that are fixed up when the DLL is loaded and the addresses are known.

This means that when a DLL is updated, the applications that use the DLL (by linking with the DLL's import library) need to be rebuilt also to ensure that the system is stable. Therefore, a build-time dependency exists between the application EXE and the DLLs that it uses.

Note

> It might be possible to update a DLL without updating the EXEs that use it, if you don't change any existing functions in the DLL. However, there is no mechanism for the EXE to gracefully recover if the DLL does become out of sync. Also, replacing an existing DLL with an older version quite often causes problems that the application cannot deal with gracefully. The ease with which this problem can occur and the lack of mechanisms to enable a graceful recovery at runtime mean that, for most practical purposes, there is a build-time dependency between an EXE and the DLLs it uses.

With traditional Win32 DLLs, you cannot simply plug a new version of the DLL into an existing system without the risk of breaking it. If you place a new DLL in an existing system without rebuilding the applications that use the DLL, the applications could crash because of changes in the functions in the DLL.

Building Software Components by Using COM

COM addresses the limitations of traditional Win32 DLLs for component development. Using COM, you build software components that

- Plug into other software systems in a modular, object-oriented fashion
- Can be updated independent of the other software in the system
- Can be used by software systems with which the component author is not intimately familiar
- Consist of a small or manageable number of files that can be distributed on disk or electronically to component users/customers.

COM uses some very nifty tricks to solve the problems of building component software. With COM components, there are none of the following:

- Requirements to export your DLL functions by name
- Incompatibilities from C++ function decorating
- Hard-coded DLL names in application EXE files
- Build-time dependencies between DLLs and EXEs

COM accomplishes these technical feats through a rather ingenious application of some relatively simple technologies. You will explore these technologies next.

Using C++ Abstract Base Classes

Modify the code that you entered from Listing 9.1 in DbComponent.h so that it looks like the code in Listing 9.3.

INPUT   **LISTING 9.3.**   THE ABSTRACT BASE CLASS DbComponent CLASS DECLARATION

```
1:  class DbComponent
2:  {
3:  public:
4:    virtual int BeepIfDbIsOk()=0;
5:  };
```

You can see that DbComponent is now an abstract base class. As you know, an abstract base class is a class that contains at least one pure virtual function.

You specify a virtual function as pure by placing = 0 at the end of its declaration. You don't have to supply a definition for a pure virtual function.

You cannot declare an instance of an abstract base class; you can use it only as a base class from which to derive other classes.

Try to build the application now. You will receive an error from the compiler indicating that you cannot instantiate abstract class DbComponent because the BeepIfDbIsOk is a pure virtual function.

Modify the code you entered from Listing 9.2 (in the OnNewDocument function) so that it looks like the code shown in Listing 9.4

INPUT **LISTING 9.4.** CALLING THE DBCOMPONENT BEEPIFDBISOK FUNCTION

```
1:  DbComponent * pDb;
2:  pDb->BeepIfDbIsOk();
3:  delete pDb;
```

Try to build the project now. It should compile and link with no errors, though you might receive a warning about using a local variable before it's initialized. Of course, you should not try to run the application, because it will fail. The DbComponent pointer defined in line 1 of Listing 9.4 is uninitialized. Line 2 tries to use this uninitialized pointer to call the BeepIfDbIsOk function.

The code will not run. However, perhaps somewhat surprisingly, the code will successfully compile and link. There is no code for the DbComponent class and its BeepIfDbIsOk function, so why did the application link successfully? How did the linker bind code that doesn't exist?

The short answer is that the linker didn't bind it. Because the DbComponent class is an abstract base class, and because BeepIfDbIsOk function is a pure virtual function, the linker knew that the code for line 2 of Listing 9.4 would be bound at runtime. Listing 9.5 is an example of runtime binding.

As you know, you can call a virtual function through a base class pointer to execute the function in a derived class. This is classic polymorphism in C++. See the code in Listing 9.5 for an example.

INPUT **LISTING 9.5.** POLYMORPHISM IN C++

```
1:  #include <iostream>
2:  using namespace std;
3:  class myBaseClass
4:  {
```

continues

LISTING 9.5.   CONTINUED

```
 5:  public:
 6:    virtual ~myBaseClass() { };
 7:    virtual void myFunc();
 8:  };
 9:
10:  class myDerivedClass : public myBaseClass
11:  {
12:  public:
13:    void myFunc();
14:  };
15:
16:  void myBaseClass::myFunc()
17:  {
18:    cout << "Executing myFunc in myBaseClass" <<endl ;
19:  }
20:
21:  void myDerivedClass::myFunc()
22:  {
23:    cout << "Executing myFunc in myDerivedClass" <<endl ;
24:  }
25:
26:  int main()
27:  {
28:    myBaseClass * myBaseClassPtrs[4];
29:    myBaseClassPtrs[0] = new myBaseClass;
30:    myBaseClassPtrs[1] = new myDerivedClass;
31:    myBaseClassPtrs[2] = new myBaseClass;
32:    myBaseClassPtrs[3] = new myDerivedClass;
33:
34:    for( int i = 0; i < 4; i++)
35:    {
36:      myBaseClassPtrs[i]->myFunc();
37:    }
38:
39:    delete myBaseClassPtrs[0];
40:    delete myBaseClassPtrs[1];
41:    delete myBaseClassPtrs[2];
42:    delete myBaseClassPtrs[3];
43:    return 0;
44:  }
```

Create a new Win32 console project in Visual Studio named Polymorph. Specify that
AppWizard should create an empty project. Create a source file called main.cpp (specify
that main.cpp should be added to the Polymorph project). Enter the code shown in
Listing 9.5 in main.cpp

Lines 3–8 declare a base class named `myBaseClass` that has a virtual function named `myFunc`. Lines 10–14 derive a class from `myBaseClass` named `myDerivedClass`. Line 13 places a function named `myFunc` in `myDerivedClass`, which overrides `myFunc` in `myBaseClass`.

Lines 16–24 define the `myFunc` functions to simply output a string indicating that they are being executed. Line 28 defines an array of four pointers to `myBaseClass` class. Lines 29–32 initialize the pointers in the array by creating alternating instances of `myBaseClass` and `myDerivedClass`. Lines 39–42 delete the instances of the classes to free up the memory.

Lines 34–37 call the `myFunc` function through the pointers to `myBaseClass`. Note that you are calling a function in a derived class through a base class pointer. `MyBaseClassPtrs[1]` and `myBaseClassPtrs[3]` are pointers to `myBaseClass` but actually point to instances of `myDerivedClass`.

Build the Polymorph project. It should build without errors or warnings. Run Polymorph. The code in Listing 9.5 will produce this output:

```
Executing myFunc in myBaseClass
Executing myFunc in myDerivedClass
Executing myFunc in myBaseClass
Executing myFunc in myDerivedClass
```

Which class's `myFunc` was executed? This was determined at runtime, using C++ virtual function tables, or vtables (pronounced *vee-tables*).

In instances of `myBaseClass`, the vtable entry for `myFunc` points to `myBaseClass`'s `myFunc`. In instances of `myDerivedClass`, the vtable entry for `myFunc` points to `myDerivedClass`'s `myFunc`.

Using vtables, the question of which class's `myFunc` to execute is resolved at runtime. Therefore, the binding of that code doesn't happen at link time. It happens at runtime.

This is a cool trick. Polymorphism is one of the pillars of object-oriented programming. Polymorphism's runtime binding is also one of the pillars of COM.

> **Note**
>
> Calling a derived class's functions through a pointer to its base class is an essential feature of COM.

Open your ADOMFC1 project in Visual Studio. You will recall that the code in the `OnNewDocument` function defines a pointer to the abstract base class, `DbComponent` (refer to Listing 9.4).

You made it an abstract base class because if a DLL existed with the DbComponent object code in it, the DLL would need to have the DbComponent BeepIfDbIsOk function with the exact decorated name that the Visual C++ linker expects. Otherwise, the linker would not find it and would generate an unresolved external symbol error. Using an abstract base class eliminates this need for a compiled symbol with a name decorated the way Visual C++ expects.

 Note

> Using abstract base classes eliminates the problem of incompatible C++ function decorating between C++ compilers. Also, the code that implements these abstract base classes doesn't need to be present when applications that use the abstract base classes are built.

The code in your OnNewDocument function in Listing 9.4 attempts to call the BeepIfDbIsOk function through the DbComponent pointer, but there is another problem. The DbComponent pointer in the OnNewDocument function is uninitialized—and you can't create an instance of the DbComponent class because it's an abstract base class.

How can the code in your OnNewDocument function get a valid DbComponent pointer so that it can call the BeepIfDbIsOk function?

Creating Objects by Using an API Function

It is impossible to create an instance of DbComponent (because it's an abstract base class). However, it is possible to create an instance of a class that is derived from DbComponent. That derived class could reside in a COM DLL (I will describe what a COM DLL entails later today in the section on COM servers).

The derived class could override the BeepIfDbIsOk function in DbComponent and implement it with code to beep if the database is okay. The derived class could be named something like DbComponentImpl.

If you could somehow create an instance of DbComponentImpl, and if you could assign its address to the DbComponent pointer in your OnNewDocument function, you could call the DbComponentImpl's BeepIfDbIsOk function through your DbComponent pointer.

It would be very handy in this case to have some Windows API function that creates instances of classes for you. You could tell it that you want an instance of DbComponentImpl and that you want to assign its address to the DbComponent pointer in your OnNewDocument function.

For example, the code could look something like that shown in Listing 9.6.

LISTING 9.6. CALLING THE DBCOMPONENT BEEPIFDBISOK FUNCTION

```
1:  DbComponent * pDb;
2:  ::CreateInstance(DbComponentImpl_ID, (void**)&pDb);
3:  pDb->BeepIfDbIsOk();
4:  pDb->Release();
```

Line 2 in Listing 9.6 calls an imaginary Windows API function named CreateInstance. Line 2 passes an (imaginary) identifier to the CreateInstance function to indicate that it should create an instance of DbComponentImpl. The function returns a pointer to the DbComponentImpl instance in the second parameter, pDb.

This CreateInstance function would load the DLL containing the DbComponentImpl code, create an instance of the DbComponentImpl class, and assign its address to pDb. After the CreateInstance call, you would have a valid pDb pointer (which is a pointer to DbComponent) that you could use to call the DbComponentImpl BeepIfDbIsOk function, as shown in line 3.

Line 4 in Listing 9.6 calls an imaginary Release function to delete the object. You shouldn't use the delete operator on pDb because DbComponent doesn't have a virtual destructor. The destructor for DbComponent probably wouldn't be capable of properly cleaning up an instance of the DbComponentImpl class. The Release function in line 4 is an imaginary function that is capable of cleaning up an instance of DbComponentImpl.

Using a CreateInstance function like this would enable you to call the member functions of the DbComponent class. You would actually be executing code that resides in the DbComponentImpl class. The really big news is that the code for the DbComponentImpl class would not have to be present when you build your application. Also, the name of the DLL is not hard-coded into your application's EXE file image. Your application can use the code in the DLL without being tied to that particular DLL file.

Note Calling an API function in your application code to create instances of components eliminates the problem of having DLL names hard-coded into the EXE file image of your application.

There are, in fact, Windows API functions that work like the CreateInstance function in Listing 9.6. These functions are part of the Windows COM libraries. The most frequently used function like this is the COM CoCreateInstance function.

Also, the Release function shown in line 4 of Listing 9.6 is authentic. COM components always implement a Release function to enable applications to delete (or free) them.

Actually, COM components free themselves. The purpose of Release is to allow the client application to announce that it won't be using the component anymore. This might result in the component deleting itself, if no other client applications are using it.

You will recall that in Day 4, you used the CoCreateInstance function. The smart pointer class's CreateInstance function internally calls CoCreateInstance. It also calls Release when the pointer goes out of scope, so you don't have to call it. Refer to the following days and their listings for examples of where you used a smart pointer class's CreateInstance function:

Day	Listings
4	4.1, 4.2, 4.6, and 4.8
5	5.1, 5.2, and 5.3
6	6.7 and 6.8

Using abstract base classes to declare the class in the client application, and calling API functions to load the DLL and instantiate the class, makes the application and the COM DLLs that it uses independent of each other.

Because all the code doesn't need to be present at the time the software is built and because the DLL names are not hard-coded in the EXE file image, you have more flexibility in updating the software. Single EXE or DLL files can be replaced with newer versions, without the need to rebuild and replace all the EXE and DLL files in the system every time.

 Note　Breaking the build-time and load-time dependence between EXE files and DLL files enables them to be updated independently of each other.

COM Clients and COM Servers

In previous Days, you learned a few things about client/server systems. You learned that in client/server database applications, which run on multiple computers over a network, the machine where the database resides is called the *server*, and the machines that run the apps that use the database are called the *clients*.

A similar terminology exists in the COM world. In this example, the application that calls the BeepIfDbIsOk function would be called the COM client. The DLL that contains the DbComponentImpl class (and the BeepIfDbIsOk code) would be called the COM server.

NEW TERM   In COM, a component that provides functions for other applications to call is a *server.*

NEW TERM   An application that calls functions provided by COM components is a *client.*

So far today, you've learned a little about what the code looks like in COM clients. COM clients use abstract base classes to declare the COM components they use.

NEW TERM   The abstract base classes that applications use to declare COM components are called COM *interfaces.*

COM clients call Windows API functions to create instances of the (server) component classes. COM clients typically must call `Release` to free the components when they are done with them. COM clients written in Visual C++ can also use a smart pointer class that internally calls `CoCreateInstance` and `Release`.

You haven't yet had much opportunity to see what the code looks like for COM servers. That is the topic of the next section.

COM Servers

COM servers have some required functions that they must implement and export and some required registry entries that they must make. The next two sections explain these requirements.

Registry Entries

You will recall that COM clients call a Win32 API function to create instances of classes from COM DLLs. How does the Win32 subsystem know which DLL contains the code for the classes?

The answer is that the COM libraries (part of the Win32 subsystem) look in the registry for the name of the DLL and the DLL's location. You will recall that in Listing 9.6, when the COM client called the API function to create the class instance, it passed in an identifier to tell the API function which class it wanted an instance of. That identifier is called a GUID.

NEW TERM   A *GUID* is a globally unique identifier. It is a 128-bit number that is guaranteed to be unique. Microsoft provides a tool for generating GUIDs, called Guidgen.exe. It uses the worldwide unique ID of the computer's network card, combined with the current date and time, to create numbers that are always unique.

If the computer doesn't have a network card, the GUID is guaranteed to be unique on that computer and statistically unique across computers. This means it's very unlikely, but possible, for such a GUID to duplicate an existing GUID.

You can typically find Guidgen.exe in your Visual C++ Tools\Bin directory. Run Guidgen so that you can see what a GUID looks like (see Figure 9.3).

FIGURE 9.3

Guidgen.

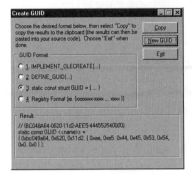

As you can see in the Result pane in the Guidgen window, GUIDs are simply 128-bit (16-byte) numbers. Guidgen makes it easy for you to generate GUIDs and copy them to the Clipboard. From there, you can easily paste them into your source code for use in building COM components.

NEW TERM A *CLSID* is a GUID that identifies a class. In every COM component, each class and each interface (remember, COM interfaces are C++ abstract base classes) is assigned a GUID. When a GUID is used in this context, it is called a CLSID.

The CLSIDs of the COM server classes are stored in the registry, under HKEY_CLASSES_ROOT\CLSID. You can best understand these registry entries by looking at a real-life example.

Suppose you want to create an instance of an ADO Connection object, as you did in Day 4 in Listing 4.1 and Listing 4.6. In this scenario, the ADO Connection object would be the COM server, and the application you are writing would be the COM client.

To create the object, you write some code that calls `CoCreateInstance` or the smart pointer class's `CreateInstance` function and pass it the CLSID of the ADO Connection object.

The code for the `CoCreateInstance` (in COM library) looks up that CLSID in the registry. Figure 9.4 shows the information in the registry for that CLSID.

As you can see in Figure 9.4, under this CLSID, there is an entry called InprocServer32. The InprocServer32 entry indicates that the ADO Connection object is an in-process server, meaning the COM server is contained in a DLL. The location of the DLL is shown as

```
"C:\Program Files\Common Files\System\ado\msado15.dll"
```

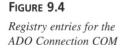

FIGURE 9.4

Registry entries for the ADO Connection COM object.

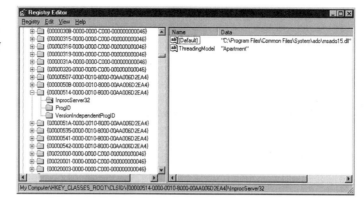

When ADO was installed on this machine, this entry for ADO Connection object was placed in the registry. This registry entry is what enables applications to use the code in the DLL, without hard-coding the DLL name in the application EXE file image.

You can find this entry yourself on your machine. Open the Registry Editor and do a Find on the key ADODB.Connection. Under the ADODB.Connection key is a CLSID sub-key. This entry contains the ADO Connection's CLSID. Next, do a Find on the key for this CLSID. You will find the entry shown in Figure 9.4.

The COM libraries use this registry entry for the CLSID to find the DLL filename and location. COM then calls LoadLibrary to load the DLL.

After the DLL is loaded, COM needs to create an instance of the ADO Connection object. To do this, COM needs some help from functions in the DLL.

Required Server Functions

When you call CoCreateInstance to create an instance of the ADO Connection object, how does COM know how to create instances of the ADO Connection object?

The answer is, it doesn't. However, COM does know how to call a standard function, which is implemented in all COM server DLLs, to get a pointer to an interface for an object that can create instances of ADO Connection. In other words, every COM DLL must export a standardized function that the OS can call to create instances of its classes.

The function name is DllGetClassObject. Its prototype is

```
STDAPI DllGetClassObject(REFCLSID rclsid, REFIID riid, LPVOID* ppv)
```

STDAPI is merely a macro that resolves to an HRESULT and a calling convention. DllGetClassObject actually takes two GUIDs as parameters, the first one being the CLSID and the second one being the GUID for a particular interface that object supports. COM calls DllGetClassObject with the parameters necessary to get a pointer to a class factory interface from the DLL.

NEW TERM   A *class factory* is a class that knows how to create instances of other classes.

A class factory is implemented in every COM server. The class factory implements the IClassFactory interface, which includes the CreateInstance function. COM can call the CreateInstance function to create COM objects (instances of COM server classes).

The class factory in msado15.dll knows how to create ADO Connection objects. After COM loads the DLL by calling LoadLibrary, it calls GetProcAddress to get the address of DllGetClassObject. COM then calls DllGetClassObject to get a pointer to the IClassFactory interface.

After COM gets a pointer to the class factory in msado15.dll, COM calls the class factory CreateInstance function, passing it the ADO Connection CLSID to create an instance of the ADO Connection class. Finally, COM returns the pointer to the ADO Connection object the client application that called CoCreateInstance.

The process of a client calling CoCreateInstance to get a pointer to a COM server is illustrated in Figure 9.5.

FIGURE 9.5

How a COM client obtains a pointer to a COM server.

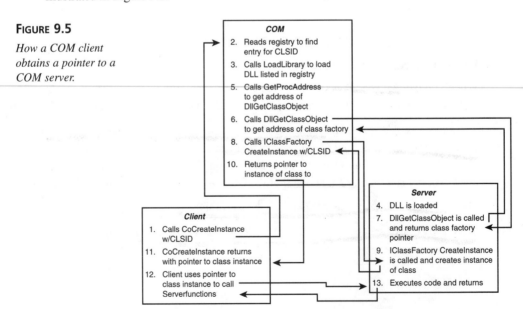

You can see from Figure 9.5 that two calls are made into the COM server DLL. The `DllGetClassObject` function is called and the class factory `CreateInstance` function is called. That means a DLL that contains COM server(s) must implement the `DllGetClassObject` function, as well as a class factory class, in order to work.

A COM DLL needs three other functions in order to implement and expose. These functions are

- `DllRegisterServer`—which contains the code to make the registry entries for the COM servers that reside in the DLL. This makes the COM DLL easy to install and use. The DLL's COM servers can be registered by running RegSvr32.exe and passing the DLL name and path as an argument.

- `DllUnregisterServer`—which contains the code to remove the registry entries for the COM servers that reside in the DLL. This function is called when RegSvr32.exe is run with an argument to specify that it should remove the registry entries for the COM servers.

- `DllCanUnloadNow`—which the OS calls to see whether it can safely unload the DLL from memory. If COM clients are currently using servers from this DLL, the DLL needs to stay loaded (and mapped into the address space of the client applications). However, if all the clients are done with its COM servers, the DLL could be unloaded to free up resources. A global reference count is kept by COM DLLs to track how many of its COM servers are being used. If that reference count is zero, the DLL can unload. If it is not, it can't. This function reports to the OS whether it can be safely unloaded. The DLL unloading functions exist to enable the OS to unload an inproc DLL when system resources are low. The DLL is always unloaded when the process it's attached to ends. While the process is running, the DLL can veto the unloading by returning `FALSE` from `DllCanUnloadNow`. When the process stops, the DLL doesn't get to vote.

Therefore, a DLL that contains COM server(s) must implement four functions (`DllGetClassObject`, `DllRegisterServer`, `DllUnregisterServer`, and `DllCanUnloadNow`) and one class (the class factory).

You can implement all this code yourself in every COM DLL you create, or you can use a tool that implements this code for you. You will next explore a tool that does most of this work for you. That tool is called ATL.

The Active Template Library (ATL)

You will learn more about ATL in Day 11, "Multitier Architectures." Today you will simply use the ATL Wizard to create a COM DLL that contains a COM server. You will see that ATL writes the code for you for the four required functions and the required class factory class in a COM DLL.

ATL is inspired by the C++ Standard Template Library (STL). To make it easy to create COM components, ATL uses C++ templates.

Despite ATL's use of templates, you don't need to use templates in your own code in order to use ATL. ATL provides two wizards and several default COM object types that generate much of the template code for you. With ATL, you are able to concentrate primarily on the implementation of your code and don't have to worry about writing very much of the plumbing that COM needs.

Create a new project in Visual Studio. Specify an ATL COM AppWizard application and ATLTest1 as the project name, as shown in Figure 9.6.

FIGURE 9.6

A new ATL COM AppWizard project.

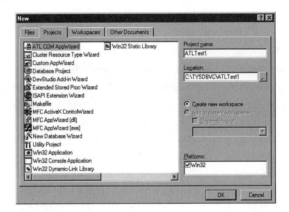

Click the OK button. In the next dialog, specify a server type of DLL, as shown in Figure 9.7. You can build COM servers into an EXE or an NT service, but don't worry about that yet. You will learn about COM servers in EXEs later today.

Check the check boxes for Allow Merging of Proxy/Stub Code and for Support MFC. Don't check the box for supporting MTS. You will learn more about MTS in Day 12, "Using Microsoft Transaction Server to Build Scalable Applications." Click the Finish button and then click the OK button to generate code for the project.

After the wizard generates the code, select the Class View and expand the list of Globals in the tree control. You will see that the four required functions for COM DLLs have been generated for you.

Now you can build your own COM server(s) in this DLL. Select the InsertNew ATL Object... menu to open the ATL Object Wizard shown in Figure 9.8. The icons in the wizard might look different from those in Figure 9.8, depending on which version of Visual Studio you are using.

FIGURE 9.7

Options for the ATL COM AppWizard project.

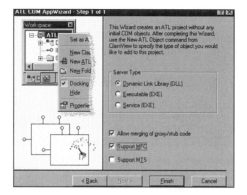

FIGURE 9.8

The ATL Object Wizard.

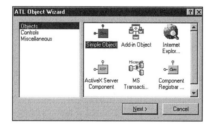

Select Simple Object from the pane on the right and click the Next button. You will then be presented with the ATL Object Wizard Properties dialog shown in Figure 9.9.

FIGURE 9.9

The ATL Object Wizard Properties Names tab.

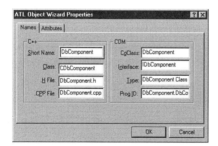

The Names tab is initially selected, as in Figure 9.9. Enter DbComponent as the short name. The other text boxes should fill in automatically.

Select the Attributes tab and select the radio buttons shown in Figure 9.10.

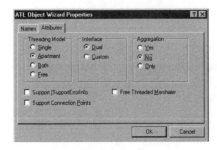

FIGURE 9.10

The ATL Object Wizard Properties Attributes tab.

Threading Model refers to the type of threading your COM server will support. Apartment is the default and will be fine for now.

Interface refers to whether your COM server will provide a dual interface so that it can be used both from scripting languages and from C++ or whether it will provide a custom interface only, which cannot be used from scripting languages. ATL gives you the dual interface for free, so you might as well take it.

Aggregation refers to whether your COM server will be aggregated inside other COM servers. It will not, so select No.

You also will not need support for ISupportErrorInfo, Connection Points, or the Free Threaded Marshaler. Do not check any of these check boxes.

When you click the OK button, the wizard will generate code for the DbComponent class, which will be a COM component that's housed in the DLL.

After the code is generated, you will see in the Class View an entry in the tree control called IdbComponent. *I* stands for *Interface*. This is the interface for the DbComponent COM server. IDbComponent will become a C++ abstract base class for clients that want to use DbComponent.

Right-click IDbComponent in the tree control and select the Add Method... menu. This will open the Add Method to Interface dialog shown in Figure 9.11.

FIGURE 9.11

The Add Method to Interface dialog.

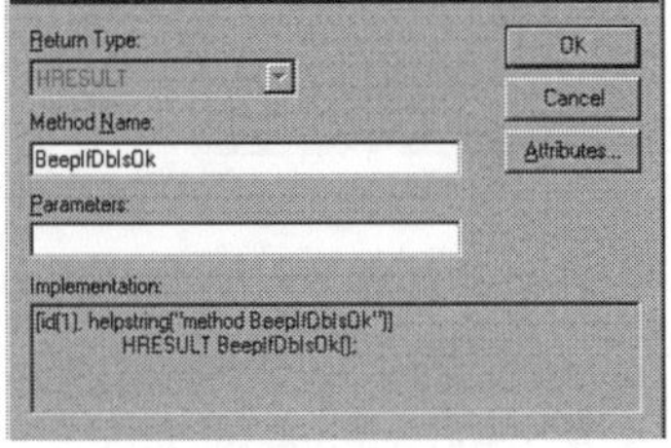

Enter `BeepIfDbIsOk` for Method Name. Return Type is always an `HRESULT` for ATL COM functions. Leave the Parameters edit box empty. Click OK.

After you click OK, ATL will generate the infrastructure for this function. In the Class View, expand the `CdbComponent`; then expand the `IDbComponent` under `CDbComponent`. Under `IdbComponent`, you will see an entry in the tree control for the `BeepIfDbIsOk` function. This points to the code for this function in the COM server. Double-click `BeepIfDbIsOk` to edit its source code.

Edit the code for the `BeepIfDbIsOk` function so that it matches the code in Listing 9.7.

LISTING 9.7. THE BEEPIFDBISOK FUNCTION

```
1:  STDMETHODIMP CDbComponent::BeepIfDbIsOk()
2:  {
3:    AFX_MANAGE_STATE(AfxGetStaticModuleState())
4:
5:    // Good'Die Mite. 'Looks lock the die-ta bise is oak eye.
6:    ::MessageBeep(MB_OK);
7:
8:    return S_OK;
9:  }
```

You can see that this code isn't really doing anything to check a database to see whether it's okay. This is just a simple function that you can use to begin your discovery of COM programming.

Lines 5 and 6 are the only lines you need to add. The ATL Wizard automatically puts the rest of them there. You can see from line 5 that this code could be written in the land down *undah*. COM components can be written and used anywhere on the planet. Line 6 simply beeps.

Build your ATLTest1 project. It should build without errors or warnings. The build process will generate an ATLTest1.h file that contains the abstract base class (`IDbComponent`) that the COM clients will use. The build process will generate another file called ATLTest1_i.c, which holds the GUIDs that the COM clients will need in order to use this COM server.

The build process will run RegSvr32.exe for you to register the COM server DLL. This means that after each successful build, you have a COM server that has been registered on your machine and is ready to be used by COM clients.

9

You have now created a COM server component that can be called from COM clients. To try it out, copy the ATLTest1.h file and the ATLTest1_i.c file into the directory with your ADOMFC1 project. Open your ADOMFC1 project in Developer Studio.

Change the CADOMFC1Doc.cpp file so that it includes the ATLTest1.h file and the ATLTest1_i.c file (instead of the DbComponent.h file), like this:

INPUT
```
#include "ATLTest1_i.c"
#include "ATLTest1.h"
```

Change the code in the OnNewDocument function so that it calls the BeepIfDbIsOk function in your COM server (see Listing 9.8). (You should, of course, leave the existing code in OnNewDocument and merely add this code to it—perhaps near the beginning of the function.)

INPUT

LISTING 9.8. CALLING THE COM SERVER BEEPIFDBISOK FUNCTION FROM THE ONNEWDOCUMENT FUNCTION

```
1:  hr = CoCreateInstance(CLSID_DbComponent, NULL,
 2:  CLSCTX_INPROC_SERVER, IID_IDbComponent,
 3:  (void**) &pDb);
 4:
 5:  if (SUCCEEDED(hr))
 6:  {
 7:    pDb->BeepIfDbIsOk();
 8:    pDb->Release();
 9:  }
```

Line 3 of Listing 9.8 defines a pointer to IDbComponent, the abstract base class that is the interface to the COM object. IDbComponent is declared in ATLTest1.h.

Lines 5, 6, and 7 call CoCreateInstance. The first parameter is the CLSID for this component. The second parameter is for the aggregating IUnknown interface and is NULL (except when using aggregation). The third parameter tells COM that you are working with a COM server in a DLL. The fourth parameter is the GUID for the interface you are requesting. (In this case, the CLSID for this component and the GUID for the interface are actually the same.) The last parameter is where the pointer to the instance of the class will be returned.

If the call to CoCreateInstance succeeds, line 10 calls BeepIfDbIsOk, and line 11 calls Release to free the COM server. Listing 9.8 does not check for or handle errors for the sake of code brevity and clarity.

Remember that you called the `AfxOleInit` function in `CADOMFC1App::InitInstance` to initialize the COM libraries. You must always do this before calling COM functions (such as `CoCreateInstance`), or they will fail.

The software should run without a hitch. You should be able to set a break point in the client code and step into the server code in the DLL, just as you can when COM isn't involved. Also, of course, the program should beep as expected. No worries.

You have now written a COM server component and a COM client application. Congratulations. You also understand COM at its foundation, which will enable you to understand more about COM later.

IUnknown, QueryInterface, AddRef, and Release

You might be wondering about that `Release` function call in line 12 of Listing 9.8. You didn't declare or implement a `Release` function in your `DbComponent` class for the COM server. How did `Release` become part of `IDbComponent`?

It might not be readily apparent in this example, but every COM interface (`IDbComponent` included) is derived from an abstract base class called `IUnknown`. `IUnknown` has three member functions: `QueryInterface`, `AddRef`, and `Release`.

> **Note**
>
> Every COM interface is inherited from `IUnknown`, which has three functions: `QueryInterface`, `AddRef`, and `Release`.

`QueryInterface` enables a COM client to query a COM server to see whether the server supports the requested interface. The implementation of `QueryInterface` is standard among COM servers, and ATL implements it for you. If you weren't using ATL (or some other tool that automates the process of creating COM server code), you would have to write an implementation of `QueryInterface` into your server code.

The same thing goes for `AddRef` and `Release`. These two functions provide usage counts for COM servers. Their implementations are pretty standard. ATL writes the code for these functions as well, so you don't have to in your COM server code.

Interface Definition Language

I mentioned earlier today that you could build COM servers into an EXE. This means that the COM client, which is an EXE in the example you just went through, can call functions in another EXE. COM enables function calls across process boundaries.

The programming model is identical, whether your COM client is talking to a COM server in a DLL or in an EXE. About the only difference on the client side is the third parameter it passes to CoCreateInstance—CLSCTX_LOCAL_SERVER instead of CLSCTX_INPROC_SERVER. The difference at runtime is that making function calls across process boundaries can be about 50 times slower than making function calls within the same process. Nevertheless, the ability to call functions in an EXE from another EXE is quite a feat.

To accomplish this feat, COM has to make each EXE believe it's talking to code inside its own address space. COM creates a local proxy of a server inside the client's address space. The client talks to the proxy, the proxy talks to COM, and COM talks to the server EXE.

NEW TERM With COM crossing process boundaries like this, it was necessary to create some standard formats for sending function calls and their parameter values and types between client and server EXEs. Also needed was an object that understands how to pack and unpack the specific parameters of an interface's functions. This is called *marshalling*.

Proxy/stub objects, which are created by the MIDL compiler, handle this marshalling. The input to the MIDL compiler is Interface Definition Language (IDL).

You can see what IDL looks like by opening the ATLTest1 project and double-clicking the IDbComponent interface in the Class View. This will open ATLTest1.idl.

You can think of IDL as C++ header files on steroids. IDL defines the interface classes, their functions, and the functions' parameters, just as C++ headers do. IDL also specifies whether the parameters are In, Out, or Both, indicating whether a parameter is used by the client to pass in a variable that's filled in or modified by the server.

Automation (Formerly Called *OLE Automation*)

Automation is the name for a standard COM interface named IDispatch. If you look at ATLTest1.idl, you will notice that IDbComponent is derived from IDispatch (IDispatch is derived from IUnknown).

Remember that you told ATL that you wanted this COM server to provide a dual interface (refer to Figure 9.10). A dual interface enables your server to be used by clients such as scripting languages.

The IDispatch interface has a member function named Invoke. Invoke takes a function name, or ordinal value that represents a function, as a parameter and invokes the function on behalf of a COM client that can't call the function directly itself.

Calling functions in a COM server through `IDispatch Invoke` is a bit slower than making direct calls to a function through a pointer. However, the `IDispatch` interface opens up a COM server so that languages without pointers can use it.

If your COM server has a dual interface, it supports both the direct method through pointers and the indirect method though the `IDispatch` interface. ATL does all the work of implementing the `IDispatch` functions, so there's often no cost to supporting Automation in your COM server.

There is a need, however, for your COM server to use only the data types supported by Automation in its function parameters. This typically isn't a problem, but you should check the Automation types in the COM/VC++ documentation to make sure they meet the requirements of your server.

COM Type Libraries

If a COM server supports Automation, it can be used from client applications written in a wide variety of programming languages. If all that a COM server provides to document its interface is a C++ header file, that might not help some of the clients that want to use that server.

| NEW TERM | A *type library* is a language-independent header file.

A type library describes the interfaces to a COM server in a way that can be understood by most modern programming languages (on the Windows platform). ATL automatically creates a type library for COM servers. The type library ATL created for ATLTest1 is in the file ATLTest1.tlb.

You have actually used a type library already. When you used the `#import` directive with ADO in Days 4, 5, and 6, you were using the ADO type library. The ADO type library is stored as a resource in the ADO DLL file. The `#import` directive reads the type library from the resource and creates C++ classes for you that correspond to the interfaces described.

Summary

Today you learned the basics of COM. You learned that COM is based on C++ abstract base classes, called *interfaces*. You also learned that the COM libraries (part of the Win32 API) provide a way to create instances of classes indirectly, thereby avoiding any build-time dependencies between clients and servers.

Traditional DLLs are good for sharing common code among concurrently running applications. However, to build real component-based software, the capabilities afforded by COM are essential.

Q&A

Q What is the difference between COM and OLE?

A These names (acronyms) are a bit historical. OLE is the name for the original technology when it was introduced several years ago. OLE now applies mostly when talking about controls, in-place activation, and other application-level technologies. COM is more foundational and deals with the base parts of the technology. Today you learned about COM, not OLE.

Q How does COM compare to other object technologies, such as CORBA and OpenDoc?

A These object technologies have incredible depth and breadth. It would be difficult to provide an adequate comparison. However, in general, COM provides the easiest development model but not always the most robust performance. COM is most popular on the Windows platforms. CORBA finds most of its adherents on the UNIX platforms. For a while, it looked as though OpenDoc would be supported on the IBM platforms (OS/2 and mainframes) and on the Macintosh platform, but support for OpenDoc has waned considerably.

Q Does MFC provide classes and wizards for COM?

A Yes, it does. However, much of MFC's support is in two areas: OLE controls, both for building them and for using them, and Automation, both for building Automation servers and for building Automation clients. The OLE support in MFC is particularly helpful when you are building OLE components that have heavy user interface (UI) requirements. ATL is best used for COM components that have few, or no, UI requirements.

Workshop

The Workshop quiz questions test your understanding of today's material. (The answers appear in Appendix F, "Answers.") The exercises encourage you to apply the information you learned today to real-life situations.

Quiz

1. Why can't you load a DLL into memory and send messages to it from your application?

2. What makes a C++ class an abstract base class?

3. What is a class factory?

4. Why is it necessary for a COM client to call `Release` on a COM server after it's finished with it?

5. What is a CLSID, and why must all CLSIDs be unique?

Exercises

1. Add another method to the `IDbComponent` interface. Make this method take, as a parameter, an address to a variable of some sort. Modify this variable in the server code and make sure it gets back okay to the client.

2. Use the ATL COM AppWizard to create a COM server in an EXE. Expose a function in its interface, similar to one in the DLL COM server. Compare the performance of the EXE-based COM server (the out-of-proc server) versus the DLL-based COM server (the inproc server).

9

DAY **10**

Database Client Technologies and the Secrets of ADO

Database client technologies for the Windows platform have rapidly evolved during the past few years. Technologies for doing database client development include ODBC, the MFC ODBC classes, DAO, RDO, OLE DB, and ADO. Each of these technologies can be a useful tool for developing database client applications.

The question of when and where to use each client technology can be very confusing—unless you understand each technology and how it relates to the others. Today, the murky waters of database client technologies will become clear.

After examining the context of database client technologies and the relationships between them, you will spend some time learning more about ADO.

Today you will learn

- An overview of the database client technologies, such as ODBC, DAO, RDO, OLE DB and ADO
- A comparison of the strengths and weaknesses of each technology
- The secrets of ADO

You won't be writing new code today. Rather, you will concentrate on gaining a deeper understanding of the ADO code you wrote in Day 4, "Retrieving SQL Data Through a C++ API," Day 5, "Adding, Modifying, and Deleting Data," and Day 6, "Harnessing the Power of Relational Database Servers."

An Overview of Database Client Technologies

Database client technologies provide abstractions. That is their purpose. A database is a very complex piece of software. Writing programs to communicate with a database through its native interface can be very complicated. Database client technologies simplify this process.

Database client technologies provide an interface that is less complex than the underlying database. Database client interfaces provide leverage for you, the developer. They enable you to write relatively simple programs that leverage an enormous amount of code (code that resides in the database) to perform very complex tasks.

A good database interface is like a magnifying glass for your code, as shown in Figure 10.1.

FIGURE 10.1

A database interface as a code magnifier.

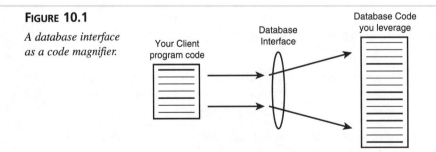

Writing programs to communicate with a database through its native interface not only can be complex but also can result in limited and inflexible applications. An application written to use a particular database's native interface is limited, of course, to using only that particular database. The process of enabling such an application to use another database can be very difficult and time-consuming, if not impossible.

Database client technologies provide a uniform interface for communicating with different and disparate database systems. With modern database client interfaces, you can write a single program that performs complex operations using multiple types of databases, as shown in Figure 10.2.

FIGURE 10.2

A uniform interface to disparate database systems.

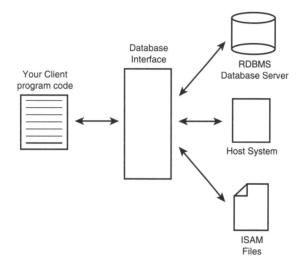

10

A good database interface magnifies your code and provides a uniform interface to different database systems. In the recent past, several database interfaces have been developed. These database interfaces differ from each other in the things they accomplish and the way they go about them.

The popular database interfaces on the Windows platforms include

- ODBC (open database connectivity)
- MFC (Microsoft Foundation Classes) ODBC classes
- DAO (Data Access Objects)
- RDO (Remote Data Objects)
- OLE DB (object-linking and embedding database—the expanded acronym makes no sense unless you know its historical context, which you will learn shortly)
- ADO (ActiveX Data Objects)

You will learn database client technologies in more depth in Days 14–21. However, here is a brief explanation of each technology to give you an understanding of the context of each.

ODBC

ODBC was created in the late '80s and early '90s to provide a uniform interface for writing client software for relational databases. ODBC provides a single API for client applications to work with different databases. Applications that use the ODBC API can communicate with any relational database for which there is an ODBC driver.

Compared to other database interfaces, the ODBC API could be classified as a low-level database interface. The ODBC API enables client applications to configure and control the database at a relatively low level.

Figure 10.3 illustrates the architecture of ODBC.

FIGURE 10.3

The ODBC architecture.

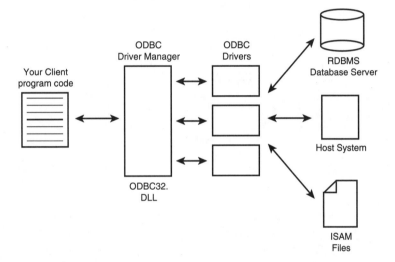

ODBC was designed to provide an interface to relational databases. ODBC has become quite popular and is generally accepted as a standard for interfacing with relational database systems.

ODBC is limited to relational databases. Because of the relational nature of ODBC, it's difficult to use ODBC to communicate with nonrelational data sources, such as object databases, network directory services, email stores, and so on.

ODBC provides the ODBC Driver Manager (ODBC32.DLL), an import library (ODBC32.LIB), and ODBC header files for the ODBC API. Client applications link with the import library to use the functions exposed by the ODBC Driver Manager. At runtime, the ODBC Driver Manager calls functions in the ODBC drivers (which are also DLLs) to perform operations on the databases, as shown in Figure 10.3.

NEW TERM ODBC does not provide an *embedded SQL* interface. With embedded SQL, the SQL code is embedded in the application program source code. A precompiler transforms the SQL code at build time into native function calls that call the database's runtime library.

NEW TERM ODBC provides a *call-level interface (CLI)*. A CLI is a special kind of database API. A CLI, like a typical API, provides functions for client applications to call. However, in a CLI, the SQL code in the client application is not precompiled. Rather, the API provides functions that enable the application to send the SQL code to the database at runtime. The SQL code is interpreted at runtime.

ODBC is a nontrivial topic. You will explore the architecture of ODBC (and write some ODBC code) in Day 14, "Legacy Database APIs."

MFC ODBC Classes

ODBC was created to provide a uniform interface to relational databases. However, the ODBC API isn't necessarily simple.

In Visual C++, MFC provides classes that simplify the ODBC API. The MFC ODBC classes make ODBC programming much less complex. You used the MFC ODBC classes in Day 1, "Choosing the Right Database Technology," in Listing 1.4.

The MFC ODBC classes are easier to use than the ODBC API but do not give you the low-level control that the ODBC API offers. Therefore, the MFC ODBC classes could be classified as a high-level database interface. You will learn more about using the MFC ODBC classes in Day 15, "The ODBC API and the MFC ODBC Classes."

DAO

DAO stands for *Data Access Objects*. Data Access Objects is a set of (COM) Automation interfaces for the Microsoft Access/Jet database engine. DAO talks directly to Access/Jet databases. DAO can also communicate with other databases through the Jet engine, as shown in Figure 10.4.

The COM-based Automation interface of DAO provides more than a function-based API. DAO provides an object model for database programming.

The DAO object model is better suited to object-oriented development than a straight API. Integrating a set of disparate API functions into an object-oriented application typically means that the developer must write her own set of classes to encapsulate the API functions.

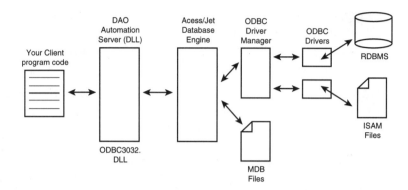

FIGURE 10.4

DAO architecture.

Rather than provide merely a bunch of functions, DAO provides a set of objects for connecting to a database and performing operations on the data. These DAO objects are easy to integrate into the source code of an object-oriented application.

In addition to including classes for connecting to a database and manipulating data, the DAO object model also encapsulates the structural pieces of an Access database, such as tables, queries, indexes, and so on. This means that DAO also enables you to directly modify the structure, or schema, of Access databases without having to use SQL DDL statements.

DAO provides a useful object model for database programming, but as you can see from Figure 10.4, several layers of software are involved. Note that if you are using DAO to talk to a database server such as Oracle or SQL Server, all the calls into the database and all the data coming out of the database must pass through the Access/Jet engine. This can be a significant bottleneck for applications that use a database server.

DAO is easier to use than the ODBC API but doesn't provide the degree of low-level control afforded by the ODBC API. Therefore, DAO could be classified as a high-level database interface.

There is a set of MFC classes that further simplify the DAO Automation interfaces. The MFC DAO classes are prefixed with CDAO. You can find information on these MFC classes in the Visual C++ documentation. On Day 14, you will learn more about DAO and the MFC DAO classes.

RDO

RDO stands for *Remote Data Objects*. RDO was originally developed as an abstraction of the ODBC API for Visual Basic programmers. Therefore, RDO is closely tied to ODBC and Visual Basic.

RDO is easier to use than the ODBC API but doesn't offer the low-level control provided by the ODBC API. Therefore, RDO could be classified as a high-level database interface.

Because RDO calls the ODBC API directly (rather than through Jet, like DAO), it can provide good performance for applications that use relational database servers.

RDO can be used with Visual C++ applications by inserting the RemoteData control in the application. The RemoteData control is an OLE Control that can be bound to controls in the application's UI. You can call RDO functions through the RemoteData control's methods. You will learn more about RDO in Day 14.

OLE DB

As I mentioned earlier, OLE DB stands for *object-linking and embedding database*. The *OLE DB* name makes more sense as an acronym. You will understand why in a moment.

OLE DB expands on ODBC in two important ways. First, OLE DB provides an OLE—actually, a COM—interface for database programming. Second, OLE DB provides an interface to both relational and nonrelational data sources.

OLE DB provides an OLE (COM) interface. *OLE* was the original name for COM. When OLE DB was being created, *OLE* was still used as the name for COM. Since that time, *COM* has become the name for the foundation of Microsoft's component technology (which you explored yesterday), and *OLE* has come to be associated with UI components such as OLE Controls (OCX Controls).

Used as an acronym, the *OLE DB* name invokes an image of OLE/COM and databases, which is accurate. However, the expanded *object-linking and embedding database* name makes no sense. This is why I say the *OLE DB* name makes more sense as an acronym.

I think the technology might best be named *COM DB* instead of *OLE DB* because OLE DB has little to do with UI components such as OLE Controls. Unfortunately, Microsoft has yet to seek my approval of the *OLE DB* name and seems committed to using the *OLE DB* term.

OLE DB's provision of a COM interface for database programming is important because a COM interface can be much more robust and flexible than a traditional call-level interface, such as the ODBC interface. This flexibility can result in better performance and more robust error handling and can enable interfacing with nonrelational data sources.

Like ODBC, OLE DB could be classified as a low-level database API. OLE DB incorporates the functionality of ODBC for relational databases and expands on it by providing access to nonrelational data sources.

10

There are two kinds of OLE DB software: OLE DB consumers and OLE DB providers.
Figure 10.5 illustrates the relationship between OLE DB consumers and OLE DB
providers.

FIGURE 10.5

*OLE DB consumers
and providers.*

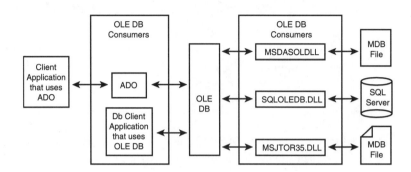

An *OLE DB consumer* is any application that uses or consumes OLE DB interfaces. For
example, any application that you write in C++ and that uses OLE DB to connect to a
database server would be an OLE DB consumer.

OLE DB providers are DLLs that implement the OLE DB interfaces and do the actual
communication with the data source. OLE DB providers are similar in function to
ODBC drivers, except that OLE DB providers implement COM interfaces instead of API
functions.

OLE DB furnishes access to any data source for which there is an OLE DB provider.
These data sources include email stores, object databases, network directories, and other
nonrelational data stores.

As you can see in Figure 10.5, there is an OLE DB provider called MSDASQL.DLL that
can talk to ODBC data sources. This is handy for those data sources that have an ODBC
driver but don't yet have an OLE DB provider.

OLE DB exposes a set of COM interfaces that can be called from C++ programs. OLE
DB doesn't offer an Automation interface.

OLE DB is the future of database client development on Windows. Microsoft's own
development efforts are focused on OLE DB. It's unlikely that we will not see any further updates of ODBC. ODBC will stick around in its present form, and all the new
database client technology from Microsoft will be applied to OLE DB. OLE DB is the
focus of Days 16–21.

ADO

ADO stands for *ActiveX Data Objects*. ADO is built on top of OLE DB. ADO is an OLE DB consumer. Applications that use ADO use the OLE DB interfaces indirectly.

ADO provides an object model for database programming that's similar to, but more flexible than, DAO's object model. For instance, you can create Recordset objects in ADO without first creating a Connection object (which is something you can't do in DAO).

ADO simplifies OLE DB. OLE DB is large and complex; a program that uses OLE DB must use some complex COM interfaces. ADO is much simpler to use than OLE DB and can be classified as a high-level database interface.

Also, ADO can be used with more programming languages than OLE DB. ADO provides an Automation interface. This enables ADO to be used from scripting languages, such as VBScript and JavaScript. (OLE DB can't be used from scripting languages because scripting languages don't have pointers and therefore can't use COM interfaces.)

You've already used ADO objects in Days 4, 5, and 6 to connect to a database, issue queries, retrieve resultsets, and execute stored procedures. You will use ADO objects more today.

10

Database Client Technology Summary

The database client technologies and how they relate to each other are shown in Figure 10.6. As you can see, several technologies are available to you for database client development.

Table 10.1 presents the relative strengths and weaknesses of the various database client technologies.

TABLE 10.1 COMPARISON OF THE DATABASE CLIENT TECHNOLOGIES

	ODBC	MFC ODBC	DAO	RDO	OLE DB	ADO
Object model	−	+	+	+	+	++
Nonrelational data sources	−	−	−	−	+	+
Low-level control	+		−	−	+	
Performance	+		−		++	
Code-to-functionality ratio	−		+		−	+

FIGURE 10.6

Database client technologies.

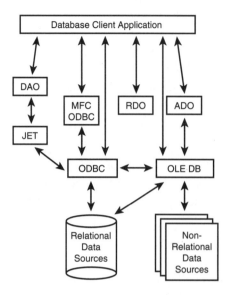

In Table 10.1, a plus sign (+) indicates a strength, two plus signs (++) indicate a special strength, a minus sign (–) indicates a weakness, and a blank indicates no particular strength or weakness.

- *Object model* indicates whether the technology provides an object model that lends itself to object-oriented programming.
- *Nonrelational data sources* refers to the technology's capability to access data stored in nonrelational data stores. (All these technologies provide access to relational databases, so relational database access isn't shown.)
- *Low-level control* refers to the amount of database configurability and low-level control the technology provides for working with relational database servers.
- *Performance* refers to the amount of execution overhead the technology imposes when accessing relational database servers.
- *Code-to-functionality ratio* refers to how much code you have to write compared to the database functionality you gain from that code.

Of all these technologies, OLE DB and ADO have the most promising future. These two technologies are where Microsoft is doing its development work. The other technologies are not being discontinued, per se, but will not be further updated by Microsoft.

OLE DB offers unparalleled power and flexibility for client database programming. However, as you can see from Table 10.1, OLE DB is a low-level interface and requires more code than a high-level interface such as ADO.

ADO offers a flexible yet simple object model with decent performance. This makes ADO the best way to start doing database client development. Next, you will explore ADO and learn how to discover details about its functions.

The Secrets of ADO

The things you are about to learn are not really secrets. They are important pieces of information about ADO that are not very clearly documented. The knowledge you are about to gain here, combined with the existing ADO documentation, should give you what you need to perform any ADO programming task.

Rather than describe all the ADO functions (as in traditional API documentation), I will show you where to find that information and how to use it. The knowledge you gain here will apply not only to ADO but also to all other dual-interface COM servers.

ADO's History

Compared to the other database client technologies, ADO is relatively new. So far, Microsoft has released three versions of ADO: 1.0, 1.5, and 2.0.

The first release, version 1.0, was a subset of the functionality of RDO. It was targeted at developers building Active Server Pages (ASP) for Internet Information Server (IIS).

The next release, version 1.5, was shipped with IIS 4.0 and Internet Explorer (IE) 4.0. It was also included in the Microsoft Data Access Components (MDAC). With version 1.5, ADO became a database interface that rivaled (or exceeded) RDO and DAO in functionality and performance.

The latest release, version 2.0, added new functionality to ADO that is not found in other database client technologies. ADO 2.0 is actually housed in MSADO15.DLL, which is the same filename as the ADO 1.5 DLL. The filename is the same, but additional ADO COM interfaces are implemented in the ADO 2.0 version of the DLL.

The new functionality in ADO 2.0 includes

- Asynchronous operations and notifications
- Recordset persistence
- Hierarchical recordsets for data shaping

Before you delve into the latest and coolest features of ADO 2.0, however, you need to understand some of the basics of ADO. You will begin with ADO's use of COM.

ADO and COM

You will recall from Day 9, "Understanding Com," that a COM server can

- Be housed in a DLL so that it runs in the client process's address space for good performance
- Provide an Automation interface so that it can be used from clients written in almost any programming language
- Sport a type library so that its objects and functions can be easily discovered by client applications

ADO does all these things as a COM server. ADO is housed in MSADO15.DLL. ADO has a dual interface, meaning it has custom (vtable) interfaces and Automation interfaces, and ADO has a type library, so you can discover the ADO objects and the functions they expose.

The ADO Type Library

You can view the ADO type library by running the OLE-COM Object Viewer. Run the OLE-COM Object Viewer now. It can be found under the Microsoft Visual Studio 6.0 Tools menu, Ole View.

From the File menu, select View TypeLib... and navigate to the MSADO15.DLL file. The MSADO15.DLL file is typically installed in the C:\Program Files\Common Files\ System\ADO directory.

The left pane of the OLE-COM Object Viewer window contains a tree control with the elements of the type library. The right pane of the window shows the Interface Definition Language (IDL) code that the MIDL compiler used to create the type library.

You will recall from yesterday that IDL is basically a language-independent C++ header file. The MIDL compiler, which runs when you build a COM server project in Visual C++, uses the IDL code to build the type library.

As you select elements in the tree control in the left pane of the OLE-COM Object Viewer window, the right pane shows the corresponding IDL code. Scroll down in the tree control and select the interface _Connection element. This is the custom COM interface for the ADO _Connection object. The ITypeLib Viewer window should look like Figure 10.7. The GUID for the _Connection interface might change between releases of ADO, so it might look similar but not identical to Figure 10.7.

The right pane shows the IDL for the ADO _Connection object. This IDL lists the _Connection object's functions and their arguments.

FIGURE 10.7

Viewing the ADO type library.

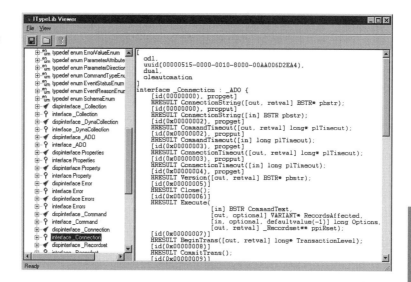

You can find documentation for IDL in the Visual C++ help system. Basically, IDL is like C++ function declarations with the addition of attributes in brackets before each function and each argument. The attributes you will see most frequently are

- id—Assigns an ordinal value, called a DISPID, to each function
- out—Indicates that the argument is an out parameter: a pointer to a variable that the server will modify and that the client will use afterwards
- in—Indicates that the argument is an in parameter and is being passed in from the client to the server and that the client is responsible for the lifetime of any storage allocated
- retval—Is used in conjunction with an out argument to indicate that this is the return value of the function (all COM interface functions return an HRESULT, so one out argument can be specified as the return value)
- optional—Indicates that this parameter can accept a NULL value
- defaultvalue—Specifies a default value for optional parameters (this attribute is not typically implemented when using #import)

Expand the tree control under the interface _Connection element. Highlight the Execute function. The right pane will show the IDL code for the ADO _Connection object's Execute function as shown in Figure 10.8.

As you can see, the type library provides documentation for the functions in the COM interfaces of a COM server. You can use the #import directive in Visual C++ to have the compiler read the type library and produce C++ header files that match it. As you will recall, that's what you did in the code you wrote in Days 4, 5, and 6. You will learn more about using #import with ADO in the next section.

FIGURE 10.8

Viewing the type library for the Execute *function of the ADO* _Connection *custom interface.*

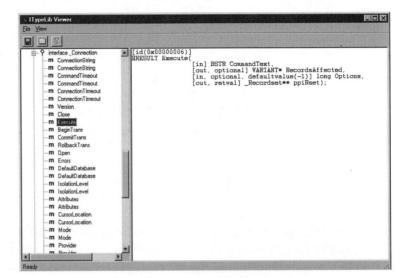

Now scroll up the left pane of the OLE-COM Object Viewer window and expand the dispinterface _Connection element in the tree control. This is the dispatch interface for the ADO _Connection object.

You will recall from yesterday that the dispatch interface (IDispatch) is the COM interface that provides an Invoke function. Programming languages that don't have pointers (but are Automation capable) can call functions in COM servers by passing the DISPID of the function to the IDispatch Invoke function. This technology was originally called *OLE Automation* but is now called simply *Automation* (with a capital *A*).

Select the Execute method under dispinterface _Connection in the OLE-COM Object Viewer. Your window will look like Figure 10.9.

You can see that the IDL for the Execute function in ADO's Automation interface in Figure 10.9 is similar to the IDL for the Execute function in the custom interface (refer to Figure 10.8). The difference between the functions is that the Automation function does not return an HRESULT. Rather, the retval argument in the custom interface is listed as the value returned from the Automation function.

FIGURE 10.9

Viewing the type library for the Execute *function of ADO* _Connection Dispinterface.

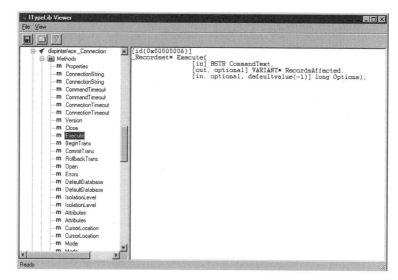

When an application uses the custom interface version of the _Connection::Execute function, the application must pass a pointer to a pointer to a Recordset as the fifth argument, and the function returns an HRESULT.

When an application uses #import, however, the _Connection::Execute function returns a pointer to a Recordset, as in the Automation version of the function.

ADO and the #import Directive

Open your ADOMFC1 project. Open the MSADO15.TLH file and the MSADO15.TLI files. You can find the MSADO15.TLH file and the MSADO15.TLI files by navigating to your build output directory (probably Debug). These are the C++ header files that the compiler created from the ADO type library at build time.

These header files contain two types of functions: high-level wrapper functions and low-level direct functions. The high-level wrapper functions have the same name as the functions in the type library. The low-level functions use the function name with a prefix of raw_.

For functions that have a retval argument, a wrapper is created with the same function name but with the retval argument removed and the return type changed to the retval pointer type. You saw the same technique used in the Automation version of the function in the type library shown in Figure 10.9.

MSADO15.TLI contains the inline implementations of the high-level wrapper functions. The low-level functions are invoked by the high-level functions, as shown in Listing 10.1.

LISTING 10.1 A HIGH-LEVEL WRAPPER FUNCTION IN MSADO15.TLI

```
 1:  inline _RecordsetPtr _Connection::Execute ( _bstr_t CommandText,
 2:    VARIANT * RecordsAffected, long Options )
 3:  {
 4:    struct _Recordset * _result;
 5:    HRESULT _hr = raw_Execute(CommandText,
 6:      RecordsAffected, Options, &_result);
 7:    if (FAILED(_hr)) _
 8:      com_issue_errorex(_hr, this, __uuidof(this));
 9:    return _RecordsetPtr(_result, false);
10:  }
```

The `raw_Execute` function in line 5 of Listing 10.1 is the low-level function being invoked by this high-level function. You can see that this code calls the low-level function (`raw_Execute`), checks the return value to see whether it's a failed `HRESULT`, and then throws an exception if it is. You can call the low-level functions from your code if you want to. This would enable you to evaluate the return values of the functions rather than have to catch exceptions.

MSADO15.TLH contains the declarations of the high-level and low-level functions. MSADO15.TLH also contains the `#include` statement for Comdef.h, the forward references for the GUIDs in the type library, smart pointer declarations, enumerated types in the type library, and the `#include` statement for MSADO15.TLI.

Listing 10.2 shows the portion of MSADO15.TLH that contains the forward references for the GUIDs in the type library. The GUID for the `_Connection` interface might change between releases of ADO, so it might look similar, but not identical, to Listing 10.2.

LISTING 10.2 FORWARD REFERENCES FOR THE GUIDs IN MSADO15.TLH

```
 1:  //
 2:  // Forward references and typedefs
 3:  //
 4:
 5:  struct __declspec(uuid("00000512-0000-0010-8000-00aa006d2ea4"))
 6:  /* dual interface */ _Collection;
 7:  struct __declspec(uuid("00000513-0000-0010-8000-00aa006d2ea4"))
 8:  /* dual interface */ _DynaCollection;
 9:  struct __declspec(uuid("00000534-0000-0010-8000-00aa006d2ea4"))
10:  /* dual interface */ _ADO;
11:  struct __declspec(uuid("00000504-0000-0010-8000-00aa006d2ea4"))
12:  /* dual interface */ Properties;
13:  struct __declspec(uuid("00000503-0000-0010-8000-00aa006d2ea4"))
14:  /* dual interface */ Property;
15:  struct __declspec(uuid("00000500-0000-0010-8000-00aa006d2ea4"))
```

```
16:   /* dual interface */ Error;
17:   struct __declspec(uuid("00000501-0000-0010-8000-00aa006d2ea4"))
18:   /* dual interface */ Errors;
19:   struct __declspec(uuid("00000508-0000-0010-8000-00aa006d2ea4"))
20:   /* dual interface */ _Command;
21:   struct __declspec(uuid("00000515-0000-0010-8000-00aa006d2ea4"))
22:   /* dual interface */ _Connection;
23:   struct __declspec(uuid("0000050e-0000-0010-8000-00aa006d2ea4"))
24:   /* dual interface */ _Recordset;
25:   struct __declspec(uuid("00000506-0000-0010-8000-00aa006d2ea4"))
26:   /* dual interface */ Fields;
27:   struct __declspec(uuid("00000505-0000-0010-8000-00aa006d2ea4"))
28:   /* dual interface */ Field;
29:   struct __declspec(uuid("0000050c-0000-0010-8000-00aa006d2ea4"))
30:   /* dual interface */ _Parameter;
31:   struct __declspec(uuid("0000050d-0000-0010-8000-00aa006d2ea4"))
32:   /* dual interface */ Parameters;
33:   struct __declspec(uuid("00000538-0000-0010-8000-00aa006d2ea4"))
34:   /* interface */ ADODebugging;
35:   struct __declspec(uuid("00000402-0000-0010-8000-00aa006d2ea4"))
36:   /* interface */ ConnectionEventsVtbl;
37:   struct __declspec(uuid("00000403-0000-0010-8000-00aa006d2ea4"))
38:   /* interface */ RecordsetEventsVtbl;
39:   struct __declspec(uuid("00000400-0000-0010-8000-00aa006d2ea4"))
40:   /* dispinterface */ ConnectionEvents;
41:   struct __declspec(uuid("00000266-0000-0010-8000-00aa006d2ea4"))
42:   /* dispinterface */ RecordsetEvents;
43:   struct __declspec(uuid("00000516-0000-0010-8000-00aa006d2ea4"))
44:   /* interface */ ADOConnectionConstruction;
45:   struct /* coclass */ Connection;
46:   struct /* coclass */ Command;
47:   struct /* coclass */ Recordset;
48:   struct __declspec(uuid("00000283-0000-0010-8000-00aa006d2ea4"))
49:   /* interface */ ADORecordsetConstruction;
50:   struct /* coclass */ Parameter;
```

10

Listing 10.2 shows the GUIDs for the ADO objects. The GUIDs defined as dual interfaces, as in lines 21 and 22, are the ones you want to pass to `CoCreateInstance` or `CreateInstance` to instantiate ADO objects. Other GUIDs are defined here that are not defined as dual interfaces. As in lines 43 and 44, these GUIDs are used internally by ADO.

After the forward references in MSADO15.TLH, you will see the declarations of the smart pointers for each ADO object. Listing 10.3 shows these declarations.

LISTING 10.3   SMART POINTER DECLARATIONS IN MSADO15.TLH

```
 1:  //
 2:  // Smart pointer typedef declarations
 3:  //
 4:
 5:  _COM_SMARTPTR_TYPEDEF(_Collection, __uuidof(_Collection));
 6:  _COM_SMARTPTR_TYPEDEF(_DynaCollection, __uuidof(_DynaCollection));
 7:  _COM_SMARTPTR_TYPEDEF(_ADO, __uuidof(_ADO));
 8:  _COM_SMARTPTR_TYPEDEF(Properties, __uuidof(Properties));
 9:  _COM_SMARTPTR_TYPEDEF(Property, __uuidof(Property));
10:  _COM_SMARTPTR_TYPEDEF(Error, __uuidof(Error));
11:  _COM_SMARTPTR_TYPEDEF(Errors, __uuidof(Errors));
12:  _COM_SMARTPTR_TYPEDEF(_Command, __uuidof(_Command));
13:  _COM_SMARTPTR_TYPEDEF(_Connection, __uuidof(_Connection));
14:  _COM_SMARTPTR_TYPEDEF(_Recordset, __uuidof(_Recordset));
15:  _COM_SMARTPTR_TYPEDEF(Fields, __uuidof(Fields));
16:  _COM_SMARTPTR_TYPEDEF(Field, __uuidof(Field));
17:  _COM_SMARTPTR_TYPEDEF(_Parameter, __uuidof(_Parameter));
18:  _COM_SMARTPTR_TYPEDEF(Parameters, __uuidof(Parameters));
19:  _COM_SMARTPTR_TYPEDEF(ADODebugging, __uuidof(ADODebugging));
20:  _COM_SMARTPTR_TYPEDEF(ConnectionEventsVtbl,
                         __uuidof(ConnectionEventsVtbl));
21:  _COM_SMARTPTR_TYPEDEF(RecordsetEventsVtbl,
                         __uuidof(RecordsetEventsVtbl));
22:  _COM_SMARTPTR_TYPEDEF(ConnectionEvents, __uuidof(IDispatch));
23:  _COM_SMARTPTR_TYPEDEF(RecordsetEvents, __uuidof(IDispatch));
24:  _COM_SMARTPTR_TYPEDEF(ADOConnectionConstruction,
                         __uuidof(ADOConnectionConstruction));
25:  _COM_SMARTPTR_TYPEDEF(ADORecordsetConstruction,
                         __uuidof(ADORecordsetConstruction));
```

The name of the smart pointer that #import generates for use in your code is the name of the first argument (with a Ptr suffix) passed to the _COM_SMARTPTR_TYPEDEF macro. For example, line 13 in Listing 10.3 creates a smart pointer derived class called _ConnectionPtr.

You can see that the second argument passed to the _COM_SMARTPTR_TYPEDEF macro uses the __uuidof keyword. The _COM_SMARTPTR_TYPEDEF macros shown in Listing 10.3 refer to the forward declaration of the GUIDs defined earlier in MSADO15.TLH. The __uuidof keyword is a Microsoft-specific C++ extension and retrieves the GUID for the argument.

Following the smart pointer declarations, MSADO15.TLH contains the enumerated types defined in the ADO type library. Listing 10.4 shows the ConnectModeEnum enumerated type as it appears in MSADO15.TLH.

LISTING 10.4   THE ENUMERATED TYPE CONNECTMODEENUM DEFINED IN THE ADO TYPE LIBRARY

```
 1:  enum ConnectModeEnum
 2:  {
 3:      adModeUnknown = 0,
 4:      adModeRead = 1,
 5:      adModeWrite = 2,
 6:      adModeReadWrite = 3,
 7:      adModeShareDenyRead = 4,
 8:      adModeShareDenyWrite = 8,
 9:      adModeShareExclusive = 12,
10:      adModeShareDenyNone = 16
11:  };
```

You will recall in Day 4 that you wrote the code shown in Listings 10.5 and 10.6 to create an instance of the ADO Connection object in your code. (Listing 10.5 duplicates Listing 4.5, and Listing 10.6 duplicates Listing 4.8.)

10

INPUT   **LISTING 10.5.**   CHANGES TO THE ADOMFC1 DOCUMENT HEADER FILE

```
 1:  class CADOMFC1Doc : public CDocument
 2:  {
 3:  // Attributes
 4:  public:
 5:      BOOL m_IsConnectionOpen;
 6:      _ConnectionPtr m_pConnection;
```

INPUT   **LISTING 10.6.**   CHANGES TO THE ADOMFC1 ONNEWDOCUMENT FUNCTION

```
 1:  BOOL CADOMFC1Doc::OnNewDocument()
 2:  {
 3:      if (!CDocument::OnNewDocument())
 4:        return FALSE;
 5:
 6:      HRESULT hr;
 7:
 8:      try
 9:      {
10:        hr = m_pConnection.CreateInstance( __uuidof( Connection ) );
11:        if (SUCCEEDED(hr))
12:        {
13:          hr = m_pConnection->Open(
14:          _bstr_t(L"Provider=Microsoft.Jet.OLEDB.3.51;
                   Data Source=c:\\tysdbvc\\vcdb.mdb;"),
15:          _bstr_t(L""),
```

continues

LISTING **10.6**   CONTINUED

```
16:            _bstr_t(L""),
17:            adModeUnknown);
18:            if (SUCCEEDED(hr))
19:            {
20:                m_IsConnectionOpen = TRUE;
21:            }
22:        }
23:    }
24:    catch( _com_error &e )
25:    {
26:        // Get info from _com_error
27:        _bstr_t bstrSource(e.Source());
28:        _bstr_t bstrDescription(e.Description());
29:        TRACE( "Exception thrown for classes generated by #import" );
30:        TRACE( "\tCode = %08lx\n", e.Error());
31:        TRACE( "\tCode meaning = %s\n", e.ErrorMessage());
32:        TRACE( "\tSource = %s\n", (LPCTSTR) bstrSource);
33:        TRACE( "\tDescription = %s\n", (LPCTSTR) bstrDescription);
34:    }
35:    catch(...)
36:    {
37:        TRACE( "*** Unhandled Exception ***" );
38:    }
39:
40:    return TRUE;
41: }
```

You can see that line 6 of Listing 10.5 defines a _ConnectionPtr instance as a member of the CDocument class. Note that the name _ConnectionPtr matches the argument (with a Ptr suffix) passed to the _COM_SMARTPTR_TYPEDEF macro in line 13 of Listing 10.3.

Line 10 of Listing 10.6 calls the CreateInstance function of the _ConnectionPtr class and passes the GUID for the ADO _Connection class (using the __uuidof keyword). CreateInstance will return a failed HRESULT rather than throw an exception.

Line 17 of Listing 10.6 passes a value in ConnectModeEnum as an argument to the Open function for the Connection object. The Open function will throw an exception if it fails (see the code for the _Connection::Open function in MSADO15.TLI).

Following the enumerated type declarations, MSADO15.TLH contains the declarations of the ADO objects in the type library. Listing 10.7 shows the portion of MSADO15.TLH that contains the declaration for the ADO _Connection object.

LISTING 10.7 THE ADO _CONNECTION OBJECT DECLARATION IN MSADO15.TLH

```
 1:  struct __declspec(uuid("00000515-0000-0010-8000-00aa006d2ea4"))
 2:  Connection : _ADO
 3:  {
 4:    //
 5:    // Property data
 6:    //
 7:
 8:    __declspec(property(get=GetConnectionString,
                                 put=PutConnectionString))
 9:    _bstr_t ConnectionString;
10:    __declspec(property(get=GetCommandTimeout,put=PutCommandTimeout))
11:    long CommandTimeout;
12:    __declspec(property(get=GetConnectionTimeout,
                                 put=PutConnectionTimeout))
13:    long ConnectionTimeout;
14:    __declspec(property(get=GetVersion))
15:    _bstr_t Version;
16:    __declspec(property(get=GetErrors))
17:    ErrorsPtr Errors;
18:    __declspec(property(get=GetDefaultDatabase,put=PutDefaultDatabase))
19:    _bstr_t DefaultDatabase;
20:    __declspec(property(get=GetIsolationLevel,put=PutIsolationLevel))
21:    enum IsolationLevelEnum IsolationLevel;
22:    __declspec(property(get=GetAttributes,put=PutAttributes))
23:    long Attributes;
24:    __declspec(property(get=GetCursorLocation,put=PutCursorLocation))
25:    enum CursorLocationEnum CursorLocation;
26:    __declspec(property(get=GetMode,put=PutMode))
27:    enum ConnectModeEnum Mode;
28:    __declspec(property(get=GetProvider,put=PutProvider))
29:    _bstr_t Provider;
30:    __declspec(property(get=GetState))
31:    long State;
32:
33:    //
34:    // Wrapper methods for error-handling
35:    //
36:
37:    _bstr_t GetConnectionString ( );
38:    void PutConnectionString (
39:       _bstr_t pbstr );
40:    long GetCommandTimeout ( );
41:    void PutCommandTimeout (
42:       long plTimeout );
43:    long GetConnectionTimeout ( );
44:    void PutConnectionTimeout (
```

10

continues

LISTING **10.7**   CONTINUED

```
45:          long plTimeout );
46:     _bstr_t GetVersion ( );
47:     HRESULT Close ( );
48:     _RecordsetPtr Execute (
49:          _bstr_t CommandText,
50:          VARIANT * RecordsAffected,
51:          long Options );
52:     long BeginTrans ( );
53:     HRESULT CommitTrans ( );
54:     HRESULT RollbackTrans ( );
55:     HRESULT Open (
56:          _bstr_t ConnectionString,
57:          _bstr_t UserID,
58:          _bstr_t Password,
59:          long Options );
60:     ErrorsPtr GetErrors ( );
61:     _bstr_t GetDefaultDatabase ( );
62:     void PutDefaultDatabase (
63:          _bstr_t pbstr );
64:     enum IsolationLevelEnum GetIsolationLevel ( );
65:     void PutIsolationLevel (
66:          enum IsolationLevelEnum Level );
67:     long GetAttributes ( );
68:     void PutAttributes (
69:          long plAttr );
70:     enum CursorLocationEnum GetCursorLocation ( );
71:     void PutCursorLocation (
72:          enum CursorLocationEnum plCursorLoc );
73:     enum ConnectModeEnum GetMode ( );
74:     void PutMode (
75:          enum ConnectModeEnum plMode );
76:     _bstr_t GetProvider ( );
77:     void PutProvider (
78:          _bstr_t pbstr );
79:     long GetState ( );
80:     _RecordsetPtr OpenSchema (
81:          enum SchemaEnum Schema,
82:          const _variant_t & Restrictions = vtMissing,
83:          const _variant_t & SchemaID = vtMissing );
84:     HRESULT Cancel ( );
85:
86:     //
87:     // Raw methods provided by interface
88:     //
89:
90:     virtual HRESULT __stdcall get_ConnectionString (
91:          BSTR * pbstr ) = 0;
92:     virtual HRESULT __stdcall put_ConnectionString (
93:          BSTR pbstr ) = 0;
```

```
 94:    virtual HRESULT __stdcall get_CommandTimeout (
 95:        long * plTimeout ) = 0;
 96:    virtual HRESULT __stdcall put_CommandTimeout (
 97:        long plTimeout ) = 0;
 98:    virtual HRESULT __stdcall get_ConnectionTimeout (
 99:        long * plTimeout ) = 0;
100:    virtual HRESULT __stdcall put_ConnectionTimeout (
101:        long plTimeout ) = 0;
102:    virtual HRESULT __stdcall get_Version (
103:        BSTR * pbstr ) = 0;
104:    virtual HRESULT __stdcall raw_Close ( ) = 0;
105:    virtual HRESULT __stdcall raw_Execute (
106:        BSTR CommandText,
107:        VARIANT * RecordsAffected,
108:        long Options,
109:        struct _Recordset * * ppiRset ) = 0;
110:    virtual HRESULT __stdcall raw_BeginTrans (
111:        long * TransactionLevel ) = 0;
112:    virtual HRESULT __stdcall raw_CommitTrans ( ) = 0;
113:    virtual HRESULT __stdcall raw_RollbackTrans ( ) = 0;
114:    virtual HRESULT __stdcall raw_Open (
115:        BSTR ConnectionString,
116:        BSTR UserID,
117:        BSTR Password,
118:        long Options ) = 0;
119:    virtual HRESULT __stdcall get_Errors (
120:        struct Errors * * ppvObject ) = 0;
121:    virtual HRESULT __stdcall get_DefaultDatabase (
122:        BSTR * pbstr ) = 0;
123:    virtual HRESULT __stdcall put_DefaultDatabase (
124:        BSTR pbstr ) = 0;
125:    virtual HRESULT __stdcall get_IsolationLevel (
126:        enum IsolationLevelEnum * Level ) = 0;
127:    virtual HRESULT __stdcall put_IsolationLevel (
128:        enum IsolationLevelEnum Level ) = 0;
129:    virtual HRESULT __stdcall get_Attributes (
130:        long * plAttr ) = 0;
131:    virtual HRESULT __stdcall put_Attributes (
132:        long plAttr ) = 0;
133:    virtual HRESULT __stdcall get_CursorLocation (
134:        enum CursorLocationEnum * plCursorLoc ) = 0;
135:    virtual HRESULT __stdcall put_CursorLocation (
136:        enum CursorLocationEnum plCursorLoc ) = 0;
137:    virtual HRESULT __stdcall get_Mode (
138:        enum ConnectModeEnum * plMode ) = 0;
139:    virtual HRESULT __stdcall put_Mode (
140:        enum ConnectModeEnum plMode ) = 0;
141:    virtual HRESULT __stdcall get_Provider (
142:        BSTR * pbstr ) = 0;
```

10

continues

LISTING 10.7   CONTINUED

```
143:    virtual HRESULT __stdcall put_Provider (
144:        BSTR pbstr ) = 0;
145:    virtual HRESULT __stdcall get_State (
146:        long * plObjState ) = 0;
147:    virtual HRESULT __stdcall raw_OpenSchema (
148:        enum SchemaEnum Schema,
149:        VARIANT Restrictions,
150:        VARIANT SchemaID,
151:        struct _Recordset * * pprset ) = 0;
152:    virtual HRESULT __stdcall raw_Cancel ( ) = 0;
153:    };
```

Line 1 in Listing 10.7 shows the interface identifier (IID) for the ADO Connection object. You can see in line 2 that the Connection class is derived from the ADO class, which is declared earlier in the MSADO15.TLH file.

COM objects can have properties, which are basically data members, in addition to member functions or methods. Visual C++ uses get, put, and putref methods to make the properties in a COM object accessible to COM clients. Lines 4–31 in Listing 10.7 assign these COM property-handling functions to the high-level wrapper functions that are created with Get, Put, and PutRef prefixes.

Lines 33–84 in Listing 10.7 declare the high-level functions for the ADO Connection object. The code for these high-level functions is found in MSADO15.TLI.

Lines 86–153 in Listing 10.7 declare the functions found in the ADO type library. They use the function name from the type library with a raw_ prefix. Low-level functions for property get, put, and putref methods are prefixed by get_, put_, and _putref.

This completes your exploration of the use of #import with ADO. You should now have a good understanding of the .tlh and .tli files generated by #import with the ADO type library.

You can use the MSADO15.TLH file and the MSADO15.TLI files in combination with the existing ADO documentation in order to understand ADO and how to effectively use it in your C++ applications.

Summary

Today you learned about database client technologies. Several database client technologies are available to C++ programmers. Each technology has its own strengths and weaknesses, and each one has an historical context that defines how it relates to the other technologies.

The two database client technologies that will be updated and improved on in the future are OLE DB and ADO. ADO offers a good balance of code size, performance, and ease of use. You can best understand the ADO object model by examining the MSADO15. TLH file and the MSADO15.TLI files, coupled with the ADO documentation.

Q&A

Q **Isn't the performance of a native database API always better than the performance of the database client technologies mentioned today?**

A Not necessarily. It depends on the implementation of the API. Some database vendors do provide a native API that is faster than the ODBC driver for their database. However, other database vendors (notably Microsoft) provide ODBC drivers and OLE DB providers that are highly optimized and are as fast as, or faster than, the native APIs for their databases.

Q **Is OLE DB just another layer on top of ODBC?**

A No. OLE DB can directly communicate with any data source for which there is an OLE DB provider. OLE DB providers do not generally communicate with data sources through ODBC. Rather, OLE DB providers directly communicate with the data source. There is one OLE DB provider, MSDASQL, that can communicate with data sources through ODBC. MSDASQL should be used only with those data sources that don't have a native OLE DB provider but do have an ODBC driver.

Q **What database client technologies are compatible with Web servers?**

A Web servers using CGI can communicate with CGI-compatible executables. The executable can conceivably talk to any data source to which it can gain access and for which it has a programming interface. However, several newer technologies provide better scalability for Web servers than CGI. These newer technologies include NSAPI on Netscape's Web servers and ISAPI on Microsoft's IIS. On the Windows platform, ODBC, OLE DB, and ADO are compatible with CGI interfaces, as well as with the newer Web server interface technologies.

10

Workshop

The Workshop quiz questions test your understanding of today's material. (The answers appear in Appendix F, "Answers.") The exercises encourage you to apply the information you learned today to real-life situations.

Quiz

1. What is the goal or purpose of ODBC?

2. How is ODBC's call-level interface different from embedded SQL?

3. Where does the ADO type library reside and how can you view it?

4. Why does ADO throw exceptions when errors occur?

5. What function that you use with `#import` does not throw exceptions but returns a failed `HRESULT` instead?

Exercises

1. Set break points in the inline functions in MSADO15.TLI, such as the `_Connection::Open` function, and run ADOMFC1 in debug mode to develop a feel for how code in MSADO15.TLH and MSADO15.TLI is executed. Debug step into all the functions to discern when you are executing code in your ADOMFC1 project and when you are executing code in the ADO DLL.

2. Modify the code in Listing 10.7 so that the call to the ADO `Command Execute` function in line 24 directly calls the low-level `Execute` function.

DAY 11

Multitier Architectures

Multitier development is transcending traditional client/server programming. The reason for this transition is the fact that multitier applications promise to combine the verve and panache of client/server applications with the ruggedness and scalability of the big iron (mainframe systems).

The tools for multitier programming are relatively new, and developers who have knowledge of multitier development are at a premium. Today's material provides you with information about some of the tools for performing multitier development on the Windows platform.

Today's development work uses Microsoft Internet Information Server (IIS) with Internet Explorer version 4.0 (IE4). If you have use of IE4 and IIS (or Microsoft Personal Web Server, which is compatible with IIS), you will be able to perform all the programming tasks described today. If not, you will have to learn some of these techniques without being able to try them yourself.

Although this is a Visual C++ book, today's work does not involve writing any C++ code. Instead, you will examine some XML code and write a little HTML code. You will also write some Active Server Page code to learn how to use Remote Data Services (RDS). You will get back to writing C++ code tomorrow when you build COM server components that run under Microsoft Transaction Server and Internet Information Server.

Today you will

- Explore some of the limitations of client/server computing that are driving the advance to multitier applications.
- Enable database data to be sent over the Internet using XML.
- Use Remote Data Services (RDS) to send database data over HTTP to thin client applications, such as Web browsers.

Layered Architecture

Creating database applications for systems where the software runs on multiple computers over a network has never been easy. The most difficult part of developing such a system is designing it. In fact, limitations in the design of typical client/server systems have hindered the growth of client/server computing.

One of the limitations in the design of typical client/server systems is that the software is generally not layered effectively. Client/server software is often monolithic.

In monolithic software, the code for the different types of operations is intermingled, and this code is all baked into traditional Windows EXEs and DLLs. Monolithic software has proven to be insufficiently flexible and scalable for many client/server applications to be successful.

Using a layered architecture is a proven alternative to monolithic software. The value of a layered architecture is best understood by examining a very successful layered architecture, the OSI model for network software.

The OSI Model

Not too many years ago, it was difficult to send data between different computer systems, because each computer manufacturer had its own standards for network communications. The computers from different manufacturers used different communications protocols, and the computers typically could not talk to each other.

In the late 1970s, the International Standards Organization (ISO) created a model to standardize the various protocols for network communications. This model is called Open Systems Interconnect, or the OSI model.

The OSI model enables network communications software to be written in layers, with well-defined interfaces between the layers. The abstractions provided by these layers now make it possible for disparate computer systems to communicate with each other over a network.

The OSI model consists of seven layers. In the OSI model, each layer was created to provide a different level of abstraction. Each layer in the model performs a well-defined type of operation and has a well-defined set of interfaces. The OSI layers are shown in Figure 11.1.

FIGURE 11.1

Layers of the OSI model.

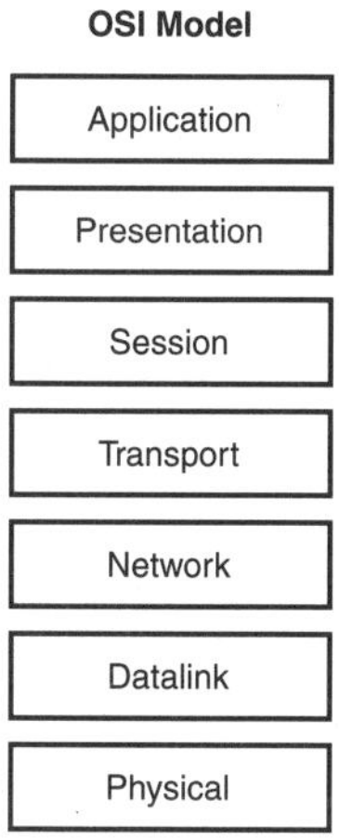

OSI Model

| Application |
| Presentation |
| Session |
| Transport |
| Network |
| Datalink |
| Physical |

11

The layers of the OSI model shown in Figure 11.1 are

- The *physical* layer, which transmits and receives unstructured bit stream data over the physical medium

- The *data-link* layer, which checks for and handles errors in the frames of bits from the physical layer

- The *network* layer, which maps physical addresses to logical addresses and handles routing of frames to adjacent nodes

- The *transport* layer, which provides reliable end-to-end data delivery with acknowledgments to ensure that messages are delivered with no losses or duplications

- The *session* layer, which enables communication sessions, or connections, to be established between processes running on different computers

- The *presentation* layer, which performs translations such as ASCII to EBCDIC or CR to CR/LF, data compression, and data encryption

- The *application* layer, which provides high-level functions such as device redirection, remote file access, remote printer access, and interprocess communication

Note | The designers of the OSI model carefully crafted the interfaces between the OSI layers so that the layers would be independent. The interfaces were created in such a way as to enable the implementation of one layer to be changed without the need to change the implementation of its neighboring layers.

The OSI model has proven to be very successful. Disparate computer systems can now readily communicate with each other using this layered approach.

TCP/IP is a protocol that adheres to the OSI model. Figure 11.2 illustrates how the layers of TCP/IP map to the layers of the OSI model.

FIGURE 11.2

How TCP/IP layers correspond to the OSI model.

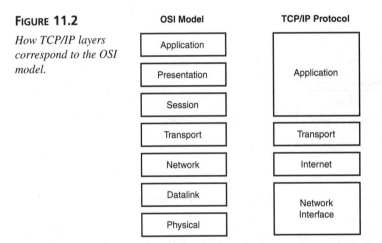

TCP/IP is the protocol of the Internet. As you will see later, the nature of TCP/IP and the nature of the OSI model figure prominently in the way multitier applications are developed.

Layered Architecture for Multitier Applications

When you build multitier applications, you can apply important lessons from the OSI model to make your applications successful.

Note

> When you build multitier applications, you must carefully craft the interfaces between the tiers so that the tiers are independent. You need to create the interfaces in such a way that the implementation of one tier can be changed without the need to change the implementation of its neighboring tiers.

Interfaces and abstractions are the two pillars on which multitier applications rest. Each tier that provides an effective level of abstraction has interfaces that are understandable and distinct. Distinct interfaces between the tiers enable the tiers to be updated independently of each other.

In traditional C++ development, programmers typically attempt to create layered architectures by using C++ classes. The classes provide the abstractions, and the public member functions provide the interfaces.

The C++ approach is good but is hampered by the fact that the C++ classes are usually compiled into Windows EXEs and DLLs, without using COM interfaces. As you discovered in Day 9, "Understanding COM," Windows EXEs and DLLs that don't support COM interfaces are invariably bound together by build-time dependencies. A non-COM Windows EXE file and the DLL files it uses must *all* come from the appropriate build of the software.

Any time you have build-time dependencies between binaries in an application, you have a monolithic application. In a multitier application, you might have client pieces running on hundreds of computers. You don't want to have to update all the software on every client machine every time you make some small alteration to the software.

11

Note

> In multitier applications, you want to avoid build-time dependencies between the tiers. You want to be able to update the software on one tier without having to update the software on its neighboring tiers.

This issue of being required to update all the client machines is a frequent problem in traditional client/server applications. In many client/server systems, even a small change in the server software can necessitate a massive update of all the client software.

These massive client software updates are often caused by the build-time dependencies between EXEs and DLLs, which make it impossible to update one binary without updating them all.

NEW TERM   Another feature in client/server applications that exacerbates the need to update
all the client software every time is *fat client* software. Fat client software does
not refer to software you write for fat clients. Rather, a fat client is a piece of software
that runs on a client computer and contains both code to process data and code to present
it to the user.

NEW TERM   As you can see in Figure 11.3, fat clients contain *business logic*. This business
logic may include code for formulas or rules to perform calculations on business
data, or it may include code that accesses tables and fields directly in a business database.

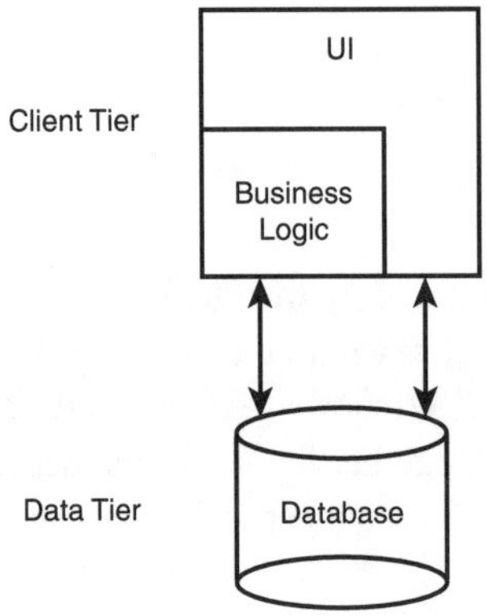

FIGURE 11.3

*Client/server architec-
ture with fat clients.*

Note in Figure 11.3 that the UI portion of the client tier communicates directly with the
database. This occurs in client applications that use direct SQL statements and/or data-
bound controls, which tie fields and records in the database directly to elements of the
user interface.

Thin Is In

Thin client software is software that runs on client machines and contains only UI (or
presentation) code. With thin clients, the need to update all the client computers every
time the application is updated is greatly reduced. Thin clients enable you to change
server software components without having to update all the client software every time.
A simple multitier architecture is illustrated in Figure 11.4.

As you can see in Figure 11.4, multitier applications use thin clients that do not contain
business logic. The business logic is typically moved to a middletier of some sort. In
some multitier applications, the middletier software runs on its own machine. In other
multitier applications, the middle-tier software runs on the same machine as the data-tier
software.

FIGURE **11.4**

Multitier architecture.

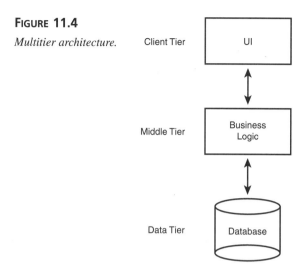

A good example of a thin client is a Web browser. All that a Web browser typically does is presentation. Contrast a Web browser with ADOMFC1.EXE, the MFC application you have been working on in this book. As you know, ADOMFC1.EXE performs more than just presentation tasks.

ADOMFC1.EXE uses ADO to connect with the database and then issues SQL statements to SELECT, UPDATE, INSERT, and DELETE data from tables in the database. ADOMFC1.EXE has intimate knowledge of the database. The code in ADOMFC1.EXE knows the names of the tables and their fields, and the relationships between the tables. If the database schema were to change, ADOMFC1.EXE would very likely need to be changed as well.

ADOMFC1.EXE is a fat client. ADOMFC1.EXE illustrates the requirement for client software to be frequently updated in client/server systems. If ADOMFC1.EXE were installed as the client software for a client/server application, a small change in the database could necessitate an update of all the instances of ADOMFC1.EXE on the client machines.

The nature of the connection that ADOMFC1.EXE uses with the database also increases its interdependence with the data tier. When ADOMFC1.EXE uses the ADO Connection object to make a connection to a database such as SQL Server, it makes an interprocess communication (IPC) connection with the database. The interprocess communication mechanism is typically named pipes or TCP/IP sockets.

It was mentioned earlier that the nature of TCP/IP and the OSI model figures prominently in the way multitier applications are developed. Here's how.

Interprocess communication with named pipes and/or sockets is done at the OSI application layer. For security reasons, interprocess communication is typically not used over the Internet. Using interprocess communications between software tiers makes a wide-open connection and enables a broad interface between the software tiers.

An IPC connection can be thought of as a hard-wired connection to the database that enables ADOMFC1.EXE and the database to have a high level of interaction. ADOM-FC1.EXE can modify data in the database almost instantaneously. Round trips between ADOMFC1.EXE and the database happen relatively fast. ADOMFC1.EXE can scroll through large sets of records very quickly. ADOMFC1.EXE can also lock records and open transactions in the database and keep them as long as it likes.

Interprocess communication between software tiers enables a broad interface between the tiers. However, a broad interface between tiers is not always desirable if you want the tiers to be somewhat independent of each other.

Web browsers and Web servers use the HTTP protocol, which is a connectionless protocol built on TCP/IP. HTTP also operates at the application layer of the OSI model. However, using HTTP for communications between software tiers provides a much narrower interface between the tiers than named pipes or TCP/IP sockets do. A client application can't make an IPC connection to a database with HTTP. This means an application that uses HTTP can't enjoy the high level of interactivity with the database that an IPC connection would provide. HTTP's narrower interface, in effect, forces the software tiers to be more independent of each other.

Web Browsers as Thin Clients

Web browsers can make a good client tier. Because Web browsers perform only UI tasks and the interface between the Web browser and the Web server (HTTP) is so distinct, the Web browser and the Web server can be quite independent of each other in terms of software update requirements.

NEW TERM   Web browsers can be used for applications that run on the Internet (more specifically, the World Wide Web) and also can be used in applications that run over a LAN in an intranet. The term *intranet* is used to describe the application of Internet technologies on internal corporate networks. With an intranet, you can have a Web server that is internal to your corporate LAN, and information from that Web server can be accessed by machines on the LAN that runs Web browsers.

Multitier applications that use Web browsers as clients use a Web server such as Microsoft (IIS) in their middle tier. In such applications, Microsoft Transaction Server (MTS) is sometimes used in conjunction with IIS on the middle tier. You will explore MTS tomorrow.

Multitier applications that use Web browsers and IIS typically use an RDBMS, such as SQL Server or Oracle, as the data tier. Later today, you will use a middle-tier software component that retrieves data from the database and sends it through IIS to software on the client tier.

Tomorrow you will write your own component that runs under MTS and IIS. You will be able to use this component on the middle tier to send data from a database to browsers over HTTP, as well as to fat DCOM clients such as ADOMFC1.EXE.

Database Data and the Internet

If you do use a Web browser for the client piece of your multitier application, how do you get the data from the database to the Web browser?

CGI—The Original Technique for Interfacing Databases with Web Servers

The tools for using a Web browser as the UI to a database application have been evolving rapidly. Figure 11.5 shows how it was done in the early days of the Web.

FIGURE 11.5

Interfacing a Web browser to a database by using CGI.

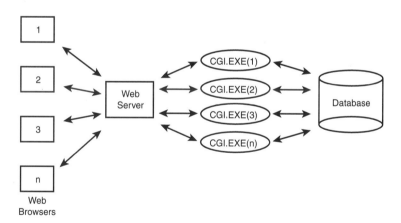

As you can see from Figure 11.5, you could write a CGI application, which is an EXE that accepts and fulfills requests from the Web server for data from the database. One drawback of CGI is the fact that for every concurrent user that is hitting your Web server, the Web server has to launch another instance of the CGI EXE. Launching an EXE for each concurrent user can put a strain on the Web server machine.

DLLs and Server Scripts—An Improved Technique for Interfacing Databases with Web Servers

Microsoft and Netscape each developed their own improvements to the CGI model. In the improved models, a DLL that runs in the Web server's process space is used instead of a CGI EXE. This is illustrated in Figure 11.6.

FIGURE 11.6

Interfacing a Web browser to a database by using DLLs.

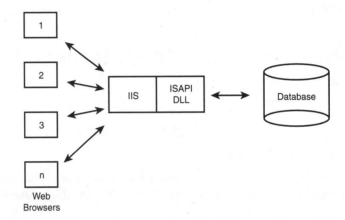

In the case of Microsoft IIS, the DLLs that provide an interface between IIS and a database are called *ISAPI DLLs*. Because DLLs run in the Web server's process, they place a lighter load on the Web server machine than CGI EXEs.

Microsoft has developed a technology called Active Server Pages (ASP), which is built on its ISAPI DLL technology. ASP has a server-side script interpreter that enables you to run JScript and VBScript scripts on the Web server. These scripts can make calls to COM servers and send the results out through the Web server to Web browsers. The ASP technology is illustrated in Figure 11.7.

FIGURE 11.7

Interfacing a Web browser to a database by using ASP.

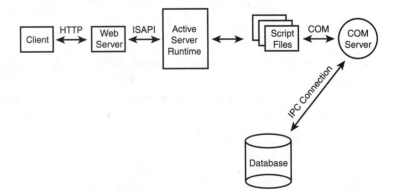

As you can see in Figure 11.7, an ASP script can call a COM server that can communicate with a database. The ASP script can then send the data from the database out through the Web server to Web browsers. Later today, you will use ASP to communicate database data to Web browsers.

The XML Files

NEW TERM *Extensible Markup Language* (XML) provides a way to describe and exchange data in Web-based applications. XML complements Hypertext Markup Language (HTML). HTML enables the *displaying* of data, whereas XML provides ways to *describe* and *transmit* data.

XML enables *metadata*, or data about data, to be imbedded with data and sent over the Web. You could think of XML as a way to describe and transmit data in an HTML-like format.

As of this writing, XML is still making its way through the standards process. XML is in its infancy now, but it will become a vital technology in multitier applications in the future.

Listing 11.1 shows some XML code. The intent here is to give you a feel for what XML looks like.

LISTING 11.1 A HIGH-LEVEL WRAPPER FUNCTION IN MSADO15.TLI

```
 1:  <?XML version="1.0" encoding="UTF-8" ?>
 2:  <Sales>
 3:  <s:schema id='SalesSchema'>
 4:
 5:    <elementType id="custnumber">
 6:       <string/>
 7:    </elementType>
 8:
 9:    <elementType id="Customer">
10:       <element id="c1" type="#custnumber"/>
11:       <key id="k1"><keyPart href="#c1"/></key>
12:    </elementType>
13:
14:    <elementType id="buyer">
15:       <string/>
16:       <foreignKey range="#Customer" key="#k1"/>
17:    </elementType>
18:
19:    <elementType id="partnumber">
20:       <string/>
```

11

continues

LISTING 11.1 CONTINUED

```
21:      </elementType>
22:
23:      <elementType id="Purchase">
24:        <element type="#partnumber"/>
25:        <element type="#buyer" occurs="ONEORMORE"/>
26:      </elementType>
27:
28:    </s:schema>
29:
30:    <Customer><custnumber>Cust003</custnumber></Customer>
31:
32:    <Customer><custnumber>Cust938</custnumber></Customer>
33:
34:    <Customer><custnumber>Cust501</custnumber></Customer>
35:
36:    <Purchase>
37:      <buyer>Cust003</buyer>
38:      <buyer>Cust938</buyer>
39:      <partnumber>CLAP-003</partnumber>
40:    </Purchase>
41:
42:    <Purchase>
43:      <buyer>Cust501</buyer>
44:      <buyer>Cust938</buyer>
45:      <partnumber>MIC-92823</partnumber>
46:    </Purchase>
47:
48:    </Sales>
```

Listing 11.1 illustrates how data from a relational database could be represented in XML. XML is text-based, and as you can see, is similar to HTML.

Line 1 indicates the version of XML. XML code is rigidly nested. An XML document is made up of XML elements, each of which consists of a start tag, such as `<Sales>` in line 2, and an end tag, such as `</Sales>` in line 48. The information between the two tags is referred to as the *contents*.

Tags annotate XML code as they do HTML code. In HTML, each tag indicates how something should look. However, in XML each tag indicates what something means.

Line 3 is the start tag for the schema called `"SalesSchema"`. Line 28 is the end tag for the schema. A schema in XML is similar to a schema in a relational database. Lines 3–28 declare a schema that relates buyers and partnumbers in a one-to-many relationship called Purchases. You will recall that you explored database design and data relationships in Day 7. (In a relational database that corresponds to the XML schema in

Listing 11.1, Purchases would be a table that contains two fields: partnumber and buyer.)

To declare the one-to-many relationship, lines 5–26 contain a series of elementType declarations. Lines 5–7 declare a class (or element type) with an id of "custnumber" that has a data type of string. Lines 9–12 declare an element type of "Customer" that has custnumber as an element (or field). Note that custnumber is the key field. (In real life, the Customer element type would have additional fields, but they are not shown here for simplicity.)

Lines 14–17 declare an element type of "buyer", which has a Customer as a foreign key field. Lines 19–21 declare a partnumber element type that is string data. Lines 23–26 declare an element type of "Purchase", which contains a partnumber and a buyer. You will notice that in line 25, buyer is indicated as ONEORMORE, meaning there can be multiple buyers per partnumber.

Line 28 marks the end of the schema. The information that comes after line 28 is the actual data. This XML data conforms to the XML schema, like records in a database.

Lines 30–34 are three instances (or records) of customers. Lines 36–46 are two instances of Purchases. Each purchase lists the partnumber and the customers who bought it. If you were to place the Purchases information in a table in a relational database, the table would consist of two fields (partnumber and buyer) and would contain four records.

A full explanation of how to parse and process XML code is beyond the scope of this book. However, you could begin to get your feet wet with XML by entering the code in Listing 11.1 into an XML file. You could then use the XML parsing sample(s) from Microsoft's Web site to process it.

To enter Listing 11.1 into an XML file, run Visual Studio, select the File, New menu, and tell it to create a new HTML page. (The HTML page needn't be part of any of your projects in Visual Studio.) Then type in the code in Listing 11.1 and save it as an XML file.

Currently, IE4 is the only XML-aware browser. Other Web browsers currently cannot read XML files.

A potentially useful tool for XML is the Microsoft XSL Processor. The XSL Processor takes XML code and converts it to HTML that can be displayed in almost any browser. This is illustrated in Figure 11.8.

Microsoft offers an XSL command-line utility and an XSL ActiveX control to make it easy and productive to get HTML from XML.

11

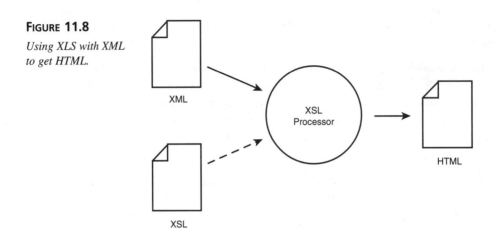

FIGURE 11.8

Using XLS with XML to get HTML.

You can find more information on XML and XSL by pointing your Web browser to `http://www.microsoft.com/XML`. You will find information and documentation on XML, as well as sample programs for parsing and processing XML code. You can obtain further XML development information as part of the Microsoft Internet Client SDK at `http://msdn.microsoft.com/developer/sdk/inetsdk`.

What Color of Edsel Would You Like?

So far today, you've read about using Web browsers as the client piece of multitier database applications. This, of course, means putting database data into HTML and sending it to Web browsers. In actual practice, using HTML to display data from a database can make a pretty lame user interface. Listing 11.2 shows a typical model for displaying and processing database data in HTML.

Note   A full explanation of HTML is beyond the scope of this work. Listing 11.2 is intended merely to familiarize you with some of the limitations of using HTML-based Web pages as the UI for a database application.

To enter Listing 11.2 into an HTML file, run Visual Studio, select the File, New menu, and tell it to create a new HTML page. (The HTML page needn't be part of any of your projects in Visual Studio.) Then type in the code in Listing 11.2 and save it as an HTM file. You can view the page in IE4 by entering the full path and filename of the HTM file in the IE4 Address text box.

INPUT   **LISTING 11.2**   DATABASE DATA IN HTML

```
1:  <HTML>
2:  <HEAD>
3:  <TITLE>Database Data in HTML</TITLE>
4:  </HEAD>
5:  <BODY>
6:  <CENTER>
7:  <H1>Database Data</H1>
8:  <BR>
9:  <TABLE BORDER=1 WIDTH=80%>
10: <THEAD>
11: <TR>
12: <TH>Field 1</TH>
13: <TH>Field 2</TH>
14: </TR>
15: <TBODY>
16: <TR>
17: <TD>Record 1, Field 1 contents.</TD>
18: <TD>Record 1, Field 2 contents.</TD>
19: </TR>
20: <TR>
21: <TD>Record 2, Field 1 contents.</TD>
22: <TD>Record 2, Field 2 contents.</TD>
23: </TR>
24: <TR>
25: <TD>Record 3, Field 1 contents.</TD>
26: <TD>Record 3, Field 2 contents.</TD>
27: </TR>
28: </TABLE>
29: <BR>
30: <TABLE>
31: <TR>
32: <TD>Field 1:<TD><INPUT NAME=Field1 SIZE=30>
33: <TD>Field 2:<TD><INPUT NAME=Field2 SIZE=30>
34: </TR>
35: </TABLE>
36:
37: <BR>
38: <INPUT TYPE=BUTTON NAME="Update" VALUE="Save Changes">
39: </CENTER>
40:
41: <SCRIPT LANGUAGE="VBScript">
42: SUB Update_OnClick
43:    MsgBox "Do some processing to update: " + Field1.Value +
       ➥ " and " + Field2.Value
44: END SUB
45: </SCRIPT>
46: </BODY>
47: </HTML>
```

11

In browser/database applications, data from a database is typically placed in static HTML tables for the browser to display to the user. Lines 1–28 in Listing 11.2 are standard HTML for displaying a table of data.

Lines 30–35 place two text boxes on the page. Line 38 puts a button on the page. Lines 41–45 contain VBScript code with an Update_OnClick function that executes when the button is clicked.

The user-interface tools in HTML for enabling the user to edit, add, and delete database data are somewhat primitive. The idea with the page in Listing 11.2 is to display the data from the database in the HTML table and accept user input for changes to the data by using the two text boxes. When the user clicks the button, the Update_OnClick function would display the user's input in the HTML table or send the data to the server, or both. Unfortunately, there is no easy way in HTML to enable the user to navigate to a particular record and edit it. As you can see, HTML makes for a somewhat primitive database UI.

Any changes that the user does make have to be sent to the server singly as they are made or cached in variables in the HTML page and sent as a batch. Sending the changes singly as they are made might result in lots of time-consuming round trips between the browser and the server. Caching the variables in the HTML page and sending them as a batch requires you to write lots of code.

With the lag time of the data's round trips to the Web server, and with browsers' primitive UI tools, your spiffy new multitier application could end up looking like an Edsel. For all the weaknesses of fat client software, a fat client does give you database connections that are responsive and quick and state of the art UI programming tools for building an elegant user interface.

Wouldn't it be nice if there were some way to build a client tier by using Web browsers that have the UI and the data handling capabilities of fat clients?

Fortunately, there is a way you can get these fat client capabilities in a browser. You can use the IE4 browser, with ActiveX controls for the UI and with ADO Remote Data Service (RDS) to handle the data on the client and middle tiers.

Using ActiveX Controls and RDS to Build Elegant Thin Clients

You can use a variety of ActiveX controls to provide an elegant UI in IE4. These ActiveX controls are available from Microsoft and from a number of independent software vendors (ISVs). Evaluation versions of many of the controls can be downloaded for free from the vendor's Web sites. These ActiveX controls enable you to create a modern and complete UI in the IE4 browser. You will use one such ActiveX control today.

To enable robust data handling in a browser, Microsoft offers Remote Data Service. RDS is included in Microsoft's Data Access Components (MDAC). When you install MDAC, RDS is installed automatically. You will find instructions for setting up RDS by searching the Platform SDK documentation (in MSDN) for a document titled "Setting Up Remote Data Service."

You need to install the RDS Address Book sample to get a particular ActiveX control required for your work today. The Sheridan grid control is an ActiveX control that (as of this writing) is included in the RDS Address Book sample.

The code that you will write today uses the Sheridan grid control. If you are unable to obtain the Sheridan grid control in the RDS samples, you can download a trial version of the Sheridan Data Widgets at `http://www.shersoft.com/`.

To test your installation of RDS, type in the code shown in Listing 11.3 and save it as an ASP file. To enter Listing 11.3 into an ASP file, run Visual Studio, select the File, New menu, and tell it to create a new Active Server Page. (The ASP page needn't be part of any of your projects in Visual Studio.) Then type in the code in Listing 11.3 and save it as an ASP file. Call it something like ClientTier.ASP. You can view the page in IE4 by entering the Web address of the ASP file in the IE4 Address text box.

> **Note**
>
> To run the code in Listing 11.3, you must have IIS or Personal Web Server running on your machine. See the "Setting Up Remote Data Service" document in the Platform SDK documentation for more information.

 INPUT

LISTING 11.3 A DATABASE CLIENT UI WITH THE ACTIVEX GRID CONTROL AND RDS

```
 1:  <HTML>
 2:  <HEAD>
 3:  <TITLE>Client Tier</TITLE>
 4:  </HEAD>
 5:  <CENTER>
 6:  <H1>Remote Data Service and Sheridan Grid Control</H1>
 7:  <BR>
 8:
 9:  <OBJECT ID="GRID" WIDTH=600 HEIGHT=200 Datasrc="#ADC"
10:    CODEBASE="http://<%=Request.ServerVariables("SERVER_NAME")%>
11:    /MSADC/Samples/ssdatb32.cab"
```

continues

LISTING 11.3 CONTINUED

```
12:     CLASSID="CLSID:AC05DC80-7DF1-11d0-839E-00A024A94B3A">
13:     <PARAM NAME="_Version"       VALUE="131072">
14:     <PARAM NAME="BackColor"      VALUE="-2147483643">
15:     <PARAM NAME="BackColorOdd"   VALUE="-2147483643">
16:     <PARAM NAME="ForeColorEven" VALUE="0">
17:     </OBJECT>
18:
19:     <OBJECT classid="clsid:BD96C556-65A3-11D0-983A-00C04FC29E33"
20:     ID=ADC HEIGHT=1 WIDTH = 1>
21:     </OBJECT>
22:
23:     <BR>
24:     <BR>
25:     <BR>
26:     <INPUT TYPE=BUTTON NAME="Execute" VALUE="Execute">
27:     <INPUT TYPE=BUTTON NAME="MoveFirst" VALUE="MoveFirst">
28:     <INPUT TYPE=BUTTON NAME="MovePrevious" VALUE="MovePrevious">
29:     <INPUT TYPE=BUTTON NAME="MoveNext" VALUE="MoveNext">
30:     <INPUT TYPE=BUTTON NAME="MoveLast" VALUE="MoveLast"> <BR><BR>
31:     <INPUT TYPE=BUTTON NAME="Update" VALUE="Update">
32:     <INPUT TYPE=BUTTON NAME="Cancel" VALUE="Cancel">
33:     </CENTER>
34:
35:     <SCRIPT LANGUAGE= "VBScript">
36:
37:     SUB MoveFirst_onClick
38:       ADC.Recordset.MoveFirst
39:     END SUB
40:
41:     SUB MovePrevious_onClick
42:       On Error Resume Next
43:       ADC.Recordset.MovePrevious
44:       IF ERR.Number <> 0 THEN
45:         ERR.Clear
46:       END IF
47:     END SUB
48:
49:     SUB MoveNext_onClick
50:       On Error Resume Next
51:       ADC.Recordset.MoveNext
52:       IF ERR.Number <> 0 THEN
52:         ERR.Clear
53:       END IF
54:     END SUB
55:
56:     SUB MoveLast_onClick
57:       ADC.Recordset.MoveLast
58:     END SUB
59:
```

```
60:  SUB Update_onClick
61:      ADC.SubmitChanges
62:      ADC.Refresh
63:      Grid.Rebind
64:  END SUB
65:
66:  SUB Cancel_onClick
67:      ADC.CancelUpdate
68:      ADC.Refresh
69:      Grid.Rebind
70:  END SUB
71:
72:  SUB Execute_onClick
73:      ADC.Server = "http://<%=Request.ServerVariables("SERVER_NAME")%>"
74:      ADC.Connect = "DSN=OrdersDb"
75:      ADC.SQL = "Select * from Products"
76:      ADC.Refresh
77:      Grid.Rebind
78:  END SUB
79:
80:  </SCRIPT>
81:  </BODY>
82:  </HTML>
```

11

Lines 1–7 in Listing 11.3 put up the title for the window and a heading. Lines 9–17 place the Sheridan ActiveX grid control in the page. Lines 19–21 place the Microsoft RDS DataControl (also called the Advanced Data Control or ADC) into the page. Lines 26–32 place several buttons on the page to enable the user to interact with the UI. Lines 35–80 contain VBScript code for handling button presses by the user. Lines 80–82 end the tags to indicate the end of the page.

The Microsoft RDS DataControl (ADC) is an ActiveX control that is instantiated on the client machine in the browser's process. When the user presses the execute button, lines 73–75 set the Server, Connect, and SQL properties in the ADC. Line 76 calls the ADC Refresh method. This method uses the Server, Connect, and SQL properties to tell the middle tier to connect to the database and issue the SQL query. The ADC then retrieves the records and caches them on the client machine.

Line 77 tells the grid control to rebind to the records. The grid actually does more than just display them. The grid enables the user to navigate through the records, using the code in lines 37 through 58. The user can edit the records' contents in the grid. The user can cancel those changes by clicking the Cancel button, which executes the code in lines 66–70. The user can commit the changes by clicking the Update button, which executes the code in lines 60–64. The output of Listing 11.3 is shown in Figure 11.9.

FIGURE 11.9

The client tier page in IE4.

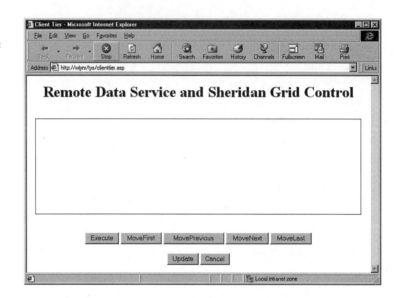

What happens behind the scenes with Remote Data Services is quite amazing. Figure 11.10 shows the architecture of RDS.

FIGURE 11.10

The RDS architecture.

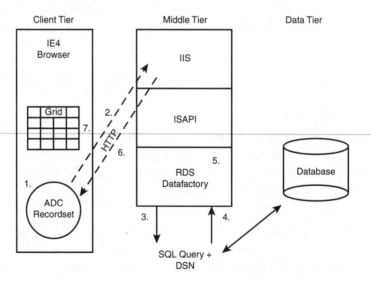

Following is an explanation of the sequence in a typical RDS operation:

1. A thin client, such as a browser, running on a client tier machine creates a local instance of the RDS.DataControl (perhaps it is bound to a grid control running in the browser).

2. When the user makes a request for the data, RDS.DataControl creates a remote instance of RDSServer.DataFactory on the middle-tier machine and issues a query to the DataFactory object.

3. The DataFactory object on the middle-tier machine uses OLE DB or ODBC to query the database on the data-tier machine.

4. The database processes the query and sends all the records to the DataFactory object on the middle-tier machine.

5. The DataFactory object stores all the records from the query in an OLE DB row set, called the *server-side cache*, which resides on the middle-tier machine.

6. The DataFactory places an ADO Recordset interface on the row set and sends it to the client machine as the RDS.DataControl requests it.

7. If configured to do so, with large amounts of data the RDS.DataControl can cause the grid control to become interactive very soon after the DataFactory begins sending data to the client machine.

Step 7 mentions a capability that RDS provides that could be crucial for applications that process large amounts of data. RDS enables the results of queries to be sent asynchronously.

The RDS.DataControl can be configured to retrieve data in the background or asynchronously. If the RDS.DataControl is retrieving the data in the background and the user tells it to MoveLast (move to the last record), user interactivity will cease until all the data is retrieved. If the RDS.DataControl is retrieving the data asynchronously and the user tells it to MoveLast, user interactivity will continue. The RDS.DataControl will move to the most recent record received and will continue to retrieve data asynchronously.

You can enable the asynchronous capabilities of RDS by using the code shown in Listing 11.4. Create a new ASP page for this code. Call it something like ClientTierAsync.ASP.

LISTING 11.4   RDS ASYNCHRONOUS OPERATIONS

```
1:  <HTML>
2:  <HEAD>
3:  <TITLE>Client Tier</TITLE>
4:  </HEAD>
5:  <CENTER>
```

continues

11

LISTING **11.4** CONTINUED

```
 6:  <H1>Remote Data Service and Sheridan Grid Control</H1>
 7:  <BR>
 8:
 9:  <OBJECT ID="GRID" WIDTH=600 HEIGHT=200 Datasrc="#ADC"
10:    CODEBASE="http://<%=Request.ServerVariables("SERVER_NAME")%>
11:    /MSADC/Samples/ssdatb32.cab"
12:    CLASSID="CLSID:AC05DC80-7DF1-11d0-839E-00A024A94B3A">
13:    <PARAM NAME="_Version"      VALUE="131072">
14:    <PARAM NAME="BackColor"     VALUE="-2147483643">
15:    <PARAM NAME="BackColorOdd"  VALUE="-2147483643">
16:    <PARAM NAME="ForeColorEven" VALUE="0">
17:  </OBJECT>
18:
19:  <OBJECT classid="clsid:BD96C556-65A3-11D0-983A-00C04FC29E33"
20:    ID=ADC HEIGHT=1 WIDTH = 1>
21:  </OBJECT>
22:
23:  <BR>
24:  <BR>
25:  <BR>
26:  <INPUT TYPE=BUTTON NAME="Execute" VALUE="Execute">
27:  <INPUT TYPE=BUTTON NAME="MoveFirst" VALUE="MoveFirst">
28:  <INPUT TYPE=BUTTON NAME="MovePrevious" VALUE="MovePrevious">
29:  <INPUT TYPE=BUTTON NAME="MoveNext" VALUE="MoveNext">
30:  <INPUT TYPE=BUTTON NAME="MoveLast" VALUE="MoveLast"> <BR><BR>
31:  <INPUT TYPE=BUTTON NAME="Update" VALUE="Update">
32:  <INPUT TYPE=BUTTON NAME="Cancel" VALUE="Cancel">
33:  <BR>
34:  <INPUT TYPE=TEXT NAME=RsState SIZE =25>
35:  </CENTER>
36:
37:  <SCRIPT LANGUAGE= "VBScript">
38:
39:  Const adcExecSync = 1
40:  Const adcExecAsync = 2
41:
42:  Const adcFetchUpFront = 1
43:  Const adcFetchBackground = 2
44:  Const adcFetchAsync = 3
45:
46:  Const adcReadyStateLoaded = 2
47:  Const adcReadyStateInteractive = 3
48:  Const adcReadyStateComplete = 4
49:
50:  SUB ADC_OnReadyStateChange
51:    Select case ADC.ReadyState
52:      case adcReadyStateLoaded: RsState.Value = "Loaded"
53:      case adcReadyStateInteractive: RsState.Value = "Interactive"
54:      case adcReadyStateComplete: RsState.Value = "Complete"
55:    END Select
```

```
 56:  END SUB
 57:
 58:  SUB MoveFirst_onClick
 59:    ADC.Recordset.MoveFirst
 60:  END SUB
 61:
 62:  SUB MovePrevious_onClick
 63:    On Error Resume Next
 64:    ADC.Recordset.MovePrevious
 65:    IF ERR.Number <> 0 THEN
 66:      ERR.Clear
 67:    END IF
 68:  END SUB
 69:
 70:  SUB MoveNext_onClick
 71:    On Error Resume Next
 72:    ADC.Recordset.MoveNext
 73:    IF ERR.Number <> 0 THEN
 74:      ERR.Clear
 75:    END IF
 76:  END SUB
 77:
 78:  SUB MoveLast_onClick
 79:    ADC.Recordset.MoveLast
 80:  END SUB
 81:
 82:  SUB Update_onClick
 83:    ADC.SubmitChanges
 84:    ADC.Refresh
 85:    Grid.Rebind
 86:  END SUB
 87:
 88:  SUB Cancel_onClick
 89:    ADC.CancelUpdate
 90:    ADC.Refresh
 91:    Grid.Rebind
 92:  END SUB
 93:
 94:  SUB Execute_onClick
 95:    ADC.ExecuteOptions = adcExecAsync
 96:    ADC.FetchOptions = adcFetchAsync
 97:    ADC.Server = "http://<%=Request.ServerVariables("SERVER_NAME")%>"
 98:    ADC.Connect = "DSN=OrdersDb"
 99:    ADC.SQL = "Select * from Products"
100:   ADC.Refresh
101:   Grid.Rebind
102:  END SUB
103:
104:  </SCRIPT>
105:  </BODY>
106:  </HTML>
```

11

The code in Listing 11.4 enables you to experiment with the asynchronous capabilities of RDS. To help understand what is happening with the asynchronous data transfer, refer again to Figure 11.10.

The code in Listing 11.4 is identical to the code in Listing 11.3, with a few additions. Line 34 adds a text box that will report on the status of the Recordset in the ADC. Lines 39–48 are constants that were copied from the RDS type library (in MSADCO.DLL). Lines 50–56 define a function that is executed automatically whenever the status of the ADC Recordset changes. Lines 95 and 96 set the ADC to asynchronous operation before the query is issued.

One apparent problem with the RDS DataControl is the fact that the client program will issue queries directly to the database. It would appear that the client application has direct knowledge of the database. However, it is important to remember that the code for the client tier actually exists on the middle tier in ASP files. Changing the database might necessitate changing the ASP files, but not the software on the client machines.

A level of abstraction could be created using stored procedures and views in the database. These database stored procedures and views could provide an interface layer to the RDS clients, underneath which the implementation of the database structure could change.

A potential problem with RDS is in the area of security. The DataFactory object on the middle tier enables anyone who can obtain a DSN, username, and password to issue SQL statements to the database. Those SQL statements could include DELETE statements to erase data in the database. For this reason, RDS is typically not used on the Internet. It could enable anyone with a browser to delete your data. Rather, RDS finds its greatest application in corporate intranets where the users are more trusted and security can be controlled more easily.

You can also use the RDS DataControl in your C++ programs. The ADC code and the type library reside in MSADCO.DLL. You can use the #import directive with MSADCO.DLL just as you do with MSADO15.DLL. The RDS DataControl interface is listed as IBindMgr in the type library.

Summary

Multitier applications promise easier updates and maintenance than traditional client/server applications. The tools for building multitier applications have evolved rapidly over the past few years. XML is a technology that will be widely used in the future to transmit data in multitier applications. Some of the more recent developments, such as ActiveX controls and RDS, promise to enable client/server-type development in an intranet environment.

Q&A

Q Can I use XML in C++ programs?

A Yes. You can use the XML parser from Microsoft to parse XML documents in C++ programs and retrieve their contents. In other words, you can use the XML parser to read the schema of XML documents and then read the data that the XML documents contain. There is at least one sample C++ program for XML parsing on the Microsoft Web site.

Q Why is it so difficult to use HTML to build a UI for a database application?

A The UI for a database application typically requires that the data be displayed in a table and that the user be able to navigate through the table and edit the content of rows in the table as needed. HTML does not provide these capabilities. This is why it is necessary to use an ActiveX control, such as a grid control, to build a good database UI.

Q Do I have to use an ODBC DSN with the RDS `DataControl`, or can I specify an OLE DB provider?

A You can use OLE DB providers as well as ODBC data sources with the RDS `DataControl`. To use an OLE DB provider, you would use `"Provider="` and specify the name of the provider and the particular OLE DB data source.

11

Workshop

The Workshop quiz questions test your understanding of today's material. (The answers appear in Appendix F, "Answers.") The exercises encourage you to apply the information you learned today to real-life situations.

Quiz

1. What are the two pillars on which multitier architectures rest?

2. Why are thin client programs often more desirable than fat client programs?

3. How does the purpose of XML differ from the purpose of HTML?

4. What COM objects are instantiated, and where are they instantiated, in a typical RDS application?

5. What is the security risk posed by the RDS COM servers?

Exercises

1. Create a table in your database that contains 10,000 records and query it with RDS to become familiar with the asynchronous operation of RDS.

2. Create a new MFC application that uses #import with MSADCO.DLL. Make this C++ application use the ADO DataControl to perform a function that is similar to the ASP code in Listing 11.4.

DAY **12**

Using Microsoft Transaction Server to Build Scalable Applications

Building a multitier application can be a daunting task. Implementing the application logic is just one part of the development process. Multitier applications require a sophisticated infrastructure. This infrastructure often includes code to synchronize access to server resources, manage server connections and thread pools, enforce security, and so on.

Without using Microsoft Transaction Server (MTS), application developers must build the infrastructure for multitier applications themselves. However, by using MTS, developers can take advantage of the infrastructure that MTS provides and are free to concentrate on implementing the application instead of its infrastructure.

Today you will learn

- The infrastructure required for scalable, multitier applications
- The foundation and infrastructure that MTS provides for multitier applications
- How to create MTS components and how to use them in applications
- Ways to integrate MTS components with IIS and Web browsers
- How to debug MTS components
- How to send ADO Recordset objects between the tiers and components of a multitier application

 Note

> Today's development work utilizes Microsoft Transaction Server (MTS), Microsoft Internet Information Sever (IIS), and Internet Explorer version 4.0 (IE4). If you have access to MTS, IE4, and IIS (or Microsoft Personal Web Server, which is compatible with IIS), you will be able to perform all the programming tasks described today. If not, you will have to learn some of these techniques without being able to try them yourself.

The Infrastructure for Multitier Applications

The move to multitier applications is being driven by the need for business applications that

- Are component-based and extensible
- Can handle large quantities of data being accessed by large numbers of concurrent users
- Are secure and provide for the safety and security of important data
- Are accessible to users who might be in diverse locations and are using the application over a LAN, WAN, or the Web

Building applications with these characteristics requires lots of code. The infrastructure, or plumbing (which includes the code for communications, resource allocation, security, and so on), has to be in place before the developer can build the application.

Developers who build multitier applications from scratch have found that building the infrastructure can be the most challenging and time-consuming portion of the project. In other words, building the plumbing can be a significant part of the development effort.

The plumbing for a multitier application typically must include code that

- Communicates with client applications over the Web, a WAN, or a LAN
- Instantiates objects and resources on the server on behalf of each client
- Queues client requests
- Manages objects' lifetimes on the server
- Tracks each user's identity and state
- Pools threads so that the server (or the middle-tier) doesn't have to dedicate a thread to each user
- Prevents unauthorized access to the application or to the data
- Manages transactions to assure the successful processing of each client's work
- Pools database connections so that the server doesn't have to dedicate a database connection to each user

This plumbing has to exist for multitier applications to work. That means that someone has to write it.

Developers who build their own plumbing for multitier applications typically must rebuild the plumbing (or parts of it) each time they build a new application. For each application, they must spend a significant portion of their time writing code that is not really part of the application.

Developers who build their own plumbing also have limited opportunities to use third-party components in their applications. For the use of third-party components in multitier applications, a common component framework must be in place, and the components and the plumbing must be compatible.

The Component Object Model (COM) provides a component framework. However, COM by itself does not provide sufficient plumbing for building multitier applications. In practice, COM by itself provides the framework for only a single tier of an application.

 Note   DCOM does provide the means to instantiate COM objects on different machines across a LAN. However, this capability alone does not provide a complete foundation for building multitier applications. Instantiating objects on a server is only part of the plumbing that a multitier application needs.

COM provides a component framework for a single tier in an application. To use COM components in a multitier application, the application must have plumbing that is compatible with COM.

MTS provides plumbing for multitier applications that is compatible with COM. COM provides the framework for using components in a single tier, and MTS provides the plumbing for these components to be used across tiers in a multitier application.

Using MTS to Build Multitier Applications

Microsoft Transaction Server extends COM to provide a multitier application framework that can shelter you from the complexities of multitier development. MTS handles object instantiation at the server, process and thread management, synchronization of shared resources, and security. MTS also supports transactions to ensure atomic updates and consistency.

Where to Find MTS and How to Install It

MTS is included in the Windows NT 4.0 Option Pack. MTS requires

- Windows NT 4.0 or Windows 98 (or Windows 95 with DCOM support)
- A hard disk with a minimum of 30MB available space
- A CD-ROM drive
- At least 32MB of RAM

You can install MTS on your computer by using the Windows NT 4.0 Option Pack Setup program. You can install MTS with or without IIS and the other Option Pack components.

To install MTS

1. Run the Option Pack Setup program.
2. Choose Custom Install.
3. Select (but do not uncheck) the check box for Transaction Server.
4. Click Show Subcomponents.
5. Check Transaction Server Core Components. This will also install the Microsoft Management Console. Note that choosing the Development Option also installs the Data Access components.
6. Click OK for the Setup program to do the install.

The Windows NT 4.0 Option Pack and MTS also are available as part of the Visual Studio Enterprise Edition Server Setup options. Select Server Setup; then select BackOffice Setup. Then you can select NT Option Pack as an installation option (along with SQL server, and so on.)

How MTS Works in Multitier Applications

To use MTS in a multitier application, you build the business logic and functionality of your application into a set of COM in-process servers. (An *in-process COM server* is a COM server that resides in a DLL.) Each of these COM servers performs some function or well-defined set of functions in your application.

The client programs in your application call these COM servers. The client programs do not perform any communications with a database server directly. The COM servers constitute a middle tier that the client programs call. This multitier architecture is illustrated in Figure 12.1.

FIGURE 12.1

Multitier architecture.

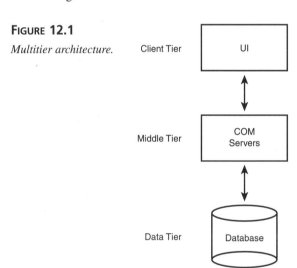

In-process COM servers by themselves can't provide an adequate middle tier. MTS extends COM by providing a wrapper for COM servers. You install these in-process COM servers in MTS, and MTS wraps them and gives them additional functionality. This additional functionality makes it possible for these COM servers to be used effectively as a middle tier in a multitier application. Figure 12.2 illustrates the role of MTS in multitier applications.

MTS wraps and extends the COM servers by intercepting the calls to them from client applications. MTS does this by causing the Registry entries for COM servers to point to the MTS runtime environment, instead of to the COM server's DLL. You will recall from Day 9, "Understanding COM," that the location of a COM server's binary (EXE or DLL) is stored in the Registry. Figure 12.3 shows a sample Registry entry for an in-process COM.

FIGURE 12.2

*MTS in multitier appli-
cations.*

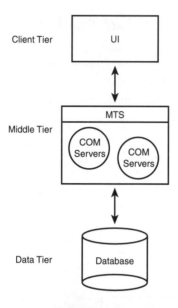

FIGURE 12.3

*The Registry entry for
an in-process COM
server.*

You can see in Figure 12.3 that the `InprocServer32` key for this particular CLSID points
to RDSATLMTS1.DLL (the filename derives from the fact that this example experiments
with RDS, ATL, and MTS) in the WorkInProgress\RDSATLMTS1\Debug directory on
the C drive.

As you will recall from Day 9, when a client application requests a pointer to an interface to a COM server (using the CLSID), the system locates the binary and loads it if
necessary. The system then calls the class factory in the binary to create an instance of
the COM server (if an instance needs to be created) and returns to the client a pointer to
an interface to the COM server. (Refer to Figure 9.5 for an illustration of this process.)

When you install an in-process COM server in MTS, the COM server becomes an MTS
component. The Registry entry for that COM server is changed so that it no longer points
to the DLL in which the COM server resides. Instead, the Registry points to MTX.EXE,
which is the MTS application binary. This is illustrated in Figure 12.4.

FIGURE 12.4

The Registry entry for an in-process COM server installed in MTS.

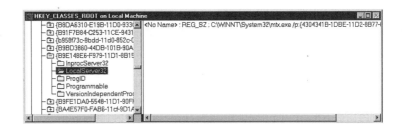

You can see in Figure 12.4 that a `LocalServer32` key that points to C:\WINNT\System32\mtx.exe has been added. Following the filename and pathname is a `/p:` command-line argument followed by a GUID. You can't see it in Figure 12.4, but the entry for the `InprocServer32` key has been emptied so that it no longer points to the COM server's DLL.

This change in the Registry means that when a client application references this COM server's CLSID to obtain an interface pointer to the COM server, the system does not look for and load the COM server's DLL. Instead, MTX.EXE is located by the system (and loaded if necessary) and is passed the `/p:` command-line argument followed by the GUID shown in Figure 12.4.

Remember that an *MTS component* is a COM server that has been installed in MTS. The GUID passed on the command line represents the particular MTS package that contains this MTS component. An *MTS package* is a collection of MTS components that run in the same process.

Managing MTS Components by Using Packages

MTS components are organized into MTS packages. Packages in MTS enable process isolation and security to be established for sets of components. Process isolation ensures that a poorly written component, which could cause errors at runtime, cannot bring down other processes running on that machine. MTS package security ensures that only authorized users can access your application.

To learn about MTS packages, and to begin today's development work, you will need to create your own package in MTS. Run the Transaction Server Explorer, which (on NT) you can run by selecting the Start, Programs, Windows NT 4.0 Option Pack, Microsoft Transaction Server, Transaction Server Explorer menu. The Transaction Server Explorer runs inside the Microsoft Management Console and is shown in Figure 12.5.

The tree control in the left pane enables you to navigate among the various MTS objects. You can double-click each element (or click the plus sign beside each element) in the tree control to expand it to view its children. The Transaction Server Explorer in Figure 12.5 has been expanded to show installed MTS packages.

FIGURE 12.5

The Transaction Server Explorer.

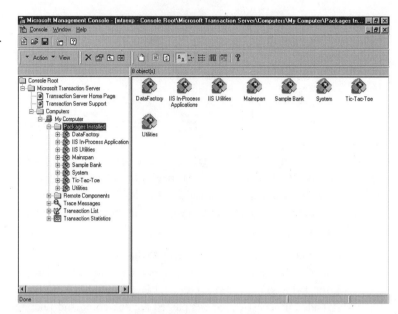

Create your own package in MTS by right-clicking the Packages Installed folder and selecting the New Packages menu. You are presented with the first window of a wizard that will help you create your package. This window is shown in Figure 12.6.

FIGURE 12.6

Using Package Wizard to create an empty MTS package.

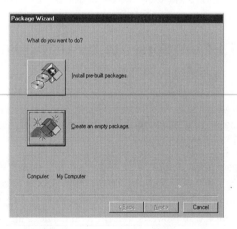

When you install a COM server in MTS, you specify which package it is to be installed in. You can create new packages anytime you need to in MTS.

Note MTS security is not as fully implemented under Windows 95 and Windows 98 as it is under Windows NT. The following explanation of how to create your own MTS package under NT might contain steps for setting up security that do not apply under Windows 95 and Windows 98.

Click the Create an Empty Package button. In the next window, you are prompted for the name of the package, which you can call MyFirst or some other appropriate name. Press the Next button. You will then be presented with a window to specify the identity under which this package will run. This window is shown in Figure 12.7.

FIGURE 12.7

Using Package Wizard to set the package identity.

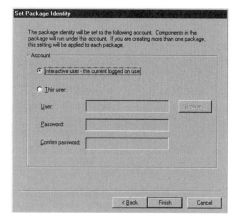

The default is to run the package under the currently logged-on user's identity. The alternative is to hard-code the package to always run under a user identity that you specify. For your work today, use the default setting of the current user's identity for your package. Click the Finish button to create the package.

Your package should appear in the tree control in the Transaction Server Explorer. Select it by clicking it, and you should see that the package contains two folders, one for components and one for roles. The Components folder will contain the in-process COM server that you will create and install later today. The Roles folder enables you to specify security to limit user access to the package and its components.

You can set the properties of your MTS package by right-clicking its element in the tree control and selecting the Properties menu from the context menu. This will show the Properties window for your package. The contents of the General tab are shown in Figure 12.8.

12

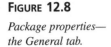

Figure 12.8

*Package properties—
the General tab.*

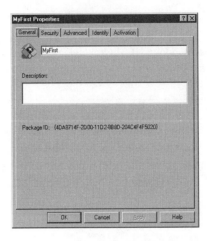

The Properties window in Figure 12.8 shows the name of the package, a description
(which you can assign), and the GUID that uniquely identifies this package. This is the
GUID that appears in the Registry as the /p: argument with MTX.EXE for the COM
servers installed in this package.

Select the Security tab, which enables you to turn on and off security for this package.
There is a check box titled Enable Authorization Checking that you should leave
unchecked to leave security off for your package while you are learning MTS.

The Advanced tab enables you to specify how long the components in your package
should live on the server after being used and released by client applications. The default
values are fine for now.

The Identity tab is the same one you saw on the Package Wizard. Use the default setting
of the current user's identity for your package.

The Activation tab enables you to specify where (in which process) the components in
your package should be instantiated. The Activation tab is shown in Figure 12.9.

The Library Package activation type is available only for client applications that run on
the computer on which the package and components are installed. In other words, the
client application and the components have to be on the same machine. Selecting this
option causes the components to be instantiated in the client application's address space.

The Server Package activation type causes the components to be instantiated in a server
process on the MTS machine. In other words, the package runs in its own process on the
MTS machine. The Server Package activation type provides process isolation. It also
enables MTS to enforce security, manage resource sharing, and track the usage of components in the package. Select Server Package activation for your package.

FIGURE **12.9**

Package properties—
the Activation tab.

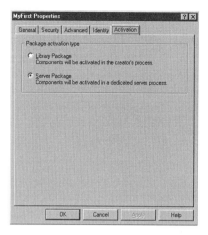

Creating an MTS Component, Using Visual C++ and the ATL

Now it is time to create your first MTS component. Run Visual Studio and select the File, New menu. On the Project tab, specify an ATL COM AppWizard project. The New Project window is shown in Figure 12.10.

FIGURE **12.10**

The new ATL COM
AppWizard project
window.

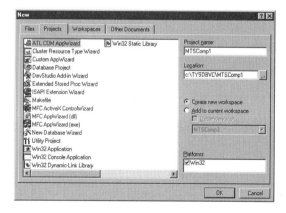

12

Call the project MTSComp1, as shown in Figure 12.10, or use whatever name you think is appropriate. Figure 12.10 shows the project being placed in the c:\tysdbvc\mtscomp1 directory. If that directory already exists on your machine, you will need to use a different directory. Click the OK button.

The next window is the ATL COM AppWizard—Step 1 of 1 window. It is shown in Figure 12.11.

FIGURE 12.11

The ATL COM AppWizard—Step 1 of 1 window.

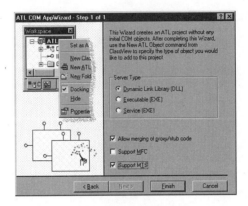

Specify merging of proxy/stub code and support for MTS, as shown in Figure 12.11. Click the Finish button and then the OK button for the wizard to create the project.

Select the Insert menu and the New ATL Object menu choice to specify an MS Transaction Server object as shown in Figure 12.12.

FIGURE 12.12

Using the ATL Object Wizard.

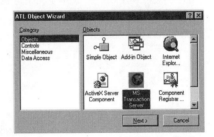

Click the Next button. The ATL Object Wizard Properties window will appear. Under the Names tab, specify a short name of Component1.

Under the MTS tab, specify a dual interface. Also, enable the check boxes for Support IObjectControl and Can Be Pooled, as shown in Figure 12.13.

FIGURE 12.13

The ATL Object Wizard Properties window and the MTS tab.

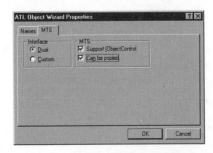

The IObjectControl and Can Be Pooled options tell MTS that your component should be returned to an instance pool after deactivation, rather than be destroyed. This enables MTS to provide access to your component in a very efficient manner as multiple client applications create and free your object. MTS provides efficient access to your component by using thread pooling and database connection pooling.

Click the OK button to generate the object. The CComponent1 class will appear in the tree view in the ClassView tab of the project workspace in Visual Studio. The IComponent1 interface will also appear there.

To add a function to your component, right-click the IComponent1 interface and choose Add Method from the context menu. The Add Method to Interface dialog will be displayed, as shown in Figure 12.14.

FIGURE 12.14

Adding the
ReturnHello *method to*
an interface.

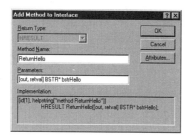

As Figure 12.14 shows, you should specify a method name of ReturnHello and the following parameters:

```
[out, retval] BSTR* bstrHello
```

Using [out, retval] tells the system that the bstrHello parameter needs to be marshaled from the server to the client and that this parameter is the return value of the function.

Click the OK button to add the method. Click the plus sign next to the IComponent1 interface, and you should see the ReturnHello method listed. Double-click the ReturnHello method to view the MTSComp1.IDL file that the ATL Wizard created for you. This IDL code declares the interface to IComponent1.

Click the plus sign next to the CComponent1 class. The IComponent1 interface will be listed there, as well as four other functions and a data member for the CComponent1 class. Click the plus sign next to the IComponent1 interface under the CComponent1 class, and you will see the ReturnHello function listed there, as shown in Figure 12.15.

12

FIGURE 12.15

The ReturnHello
function in
Component1.CPP.

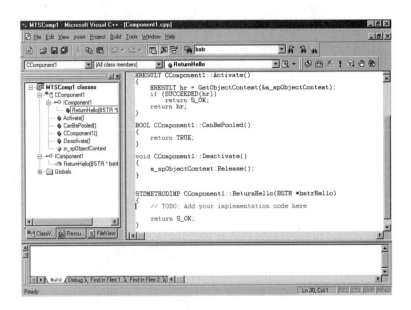

Double-click the ReturnHello function under the IComponent1 interface under the CComponent1 class to open the Component1.CPP, as shown in Figure 12.15. This is where you implement the code for IComponent1. Change the code in the ReturnHello function so that it matches the code shown in Listing 12.1.

LISTING 12.1 THE ReturnHello FUNCTION IN COMPONENT1.CPP

```
1:  STDMETHODIMP CComponent1::ReturnHello(BSTR *bstrHello)
2:  {
3:    *bstrHello = _bstr_t("Hello");
4:    return S_OK;
5:  }
```

The ATL Object Wizard generated lines 1, 2, 4, and 5. You add the code in line 3 that assigns a temporary _bstr_t instance to the pMyBSTR argument. You will also need to add

INPUT   #include <comdef.h>

to Component1.CPP so that you can use the _bstr_t class. Build the project, which should compile and link with no errors or warnings. When you build the project, Visual Studio will register the COM server for you.

Note

> To build any of the release versions of this project, you might need to remove the _ATL_MIN_CRT preprocessor definition from the compiler settings for those configurations. Search your Visual C++ documentation on _ATL_MIN_CRT, for details.

Using the OLE-COM Viewer to Instantiate Your Component

Before installing your component in MTS, you would be wise to test it. There are several ways for you to verify that your COM component works.

First, you will want to ensure that the system can instantiate your component. The easiest way to do this is to use the OLE-COM Object Viewer. You will recall from Day 10, "Database Client Technologies and the Secrets of ADO," that you can find the OLE-COM Object Viewer under the Microsoft Visual Studio 6.0 Tools menu. The menu OLE-COM Viewer is called OLE View. Run the OLE-COM Object viewer and expand the Object Classes, Grouped by Component Category elements of the tree control in the left pane. Expand the Automation Objects element. Under the Automation Objects in the left pane, you should see all the Automation objects that are registered on your system.

Scroll down until you find `Component1` Class. If you don't see `Component1` there, it probably is not registered. Visual Studio registers it for you after every successful build, so it should be there if you are doing this on your build machine. If you ever need to register the component manually (perhaps on another machine), you can run regsvr32 mtscomp1.DLL from the DOS prompt to register it.

Click Component1 Class, and the right pane of the OLE-COM Viewer will display the Registry entry for your `Component1`. Right-click Component1 in the left pane and select Create Instance from the context menu. The Component1 Class element in the tree control will appear in bold text, and the `IComponent1`, `IDispatch`, and `IUnkown` interfaces will appear under it, as shown in Figure 12.16.

If this works, you know that your `Component1` is registered properly and that the system can instantiate it. Release the instance of the `Component1` you just created, by right-clicking Component1 Class and selecting Release Instance from the context menu.

12

FIGURE 12.16

Using the OLE-COM viewer to instantiate a COM object.

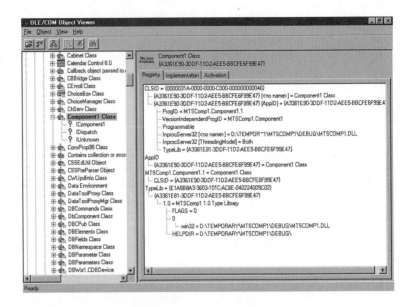

Using the Windows Scripting Host to Test Your Component

One of the easiest ways to exercise a function in your component is to write a simple script that calls it.

Until recently, the only scripting language that Windows supported was the MS-DOS command language. Compared to the scripting languages available on other platforms, the MS-DOS command language has very limited features and capabilities.

Microsoft has greatly expanded the scripting language support on the Win32 platform by introducing the ActiveX scripting architecture. Microsoft provides three hosts for running scripts in the ActiveX scripting architecture:

- Microsoft Internet Explorer (IE4), which enables scripts to be executed on client machines from within HTML pages
- Internet Information Server (IIS) and Active Server Pages (ASP), which enable server-side scripting for use over the Internet or an intranet
- Windows Scripting Host (WSH), which enables you to write scripts and execute them directly on the Windows desktop or at the MS-DOS prompt

The Windows-based host is called WSCRIPT.EXE and enables you to run scripts directly from the Windows desktop by double-clicking a script file. The command prompt-based host is CSCRIPT.EXE and enables you to run scripts from the MS-DOS prompt by simply entering the name of the script file.

WSH is included in the NT 4.0 Option Pack, Windows 98, Windows NT Workstation version 5.0, and Windows NT Server version 5.0.

Microsoft provides Visual Basic Script (VBScript) and Java Script scripting engines for WSH. Support for other script languages, such as Perl, TCL, REXX, and Python, is (or will be) provided for WSH by third-party companies.

To write a script that exercises your component, create a text file and save it as `Comptest.VBS`. The VBS extension is important because the extension tells WSH which scripting language to use. (VBS stands for VBScript.) Enter the code shown in Listing 12.2 in Comptest.VBS.

LISTING 12.2 THE VBSCRIPT FILE FOR EXERCISING Component1

```
1:  dim comp1
2:  set comp1 = WScript.CreateObject("MTSComp1.Component1.1")
3:  myStr = comp1.ReturnHello
4:  WScript.Echo "Result of ReturnHello: " & myStr
```

Line 1 in Listing 12.2 defines a variable called `comp1` that can hold a COM object. Line 2 calls the `WScript.CreateObject` function to instantiate your component. Line 3 declares a variable called `myStr` and stores the results of a call to your component's `ReturnHello` function. Line 4 displays the resulting string in a message box.

You can execute your Comptest.VBS script by double-clicking the file in Windows Explorer or by entering `cscript Comptest.VBS` at the DOS prompt in the directory that contains the file. It should run with no errors and display `Result of ReturnHello: Hello` in a message box. Testing your component with a script is one way for you to know that your component is registered properly and that the code for your component works.

Testing Your Component in an Active Server Page

You can also call your component from within an Active Server Page. However, you must make some additional entries in the Registry for IE4 to allow your component to run in its process.

IE4 has its own security to help ensure that the ActiveX (COM) components it runs are not malicious. A component must be registered as safe for scripting and safe for initialization, or IE4 will not run it. Therefore, you need to register Component1 as being safe

12

for scripting and initialization. You do this by creating a text file that has a .REG extension, such as `marksafe.REG`, and that contains the code shown in Listing 12.3.

LISTING 12.3 A REG FILE TO MARK YOUR COMPONENT SAFE FOR SCRIPTING AND INITIALIZATION

```
1:  REGEDIT4
2:  [HKEY_CLASSES_ROOT\CLSID\<GUID>\Implemented Categories\{7DD95801-
    ➥9882-11CF-9FA9-00AA006C42C4}]
3:  [HKEY_CLASSES_ROOT\CLSID\<GUID>\Implemented Categories\{7DD95802-
    ➥9882-11CF-9FA9-00AA006C42C4}]
```

Replace the text that says <GUID> in lines 2 and 3 of Listing 12.3 with the CLSID for your Component1. You can obtain the CLSID for your Component1 from several places.

One easy way to obtain the CLSID for your Component1 is to use the OLE-COM Viewer. Right-click Component1 Class and select Copy CLSID to Clipboard from the context menu. (After doing this you can exit OLE-COM Viewer.)

You can then paste the CLSID into the REG file. To add these entries to the Registry database on your machine, simply double-click the REG file in Windows Explorer.

In Visual Studio, create a new Active Server Page (the file does not need to be added to a project). Enter the code shown in Listing 12.4 and save the file as `ClientTierForMTS.ASP`.

LISTING 12.4 THE CLIENTTIERFORMTS.ASP TO RUN Component1 FROM AN ACTIVE SERVER PAGE

```
 1:  <HTML>
 2:  <HEAD>
 3:  <TITLE>Client Tier</TITLE>
 4:  </HEAD>
 5:  <CENTER>
 6:  <H1>Browser Client for MTS Component</H1>
 7:
 8:  <!-- RDS.DataSpace --><OBJECT ID="ADS1" WIDTH=1 HEIGHT=1
 9:    CLASSID="CLSID:BD96C556-65A3-11D0-983A-00C04FC29E36">
10:  </OBJECT>
11:
12:  <BR>
13:  <BR>
14:  <INPUT TYPE=BUTTON NAME="ReturnHello" VALUE="Return Hello">
15:  <INPUT NAME=ReturnedHello SIZE=10>
16:  </CENTER>
17:
18:  <SCRIPT LANGUAGE= "VBScript">
```

```
19:
20:   SUB ReturnHello_OnClick
21:
22:     Dim objMyCustomBusinessObject
23:     Set objMyCustomBusinessObject =
      ➥ADS1.CreateObject("MTSComp1.Component1.1", "")
24:
25:     ReturnedHello.Value = objMyCustomBusinessObject.ReturnHello
26:
27:     Set objMyCustomBusinessObject = Nothing
28:
29:   END SUB
30:
31:   </SCRIPT>
32:   </BODY>
33:   </HTML>
```

Lines 1– 7 and 32–33 are simple HTML. Lines 11–17 contain normal HTML code that creates a ReturnHello button and a text box.

Lines 8–10 create an instance of the Remote Data Services (RDS) DataSpace object. The database space object is used to create client-side proxies of COM components that exist on a server or middle-tier machine. RDS supports four protocols over which it can instantiate and call COM objects: HTTP, HTTPS, DCOM, and in-process.

Lines 18 through 31 contain VBScript code that uses the DataSpace object to instantiate your Component1, call its ReturnHello method, and display the results in the text box.

Line 23 calls the DataSpace CreateObject function to instantiate Component1. As you can see, the second argument passed to the CreateObject function is "". This tells the CreateObject function that the COM component is installed on this machine and to run it as an in-process COM server. You can specify a machine name in the form, "*machine name*" to have the CreateObject function instantiate the COM component over DCOM. You can specify "HTTPS://*webservername*" or "HTTP://*webservername*" to have the CreateObject function instantiate the COM component over an HTTP connection to a Web server.

Before you can have the DataSpace CreateObject function instantiate your component over HTTP or DCOM, you must add the Prog ID of your component (MTSComp1.Component1.1) as a key under the following Registry key:

```
HKEY_LOCAL_MACHINE\SYSTEM\CurrentControlSet\Services\W3SVC\Parameters\
➥ADCLaunch
```

To run the ASP shown in Listing 12.4, place the ASP file in a directory that is accessible to IIS (IIS will need to be running on the machine). Run IE4 and enter the HTTP address

12

of that directory, followed by the ASP filename. The page should load with no errors. When you click the ReturnHello button, Component1 will be called, and Hello will be displayed in the text box.

Note that you have not yet installed your component in MTS. The ability to instantiate and call your COM component over DCOM and HTTP from a browser is provided by RDS. When you install your component in MTS, it will not change the ASP code in Listing 12.4. Rather, MTS will simply make your Component1 more robust and secure when it executes on the middle-tier machine.

Installing Your Component in MTS

Now you need to install your COM server in MTS. Click the plus sign next to the MyFirst package in Transaction Server Explorer; then click the Components folder under the MyFirst package in the tree control. Right-click the Components folder and select the New Component menu. This will run the Component Wizard, shown in Figure 12.17.

FIGURE 12.17

The MTS Component Wizard.

As you can see in Figure 12.17, there is a button to install new components and a button to import components that are already registered. The button to import components that are already registered will open a window that displays all the COM servers registered on your computer. The button to install new components opens the window shown in Figure 12.18. Click the button to install new components.

Click the Add Files button and navigate to the directory that contains the MTSComp1.DLL file for the COM server that you just built and select the DLL. The Install Components window should show that it found Component1, which is the COM server in your DLL. Click the Finish button to install Component1 in MTS.

FIGURE 12.18

The Install Components window in the MTS Component Wizard.

You should now be able to see MTSComp1.Component1 in the MyFirst package. The installed component looks like a bowling ball with an X on it, as shown in Figure 12.19.

FIGURE 12.19

The MTSComp1.Component1 in the Transaction Server Explorer.

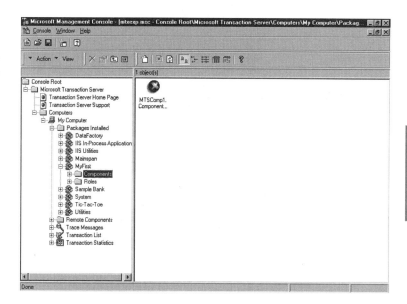

12

Using the View menu, you can see various kinds of information about the components. One interesting view is the Status view. Select the Status view, and you will be able to see information on whether MTSComp1.Component1 has been activated, how many objects of it are instantiated, and how many are handling calls from client applications. These values should all be blank now, but when a client application calls your MTSComp1.Component1, you will be able to see that the object is instantiated by using this view.

Calling Your MTS Component from an Active Server Page

You can use MTS components in Active Server Pages (ASP). However, there are two things you need to do to your Component1 MTS component to enable it to be used from an ASP.

First, just to ensure that the MTS security doesn't get in your way during development, you need to make sure it is not enabled for your Component1. You do this by right-clicking the bowling ball for Component1 and selecting Properties from its context menu. Under the Security tab, uncheck the Enable Authorization Checking check box, as shown in Figure 12.20, and press the OK button.

FIGURE 12.20

Disabling security authorization checking for Component1.

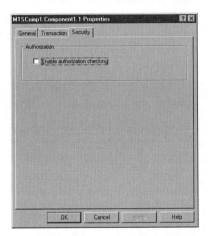

Secondly, you need to mark the component safe for scripting and initialization again. When you installed Component1 in MTS, the Registry entry was modified, and the entries that mark Component1 as safe for scripting and initialization were removed. You can put the safe-for-scripting and initialization entries back in the Registry for your component by simply double-clicking the marksafe.REG file in Windows Explorer. After you mark Component1 safe again, you might want to refresh the MyFirst package in Transaction Server Explorer, just to make sure that MTS is feeling good about things with your component.

It is important to refresh the MTS settings for components each time you recompile your project or make changes to its Registry settings. Refreshing component settings prevents your component Registry settings from being rewritten.

To refresh your component settings, in the left pane of the Transaction Server Explorer, select My Computer. On the Action menu, click Refresh All Components. This updates

MTS with any changes to the System Registry, component CLSIDs, or interface identifiers (IIDs). You can also refresh components by selecting the computer in the left pane of the Explorer and clicking the Refresh button on the MTS toolbar.

You can refresh individual packages in MTS by right-clicking the Components folder, under the package in the left pane of the Transaction Server Explorer, and selecting Refresh from the context menu.

When you build your MTSComp1 project, it will run mtxrereg.EXE as a postbuild step. Mtxrereg.EXE is a command-line version of the Refresh Components menu that you can access by right-clicking a package. If mtxrereg.EXE runs properly, you will not have to use Transaction Server Explorer to refresh your component after each build.

After making all these changes, your component will be ready to run under MTS and will be accessible to Web browsers through RDS.

Run the ASP shown in Listing 12.4 again, by clicking the Refresh button on your browser. If you have already quit IE4, run it and enter the HTTP address of that directory, followed by the ASP filename. The page should load with no errors. When you click the ReturnHello button, `Component1` will be called, and `Hello` will be displayed in the text box.

You will also be able to look at the Status view for the components of your package in Transaction Server Explorer. The Objects, Activated, and In Call columns for MTSComp1.Component1 should go from blank to 0, indicating that the object was instantiated, activated, and called. (It ran to completion too quickly to register a 1 in any of those columns.)

Returning an ADO Recordset from MTS Component to an Active Server Page

Now that you know that your component can run in MTS and can be called from an ASP, it's time to make your component do something useful. In fact, your component will do more than something useful; it will do something really cool.

As you know, ADO Recordsets are built to encapsulate the results of database queries. ADO Recordsets have functions built in for navigating through records and accessing the data in fields. You can edit the data in the Recordset, and those changes will be made to data that resides in the database. (Of course, you recall that you need to make a connection to the database first by using the ADO `Connection` object.)

ADO Recordsets are nifty because they can be disconnected from the database and returned from functions in COM components. This is because ADO Recordsets have the capability to be marshaled across process boundaries.

12

This feature of ADO Recordsets enables your middle-tier COM component to create a Recordset from a database query and then send the Recordset across the wire, using COM, DCOM, or HTTP, to the IE4 Web browser. A Recordset that is sent across the wire in this manner is called a *disconnected Recordset*.

IE4 can use a disconnected Recordset as the data source for a grid control. The browser can accept the user's changes to the data in the grid control and then submit the Recordset back to the middle-tier component, which could submit the Recordset back to the database for the user's changes to be made to the data in the database.

Web browsers that have no direct connection to the database can retrieve and edit data from the database as if they did have a connection to it. Remember, MTS can provide security for these types of applications.

Unfortunately, building a complete application like this is beyond the scope of today's work. You will, however, in today's work write the code to send a Recordset from your middle-tier MTS component to a Web browser and bind it to a grid control.

Add another method to your Component1 interface. Name the method ReturnRs and use the following for its parameters:

```
[out, retval] IDispatch ** Rs
```

After adding the ReturnRs method, implement the code for it as shown in Listing 12.5.

LISTING 12.5 THE ReturnRs METHOD FOR RETURNING AN ADO RECORDSET FROM AN MTS COMPONENT TO AN ASP

```
 1:   STDMETHODIMP CComponent1::ReturnRs(IDispatch **Rs)
 2:   {
 3:     _RecordsetPtr adoRs = NULL;
 4:
 5:     try
 6:     {
 7:       adoRs.CreateInstance(__uuidof(Recordset));
 8:       adoRs->PutCursorLocation(adUseClient);
 9:       adoRs->Open( "SELECT * FROM Customers",
10:         "DSN=OrdersDb; UID=; PWD=;",
11:         adOpenStatic, adLockBatchOptimistic, adCmdText );
12:
13:       *Rs = (IDispatch*)adoRs;
14:
15:       adoRs->AddRef();
16:
17:       //m_spObjectContext->SetComplete();
18:
19:       return S_OK;
```

```
20:    }
21:    catch (_com_error e)
22:    {
23:      ::MessageBeep(MB_OK);
24:      AtlReportError( CLSID_Component1, (LPCOLESTR)e.Description(),
25:        IID_IComponent1, e.Error());
26:    }
27:
28:    //m_spObjectContext->SetAbort();
29:    return E_FAIL;
30:  }
```

Line 3 of Listing 12.5 defines an ADO Recordset smart pointer. Line 7 uses the smart pointer class's `CreateInstance` function to create an ADO Recordset. Line 8 tells ADO to use a client-side cursor, which is necessary if you are going to make this a disconnected Recordset. Lines 9–11 open the Recordset with a `"SELECT * FROM Customers"` query.

Line 13 is where the real magic happens. It casts the Recordset smart pointer as an `IDispatch` pointer and assigns it to the `retval out` parameter. When this line of code executes, COM uses the ADO Recordset's `IMarshal` implementation to send the Recordset object (code, data, and all) to whichever client program is calling this `ReturnRs` function. After line 13 executes, the Recordset no longer exists in this process space, so it is not necessary to close or release it.

Line 15 calls `AddRef()` so that when the smart pointer goes out of scope, it won't call `Release()` on the Recordset. It will cause an error if it does, because the Recordset is already gone. (It was sent to the client and released from this end in Line 13.) Line 17 could call `SetComplete()` if you were supporting MTS transactions in this component, which you are not. Lines 21–29 are for error handling. Line 23 just beeps in case the client application is not set up to take the output of `AtlReportError()`.

You will need to add the `#import` directive for the ADO library to a source file in your project. Stdafx.h is a good file to add the `#import` directive to. (You will, of course, need to list the path to the MSADO15.DLL file on your machine.)

```
#import "C:\program files\common files\system\ado\msado15.dll" \
                    no_namespace \
                    rename( "EOF", "adoEOF" )
```

You will receive a C4530 warning unless you enable exception handling for this project. In the C++ Language Category of the C/C++ tab in the Project Settings dialog box, select the Enable Exception Handling option or simply use the /GX compiler switch.

12

After making these additions, build your MTSComp1 project. It should build with no errors or warnings. If mtxrereg.EXE ran properly in the postbuild step, it will have refreshed your MTS package for you.

Now you need to create an ASP that will use your `ReturnRs` method. Create a new ASP file in Visual Studio. (It does not need to be made part of the project.) Listing 12.6 shows the source code for the ASP.

You need to install the Sheridan grid control on your machine for the code in Listing 12.6 to run properly. As of this writing, the Sheridan grid control is included in the Microsoft RDS Address Book sample.

If you are unable to obtain the Sheridan grid control in the RDS samples, you can download a trial version of the Sheridan Data Widgets at `http://www.shersoft.com/`.

LISTING 12.6 CLIENTTIERFORMTSADORS.ASP RECEIVES AN ADO RECORDSET FROM AN MTS COMPONENT TO AN ASP

```
 1:  <HTML>
 2:  <HEAD>
 3:  <TITLE>Client Tier</TITLE>
 4:  </HEAD>
 5:  <CENTER>
 6:  <H1>Browser Client for MTS Component</H1>
 7:
 8:  <OBJECT ID="GRID" WIDTH=600 HEIGHT=200 Datasrc="#ADC"
 9:    CODEBASE="http://<%=Request.ServerVariables("SERVER_NAME")%>
10:    /MSADC/Samples/ssdatb32.cab"
11:    CLASSID="CLSID:AC05DC80-7DF1-11d0-839E-00A024A94B3A">
12:    <PARAM NAME="_Version"      VALUE="131072">
13:    <PARAM NAME="BackColor"     VALUE="-2147483643">
14:    <PARAM NAME="BackColorOdd"  VALUE="-2147483643">
15:    <PARAM NAME="ForeColorEven" VALUE="0">
16:  </OBJECT>
17:
18:  <OBJECT classid="clsid:BD96C556-65A3-11D0-983A-00C04FC29E33"
19:    ID=ADC HEIGHT=1 WIDTH = 1>
20:  </OBJECT>
21:
22:  <!-- RDS.DataSpace --><OBJECT ID="ADS1" WIDTH=1 HEIGHT=1
23:    CLASSID="CLSID:BD96C556-65A3-11D0-983A-00C04FC29E36">
24:  </OBJECT>
25:
26:  <BR>
27:  <BR>
28:  <INPUT TYPE=BUTTON NAME="ReturnHello" VALUE="Return Hello">
29:  <INPUT NAME=ReturnedHello SIZE=10>
30:  <INPUT TYPE=BUTTON NAME="ReturnRS" VALUE="Return RecordSet">
```

```
31:   </CENTER>
32:
33:   <SCRIPT LANGUAGE= "VBScript">
34:
35:   SUB ReturnHello_OnClick
36:      Dim objMyCustomBusinessObject
37:      Set objMyCustomBusinessObject =
         ➥ADS1.CreateObject("MTSComp1.Component1.1", "")
38:      ReturnedHello.Value = objMyCustomBusinessObject.ReturnHello
39:      Set objMyCustomBusinessObject = Nothing
40:   END SUB
41:
42:   SUB ReturnRS_OnClick
43:      Dim objMyCustomBusinessObject
44:      Set objMyCustomBusinessObject =
         ➥ADS1.CreateObject("MTSComp1.Component1.1", "")
45:      ADC.SourceRecordset = objMyCustomBusinessObject.ReturnRs
46:      Grid.Refresh
47:      Set objMyCustomBusinessObject = Nothing
48:   END SUB
49:
50:   </SCRIPT>
51:   </BODY>
52:   </HTML>
```

Lines 1–6 in Listing 12.6 put up the title for the window and a heading. Lines 8–16 place the Sheridan ActiveX grid control in the page. Lines 18–20 place the Microsoft RDS `DataControl` (also called the Advanced Data Control or ADC) into the page. Lines 22–24 place the RDS `DataSpace` object in the page, as you used in Listing 12.4 as well.

Line 30 adds a button called ReturnRS. Lines 42–48 are the code that executes when the user clicks the ReturnRS button. Line 45 sets the ADC Source Recordset to the disconnected Recordset returned by `Component1.ReturnRs()`.

Load this ASP in IE4. Click the ReturnHello button to make sure it still works. Then click the ReturnRs button. If everything runs properly, you should see the records from the `Customers` table appear in the grid control. It's really cool when it works. When it doesn't work, you need to debug your component.

Debugging MTS Components

You can debug your Microsoft Transaction Server component DLL in Visual C++ with the following procedure. Shut down server processes using the Transaction Server Explorer by right-clicking My Computer and selecting Shutdown Server Process.

In your Visual C++ session, under the Project, Settings, Debug, General menu, set the program arguments to the following string: `"/p: PackageName"`—for example,

12

```
/p: "MyFirst"
```

In the same property sheet, set the executable to the full path of Mtx.EXE—for example,

```
C:\WINNT\System32\MTx.exe
```

Set breakpoints in your component DLL in the `ReturnHello` and `ReturnRs` functions and run the server process (in the Build menu, select Start Debug and click Go.) Then run IE4 and load ClientTierForMTSAdoRS.ASP. Click the ReturnHello button and/or the ReturnRs button to hit your breakpoints. You should be able to step through the code just like a normal debugging session.

Summary

The infrastructure necessary for multitier applications is difficult and time-consuming to build yourself. MTS can do most of that work for you and enable you to concentrate on building your application, not its infrastructure.

MTS components are COM DLLS that you can build with ATL. In your component code, you can create ADO Recordsets from database queries and send the Recordsets to applications on the client tier.

IE4 can host ActiveX controls and, with RDS, can instantiate and communicate over COM, DCOM, and HTTP with MTS components that you build.

Q&A

Q What do transactions in MTS do?

A Some operations that you might perform in your MTS components could involve calling code in several other components or in several databases. MTS transactions enable you to ensure that all that work completes successfully.

Q What is the difference between the RDS `DataSpace` object I used today and the RDS `DataControl` object I used yesterday?

A The `DataControl` object has a `Refresh` function that enables you to query a data source behind the Web server. That `Refresh` function uses the RDS `DataFactory` object on the middle tier, which could be a security risk in some installations. The `DataSpace` object enables you to instantiate other components on the middle tier, which you can use instead of the `DataFactory` object.

Q The RDS `DataControl` `Refresh` method provides for asynchronous fetching of ADO Recordsets. Does the `DataSpace` object provide that capability?

A No. When retrieving a Recordset from a COM component that was instantiated using the `DataSpace` object, the Recordset comes across synchronously. In other words, it will block until all the data in the Recordset is fetched.

Workshop

The Workshop quiz questions test your understanding of today's material. (The answers appear in Appendix F, "Answers.") The exercises encourage you to apply the information you learned today to real-life situations.

Quiz

1. Why isn't DCOM alone sufficient for building multitier applications?
2. What does [out, retval] mean and where is it used?
3. Will MTS run on Windows 98?
4. What do MTS packages do?
5. What is a disconnected Recordset?

Exercises

1. Try to rebuild your MTSComp1.DLL while you have IE4 running with ClientTierForMTSAdoRS.ASP loaded. What happens? How do you fix the problem?
2. How would you go about removing your MTSComp1.Component1 from MTS so that you could use it as a standard COM server? Try it.

12

DAY 13

Melding Object-Oriented Programming with Relational Databases

Relational database technologies have revolutionized the way data is managed. With relational databases, you can manage huge quantities of data that are impossible to manage using other, less capable database technologies.

Object-oriented programming techniques have revolutionized the way software is developed. With object-oriented programming techniques, you can create large and complex software systems that are impossible to create using other, less capable programming methodologies.

Relational databases enable powerful data management, and object-oriented programming enables powerful software development. By combining the object model and the relational model, you can write large and complex software systems that manage huge amounts of data.

Today you will learn

- The characteristics of the relational model and the object model that make them difficult to integrate
- The factors that determine whether an application is suitable for an object/relational mix or for a pure object database
- The costs and the benefits of combining the relational model with the object model
- The techniques for integrating relational databases with object-oriented programs

Because today's work deals primarily with design issues, you won't be writing any code today. Also, it is very difficult to write a day's worth of code on this topic. The topic is so large that to write a little bit of code, you end up having to write a lot.

Relational Databases and Object-Oriented Languages, the Oil and Vinegar of Modern Application Development

Some things don't mix easily. Their characteristics are so different that they do not blend with each other naturally. Relational databases and object-oriented programming languages are like that.

Combining the object model and the relational model can enable you to write complex applications that manage huge amounts of data. However, the relational model and the object model come from different worlds and are quite dissimilar. The differences between the two models prevent them from blending easily with each other easily.

The interface between the relational model and the object model is not straightforward, but there are proven techniques for combining the two models. As a C++ database programmer, you possess knowledge of both the relational model and the object model. You are in a unique position to learn how to fuse these two disparate models to build advanced software applications.

How the Relational Model and the Object Model Differ

Relational database systems:

- Data is represented in a collection of two-dimensional tables.
- Relationships between the data in the tables are expressed by values stored in the tables.

- Using SQL, you can create relationships between the data in a dynamic fashion on-the-fly.
- The relationships between the data entities do not necessarily need to be defined or envisioned when the database is first created.

Object-oriented systems:

- The application consists of a set of objects that contain data and the code to act on that data.
- These objects are data types defined by the programmer when the system is first created.
- These data types can have complex relationships with each other through techniques such as inheritance and encapsulation.
- The relationships between data types cannot be modified easily or created dynamically after the system is built.
- The instances (or objects) of these data types can hold references to other objects and can also be stored in collections for enumerating them easily.

Relational systems and object-oriented systems differ from each other fundamentally. These differences can be categorized as

- Differences in type systems
- Differences in language
- Differences in paradigms
- Differences in basic data entities

Differences in Type Systems

The type system of a relational database is relatively simple. The database vendor establishes the data types. These data types typically consist of simple numeric, date/time, text, and binary types. Developers cannot create their own types, as they can in the object model.

The data types in a relational database are used to define fields (or columns) in the database tables. The data that goes into each column must match the data type defined for that column.

For a relational database to perform properly, the data in the database tables must conform to the first normal form. The data in each row of each column must be atomic.

The object model is based on objects, each of which can contain many data attributes and the code to act on them. Objects are instances of these data types. The application developer can create new data types as needed.

Because of the complexity of objects, you cannot create usable objects that would be considered atomic types in the relational model. In other words, you cannot store objects in relational tables because objects have many attributes and do not fit the relational definition of an atomic data type.

In addition, the type system of a relational database is established by the database itself. Data of the supported types are the all that you can store in a relational database.

The basic properties of objects are encapsulation, inheritance, and polymorphism. There is no real support for encapsulation, inheritance, and polymorphism in the type systems of relational databases.

Differences in Language

In the relational model, SQL is the only language you can use, and SQL does everything. SQL code expresses the functionality of the database. SQL statements create the tables in which the data is stored. Relationships in the data are expressed through a combination of data in key fields and SQL code. All access to the data in the database is done through SQL.

Each relational database vendor implements SQL for its own database system. Each relational database system contains a SQL engine that executes its particular implementation of SQL. In relational systems, SQL is the only language you can use, and you can use only your database's particular brand of SQL.

SQL is not an object-oriented language. It has no object-oriented constructs or capabilities. There is no real support for encapsulation, inheritance, and polymorphism in SQL. SQL's sole purpose is to store and retrieve data in tables in a relational database.

In the object model, you can use a language such as C++, which supports object-oriented mechanisms such as encapsulation, inheritance, and polymorphism. Using C++, you can define your own data types. Instances of data types (objects) can contain multiple attributes as well as code to operate on those attributes. You can use mechanisms such as encapsulation, inheritance, and polymorphism to create complex hierarchies and networks of interrelated objects.

With C++, you can implement data models that are highly complex and intricate. However, C++ provides only primitive mechanisms for persisting and retrieving objects from a permanent store such as a hard disk.

SQL was built to store and retrieve data from tables in a database and has no object capabilities. C++ was built to create complex object systems and has extremely meager data storage capabilities.

These two languages are fundamentally different from each other, and no facility is built in to either language for interfacing with the other. The two languages are as different as English and music.

Differences in Paradigms

In the relational model, the database server dictates the model, the language, and the type system. Applications must use the database server on the database server's terms. If the application wants to use a model that is different from the model provided by the database, the application must provide the interface that maps between the models.

The necessity of using a database server on its terms has been the driving force behind the creation of database interfaces such as ODBC and OLE DB. These APIs are an effort to provide an interface between databases (which use the relational model) and C++ applications (which can use either the procedural model or the object model). At the very least, what these APIs do is translate between the data types in relational databases and data types in C++.

The relational model sees the world as a set of two-dimensional tables. Data that cannot be easily represented in a tabular form is difficult to fashion in a relational database.

The *field* is the basic unit of the relational database. The field is the smallest data element in a relational database. All data access in a relational database is performed on a field basis. All data access is done through SQL, which is built to work with fields.

The relational model is built to handle large quantities of data. If you can mold your data so that it conforms to the relational model, a relational database can manage enormous quantities of data quite effectively.

By contrast, object-oriented systems try to mimic objects in the real world. You don't have to try to mold your data to fit the object model. Instead, you create objects that mimic or reproduce the attributes and characteristics of real-life objects.

This is why the object model can handle more complexity than the relational model. With the relational model, you have to make the data fit the model. With the object model, you can make the model fit the data.

Differences in Basic Data Entities

A common mapping between the object model and the relational model is the direct mapping of a class to a relational table, as shown in Figure 13.1.

As you can see in Figure 13.1, a C++ class corresponds to a relational table. The data members of the class correspond to fields in the table. Instances of the class correspond to records in the table.

12

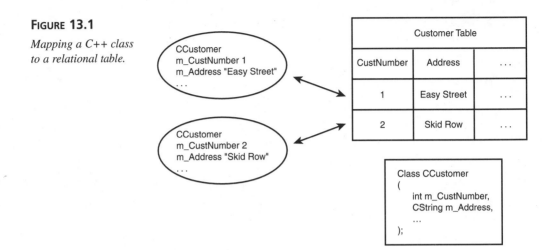

FIGURE 13.1

Mapping a C++ class to a relational table.

One thing that makes it difficult to interface the relational model with the object model is that the basic data entities of the two models do not correspond to each other. In the C++ object model, the basic data entity is the class. In the relational model, the basic data entity is the field. C++ classes do not map to fields. C++ classes map to tables.

C++ and SQL are built around their basic data entities. C++ is built to work with classes. SQL is built to work with fields. When you try to map between the two models, you end up having to make your SQL code work with tables and your C++ code work with the data members.

Object Databases Versus Relational Databases

With all the difficulty in trying to map between two such disparate models, it might seem better to simply use one model for all your application development. If you were to use an object database management system (ODBMS) instead of a relational database management system (RDBMS), you could avoid the muss and the fuss of mapping between the object model and the relational model.

However, some applications lend themselves to object databases, and some do not. Your choice of database technology should depend on the particular requirements of your application.

Object databases and relational databases each have specific characteristics, and each will provide particular capabilities in your applications.

As you learned in Day 1, "Choosing the Right Database Technology," C++ object databases directly support the type system of the C++ language. In other words, you can use a C++ object database to store instances of C++ classes right in the database.

Refer to Listing 1.5 to see how well and how easily C++ databases can integrate with C++ applications. By using simple overrides of a few C++ operators, you can easily persist and retrieve your C++ objects in an object database.

C++ object databases support

- The C++ type system, including classes that are defined by the application developer

- Inheritance, where the database understands the class hierarchy and manages the object store appropriately

- Polymorphism, where objects can be read from the database without knowing in advance their complete type information

- Object identities, where the database assigns a unique ID to each object, can readily retrieve each object by ID, and can determine whether the object has already been loaded into program memory

- References to other objects, where the database understands pointer references between objects and can store and retrieve linked objects appropriately

Using an object database means that your database will directly mirror the objects in your application. The objects in the database will be the same as the objects in your C++ code. Having a database that mirrors the objects in your C++ code is a two-edged sword with two potentially negative consequences.

First, the only data that can be retrieved from your database is the data encapsulated in the objects in your C++ source code. All the data, relationships, and uses of that data must be defined in the source code for your application. You might not be able to foresee all the potential uses of this data during your application development. This means that your application and its database could miss opportunities to be useful in the future.

Second, the only applications that will be able to access the database will be C++ programs that have an intimate knowledge of the objects in your application source code. The database will be a closed, proprietary database. This means that your database could miss opportunities to be useful in the future.

12

Note

> If your data is important to you, it is probably important to others, also. They will want access to the data through more than just your application.

It is important to remember what makes most database applications valuable is the information that they provide. Your application processes the data from the data source into
useful information and presents its view of the information. However, people will invariably want access to the data source themselves so that they can perform additional analyses for use in different applications.

Tip

Over time, applications often depreciate, while databases appreciate. The
value of a given application will decline as business needs change, but information is always valuable.

Because information is always valuable, its value often justifies the additional time and
effort required to place it in a relational database and create an object-to-relational mapping layer for your application.

Figure 13.2 illustrates the closed nature of a C++ object database and the openness and
availability of a relational database.

FIGURE 13.2

*The relative openness
of object databases
and relational data-
bases.*

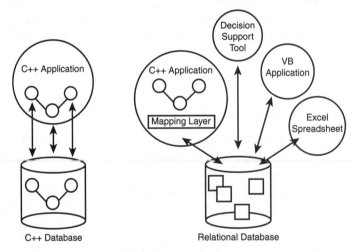

Some applications lend themselves to object databases, whereas other applications lend
themselves to relational databases. Whether an application should use an object database
or a relational database is largely determined by the need for flexibility in using the data.

A relational database will be open to other uses and other applications. It will also be
open to future versions of your application that might need to apply new analyses to data

from the database. A relational database enables you to create new relationships and collections of data that you had not envisioned at the time the database was first created. If your database conforms to the normal forms, you can simply write some new SQL code to create new relationships and to perform new analyses on the data. Relational databases provide a high degree of flexibility in defining new uses for the data.

Object databases lend themselves to applications in which the data model is complex and the relationships are well defined at the time the database is created. Some data models are too complex to be molded into a relational database. For specialized applications like this, you will need to take advantage of the object-oriented features of C++ to model the complexities of the data. An object database will enable you to easily persist those C++ objects to a data store. Defining new uses for that data and making that data available to other applications might not be easy, however.

The Costs and Benefits of Using Relational Databases with C++

To use a relational database with a C++ object-oriented application, you must create a mapping layer that translates between the object model and the relational model. Creating this mapping layer can be a costly endeavor in terms of time and effort, but can also result in significant benefits and synergies for your application.

The costs and difficulties of creating an object-to-relational mapping layer include

- Dealing with two semantic spaces where the logic for your application is manifested in two different programming models
- Creating two separate designs: a relational design and an object design
- Building an interface to translate between the relational model and the object model
- Developing the code in each object to communicate with the translation layer
- Your application not being able to handle highly complex data models because of the relational database and the need for the translation layer

Using a relational database with an object-oriented application enables you to

- Create new uses for the data in the database because the data itself is valuable.
- Use the strengths of the relational model, by using the relational database to obtain aggregate totals directly from the server without having to instantiate lots of objects and access each of the data members of each object.

12

- Use the strengths of the object model by using C++ objects to handle nested relationships that are difficult to model in a relational database, such as a bill of materials.

- Take advantage of the many server management tools available for relational database servers.

Techniques for Integrating Relational Databases with Object-Oriented C++ Programs

There are a few general strategies you can use to build an object-oriented application that uses a relational database.

Begin by Designing the Relational Database

In general, when you are creating the object-oriented application that uses a relational database, it is not a good idea to create the object model first and then try to map it to relational tables. Object models can be significantly more complex than relational models. If you build the object model first, you might not be able to create a relational model that matches it.

Even in relatively simple object models, an object might need to be stored across several relational tables, and many joins might be required to construct the objects. This can cause application performance to deteriorate.

Because the relational database is the foundation of your application, and because the relational model might ultimately limit the degree of complexity that your application can handle, you should begin with the design of the relational database.

If you are able to model the data for your application effectively in a relational database, you will know that your application can indeed handle the level of complexity that is required. Refer to Day 7, "Database Design," for information on designing relational databases.

Relational models tend to be simpler than object models. Therefore, entities in a relational model can usually be converted to entities in an object model quite readily. If you use this approach, the relational database schema becomes the basis for the object model.

Create Simple Object/Relational Mappings

Simple mappings between the relational and object models provide the best performance. Remember KISS (Keep It Simple, Sweetie).

Map Tables to Classes

As shown in Figure 13.1, the simplest and most straightforward mapping is to map a class to each relational table. The class absolutely must contain the primary key and foreign key fields from the table as data members and would probably contain data members for all the fields in the table as well.

Routines need to be developed for reading and persisting objects to and from the database. These routines will need to have intimate knowledge of the C++ classes and of the database. These routines could exist in each class, or they could be implemented in friend classes.

Encapsulating disconnected ADO Recordsets (which you learned about in Day 12, "Using Microsoft Transaction Server to Build Scalable Applications") in your classes can go a long way toward encapsulating the field data members, as well as the reading and persisting routines that each of your classes needs.

Use Primary and Foreign Keys to Map Relationships Between Objects

The simplest approach for defining a relationship between two objects is to embed the primary key of one object as a data member of the other object. (As you will recall from Day 2, "Tools for Database Development in Visual C++ Developer Studio," and Day 3, "Retrieving Data Through Structured Query Language (SQL)," a primary key from another table is called a *foreign key*.) This approach works well for one-to-one and one-to-many relationships.

For many-to-many relationships, it is necessary to have a link table in the database that contains the primary keys of the two related entities. This is illustrated in Figure 13.3.

Figure 13.3 shows a relational database schema. It has a Customers table, with CustomerNumber as the primary key, a Products table, with ProductNumber as the primary key, and a Purchases table, with a composite key of CustomerNumber and ProductNumber. The Purchases table's CustomerNumber and ProductNumber fields are also foreign keys from the other two tables. The Purchases table defines a many-to-many relationship between records in the Customers table and the Products table. A customer can purchase many products, and a product can be purchased by many customers.

Modeling many-to-many relationships in an object system might involve storing a collection (or disconnected Recordset) containing foreign keys inside the objects involved in the relationships.

12

FIGURE 13.3

Many-to-many relationships in a relational database.

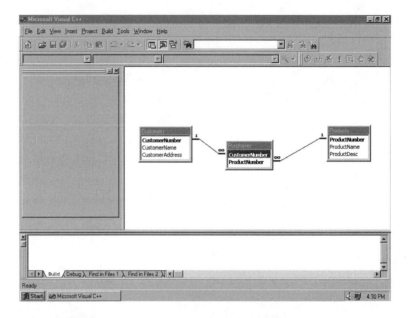

Don't Try to Map Object Inheritance in Relational Databases

Object inheritance is all but impossible to implement in relational databases. The best approach generally is to map only the leaf classes (the concrete classes at the bottom of the hierarchy) to tables in the database. For example, refer to the C++ classes declared in Listing 13.1

LISTING 13.1 CREATING C++ CLASSES WITH INHERITANCE

```
 1:  class shoe
 2:  {
 3:  public:
 4:    int sole;
 5:    int upper;
 6:  };
 7:
 8:  class athleticshoe : public shoe
 9:  {
10:  public:
11:    int tongue;
12:    int laces;
13:  };
14:
15:  class basketballshoe : public athleticshoe
```

```
16:    {
17:    public:
18:       int archsupport;
19:    };
```

In this case, it would probably be best to create a single table in the database, called BasketballShoes. The BasketballShoes table would contain fields for sole, upper, tongue, laces, and archsupport. You would also need to have an additional field for the primary key in the BasketballShoes table. You should also add a data member to the shoe class to hold the primary key from the database table.

If other classes derive from athleticshoe, such as crosstrainer, you would want to create a CrossTrainers table that contains fields for sole, upper, tongue, laces, the primary key, and whatever data members are in the crosstrainer class.

Sometimes, however, it might be necessary to get a count all of the shoes. That would mean that you would have to tell the database to count the records in the BasketballShoes table, count the records in the CrossTrainers table, and add those two numbers together. That would not be very elegant and will become uglier if the number of different types of shoes increases.

One possible solution is to create a Shoes table that contains fields for the primary key, sole, and upper and remove the sole and upper fields from the BasketballShoes table and the CrossTrainers table. You would need to add a field to the Shoes table to indicate the shoe type.

The idea then would be to add a record for each shoe to the Shoes table and also add a record to whatever additional table is appropriate.

For instance, a basketball shoe would have a record in the Shoes table, which indicates its sole and upper. It would also have a record in the BasketballShoes table that indicates its tongue, laces, and archsupport. The Shoes table and the BasketballShoes table would have a one-to-one relationship with each other, based on the primary key in each table. Likewise, a cross-trainer shoe would have a record in the Shoes table and a record in the CrossTrainers table.

The database schema would look like the one shown in Figure 13.4.

Data in the database would look something like the data shown in Figure 13.5.

As you can see in Figure 13.5, there are two records in the Shoes table and one record each in the BasketballShoes table and the CrossTrainers table.

12

FIGURE 13.4

A relational database schema to model a single level of inheritance.

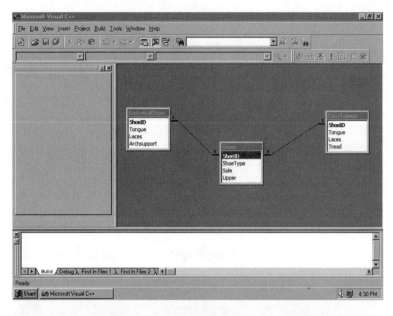

FIGURE 13.5

Data in a relational database schema that models a single level of inheritance.

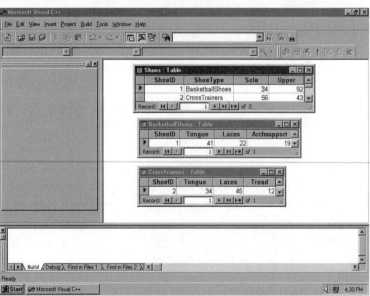

The class definition for the shoe type would have two data members added to it, as shown in Listing 13.2.

LISTING 13.2 CHANGES TO THE BASE Shoe CLASS

```
1:  class shoe
2:  {
3:  public:
4:    int shoeID;
5:    int shoeType;
4:    int sole;
5:    int upper;
6:  };
```

To get a count of all the shoes using this schema, you needn't count the records from multiple tables and add up the counts to get the total number of instances. You merely get a count of the records in the Shoes table.

This schema also enables you to look up a shoe by its ID (without knowing its type in advance) and discover its type. You can then use its type to execute the proper SQL query to perform a join with the appropriate table to get all the shoe's attributes.

Note that in relational database servers, you cannot use a variable for a table name in a compiled stored procedure. Therefore, in a stored procedure you could not put the name of the table from the ShoeType field in a variable and use that variable in the FROM clause of a SELECT statement to get the rest of the shoe's attributes. However, you could use that variable as a flag in a case-type or switch-type statement in a SQL query to execute the appropriate query to retrieve the attributes from the appropriate table.

As you can see, mapping object-oriented concepts to the relational model requires imagination and potentially lots of code.

Create a Live Object Cache

The biggest performance hit in database applications is database access. If you can minimize the number of times the application must access the database, the performance will be dramatically faster than if the application has to hit the database frequently.

To reduce the number of database hits, applications can use an object cache. The idea is to cache objects read from the database in RAM so that the next time the objects are needed, they can be read from the cache instead of the database.

Using a cache provides significant performance benefits because accessing data in RAM is much faster than accessing data in a database. A cache can also reduce the number of costly network roundtrips between a client application and a database server.

When the client application asks for an object, the translation layer should look to see whether that object already exists in the cache. The translation layer can use the primary

12

key as the object identifier. If the object is in the cache, the translation layer can give the application a pointer to the existing object without having to query the database. This is a huge optimization, but requires a bit of code.

Unfortunately, describing the code required to implement an object cache is beyond the scope of the book. Some technical white papers on this topic are available from programming tool vendors who specialize in this kind of work.

Use the Strengths of Both Models

Take advantage of objects when you can, and take advantage of the RDMS server when you can—use both.

For example, if you need to get the total number of instances in the database, do not count them by instantiating every object inside a loop in the client code. Instead, ask the database server to simply count the records and return the figure to the client application that needs it. The performance will be much better with this approach.

Another example is if you need to traverse a tree of nested objects, such as in a bill of materials. It would probably be inefficient to have the relational database server traverse the tree. Instead, you should instantiate the appropriate objects and have the object code traverse the tree.

Summary

Relational databases and object-oriented programming languages are powerful tools for managing data and writing software. Unfortunately, melding these two technologies is not straightforward. This is because relational databases were not designed to store objects, and objects were not designed to be stored in relational databases.

Melding an object-oriented application with a relational database requires you to write a translation layer between the object code and the relational database. Writing this translation layer can be difficult and time-consuming. However, your application and your database can derive great benefits from the synergies of these two technologies.

Q&A

Q **Are any software tools available that make the task of writing the translation layer easier?**

A Yes. There are independent software vendors who produce tools for just this purpose. You can find them by perusing the advertisements in the various relational database or C++ technical journals. You can also search the Web for terms such as *object database*, *RDBMS*, *ODBMS*, *persistence*, *mapping*, *translation layer*, and so on.

Q Aren't the vendors of relational databases extending their databases to support the storage of objects?

A Yes. Relational database vendors such as Informix, Oracle, and others have made efforts to extend their databases to support object storage. However, there is no clear indication of significant market acceptance of any of their approaches so far. Let the buyer beware.

Q Can't I just create a set of C++ base classes that talk to the translation layer and derive the classes in my application from these base classes to get easy communication with a relational database?

A If only it were that simple. One of the problems you will encounter is that a C++ base class will have trouble persisting an instance of a derived class, because the derived class might contain data that the base class does not know about. The derived classes themselves will probably need to participate in some way in their being persisted to the database.

Q What is Microsoft's approach to object storage?

A Microsoft does not seem to be trying to extend its SQL Server database to make it store objects. Rather, Microsoft has provided OLE DB as an object-oriented API that can communicate with relational as well as object-oriented data stores.

Workshop

12

The Workshop quiz questions test your understanding of today's material. (The answers appear in Appendix F, "Answers.") The exercises encourage you to apply the information you learned today to real-life situations.

Quiz

1. What prevents you from being able to store C++ objects in relational database fields?

2. Why can't you use SQL for object-oriented programming tasks?

3. What are the primary differences between C++ object databases and relational databases?

4. When designing an application that will use object and relational technology, where do you start?

5. What are the benefits of a live object cache?

Exercises

1. Write a SELECT statement that retrieves the shoe type based on the shoe ID from the Shoes table shown in Figure 13.5.

2. Write a SELECT statement that retrieves all the attributes of basketball shoes from the tables shown in Figure 13.5.

DAY **14**

Legacy Database APIs

Although considered legacy, the APIs that you will learn about today provide some valuable insight into the structured nature of developing database applications. Merriam Webster defines legacy as "being from the past," but you can hardly limit the content of this chapter to dusty old relics that need only cursory explanation. Although ODBC and DAO APIs might no longer be applicable in mainstream coding circles, the technology provides the foundation for most databases supported today.

Today you will

- Learn about the ODBC Architecture and API.
- Receive an introduction to the ODBC API calls.
- Learn about the DAO API.
- Receive an introduction to the DAO API calls.
- Explore the similarities and differences between ODBC and DAO.
- Understand the MFC wrapper classes for each API.

| **Note** | This book focuses primarily on the newer OLE DB (ADO) technologies, but remember that it is still in its infancy and OLE DB providers for many databases are still in development. With this in mind, it is easy to see the importance of understanding these legacy interfaces. Who knows, you might have to provide support for an application using these APIs. |

ODBC

Databases, and their programming APIs, come in a variety of flavors. Many different databases are available to the developer, and each has a specific set of programming APIs. SQL was an attempt to standardize the database programming interface. However, each database implementation of SQL varies slightly.

| **Note** | ANSI SQL-92 is the latest and most supported version of SQL, but the specification only provides a guideline. It is up to the database vendor to support all or part, as well as additional elements of the specification. |

ODBC was the first cohesive attempt to provide an application layer that would allow access to many different databases. ODBC provided a consistent specification for database vendors to develop ODBC drivers that applications could connect to. Applications can make function calls to the ODBC driver to send data to and receive data from a database, or in some cases multiple databases.

ODBC provides standardized access to databases. This enables the application developer to better concentrate on the application and its user interface and not have to worry about database specifics for every possible database on the market. To make things even simpler, the developers of ODBC decided to implement the API layer as a SQL translation mechanism. By passing ODBC SQL to an ODBC driver, the application can communicate with the database using SQL. Because there are many different flavors of SQL, ODBC provides a single flavor that would be translated into a flavor that the database could read.

Note You might have heard that an ODBC driver is Level X–compliant as related to the API. What does this mean? There are three levels of compliance:

Core Level—All drivers must support this level. Must be able to support connections, SQL statement preparation and execution, data set management, and transaction management.

Level 1—Must support all core-level compliance, as well as dialog-based connectivity, and be able to obtain driver/datasource information, which includes advanced connections using get and set options.

Level 2—Must support all the previous levels, plus the capability to list and search the datasource connections, and advanced query mechanisms and have support for scrollable cursors, among other things.

FIGURE 14.1

The ODBC architecture overview.

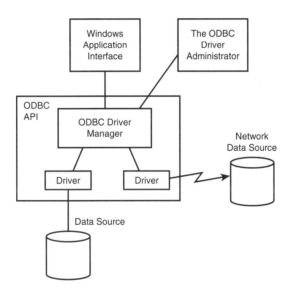

The ODBC Driver Administrator

The Driver Administrator is a Control Panel applet responsible for defining the ODBC data sources. A *data source* is simply the connection definition to a specific database. The connection definition contains information about the type of database, as well as the pertinent location information for the database. It then assigns a common name, called the Data Source Name (DSN), to the definition. The ODBC Driver Manager and drivers use the name as an index into the data source table to find the database-specific information.

14

Refer to Day 2, "Tools for Database Development in Visual C++ Developer Studio," for a description of the steps to define DSNs.

The ODBC Driver Manager

The ODBC Driver Manager is a set of functions that receives requests from the application and manages the subsequent driver actions for those requests. The primary functions of the Driver Manager are to load and unload database drivers and pass function calls to the driver. You might be thinking that this is a little bit of overkill. Why not just call the driver directly? Wouldn't it be faster? Just imagine, however, if the Driver Manager didn't exist, and your application was responsible for loading, unloading, and maintaining driver connections. Your application would be responsible for every possible driver configuration available, including the data source definitions. (Registry programming, anyone?) The Driver Manager makes the application developer's life easy, by compartmentalizing this functionality.

If you look a little closer at the Driver Manager, you see that it does perform some processing related to your application's requests. It implements some of the functions of the ODBC API. These include `SQLDataSources`, `SQLDrivers`, and `SQLGetFunctions`. It also performs some basic error checking, function call ordering, checking for null pointers, and validating of function arguments and parameters.

 Note

> Note that the ODBC API calls start with SQL. There is good reason for this. The ODBC API communicates through the SQL database interface instead of calling the database's lower layer. This is done primarily to add some level of consistency and standardization. ODBC does this by mapping ODBC SQL to the database driver's specific SQL standard. Hence, the naming convention for ODBC API function calls.

When the Driver Manager loads a driver, it stores the address of each function call in the driver and then tells the driver to connect to the data source. The application specifies which data source to connect to, using the data source name. The Driver Manager searches the DSN definition file for the particular driver to load. When the application is done, it tells the Driver Manager to disconnect (`SQLDisconnect`). The Driver Manager in turn hands this to the connected driver, which disconnects from the data source. The Driver Manager will unload the driver from memory only when the application frees the connection. The driver is kept in memory in case the application developer decides he needs further access.

The ODBC Driver

To adequately discuss every aspect of developing ODBC drivers would require another book. However, a cursory discussion is warranted. An ODBC driver must perform the following:

- Connecting to and disconnecting from the data source.
- Error checking not performed by the Driver Manager.
- Transaction management.
- Submitting SQL statements. This involves transposing the ODBC SQL to the SQL "speak" of the database that is supported.
- Processing data.

A driver can be defined as one of two types. A file-based driver accesses the physical data directly. A DBMS-based driver doesn't access the data directly but performs SQL functions on another wrapper. This wrapper is referred to as an engine. The database *engine* for Microsoft Access is the Jet engine.

Programmatic Sequence for the ODBC API

Now that I've discussed the architecture of the ODBC specification, let's take a look at how to develop an application by using the ODBC API.

 Note Although this section introduces certain steps in developing an ODBC application, it isn't intended to be a complete reference. Many ODBC programming references are available that provide in-depth discussions about the API function calls.

Before I discuss the API function calls, let's make some sense out of processing a data request. First you have to know where the data is (data source definition). Then you have to connect to it. After you are connected, you need to ask the data source for information. After the information is in hand, you process it and in most cases hand it back to the data source for safe keeping. When you are finished, you disconnect from the data source.

14

FIGURE 14.2

*The ODBC program-
matic flow chart.*

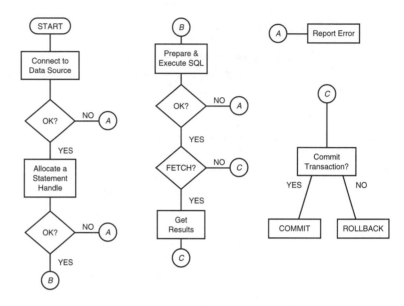

Step 1: Connect to a Data Source

First you have to acquire an environment handle. Do this by calling `SQLAllocHandle`. At this point you might be asking what an environment handle is. A *handle* is nothing more than a pointer to a special structure. The *environment* mentioned here is generally considered the system and data source information that the Driver Manager needs to store for the driver. You might also be asking why the Driver Manager does this, not the driver. Recall that you have not connected yet, and therefore the Driver Manager doesn't know what driver you will be using and will hold this information until it is needed. Some applications might need to connect to multiple databases. If the Driver Manager did not exist, the application would have to keep track of all the environment handles.

```
SQLHENV envHandle1;
SQLAllocHandle(SQL_HANDLE_ENV,SQL_NULL_HANDLE, &envHandle1);
```

After the Environment Handle is allocated, the application must then determine the attributes for the handle. The most important of these attributes is the ODBC version attribute (`SQL_ATTR_ODBC_VERSION`). Different versions of ODBC support different SQL statements and parameters. In some cases, it is important to determine the ODBC version that the driver supports and to know the differences.

Step 2: Allocate a Statement Handle

You can think of a statement in ODBC as being a SQL statement. As discussed earlier, ODBC communicates with the SQL interface to the database. The Driver Manager maps the ODBC SQL to the driver's SQL. However, a statement also carries attributes with it that define it in the context of the connection to the data source. This includes, but is certainly not limited to, the resultsets that the statement creates. Some statements require specific parameters in order to execute. These parameters are also considered attributes of the statement. Therefore, each statement has a handle that points to a structure that defines all the attributes of the statement. This handle also assists the driver in keeping track of the statements, because a multitude of statements can be associated with a connection.

Statement handles are defined and allocated similarly to the environment handle. However, the handle type is HSTMT. Remember that the Driver Manager allocates the handle structure and hands this off to the driver whenever the connection to the driver is made.

Step 3: Prepare and Execute the SQL Statements

Here's where things can differ depending on what the application requires. If an application just wants to read data from the database and display it to the user (that is, database viewer application), it won't require some of the more complex SQL UPDATEs, INSERTs, or DELETEs.

Note

> Because Day 15, "The ODBC API and the MFC ODBC Classes," discusses the binding of parameters, this section skips the explanation and demonstration of how to bind SQL parameters to the application's data. However, it is important to bear in mind that when you are preparing a SQL statement, this binding must take place.

There are two primary ways to prepare and execute the statements. The first is SQLExecDirect, which essentially executes a SQL statement in a single step. For many application requirements, this is okay. Some applications, however, might need to execute the same statement several times. To do this, you should use the SQLPrepare and then the SQLExecute functions. You call SQLPrepare once and then call SQLExecute as many times as necessary to execute the prepared statement.

Step 4: Get the Results

After the SQL statement has been executed, the application must be prepared to receive the data. The first part of this takes place when the application binds the results to the local variables. However, the results aren't passed back to the application directly. The application has to tell the Driver Manager that it is ready to receive the results. The application does this by calling SQLFetch. SQLFetch only returns one row of data.

14

Because the data is returned in columns, the application has to bind those columns with the SQLBindCol call. Essentially, you have to do the following statements, in order, to receive the resultset:

- SQLNumResultCols—Returns the number of columns.
- SQLDescribeCol—Gives you information about the data in the columns (name, data type, precision, and so on).
- SQLBindCol—Binds the column data to a variable in the application.
- SQLFetch—Gets the data.
- SQLGetData—Gets any long data.

First the application calls SQLNumResultCols to find out how many columns are in each record. SQLDescribeCol tells the application what type of data is stored in each column. The application has to bind the data to variables in its address space in order to receive the data. Then the application calls SQLFetch or SQLGetData to obtain the data. The application repeats this sequence for any remaining statements.

Step 5: Committing the Transaction

When all the statements have been executed and the data received, the application calls SQLEndTran to commit or roll back the transaction. This takes place if the commit mode is manual (application-directed). If the commit mode is set to be automatic (which is the default), the command will be committed whenever the SQL statement is executed.

Note

Think of a transaction as a single entity that contains any number of steps. If any step or part of the transaction fails, the entire transaction fails. A transaction can be either committed or rolled back. *Committed* indicates that every part/step of the transaction was successful. If any part fails, then the transaction is *rolled back*, which indicates that the original data is preserved. Changing the commit mode to manual will assist in preserving data integrity.

A Simple Example

Because Day 15 presents a more detailed example, this section shows only a portion of the program flow. This example will fetch the last name for all the records stored in the AddressBook database.

LISTING 14.1 A SIMPLE ODBC EXAMPLE TO RETRIEVE THE LAST NAME FROM THE ADDRESSBOOK DATABASE

```
 1:  #include <SQL.H>
 2:  #include <SQLEXT.H>
 3:  void CAddressBookView::OnFillListBox()
 4:  {
 5:    RETCODE rcode;
 6:
 7:    HENV henv1;
 8:    HDBC hdbc1;
 9:    HSTMT hstmt1;
10:
11:    char szFirstName[50];
12:    char szLastName[50];
13:    char szPhoneNum[20];
14:
15:    SDWORD sdODataLength;
16:    unsigned char conStringOut[256];
17:
18:    rcode = ::SQLAllocEnv(&henv1);
19:    if (rcode == SQL_SUCCESS)
20:    {
21:      rcode = ::SQLAllocConnect(henv1, & hdbc1);
22:      if (rcode == SQL_SUCCESS)
23:      {
24:          rcode = ::SQLDriverConnect(hdbc1, 0,
25:          (unsigned char *)"DSN=AddressBookDb",
26:          SQL_NTS, conStringOut, 256, NULL,
27:          SQL_DRIVER_NOPROMPT);
28:        if (rcode == SQL_SUCCESS)
29:        {
30:          rcode = ::SQLAllocStmt(hdbc1, &hstmt1);
31:          if (rcode == SQL_SUCCESS)
32:          {
33:              rcode = ::SQLExecDirect(hstmt1,
34:              (unsigned char *)
35:              "SELECT szLastName FROM AddressTable",
36:              SQL_NTS);
37:
38:            for (rcode = ::SQLFetch(hstmt1);
39:              rcode == SQL_SUCCESS;
40:              rcode = SQLFetch(hstmt1))
41:            {
42:              ::SQLGetData(hstmt1, 1, SQL_C_CHAR,
43:                szLastName, 50,  & sdODataLength);
44:              ::MessageBox(NULL, szLastName,
45:                " from AddressBookDb ", MB_OK);
46:            }
47:            ::SQLFreeStmt(hstmt1, SQL_DROP);
```

14

continues

LISTING **14.1**   CONTINUED

```
48:             }
49:             ::SQLDisconnect(hdbc1);
50:         }
51:         ::SQLFreeConnect(hdbc1);
52:     }
53:     ::SQLFreeEnv(henv1);
54:   }
55: }
```

Line 18 in Listing 14.1 calls SQLAllocEnv to instruct the ODBC Driver Manager to allocate variables for this application and return an environment handle. Line 21 calls
SQLAllocConnect, which tells the Driver Manager to allocate variables to manage a connection and to obtain a connection handle. Line 24 calls SQLDriverConnect to make a
connection to the AddressBookDb data source name.

You might have noticed that the section "Step One: Connect to a Data Source" discusses
using the SQLAllocHandle call to allocate any handle, including the environment handle.
SQLAllocHandle is an ODBC 3.0 call that replaces SQLAllocEnv, SQLAllocConnect, and
SQLDriverConnect. This was presented in this fashion to make the point that some legacy applications might contain ODBC version 2.0 code.

Notice the #include declarations:

```
#include <SQL.H>
#include <SQLEXT.H>
```

These #include files are required for any function implementing the ODBC API.

Obviously, this listing is very simplistic and is presented here to assist you in understanding programmatic flow of the ODBC API and working with databases.

MFC Wrappers for ODBC

As you can see from this simplistic listing, you must perform many steps just to obtain
some data from a database. There is an easier way.

Note   Although the MFC class library provides class wrappers for database functions, the ODBC API function calls are still accessible from within the application. Remember to include the SQL.H and the SQLEXT.H files.

The Microsoft Foundation Classes (MFC) are designed to make life simple for developers. They enable developers to create Windows-based applications without having to

know the underlying Windows architecture. Because database applications are an important aspect of managing data, Microsoft developed the MFC wrappers for the ODBC API. These classes present an object-oriented approach to using the ODBC API.

> **Note**
>
> The MFC class wrappers for the ODBC API make life easier on the programmer, linking to the MFC can make the application quite large. Depending on how the MFC library is linked with the application, the MFC DLLs might need to be distributed with the application's executable and libraries.

CDatabase

The CDatabase class represents a connection to the database. It contains the m_hdbc member variable, which represents the connection handle to a data source. To instantiate the CDatabase class, call the constructor and then the OpenEx or Open member function. This will initialize the environment handle and perform the connection to the data source. To close the connection, call the Close member function.

> **Note**
>
> The application can use the CDatabase class for more than just one database. If the application finishes using a database but needs to connect to another database, the same instance of the CDatabase class can be reused. Simply call Close to close the connection to the original data source; then call the OpenEx member function to a different data source.

There are member functions that perform work on the connected database. After the application is connected to a database, it is ready to begin work with the CDatabase instance. To begin a transaction, the CDatabase class contains a member function called BeginTrans. After all the processing is completed, the application will call the CommitTrans to commit the transaction or Rollback to rollback the changes. Both CommitTrans and Rollback are member functions of the CDatabase class.

> **Note**
>
> The CDatabase class also contains a member function that can execute SQL statements that don't require a returned resultset (recordset). This function member is the ExecuteSQL function.

14

There are also member functions that will return specific information about the data source. Some of these are

- GetConnect—Is the ODBC connection string used to connect the CDatabase instance to a specific data source.
- IsOpen—Indicates whether the CDatabase instance is connected to a data source.
- GetDatabaseName—Returns the data source name that the CDatabase instance is currently connected to.
- CanTransact—Indicates whether the data source uses transactions.

As you can see, the CDatabase class provides the C++ programmer with an object-oriented interface to the ODBC environment and connection API calls.

CRecordSet

The CRecordSet class defines the data that is received from or sent to a database. The recordset could be defined as an entire table or simply one column of a table. The recordset is defined by its SQL statement.

The m_hstmt member variable of the CRecordSet contains the statement handle for the SQL handle that defines the recordset. The m_nFields member variable holds the number of fields in the recordset. The m_nParams member variable holds the number of parameters used to define the recordset. The recordset is connected to the data source through a pointer to the CDatabase object. This pointer is the CRecordSet member variable m_pDatabase.

Other member variables are defined in the CRecordSet class declaration. The m_strFilter member variable defines the WHERE clause used in the SQL statement. The m_strSort member variable is used if the SQL statement uses an ORDER BY clause.

There are many ways that recordsets can be opened or defined. CRecordSet has an Open member function that will actually perform the recordset query. The application can format a SQL SELECT statement to pass in the Open function member of the CRecordSet class.

The first parameter for the Open member function defines how the recordset will be opened. You can define and open a recordset by the following three methods:

- CRecordSet::dynaset—Dynamic recordsets that support bi-directional cursors and synchronize with the underlying data of the database.
- CRecordSet::snapshot—A static snapshot of the table to be queried. Doesn't reflect any other changes made to the table from other sources. The application must re-query the database to obtain updates to the recordset. Supports bidirectional cursors.
- CRecordSet::forwardOnly—Similar to snapshot but doesn't support bidirectional, scrollable cursors.

DAO

In 1995, Microsoft introduced the DAO API. This API was developed as the API for the Microsoft Jet Database engine. The Microsoft Jet Database Engine is the database engine for Microsoft Access. The Jet Database Engine contains an ODBC interface that enables both direct and indirect ODBC access to other databases.

As opposed to being a layered API similar to ODBC, DAO was based on OLE Automation objects. Coding directly to the ODBC API was a matter of calling API functions directly within the application or using the MFC wrappers. This wasn't the case with DAO objects. If the programmer is proficient in COM, programming directly to the API can be more convenient. Not all programmers are proficient with COM, so Microsoft developed DAO wrappers within the Microsoft Foundation Classes (MFC). To ease the transition from one API to another, the MFC classes are similar to the MFC ODBC wrappers.

Not only does the DAO API provide an object-oriented method for accessing a database, but it also provides the capability for database management. DAO has the capability to modify the database schema. It does this by enabling the application to define queries and table structures within the database and then applying SQL statements against those structures. New relationships and table unions can also be defined from within the DAO API.

This section presents pertinent information for understanding the DAO objects and introduces key steps in working with these objects. After this introduction, you will explore the MFC wrapper classes for the DAO objects.

The Jet Database Engine

Before you jump into the DAO API object description, let's take a quick look at the underlying engine that DAO was created for. The Jet Engine was primarily developed as the engine for the Microsoft Access database. Microsoft, understanding that a proprietary database might not succeed, decided to add two types of ODBC support to the engine.

DAO's Direct ODBC is similar in nature to pass-through SQL. ODBC calls are passed through the engine and handed directly to the ODBC Driver Manager. Indirect ODBC requires that the ODBC layer of the Jet Engine process the request. Access, for example, supports SQL statements.

The Jet Engine is also designed to interface to ISAM (indexed-sequential access files) as shown in Figure 14.3. If an ISAM driver exists for the file database, it can be accessed through the ISAM layer of the Jet engine.

14

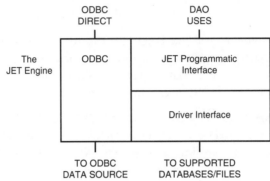

FIGURE **14.3**

The Jet Database Engine interface diagram.

CdbDBEngine: **The Root of It All**

The relationship between the DAO classes is shown in Figure 14.4.

FIGURE **14.4**

DAO class diagram.

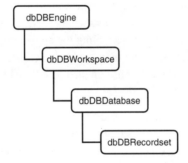

Note that the classes shown in Figure 14.4 are not MFC classes; they are classes provided in the DAO SDK.

The CdbDBEngine class is the base class for the DAO classes. It contains and controls all other DAO classes. You must create an instance of this class before any connections to the Jet database can be performed. The DBEngine class is the class that contains the logic to connect to the Jet database engine. For an application to connect to the Jet database, it must create a DBEngine object.

CdbDBWorkspace

Directly underneath the CdbDBEngine object is the CdbDBWorkspace object. The workspace object manages the database. Remember that DAO provides the ability to modify the actual database schema. This is done through the database object. The database that the workspace owns can contain QueryDefs and TableDef objects that can be used to modify the database structure. The workspace object also contains group and user objects that further define the database permissions structures, and allows the application to add or modify them.

CdbDBDatabase

The workspace might contain any number of databases that it is connected to. A typical application can access one database for employee information and another for payroll information to create a history report. This would be done by instantiating the CdbDBDatabase object for each database and assigning it to the workspace already created to manage the payroll history reporting.

CdbDBRecordsets

CdbDBRecordsets are similar in nature to the ODBC wrapper for the ODBC recordset. For each SQL statement that is executed on any database, a recordset must exist to receive the data. Therefore, a CdbDBRecordset object will be instantiated for each query or action.

MFC Wrappers for DAO

If you look at the MFC wrapper classes supplied for DAO, you will notice that they are similar in some respects to the wrappers for ODBC. This was done to aid developers in migrating ODBC applications that connected to databases designed to use the Jet engine. Because the object model for DAO was developed with some of this in mind, some correlation exists between the DAO API and its corresponding MFC wrapper classes. Because the DAO API is object-oriented, the wrapper classes are much easier to comprehend.

Caution

> The DAO API provides database security through the groups object and the users object. The MFC wrapper, CDaoDatabase, doesn't grant access to these objects, so a security risk could exist. See Technote 54 in the Visual C++ documentation for details.

CDaoWorkspace

The CDaoWorkspace encapsulates the CdbDBWorkspace object. However, it doesn't stop there. The application uses the workspace to manage the database itself.

14

CDaoDatabase

The CDaoDatabase wrapper class encapsulates the CdbDBDatabase object, and all connection information is contained within it. An application will declare and instantiate the CDaoDatabase and then store this connection information within the application for all processing related to the database.

CDaoRecordSet

Like the ODBC MFC wrapper class, the recordset is managed and maintained by the CDaoRecordSet class. There are many similarities to the ODBC wrapper, and at first glance it would appear that applications programmatically perform the same functions.

A Simple Example

Listing 14.2 merely shows the general sequence for developing database applications; it doesn't really do anything.

LISTING 14.2 AN EXAMPLE SHOWING THE GENERAL SEQUENCE FOR DEVELOPING DATABASE APPLICATIONS

```
 1:   #include <stdafx.h>
 2:   #include <afxdao.h>
 3:
 4:   void CAddressBookView::OnFillListBox()
 5:   {
 6:     CString lpszSQL_SELECT_ALL = "SELECT * FROM ADDRESSES";
 7:     CString message;
 8:     int nRetCode = 1;
 9:
10:     CString filename = "c:\\tysdbvc\\AddressBook.mdb";
11:
12:     // construct new database
13:     CDaoDatabase     *ppDatabase = new CDaoDatabase;
14:
15:     if (ppDatabase == NULL) return -1; // fatal error
16:
17:     try
18:     {
19:       (*ppDatabase)->Open(fileName);
20:     }
21:     catch (CDaoException *e)
22:     {
23:       // create a message to display
24:       message = _T("Couldn't open database—Exception: ");
25:       message += e->m_pErrorInfo->m_strDescription;
26:       AfxMessageBox(message);
```

```
27:        nRetCode = -1;
28:    }
29:
30:    CDaoRecordSet *ppRecSet = new CDaoRecordSet(ppDatabase);
31:
32:    try
33:    {
34:        ppRecSet->Open(dbOpenSnapshot,lpszSQL_SELECT_ALL,dbReadOnly);
35:    }
36:    catch(CDaoException *e)
37:    {
38:        // create a message to display
39:        message = _T("Couldn't open RecordSet—Exception: ");
40:        message += e->m_pErrorInfo->m_strDescription;
41:        AfxMessageBox(message);
42:        nRetCode = -1;
43:    }
44:    }
```

Line 19 of Listing 14.2 attempts to open the database file (in this case, an Access database file). Line 34 opens a recordset defined by

```
SELECT * FROM ADDRESSES
```

This SQL statement will retrieve all columns in the Addresses table of the AddressBook.mdb Access database. Notice the dbReadOnly flag passed as the last parameter. Table 14.1 shows some of the option flags available in the DAO MFC wrapper CDaoRecordSet wrapper class.

TABLE 14.1 OPTIONS TO RECORDSETS

Flag	Description
dbAppendOnly	Allows additional records but doesn't permit existing records to be modified. (Dynasets only.)
dbDenyWrite	Prevents data from being modified while a recordset is active. (All)
dbDenyRead	Basically locks the tables and doesn't allow records to be read by other applications or users while the recordset is active. (Tables)
dbSQLPassThrough	Passes the SQL statement directly to the data source (ODBC). The DAO API won't perform any processing on the SQL statement. (Dynaset and snapshots)
DbForwardOnly	Allows the recordset to have forward-scrolling only. (Snapshot)
DbFailOnError	The workspace will roll back any changes made if an error occurs during the recordset processing. (All)

14

One thing that you will notice from Listing 14.2 is that the recordset was opened, but the data wasn't mapped to any application variables. This is referred to as *data binding* and is covered in the next chapter.

Again, this example is extremely simplistic, but it's presented to show the object-oriented nature of the DAO MFC wrapper classes. In the next chapter you will actually build the simple Address Book application. You will build it twice, once for the ODBC wrapper classes and once for the MFC wrapper classes.

| Tip | It is always good practice to use try/catch blocks for processing errors. |

Summary

ODBC was the first good attempt at shielding the application programmer from all the nitty-gritty of developing database applications. DAO was the follow-up API aimed at closely matching the object-oriented programming nature of C++ with the relational nature of databases.

You might run across older applications that use the ODBC or DAO APIs. It helps to gain enough understanding of the ODBC architecture and the API to be able to support legacy applications.

Today you the big picture of the two APIs. By understanding the environment of these APIs, you become more proficient at migrating to the newer OLE DB and ADO technologies.

Q&A

Q How do I determine which MFC wrapper classes to use?

A The DAO API is designed to sit on top of and interface with the Jet database engine. It is optimized for this. However, it enables the programmer to access other data sources through the ODBC layer of the engine. This pass-through method is slower than using the ODBC API directly. If the database is a Jet engine database or a local ISAM database, use DAO; otherwise, use ODBC.

Q Why is the dbDBEngine object not directly mapped into the MFC DAO wrapper classes?

A The MFC DAO wrapper class for CDaoWorkspace encapsulates this functionality. The concept of the workspace is to present a transaction manager.

Q Can I create a data source directly from my application?

A Yes. The ODBC API function `SQLConfigDataSource` will do this for you. The function takes four arguments. The first argument is the handle of the parent window. The second argument is used to designate whether you want to add a DSN (`ODBC_ADD_DSN`) or configure an existing one (`ODBC_CONFIG_DSN`). You might also remove a DSN by passing `ODBC_REMOVE_DSN`. The third argument names the driver, whereas the fourth argument names the data source.

Q Does the ODBC API have any built-in exception handling?

A Yes. Typically, the application should perform all database processing inside `try/catch` blocks. Both the ODBC and the DAO will throw the `CDBException` error. The application must provide the error handling inside the catch block.

Workshop

The Workshop quiz questions test your understanding of today's material. (The answers appear in Appendix F, "Answers.") The exercises encourage you to apply the information you learned today to real-life situations.

Quiz

1. Name the MFC wrapper class that encapsulates the `SQLConnect` logic.
2. What is the environment handle used for, and who maintains it?
3. What is the root object in the DAO API? Does it have a corresponding MFC wrapper class?
4. What parameter should be passed to the recordset for it to be dynamic and allow the data in the recordset to be synchronized with the data source?

Exercises

1. Use the OLE/COM Object Viewer to find the DAO classes on your system. View the type library to see all the methods exposed by the DAO classes.

14

WEEK 2

In Review

On Day 8, you learned some power tools that relational database servers have to offer. You learned about transactions, triggers, aggregate functions, and views. These tools can enable you to build highly advanced database applications. Transactions enable reliable changes to the data. Triggers make the database react automatically to changes in the data. Aggregate functions cause the bulk of the data processing to happen at the server. Finally, views enable you to customize the way people see your database.

In Day 9's lesson, you learned the basics of COM. You learned that COM is based on C++ abstract base classes, called *interfaces*. You also learned that the COM libraries (part of the Win32 API) provide a way to create instances of classes indirectly, thereby avoiding any build-time dependencies between clients and servers. Traditional DLLs are good for sharing common code among concurrently running applications. However, to build real component-based software, the capabilities afforded by COM are essential.

You learned in Day 10 how to program Microsoft's database client technologies. Several database client technologies are available to C++ programmers. Each technology has its own strengths and weaknesses, and each one has an historical context that defines how it relates to the other technologies. The two database client technologies that will be updated and improved on in the future are OLE DB and ADO. ADO offers a good balance of code size, performance, and ease of use. You can best understand the ADO object model by examining the MSADO15.TLH file and the MSADO15.TLI files, coupled with the ADO documentation.

On Day 11, you learned how multitier applications promise easier updates and mainte-nance than traditional client/server applications. The tools for building multitier applica-tions have evolved rapidly over the past few years. XML is a technology that in the future will be widely used to transmit data in multitier applications. Some of the more recent developments, such as ActiveX controls and RDS, promise to enable client/server-type development in an intranet environment.

In Day 12's lesson, you learned that the infrastructure necessary for multitier applica-tions is difficult and time-consuming to build yourself. MTS can do most of that work for you. MTS components are COM DLLS that you can build with ATL. In your compo-nent code, you can create ADO Recordsets from database queries and send the Recordsets to applications on the client tier. IE4 can host ActiveX controls and, with RDS, can instantiate and communicate over COM, DCOM, and HTTP with MTS com-ponents that you build.

You learned, on Day 13, that melding an object-oriented application with a relational database requires you to write a translation layer between the object code and the rela-tional database. This translation layer can be difficult and time-consuming to write. However, your application and your database can derive great benefit from the synergies of these two technologies.

On Day 14, you learned a history lesson in technology progression. ODBC was the first good attempt at shielding the application programmer from all the nitty-gritty associated with developing database applications. DAO was the follow-up API that was aimed at closely matching the object-oriented programming nature of C++ with the relational nature of databases. Hopefully, after reading this chapter, you can come closer to under-standing the big picture of the two APIs. By understanding the steps and environment of these APIs, you will become more proficient at migrating to the newer OLE DB and ADO technologies.

Week 3

At a Glance

This week, you expand your understanding of database programming by learning additional database APIs.

- Day 15   You learn to use the ODBC API and the MFC ODBC classes.
- Day 16   You receive an introduction to OLE DB, the latest and most powerful database API from Microsoft.
- Day 17   You learn to connect with a data source by using the OLE DB API.
- Day 18   You learn to retrieve data from a data source by using OLE DB.
- Day 19   You learn to scroll through data that you retrieve from a data source.
- Day 20   You learn OLE DB properties, transactions, and the Index object.
- Day 21   You learn mechanisms for integrating error handling into your OLE DB applications.

15

16

17

18

19

20

21

The ODBC API and the MFC ODBC Classes

Yesterday, you explored the ODBC and DAO APIs and were introduced to the MFC wrapper classes for both. Today, you will create a simple application using the wrapper classes and discuss the data binding that takes place. You will also look at what the API is doing through the use of the wrapper classes.

Today you will

- Bind data with the ODBC API.
- Implement ODBC MFC wrappers in an application.
- Bind data with the DAO API.
- Implement DAO MFC wrappers in an application.

The Address Book

This chapter focuses on using the wrapper classes that MFC provides for the ODBC and DAO APIs. You do this by creating a simple application to list addresses for your friends, like the one in Figure 15.1. The database that you will be using was created with Access 97 and will contain a single table (Addresses). This table will contain the fields shown in Figure 15.1:

FIGURE 15.1

The Address book table (Addresses) structure.

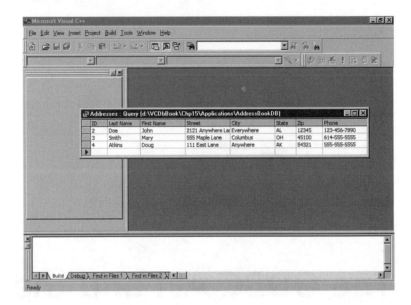

To simplify things, you examine the application development code, using the MFC AppWizard for creating your data bindings. After you do this, you will take a closer look at how the table data can be manually bound to the application's variables.

Using the MFC ODBC Wrapper Classes

Day 14, "Legacy Database APIs," provides an introduction to the ODBC API and to the MFC wrappers for the API. One important item that Day 14 doesn't discuss is the CRecordView class. This class doesn't really wrap the API so much as it creates a go-between data-binding class that fits into the MFC's Document/View architecture. CRecordView is derived from the CFormView class, which ultimately is derived from CView. The view classes provide the user interface mechanisms to display the data and handle Windows messages. The CRecordSet and CDatabase classes are closely coupled with CRecordView, as you will see in your application code. It contains a member variable to handle the actual data cursor. It does this in the form of a record pointer. If you have had the opportunity to program database applications the hard way, you will definitely appreciate this class. The CRecordView also contains a pointer to the CRecordSet class.

Note

If you are unfamiliar with MFC and the MFC Document/View architecture, the following sections might appear to be a broad step from the explanation of the API to the actual implementation of the application. This chapter does this to highlight certain aspects of implementing database applications; however, it does so using the most widely used approach.

15

Let's jump right in and create the sample application.

Creating the Application

Before the AppWizard creates the application, the database and ODBC data source must exist. You can use the Control Panel ODBC applet to determine whether a database and ODBC data source exist for the targeted application.

Note

The application code is included on the accompanying CD-ROM, which includes the AddressBook database.

From the File menu, select New to start the MFC AppWizard. The screen shown in Figure 15.2 appears. Based on your system file structure and where your database and application files reside, fill in the appropriate information shown in Figure 15.2. In this case, you are creating an executable that will be MFC-based.

FIGURE 15.2

MFC AppWizard Step 1: Creating the application.

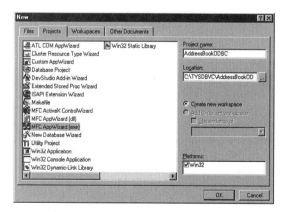

Figure 15.3 shows the screen where you specify the database support for your application. At this point, it is asking whether you want database support. (You can choose to skip this selection, by choosing None, and then put it in later.) Select Database View

Without File Support. After you select the database support, the next step is to set the data source. For your example, select ODBC as shown in Figure 15.3.

FIGURE 15.3

*MFC AppWizard Step
2: Defining database
requirements.*

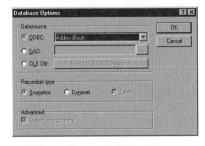

You then select the table(s) that you would like to have support for.

The AppWizard will build the data relationships for the recordset that relates to the tables you select. For every table that you select, the wizard will create a `CRecordSet`-based class that wraps the table. You'll come back to this when you look at the code. Figure 15.4 shows the classes that AppWizard will create.

FIGURE 15.4

*MFC AppWizard Step
6: Files created.*

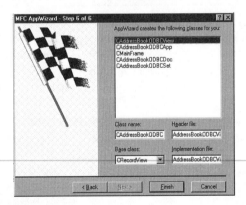

You only need to concern yourself with the `CAddressBookODBCView` class and the `CAddressBookODBCSet` class. These two classes contain the information that will help you understand how the data is passed from the data source to the application. Listing 15.1 is the definition file for the `CAddressBookODBCSet` class.

LISTING 15.1   THE `CAddressBookODBCSet` CLASS DECLARATION

```
1:  // AddressBookODBCSet.h : interface of the
2:  // CAddressBookODBCSet class
3:  /////////////////////////////////////////////////////////////
```

```
 4:
 5: #if !defined(AFX_ADDRESSBOOKODBCSET_H__D21600E1_4140_
    ➥11D2_9D78_000000000000__INCLUDED_)
 6: #define AFX_ADDRESSBOOKODBCSET_H__D21600E1_
    ➥4140_11D2_9D78_000000000000__INCLUDED_
 7:
 8: #if _MSC_VER >= 1000
 9: #pragma once
10: #endif // _MSC_VER >= 1000
11:
12: class CAddressBookODBCSet : public CRecordset
13: {
14: public:
15:   CAddressBookODBCSet(CDatabase* pDatabase = NULL);
16:   DECLARE_DYNAMIC(CAddressBookODBCSet)
17:
18:   // Field/Param Data
19:   //{{AFX_FIELD(CAddressBookODBCSet, CRecordset)
20;   long   m_ID;
21:   CString   m_Last_Name;
22:   CString   m_First_Name;
23:   CString   m_Street;
24:   CString   m_City;
25:   CString   m_State;
26:   long   m_Zip;
27:   CString   m_Phone;
28:   //}}AFX_FIELD
29:
30:   // Overrides
31:   // ClassWizard generated virtual function overrides
32:   //{{AFX_VIRTUAL(CAddressBookODBCSet)
33:   public:
34:   virtual CString GetDefaultConnect();  // Default connection string
35:   virtual CString GetDefaultSQL();   // default SQL for Recordset
36:   virtual void DoFieldExchange(CFieldExchange* pFX);  // RFX support
37:   //}}AFX_VIRTUAL
38:
39:   // Implementation
40:   #ifdef _DEBUG
41:     virtual void AssertValid() const;
42:     virtual void Dump(CDumpContext& dc) const;
43:   #endif
44:
45: };
46:
47: //{{AFX_INSERT_LOCATION}}
48: // Microsoft Developer Studio will insert additional
49: // declarations immediately before the preceding line.
50:
51: #endif // !defined(AFX_ADDRESSBOOKODBCSET_H__D21600E1_
    ➥4140_11D2_9D78_000000000000__INCLUDED_)
```

Notice that line 19 is where the data mapping starts. The AFX_FIELD declaration indicates that this is field data for the recordset. Just think of the number of SQLBindColumn calls that you would have to make to declare each field if the table were very large.

The MFC DDX/DDV message-handling mechanism defines the connection between the table column data and the applications variable used to present that data. The other part of the binding that takes place here is the actual data attribute definition. The CString class is a wrapper for a C character string. The CString class is mapped to the character data represented in the columns. The long is mapped to the data type for the Zip code in the Access database. In this case, it is defined as an integer.

Let's take a look at the CRecordView-based class. Here you see the implementation file for the CAddressBookODBCView class in Listing 15.2.

LISTING 15.2   THE CAddressBookODBCView CLASS DECLARATION

```
 1:    // AddressBookODBCView.h : interface of the
 2:    // CAddressBookODBCView class
 3:    /////////////////////////////////////////////////////
 4:
 5:    #if !defined(AFX_ADDRESSBOOKODBCVIEW_H__D21600DF_4140_
       ➥11D2_9D78_000000000000__INCLUDED_)
 6:    #define AFX_ADDRESSBOOKODBCVIEW_H__D21600DF_4140_11D2_
       ➥9D78_000000000000__INCLUDED_
 7:
 8:    #if _MSC_VER >= 1000
 9:    #pragma once
10:    #endif // _MSC_VER >= 1000
11:
12:    class CAddressBookODBCSet;
13:
14:    class CAddressBookODBCView : public CRecordView
15:    {
16:    protected: // create from serialization only
17:        CAddressBookODBCView();
18:        DECLARE_DYNCREATE(CAddressBookODBCView)
19:
20:    public:
21:        //{{AFX_DATA(CAddressBookODBCView)
22:        enum{ IDD = IDD_ADDRESSBOOKODBC_FORM };
23:        CAddressBookODBCSet* m_pSet;
24:            // NOTE: the ClassWizard will add data members here
25:        //}}AFX_DATA
26:
27:    // Attributes
28:    public:
29:        CAddressBookODBCDoc* GetDocument();
30:
31:    // Operations
32:    public:
```

15

```
33:
34:     // Overrides
35:         // ClassWizard generated virtual function overrides
36:         //{{AFX_VIRTUAL(CAddressBookODBCView)
37:     public:
38:         virtual CRecordset* OnGetRecordset();
39:         virtual BOOL PreCreateWindow(CREATESTRUCT& cs);
40:     protected:
41:         virtual void DoDataExchange(CDataExchange* pDX);     // DDX/DDV
                                                                 // support
42:         virtual void OnInitialUpdate(); // called first time after
                                             // construct
43:         virtual BOOL OnPreparePrinting(CPrintInfo* pInfo);
44:         virtual void OnBeginPrinting(CDC* pDC, CPrintInfo* pInfo);
45:         virtual void OnEndPrinting(CDC* pDC, CPrintInfo* pInfo);
46:         //}}AFX_VIRTUAL
47:
48:     // Implementation
49:     public:
50:         virtual ~CAddressBookODBCView();
51:     #ifdef _DEBUG
52:         virtual void AssertValid() const;
53:         virtual void Dump(CDumpContext& dc) const;
54:     #endif
55:
56:     protected:
57:
58:     // Generated message map functions
59:     protected:
60:         //{{AFX_MSG(CAddressBookODBCView)
61:             // NOTE - The ClassWizard will add and remove member
                 // functions here.
62:             //    DO NOT EDIT what you see in these blocks of generated
                 //    code!
63:         //}}AFX_MSG
64:         DECLARE_MESSAGE_MAP()
65:     };
66:
67:     #ifndef _DEBUG  // debug version in AddressBookODBCView.cpp
68:     inline CAddressBookODBCDoc* CAddressBookODBCView::GetDocument()
69:        { return (CAddressBookODBCDoc*)m_pDocument; }
70:     #endif
71:
72:     /////////////////////////////////////////////////////////////////
73:
74:     //{{AFX_INSERT_LOCATION}}
75:     // Microsoft Developer Studio will insert additional declarations
76:     // immediately before the preceding line.
77:
78:     #endif // !defined(AFX_ADDRESSBOOKODBCVIEW_H__D21600DF_4140_
        ➥11D2_9D78_000000000000__INCLUDED_)
```

The `CAddressBookODBCView` class contains quite a few more function members, but most are related to the Document/View architecture of MFC. Notice on line 23 that you have a pointer to the `CAddressBookODBCSet` class in the `CAddressBookODBCView` class. This pointer is the primary link between the API wrapping and the Document/View architecture. The `CAddressBookODBCView` class contains a document that is the application's data keeper. Data is passed between the view and dialog classes and the GUI via the MFC DDX/DDV data exchange mechanisms. The view gets access to the document directly via `GetDocument`; the document pumps notifications (and hints) to the view via the `CDocument::UpdateAllViews`/`CView;;OnUpdate` coupling. For data to be bound from a database to the application, the application's view must know about the data structure. The `m_pSet` pointer is the mechanism that accomplishes this. Let's take a look at what the `Document` class contains. Notice that the document contains the `RecordSet` (line 21).

Something very interesting happens in Listing 15.3. By looking at the wrapper declarations for your application, you have learned how the data binding takes place. The document class represents the application's memory. The view class is your window into that data. But you are working with databases, and the data in this case is stored on disk. The `RecordSet` is the API wrapper that will provide the link to the data in the database. By containing the recordset, the document class essentially maps the data into the application's memory.

LISTING 15.3 THE `CAddressBookODBCDoc` CLASS DECLARATION

```
 1:  // AddressBookODBCDoc.h : interface of the CAddressBookODBCDoc
     // class
 2:  //
 3:  /////////////////////////////////////////////////////////////////////
 4:
 5:  #if !defined(AFX_ADDRESSBOOKODBCDOC_H__D21600DD_4140_11D2_9D78_
     ➡000000000000__INCLUDED_)
 6:  #define AFX_ADDRESSBOOKODBCDOC_H__D21600DD_4140_11D2_9D78_
     ➡000000000000__INCLUDED_
 7:
 8:  #if _MSC_VER >= 1000
 9:  #pragma once
10:  #endif // _MSC_VER >= 1000
11:
12:
13:  class CAddressBookODBCDoc : public CDocument
14:  {
15:  protected: // create from serialization only
16:      CAddressBookODBCDoc();
17:      DECLARE_DYNCREATE(CAddressBookODBCDoc)
18:
```

```
19:     // Attributes
20:     public:
21:         CAddressBookODBCSet m_addressBookODBCSet;
22:
23:     // Operations
24:     public:
25:
26:     // Overrides
27:         // ClassWizard generated virtual function overrides
28:         //{{AFX_VIRTUAL(CAddressBookODBCDoc)
29:         public:
30:         virtual BOOL OnNewDocument();
31:         //}}AFX_VIRTUAL
32:
33:     // Implementation
34:     public:
35:         virtual ~CAddressBookODBCDoc();
36:     #ifdef _DEBUG
37:         virtual void AssertValid() const;
38:         virtual void Dump(CDumpContext& dc) const;
39:     #endif
40:
41:     protected:
42:
43:     // Generated message map functions
44:     protected:
45:         //{{AFX_MSG(CAddressBookODBCDoc)
46:             // NOTE - The ClassWizard will add and remove member
47:             // functions here. DO NOT EDIT what you see in these
48              // blocks of generated code !
49:         //}}AFX_MSG
50:         DECLARE_MESSAGE_MAP()
51:     };
52:
53:     //////////////////////////////////////////////////////////////////////
54:
55: //{{AFX_INSERT_LOCATION}}
56: // Microsoft Developer Studio will insert additional declarations
57: // immediately before the previous 57: line.
58:
59:     #endif // !defined(AFX_ADDRESSBOOKODBCDOC_H__D21600DD_4140_11D2_
        ➡9D78_000000000000__INCLUDED_)
```

You have now created an application that contains the ODBC wrappers that you will need to interface to your database. However, the AppWizard really can't determine what you plan to do with the data. If the application were to be built and executed at this point, you would see something similar to Figure 15.5.

FIGURE 15.5

*The Address Book
ODBC application.
First run.*

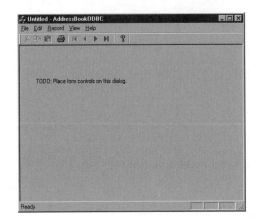

For the application to do any real work, you first have to create controls for the data to be displayed in.

Getting Data

Look at Listing 15.4 to see how much the AppWizard really does for you.

LISTING 15.4   THE `OnInitialUpdate` IMPLEMENTATION

```
1:    void CAddressBookODBCView::OnInitialUpdate()
2:    {
3:        m_pSet = &GetDocument()->m_addressBookODBCSet;
4:        CRecordView::OnInitialUpdate();
5:    }
```

The `OnInitialUpdate` function member of your view class will set your recordset pointer. Notice that it gets the `RecordSet` information from the document—remember our discussion about the Document/View and how the `RecordView` tied everything together.

In Listing 15.5, the two functions `GetDefaultConnect()` and `GetDefaultSQL()` are used. The `GetDefaultConnect` function member will provide the data source information that you need to pass to the database open command. The `GetDefaultSQL` function member will pass back the defining information for your fetch routines. (In this case, the SQL statement that queries the `Addresses` table).

LISTING 15.5   THE `GetDefaultConnect` AND `GetDefaultSQL` IMPLEMENTATIONS

```
1:    CString CAddressBookODBCSet::GetDefaultConnect()
2:    {
3:        return _T("ODBC;DSN=AddressBook");
4:    }
```

15

```
 5:
 6:    CString CAddressBookODBCSet::GetDefaultSQL()
 7:    {
 8:        return _T("[Addresses]");
 9:    }
10:
11:    void CAddressBookODBCSet::DoFieldExchange(CFieldExchange* pFX)
12:    {
13:        //{{AFX_FIELD_MAP(CAddressBookODBCSet)
14:        pFX->SetFieldType(CFieldExchange::outputColumn);
15:        RFX_Long(pFX, _T("[ID]"), m_ID);
16:        RFX_Text(pFX, _T("[Last Name]"), m_Last_Name);
17:        RFX_Text(pFX, _T("[First Name]"), m_First_Name);
18:        RFX_Text(pFX, _T("[Street]"), m_Street);
19:        RFX_Text(pFX, _T("[City]"), m_City);
20:        RFX_Text(pFX, _T("[State]"), m_State);
21:        RFX_Long(pFX, _T("[Zip]"), m_Zip);
22:        RFX_Text(pFX, _T("[Phone]"), m_Phone);
23:        //}}AFX_FIELD_MAP
24:    }
```

In Listing 15.6, notice line 4 from the modified OnInitialUpdate function. To open the recordset, simply call the Open function member of the recordset and pass the SQL string. This isn't always necessary. The GetDefaultSQL function member contains a shorthand version of the statement listed previously. If the SELECT statement needs to change, simply insert the SQL statement in the recordset's OPEN function.

LISTING 15.6 THE MODIFIED OnInitialUpdate IMPLEMENTATION

```
1:    void CAddressBookODBCView::OnInitialUpdate()
2:    {
3:        m_pSet = &GetDocument()->m_addressBookODBCSet;
4:        m_pSet->Open(CRecordSet::snapshot,"SELECT * FROM Addresses");
5:        CRecordView::OnInitialUpdate();
6:    }
```

 Note

It is important to note here that the OnInitialUpdate routine will actually perform the connecting and opening of the data source. It then will set the pointer to the recordset.

Updating the Application's Variables

By using the AppWizard to generate this application, you didn't use the CDatabase class
to connect or open the data source. By letting AppWizard define the recordset parameters, the code generated gets around this. If the support selected during the AppWizard
phase does not include this support, the application developer would have to add a
CDatabase class and CRecordSet class implementation in the CRecordView. More work,
but essentially the same result.

What you haven't learned is how the table data is transferred to the application's data.
Inside MFC database support is the Record Field Exchange (RFX) mechanism. Similar
to Dynamic Data Exchange (DDX), the RFX layer performs the underlying field-to-data
transfers. This is done at the message interface level.

You have now created an application that uses the ODBC API. You will next explore the
DAO API.

Using the MFC DAO Wrapper Classes

The steps needed to create the DAO application are similar to the steps needed to create
an MFC ODBC application. However, there are some minor differences. When asked for
database support (refer to Figure 15.3), select Database Support with File Support (the
last selection). Remember the discussion in Day 14 concerning the two APIs. ODBC
uses a data source, which can be network-resident and doesn't rely on the file system.
DAO uses the Jet engine, which is file-based. After this selection is made, the steps are
identical to those for the ODBC application.

Many applications that you might run across will obviously have more than one recordset defined to accept a query on just one table. The AppWizard gives the application
developer a starting point. As the application is created, notice that the files produced by
the AppWizard are almost identical to those created when you built the ODBC application. The MFC wrapper classes for the DAO API were designed to closely match those
created for the ODBC API, even though the APIs are completely different. Taking a good
look under the hood is beyond the scope of this book, but if you have the opportunity,
look at the MFC wrapper code for the DAO API classes that AppWizard creates. If you
compare the implementation of the CDaoRecordView class and the CRecordView class,
you will also see the similarities. Remember that the view is the coupling class to the
MFC Document/View architecture. Most of the differences will appear at the recordset
class wrappers.

Taking a Closer Look

Let's take a look at in Listing 15.7 the class implementations that the AppWizard generated for us. First, look at the Record Set class.

LISTING 15.7 THE DAO CAddressBookDAOSet CLASS DECLARATION

```
 1:    // AddressBookDAOSet.h : interface of the CAddressBookDAOSet class
 2:    //
 3:    /////////////////////////////////////////////////////////////////////
 4:
 5:    #if !defined(AFX_ADDRESSBOOKDAOSET_H__990F28BF_41F8_11D2_9D79_
       ➡000000000000__INCLUDED_)
 6:    #define AFX_ADDRESSBOOKDAOSET_H__990F28BF_41F8_11D2_9D79_
       ➡000000000000__INCLUDED_
 7:
 8:    #if _MSC_VER >= 1000
 9:    #pragma once
10:    #endif // _MSC_VER >= 1000
11:
12:    class CAddressBookDAOSet : public CDaoRecordset
13:    {
14:    public:
15:        CAddressBookDAOSet(CDaoDatabase* pDatabase = NULL);
16:        DECLARE_DYNAMIC(CAddressBookDAOSet)
17:
18:    // Field/Param Data
19:        //{{AFX_FIELD(CAddressBookDAOSet, CDaoRecordset)
20:        long     m_ID;
21:        CString    m_Last_Name;
22:        CString    m_First_Name;
23:        CString    m_Street;
24:        CString    m_City;
25:        CString    m_State;
26:        long     m_Zip;
27:        CString    m_Phone;
28:        //}}AFX_FIELD
29:
30:    // Overrides
31:        // ClassWizard generated virtual function overrides
32:        //{{AFX_VIRTUAL(CAddressBookDAOSet)
33:        public:
34:        virtual CString GetDefaultDBName();  // REVIEW:  Get a comment
                                               // here
35:        virtual CString GetDefaultSQL();     // default SQL for
                                               // Recordset
36:        virtual void DoFieldExchange(CDaoFieldExchange* pFX);
                                               // RFX support
```

continues

LISTING 15.7 CONTINUED

```
37:        //}}AFX_VIRTUAL
38:
39:    // Implementation
40:    #ifdef _DEBUG
41:        virtual void AssertValid() const;
42:        virtual void Dump(CDumpContext& dc) const;
43:    #endif
44:
45:    };
46:
47:    //{{AFX_INSERT_LOCATION}}
48:    // Microsoft Developer Studio will insert additional declarations
49:    // immediately before the previous line.
50:
51:    #endif //
    ➥!defined(AFX_ADDRESSBOOKDAOSET_H__990F28BF_41F8_11D2_9D79_
    ➥000000000000__INCLUDED_)
```

On line 34, notice the declaration of GetDefaultDBName(). This is different from the ODBC configuration. Again, it's the file or data source difference between the two APIs. Other than that difference, the declarations appear identical.

In Listing 15.8, you can explore the document class declaration.

LISTING 15.8 THE DAO CAddressBookDAODoc CLASS DECLARATION

```
1:    // AddressBookDAODoc.h : interface of the CAddressBookDAODoc class
2:    //
3:    /////////////////////////////////////////////////////////////////
4:
5:    #if !defined(AFX_ADDRESSBOOKDAODOC_H__990F28BB_41F8_11D2_9D79_
    ➥000000000000__INCLUDED_)
6:    #define AFX_ADDRESSBOOKDAODOC_H__990F28BB_41F8_11D2_9D79_
    ➥000000000000__INCLUDED_
7:
8:    #if _MSC_VER >= 1000
9:    #pragma once
10:    #endif // _MSC_VER >= 1000
11:
12:
13:    class CAddressBookDAODoc : public CDocument
14:    {
15:    protected: // create from serialization only
16:        CAddressBookDAODoc();
17:        DECLARE_DYNCREATE(CAddressBookDAODoc)
18:
```

```
19:    // Attributes
20:    public:
21:        CAddressBookDAOSet m_addressBookDAOSet;
22:
23:    // Operations
24:    public:
25:
26:    // Overrides
27:        // ClassWizard generated virtual function overrides
28:        //{{AFX_VIRTUAL(CAddressBookDAODoc)
29:        public:
30:        virtual BOOL OnNewDocument();
31:        virtual void Serialize(CArchive& ar);
32:        //}}AFX_VIRTUAL
33:
34:    // Implementation
35:    public:
36:        virtual ~CAddressBookDAODoc();
37:    #ifdef _DEBUG
38:        virtual void AssertValid() const;
39:        virtual void Dump(CDumpContext& dc) const;
40:    #endif
41:
42:    protected:
43:
44:    // Generated message map functions
45:    protected:
46:        //{{AFX_MSG(CAddressBookDAODoc)
47:        // NOTE - The ClassWizard will add and remove member functions
           // here.
48:        //     DO NOT EDIT what you see in these blocks of generated
           //     code !
49:        //}}AFX_MSG
50:        DECLARE_MESSAGE_MAP()
51:    };
52:
53:    ////////////////////////////////////////////////////////////////////
54:
55:    //{{AFX_INSERT_LOCATION}}
56:    // Microsoft Developer Studio will insert additional declarations
57:    // immediately before the preceding line.
58:
59:    #endif //
       ➥!defined(AFX_ADDRESSBOOKDAODOC_H__990F28BB_41F8_11D2_9D79_
       ➥000000000000__INCLUDED_)
```

Notice that this again appears identical to the ODBC MFC Document wrapper class.
Notice on line 21 that the document owns the recordset (your coupling).

Finally, the view class is explored in Listing 15.9.

```
 1:    // AddressBookDAOView.h : interface of the CAddressBookDAOView
       // class
 2:    //
 3:
 ////////////////////////////////////////////////////////////////////////
 4:
 5:    #if !defined(AFX_ADDRESSBOOKDAOVIEW_H__990F28BD_41F8_11D2_9D79_
       ➥000000000000__INCLUDED_)
 6:    #define AFX_ADDRESSBOOKDAOVIEW_H__990F28BD_41F8_11D2_9D79_
       ➥000000000000__INCLUDED_
 7:
 8:    #if _MSC_VER >= 1000
 9:    #pragma once
10:    #endif // _MSC_VER >= 1000
11:
12:    class CAddressBookDAOSet;
13:
14:    class CAddressBookDAOView : public CDaoRecordView
15:    {
16:    protected: // create from serialization only
17:        CAddressBookDAOView();
18:    DECLARE_DYNCREATE(CAddressBookDAOView)
19:
20:    public:
21:        //{{AFX_DATA(CAddressBookDAOView)
22:        enum{ IDD = IDD_ADDRESSBOOKDAO_FORM };
23:        CAddressBookDAOSet* m_pSet;
24:            // NOTE: The ClassWizard will add data members here
25:        //}}AFX_DATA
26:
27:    // Attributes
28:    public:
29:        CAddressBookDAODoc* GetDocument();
30:
31:    // Operations
32:    public:
33:
34:    // Overrides
35:        // ClassWizard generated virtual function overrides
36:        //{{AFX_VIRTUAL(CAddressBookDAOView)
37:        public:
38:        virtual CDaoRecordset* OnGetRecordset();
39:        virtual BOOL PreCreateWindow(CREATESTRUCT& cs);
40:        protected:
41:        virtual void DoDataExchange(CDataExchange* pDX);
        // DDX/DDV support
```

```
42:        virtual void OnInitialUpdate(); // called first time after
                                          // construct
43:        virtual BOOL OnPreparePrinting(CPrintInfo* pInfo);
44:        virtual void OnBeginPrinting(CDC* pDC, CPrintInfo* pInfo);
45:        virtual void OnEndPrinting(CDC* pDC, CPrintInfo* pInfo);
46:        //}}AFX_VIRTUAL
47:
48:    // Implementation
49:    public:
50:        virtual ~CAddressBookDAOView();
51:    #ifdef _DEBUG
52:        virtual void AssertValid() const;
53:        virtual void Dump(CDumpContext& dc) const;
54:    #endif
55:
56:    protected:
57:
58:    // Generated message map functions
59:    protected:
60:        //{{AFX_MSG(CAddressBookDAOView)
61:            // NOTE - The ClassWizard will add and remove member functions
                // here.
62:            //    DO NOT EDIT what you see in these blocks of generated
                //    code !
63:        //}}AFX_MSG
64:        DECLARE_MESSAGE_MAP()
65:    };
66:
67:    #ifndef _DEBUG  // debug version in AddressBookDAOView.cpp
68:    inline CAddressBookDAODoc* CAddressBookDAOView::GetDocument()
69:       { return (CAddressBookDAODoc*)m_pDocument; }
70:    #endif
71:
72:
//////////////////////////////////////////////////////////////////////
73:
74:    AFX_INSERT_LOCATION}}
75:    // Microsoft Developer Studio will insert additional declarations
76:    // immediately before the preceding line.
77:
78:    #endif //
       ➥!defined(AFX_ADDRESSBOOKDAOVIEW_H__990F28BD_41F8_11D2_9D79_
       ➥000000000000__INCLUDED_)
```

Again, this looks identical to the ODBC implementation, and in many respects it is.

Getting Data

If you look implementation>at the OnInitialUpdate routine of your view class, you see that it, too, is identical to the ODBC implementation. Do you see a pattern?

The GetDefaultDBName will return a string indicating the file and path information to the database (see Listing 15.10). In the ODBC implementation, you had to go to the DSN table to find this information.

LISTING 15.10   DAO GetDefaultDBName IMPLEMENTATION

```
1:    CString CAddressBookDAOSet::GetDefaultDBName()
2:    {
3:        return _T("E:\\Teach_Yourself_stuff\\Database_21\\Day
      ➥ 15\\Applications\\AddressBookDB.mdb");
4:    }
```

Tip

It's not generally good practice to hard-code string information. Modify this to return a string variable that will contain the file and path declaration.

The DoFieldExchange, shown in Listing 15.11, is similar to the DoDataExchange for a dialog-based view. The data from the database's columns are mapped to the application's memory by this mechanism.

LISTING 15.11   THE DAO GetDefaultSQL AND DoFieldExchange IMPLEMENTATIONS

```
1: CString CAddressBookDAOSet::GetDefaultSQL()
2: {
3:     return _T("[Addresses]");
4: }
5:
6: void CAddressBookDAOSet::DoFieldExchange(CDaoFieldExchange* pFX)
7: {
8:     //{{AFX_FIELD_MAP(CAddressBookDAOSet)
9:     pFX->SetFieldType(CDaoFieldExchange::outputColumn);
10:    DFX_Long(pFX, _T("[ID]"), m_ID);
11:    DFX_Text(pFX, _T("[Last Name]"), m_Last_Name);
12:    DFX_Text(pFX, _T("[First Name]"), m_First_Name);
13:    DFX_Text(pFX, _T("[Street]"), m_Street);
14:    DFX_Text(pFX, _T("[City]"), m_City);
15:    DFX_Text(pFX, _T("[State]"), m_State);
16:    DFX_Long(pFX, _T("[Zip]"), m_Zip);
17:    DFX_Text(pFX, _T("[Phone]"), m_Phone);
18:    //}}AFX_FIELD_MAP
19: }
```

15

Other DAO Classes

Both the ODBC and the DAO Address Book applications, as presented, are quite simplistic, and they really don't do much. What if you decided that you need to add another phone number field to the database? You could use Microsoft Access to add the field and rebuild these applications to read in that field. You would also have to place controls on the views to display your new field. This is a little bit of work, but what if you needed to let the application's users define temporary tables and queries? Except for SQL DDL statements, ODBC doesn't give the programmer a method for modifying the data source's schema. Because DAO is file-based, the programmer is able to easily modify the schema programmatically.

MFC provides two class wrappers that enable the programmer to easily modify the structure of the database. These are CDaoTableDef and CDaoQueryDef. These wrappers map to the TableDef and QueryDef objects directly. These classes contain member functions that enable the programmer to build new database structures as well as modify any database structures deemed as updatable.

In many cases, a database schema might be too limited to provide the application with the exact query information that it needs. Instead of doing multiple queries and saving all this information locally within the application for processing, the CDaoQueryDef function member will enable the programmer to add a query definition to the database and then perform a query on the temporary query just created.

If the database is large, temporary tables can be defined for the application that can hold temporary indexes, report results, running totals, and other such items that might be expensive in the application.

 Tip

Although this book isn't intended to instruct the database application developer on programming the older APIs, you would be well adivsed to build a few test applications to solidify your learning. The MFC source code is distributed with the Developer Studio, and it is recommended that the database application programmer review and investigate the wrapper classes.

Summary

After reading this chapter, you will be able to view ODBC and DAO API applications and understand the mechanisms used in ODBC and DAO applications.

MFC AppWizard provides a good start in creating ODBC and DAO appliations. The MFC wrapper classes do much of the work for you as well. The MFC classes automatically perform the data and provide the RFX mechanism. After you define the user interface controls to view the data, your application is off and running. The only code that you have to write is code for reports and other data manipulation.

Q&A

Q How do I determine which database support I need?

A On the MFC AppWizard, the database support without file support is primarily for the ODBC API. Remember that ODBC works with data sources, and DAO works with files. If file support is selected, you are essentially using the Jet database engine.

Q Can I modify the database table by adding fields (columns)?

A If the application is a DAO application, use the CDaoTableDef class to define a table. The CDaoTableDef has a member function, CanUpdate, that can determine whether field information in the table can be modified. CDaoTableDef can be used to open an existing table or create a new table in a database schema.

Workshop

The Workshop quiz questions test your understanding of today's material. (The answers appear in Appendix F, "Answers.") The exercises encourage you to apply the information you learned today to real-life situations.

Quiz

1. What is the mechanism that binds the column data in the database with the data in the database?
2. How is the API attached to the MFC Document/View architecture?
3. What routine would have to be modified to change the database SQL Query?

Exercises

1. Taking the ODBC Address Book application, add controls to display the fields to the RecordView. Is the data updated whenever the cursor selectors are pressed to move up and down the list?
2. Repeat exercise 1 for the DAO application.
3. What would the code look like for adding another record to the table? Use (Smith, Jennifer, 234 WayWay St., Dublin, OH, 45400, 614-555-0101).

DAY 16

The Ultimate Database API: OLE DB

Today's material introduces OLE DB and explains the OLE DB object hierarchy. Today's material also relates the basic concepts of ODBC to concepts of OLE DB, enabling you to build on your knowledge of database APIs and expand it to include OLE DB.

Today you will

- Look at the architecture of OLE DB.
- Explore the ODBC concepts found in OLE DB.
- Learn the OLE DB object hierarchy.
- Find sources for the latest information on OLE DB.

An API for All Data Sources

OLE DB is designed to provide a means for accessing data regardless of the data source. As shown in Figure 16.1, OLE DB becomes the data access bridge for documents, email systems, file systems, spreadsheets, COM components, and relational databases.

FIGURE 16.1

The topology of OLE DB applications.

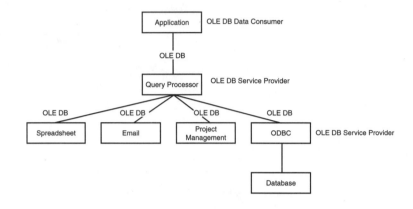

As you can see in Figure 16.1, an application that uses OLE DB can communicate with any data source for which there is an OLE DB data provider. Because of the object-oriented (and COM) nature of OLE DB, OLE DB data providers can be written to accommodate relational as well as nonrelational data sources.

The Components of an OLE DB Application

Two basic components of an OLE DB implementation are the data provider and the data consumer. An OLE DB data provider is an application that responds to queries and returns data in a usable form. An OLE DB data provider responds to various OLE DB calls to provide the information from the data source in a usable tabular form.

An OLE DB consumer is an application, or other COM component, that uses the OLE DB API to access a data source. OLE DB enables an application to access the entire range of enterprise data, regardless of where it is stored.

Making Data Sources Available

The key feature of OLE DB is that it simplifies the requirements for implementing a data provider. With OLE DB, the only requirement for a data provider is to return data in a tabular form; the data provider is not required to support a SQL language interface.

Note

To create an ODBC driver for a data source, it's necessary to build an SQL processing engine that can interpret and execute SQL queries. However, to create an OLE DB data provider, it's not necessary to build an SQL processing engine.

An important component of OLE DB is the service provider. As shown in Figure 16.1, a service provider is a middleman in the OLE DB architecture. Acting as a consumer of raw OLE DB data sources and as a provider to other OLE DB consumers, a service provider can provide functionality that OLE DB data providers don't implement themselves.

For instance, OLE DB service providers alleviate the need for OLE DB data providers to implement their own SQL database engine. OLE DB offers a query-processing component as a service provider. Developers of OLE DB data providers can use the query-processing service provider if they don't want to implement a query-processing engine themselves.

Because OLE DB components provide a consistent interface, OLE DB data providers can use OLE DB service providers if they need to, in order to offer complete OLE DB functionality to applications. Also, some OLE DB service providers provide cursor engines, besides query-processing engines. Other service providers built to provide additional functionality will be available in the future.

OLE DB extends the capabilities of ODBC by enabling less sophisticated data sources to have data providers written for them. OLE DB extends ODBC, but many concepts of ODBC programming have their counterparts in OLE DB.

Comparing OLE DB to ODBC

Open your ADOMFC1 project. Add a menu titled ODBC and add a drop-down menu item called Simple. Use ClassWizard to implement a command handler in the View class for that menu choice.

You need to include the files SQL.H and SQLEXT.H in ADOMFC1View.cpp, as shown here:.

```
#include <SQL.H>
#include <SQLEXT.H>
```

You also need to use the ODBC import library, called Odbc32.lib, in your linker input (found under the Project Settings menu), shown in Figure 16.2.

Inside your command handler, add the code in Listing 16.1.

FIGURE 16.2

ODBC import library.

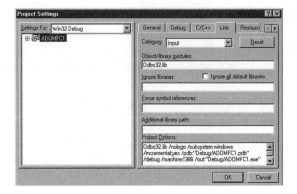

INPUT   **LISTING 16.1**   ODBC API PROGRAMMING

```
1:   void CADOMFC1View::OnOdbcSimple()
2:   {
3:     RETCODE retcode;
4:     HENV henviron;
5:     HDBC hdbconn;
6:     HSTMT hstmt;
7:     char szCustFirstName[50];
8:     SDWORD sdOutputDataLen;
9:     unsigned char connStrOut[256];
10:
11:    retcode = ::SQLAllocEnv(&henviron);
12:    if (retcode == SQL_SUCCESS)
13:    {
14:      retcode = ::SQLAllocConnect(henviron, &hdbconn);
15:      if (retcode == SQL_SUCCESS)
16:      {
17:        retcode = ::SQLDriverConnect(hdbconn, 0,
18:          (unsigned char *)"DSN=OrdersDb",
19:          SQL_NTS, connStrOut, 256, NULL,
20:          SQL_DRIVER_NOPROMPT);
21:        if (retcode == SQL_SUCCESS)
22:        {
23:          retcode = ::SQLAllocStmt(hdbconn, &hstmt);
24:          if (retcode == SQL_SUCCESS)
25:          {
26:            retcode = ::SQLExecDirect(hstmt,
27:              (unsigned char *)
28:              "SELECT CustFirstName FROM Customers",
29:              SQL_NTS);
30:
31:            for (retcode = ::SQLFetch(hstmt);
32:              retcode == SQL_SUCCESS;
33:              retcode = SQLFetch(hstmt))
```

16

```
34:                {
35:                    ::SQLGetData(hstmt, 1, SQL_C_CHAR,
36:                        szCustFirstName, 50,
37:                        &sdOutputDataLen);
38:                    ::MessageBox(NULL, szCustFirstName,
39:                        "Simple ODBC", MB_OK);
40:                }
41:                ::SQLFreeStmt(hstmt, SQL_DROP);
42:            }
43:            ::SQLDisconnect(hdbconn);
44:        }
45:        ::SQLFreeConnect(hdbconn);
46:    }
47:    ::SQLFreeEnv(henviron);
48:    }
49: }
```

As you know, the code in Listing 16.1 is unrealistically simple. Listing 16.1 is intended merely to provide a simple ODBC program for comparison with the simple OLE DB program that you will see later in Listing 16.2.

Line 11 in Listing 16.1 calls SQLAllocEnv to instruct the ODBC driver manager to allocate variables for this application and return an environment handle. Line 14 calls SQLAllocConnect to instruct the ODBC driver manager to allocate variables to manage a connection and to obtain a connection handle. Line 17 calls SQLDriverConnect to make a connection, using the OrdersDb data source name. (SQLAllocEnv, SQLAllocConnect, and SQLDriverConnect are ODBC 2.0 functions that have been replaced in ODBC 3.0 with the SQLAllocHandle function.)

Line 23 allocates a statement handle. Line 26 calls SQLExecDirect, using that statement handle, to execute a query against the database. Lines 31–40 use SQLFetch and SQLGetData to retrieve the results of the query and display the first field in a series of message boxes. Lines 41–47 release all the resources allocated earlier in the routine.

Compile the application and run it. Yes, the message boxes do make a lovely interface.

OLE DB programming is quite different from ODBC programming. OLE DB uses COM and COM interfaces extensively.

To write a routine similar to Listing 16.1 for OLE DB is quite a bit more involved, so much more involved that all I can show you today is the OLE DB code to load the OLE DB provider and initialize it.

Add to your ADOMFC1 project a menu titled OLE DB and add a drop-down menu item called Simple. Use ClassWizard to implement a command handler in the View class for that menu choice.

You need to include the files oledb.h, oledberr.h, msdaguid.h, and msdasql.h in ADOM-FC1View.cpp, as shown here:

```
#include <oledb.h>
#include <oledberr.h>
#include <msdaguid.h>
#include <msdasql.h>
```

You also need to use the OLE DB import library, called oledb.lib, in your linker input (found under the Project Settings menu), as shown in Figure 16.3.

FIGURE 16.3

OLE DB import library.

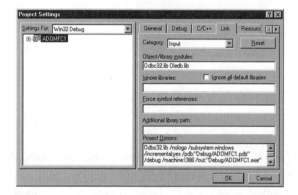

You also need to add a preprocessor definition of DBINITCONSTANTS under the C/C++ tab of the Project Settings menu, as shown in Figure 16.4.

FIGURE 16.4

The DBINITCONSTANTS preprocessor definition.

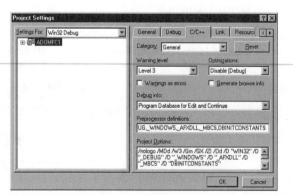

Inside your OLE DB Simple command handler, add the code in Listing 16.2.

```
 1:  void CADOMFC1View::OnOledbSimple()
 2:  {
 3:    IDBInitialize* pIDBInitialize = NULL;
 4:
 5:    // Initialize The Component Object Module Library
 6:    //CoInitialize(NULL);
 7:
 8:    // Obtain Access To The OLE DB - ODBC Provider
 9:    CoCreateInstance(CLSID_MSDASQL, NULL, CLSCTX_INPROC_SERVER,
10:            IID_IDBInitialize, (void **) &pIDBInitialize);
11:    pIDBInitialize->Initialize();
12:
13:    // This Is Where You Would Utilize OLE DB . . .
14:
15:    // Free Up Allocated Memory
16:    pIDBInitialize->Uninitialize();
17:    pIDBInitialize->Release();
18:
19:    // Release The Component Object Module Library
20:    //CoUninitialize();
21:
22:  }
```

16

As you can see, the code in Listing 16.2 is unrealistically simple. Listing 16.2 is intended merely to get you started with OLE DB programming. For the sake of code brevity, error checking is not performed.

Line 3 in Listing 16.2 declares an IDBInitialize pointer. IDBInitialize is an interface used to initialize and uninitialize data source objects and enumerators.

Lines 6 and 20 show the calls to CoInitialize and CoUninitialize. These calls are commented out because the COM libraries are already being initialized elsewhere in the code in ADOMFC1. They are shown in Listing 16.2 to illustrate the fact that the COM libraries must be initialized when you are doing OLE DB programming, but not when doing ODBC programming.

Lines 9 and 10 call CoCreateInstance to load the OLE DB provider for ODBC data sources; the provider resides in MSDASQL.DLL. The CoCreateInstance call requests a pointer to the IDBInitialize interface for the MSDASQL object and stores it in pIDBInitialize. As you know, the CoCreateInstance call will load MSDASQL.DLL into memory. Line 11 calls the IDBInitialize::Initialize function to initialize the provider.

From here you could make calls directly into the OLE DB provider. You would use `QueryInterface` to obtain pointers to the OLE DB interfaces exposed by the provider and would call its member functions to perform operations on the database.

ODBC programming and OLE programming are similar in that the application, in both environments, does the following:

- Calls API functions to load the appropriate DLL(s)
- Uses functions in the DLL(s) to connect to a data source
- Creates and executes queries
- Processes results
- Cleans up

For ODBC, to load the appropriate DLL(s), the application links with Odbc32.lib, which is the import library for the ODBC Driver Manager. The Driver Manager DLL, Odbc32.dll, loads when the application loads. The application calls ODBC API functions in the Driver Manager DLL, and the Driver Manager in turn calls functions in the appropriate ODBC driver.

For OLE DB, the application initializes the COM libraries. The application loads the proper data provider according to the `CLSID` parameter that it passes to the `CoCreateInstance` function. After that, the application can obtain pointers to the interfaces that the provider exposes and can call functions directly in the provider.

For ODBC, the application connects to the data source by calling `SQLAllocEnv`, `SQLAllocConnect`, and `SQLDriverConnect` (or by calling `SQLAllocHandle`) to allocate a connection handle. The application then builds a connection string containing the user ID, password, and the name of the data source.

For OLE DB, the application connects to the data source by building an array of property structures that contain the user ID, password, and the name of the data source. The application then calls `IDBProperties::SetProperties` to set initialization properties. (Listing 16.2 doesn't show this step, but tomorrow you will see the code for this.) Then the application calls `IDBInitialize::Initialize` to initialize the data source object.

The fundamental differences between the model for OLE DB and the model for ODBC are

- OLE DB uses COM interfaces, whereas ODBC uses traditional DLLs and static linking with an import library.
- OLE DB uses structures that contain the user ID, password, and DSN, whereas ODBC uses keywords in a string variable.

- In OLE DB, setting the user ID, password, and DSN is separate from actually connecting to the data source, which enables the connection properties to be persisted by the application more easily than in ODBC.

- In OLE DB, the application uses COM interfaces to set properties in a query object and then calls a member function to execute the query (you will see code for this later this week), whereas ODBC uses the `SQLAllocStmt` and `SQLExecDirect` functions to send SQL strings to the database.

- In OLE DB, the application receives results from queries in `Rowset` objects, whereas ODBC uses the `SQLGetData` and `SQLGetData` functions to retrieve the data from queries.

As you can see, OLE DB takes an object-oriented, or COM, approach, whereas ODBC takes a traditional API-based approach to database client programming.

The OLE DB Object Hierarchy

The OLE DB interface is composed of several major objects: `Enumerator`, `DataSource`, `Session`, `Command`, `Rowset`, `Index`, `Error`, and `Transaction`. In Figure 16.5, you can see the hierarchy of the OLE DB objects. During this week you will have a chance to look at each object in detail. A brief survey of the major OLE DB objects follows.

FIGURE 16.5

The OLE DB object hierarchy.

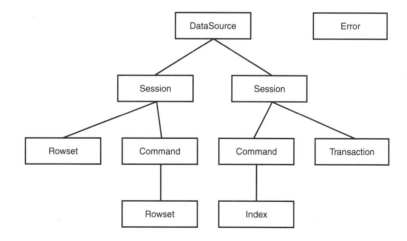

Enumerator

The `Enumerator` object retrieves information regarding the OLE DB providers and enumerators available on this system. Much of the information about OLE DB providers is stored in the registry. An `Enumerator` exposes the `ISourcesRowset` interface and returns a `Rowset` describing all data sources and enumerators visible to the `Enumerator`.

Using the `Enumerator` object is better than directly accessing the registry, because in the future this information might be stored somewhere else. The `Enumerator` object abstracts the source of the data provider information from an application, enabling it to work even if a new enumeration method is created.

DataSource

A data consumer uses a `DataSource` object to connect to a data provider. A data provider can be an OLE DB application, a database, or an ODBC data source using the OLE DB ODBC data source provider. When connecting to a database, a `DataSource` object encapsulates the environment and connection information, including a username and password. A `DataSource` object can be made persistent by saving its state to a file.

Session

A `Session` object provides a context for transactions. `Sessions` create an environment to encapsulate transactions, generate rows of data from a data source, and generate commands that can query and manipulate the data source. A `DataSource` object creates a `Session` object; a `DataSource` object can create multiple `Session` objects.

Command

A `Command` object processes commands. An OLE DB data provider isn't required to process commands. A `Command` object can create commands that can query or manipulate a data source. The result of a query creates a `Rowset` object. A `Command` object can also create multiple row sets. When accessing a data source, `Command` objects can create prepared statements and queries that return multiple row sets.

Rowset

A `Rowset` object accesses information from a data source in a tabular form. A `Rowset` object can be created as the result of executing a command. If the data provider doesn't support commands (which it is not required to provide), a row set can be generated directly from the data provider. The capability to create row sets directly is a requirement of all data providers. A `Rowset` object also is used when accessing data source schema information. Depending on the functionality of the data provider, a `Rowset` object can also update, insert, and delete rows.

Index

An `Index` object is a special case of a `Rowset` object. An `Index` object creates a row set that uses an associated index, which allows ordered access to a data source row set.

Error

An Error object encapsulates errors that occur when accessing a data provider. An Error object can be used to obtain extended return codes and status information. OLE DB Error objects use the standard OLE Automation methodology of error handling. Although all OLE DB methods return error codes indicating the success or failure of the method call, they are not required to support the extended information provided by the Error object.

Transaction

A Transaction object encapsulates transactions with a data source. A transaction buffers changes to the data source, giving the application the opportunity to commit or abort these changes. Transactions can improve application performance when accessing a data source. If the OLE DB provider supports them, distributed transactions, which enable multiple OLE DB data consumers to participate in shared transactions, are possible. An OLE DB provider is not required to support the transaction interface.

Getting the Latest OLE DB Information

The following Microsoft Web sites can help you keep up with the latest developments of OLE DB:

- http://www.microsoft.com/data/—The latest information on Microsoft's Universal Data Access (MDAC) strategy
- http://www.microsoft.com/data/oledb/—The latest OLE DB information
- http://www.microsoft.com/data/ado/—The ADO Web site

The following Internet newsgroups might also be helpful:

- microsoft.public.oledb—General OLE DB information
- microsoft.public.oledb.sdk—Specific OLE DB SDK–related information
- microsoft.public.ado—ADO information

Summary

OLE DB builds on and expands the capabilities of ODBC.

Because of the need to implement a SQL processor in an ODBC driver, writing an OLE DB provider for a data source is generally easier than writing an ODBC driver. Because OLE DB providers can be written for nonrelational data sources, OLE DB provides an interface to relational as well as nonrelational data sources.

16

OLE DB takes an object-oriented approach to database client development, whereas ODBC takes a function-based API approach. The OLE DB object hierarchy consists of just a few objects, which expose COM interfaces to perform well-defined sets of functions.

Q&A

Q I can see how OLE DB technology can help a large enterprise access all the information it stores in disparate locations, but what about a small organization? Small organizations don't have data stored all over the place, so what can OLE DB do in that environment?

A The data in a small organization might not be stored in many different locations, but OLE DB technology can certainly be of help to everyone. First, OLE DB provides a consistent and scalable interface to access data providers, no matter what the source. Second, OLE DB enables you to use this consistent interface to retrieve information previously inaccessible in a programmatically consistent manner. OLE DB potentially opens all information in an organization to any application.

Q Does OLE DB support security?

A The security mechanisms in OLE DB are currently incomplete. OLE DB will permit authentication, authorization, and the management of security options. Authentication makes sure users are who they say they are and is generally implemented by a username and password mechanism. When it's complete, OLE DB will support domain-based and distributed authentication methodologies. Authorization methods make sure users access only what they have privileges to access. The current version of OLE DB supports local authorization methods by returning a flag if security restrictions cause a call to fail. When it's complete, OLE DB will support Distributed Component Object Model (DCOM) authorization methods. Finally, the complete OLE DB will support mechanisms to manage permissions for users and groups.

Q Many complaints about using ODBC to access a database concern performance issues. How will the additional layer of an OLE DB ODBC provider affect performance? Are my applications going to run even more slowly?

A You should not notice much of a performance difference between the OLE DB ODBC provider and using the ODBC API directly. Remember that OLE DB is based on COM technology. COM is a way to provide a consistent interface so that two applications can share functionality. The OLE DB ODBC provider is simply a mechanism that remaps ODBC-specific calls into the OLE DB model; it doesn't add any overhead to this process. As the OLE DB technology matures, you are sure to see more pure OLE DB providers for data sources. Because the goal of COM and OLE DB is to create a plug-and-play architecture for application components, applications designed today using the OLE DB ODBC provider should be capable of using a pure OLE DB data provider with very few modifications.

Workshop

The Workshop quiz questions test your understanding of today's material. (The answers appear in Appendix F, "Answers.") The exercises encourage you to apply the information you learned today to real-life situations.

16

Quiz

1. What are the two basic OLE DB components?

2. How does OLE DB currently enable access to ODBC data sources for which no OLE DB provider is yet available?

3. What are the major OLE DB objects?

4. Which header files must be included to access OLE DB objects?

5. What is the URL for the OLE DB home page?

Exercises

1. Browse the OLE DB documentation and become familiar with it.

2. Visit the OLE DB Web site at `http://www.microsoft.com/oledb`.

DAY 17

Accessing a Data Source with OLE DB

As you learned yesterday, OLE DB is based on the Component Object Model (COM) architecture. Today begins the process of integrating OLE DB into applications. You will explore the relationship between COM and OLE DB and learn how COM technology influences the OLE DB programming model.

Note

> Much of today's material deals with COM and will help you understand and integrate COM components, including OLE DB, into your applications.

Today you will

- Explore what OLE DB data consumers and providers are.
- Learn how to obtain an OLE DB interface.
- Understand the structure of an OLE DB application.
- Observe the flow of information from object to object.
- Work with enumerators.

- Use `DataSource` objects.
- Use properties to change the state of COM and OLE DB ODBC provider objects in a particular object.
- Integrate the OLE DB objects discussed today.

Data Consumers and Providers

As you learned yesterday, OLE DB applications in their simplest form are composed of a data provider and a data consumer. A *data provider* is a COM component that provides an OLE DB–compliant interface. A *data consumer* is an application or component that uses an OLE DB interface to access a data source. Figure 17.1 shows how OLE DB applications are structured in a give-and-take manner:

- A data provider gives access to a data source through an interface.
- A data consumer takes the data from a data source by using that interface.

FIGURE 17.1

The give-and-take nature of OLE DB applications.

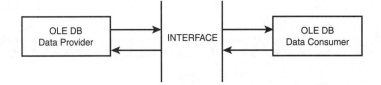

OLE DB extends the key concept of the COM architecture. That is, it provides a well-defined and structured mechanism for application components to "talk" with each other in order to access data. An OLE DB data provider is not required to support the complete OLE DB interface; for example, a data provider does *not* have to support commands. Lowering this barrier makes it easier to write OLE DB data providers.

The interface layer of the COM architecture can tell you which aspects of the OLE DB specification a given data provider supports. By querying a data provider's interfaces, you can determine which portions of the OLE DB specification the data provider supports and how to write an application to take full advantage of that provider.

Interfaces

The idea behind interfaces is best described through a real-world example. A standard electrical wall outlet is a good example of an interface. The top two holes in the outlet provide the power to an electrical device, and the bottom hole provides grounding.

Because an electrical outlet is a standard interface, it can support the power needs of any device, current or future, that conforms to its standards, that is, has a compatible plug (one that fits in the outlet's holes) and can use the standard 120 volts of power. A standard electrical outlet can supply power to a diverse set of devices, from a device as simple as a toaster to something as complex as a personal computer.

Another key aspect of an electrical outlet is the grounding receptacle. As you probably know, not every electrical device uses the ground provided by the outlet, but that doesn't prevent the device from being able to use the outlet. An electrical outlet provides a set of features, just like a well-designed software component. A device doesn't have to use all the features of the interface in order to use the interface.

You learned about COM interfaces in Day 9, "Understanding COM." Interfaces are the key aspect of the COM architecture, as you can see in Figure 17.2. *Interfaces* describe the functionality provided by the component and also supply the structured mechanism by which the components talk with each other. You can think of a *component* as a collection of code that supports the functionality described by the interface. The code is separate from the interface, and the details are hidden from the user of the component.

17

FIGURE 17.2

The role of the interface in an application that uses COM components.

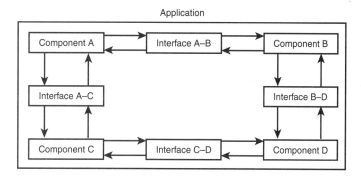

If you have any previous experience with object-oriented programming, the preceding description of a COM component should remind you of an object. In fact, a *COM component* is an object that uses the rules in the COM specification to provide access to the component's interface.

Interface Factoring

One of the most important aspects of COM interfaces is that they don't change. After a COM component interface is published, it remains static. When a new version of a component is released, a new interface is created; however, the old version of the interface is still supported. Like the electrical outlet that has two interfaces, one for two-pronged devices and another for three-pronged devices, a COM component can support multiple interfaces.

A COM component can support any number of interfaces. Multiple interfaces enable older applications to continue to use a COM component that has been upgraded with additional functionality, even though the older applications were developed before the component was upgraded and have no knowledge of the additional features. Figure 17.3 shows how a set of COM components and their interfaces can define an application. Each set of interfaces defines a set of methods specific to it.

FIGURE 17.3

The partitioned nature of a COM application.

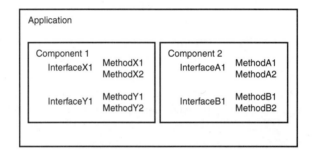

You can determine the interfaces that a COM component supports by calling the QueryInterface method. When an application determines whether a component supports a specific interface, it is guaranteed the functionality of that interface. Because an interface defines a complete set of functions, interfaces are separated, or *factored,* by the functionality they support.

OLE DB uses *interface factoring* extensively. The OLE DB specification requires certain interfaces, but OLE DB objects can support additional functionality. OLE DB consumers use the QueryInterface method to determine the level of functionality an OLE DB object supports.

If you have previous experience with object-oriented programming, you might recognize the term *polymorphism.* Polymorphism is the use of the same methods when you are accessing different objects. The capability of COM components to support multiple interfaces helps to facilitate polymorphism. Figure 17.4 shows that OLE DB applications designed to support the base level of functionality can also be used with different OLE DB data providers. Various OLE DB providers can be *plugged* into the same application, like the electrical outlet described earlier, and still be guaranteed to work.

FIGURE 17.4

The plug-in orientation of COM and the OLE DB architecture.

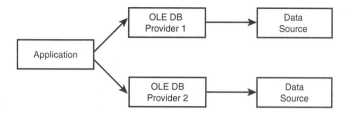

Interface Negotiations

How does an application determine which interfaces an object supports? The QueryInterface method of the COM IUnknown interface checks whether an object supports an interface. The QueryInterface method returns a pointer to the interface (in an out parameter) if the object supports it; otherwise, the QueryInterface method places NULL in the out parameter. An application uses this mechanism to determine the interface functionality that a component supports. At a minimum, every COM component must support the IUnknown interface. (Ideally, a component also supports other interfaces, or the component won't have any functionality!) All interfaces are inherited from the IUnknown interface.

The IUnknown Object

The IUnknown interface is declared in the UNKNWN.H header file, which is part of the Win32 SDK. The IUnknown interface is essentially defined as this:

```
interface IUnknown
{
    virtual HRESULT stdcall QueryInterface(const IID &riid,
                                  void **ppvObject) = 0;
    virtual ULONG stdcall AddRef() = 0;
    virtual ULONG stdcall Release() = 0;
};
```

The actual declaration looks more complex, but this the essence of it.

> **Note**
>
> The stdcall option in the IUnknown definition tells the C++ compiler to use the standard Pascal calling convention. Most Win32 API functions use the Pascal calling convention. Most COM functions use this method, also. With the Pascal calling convention, the function called is responsible for removing calling arguments from the stack before it returns. If the function takes a variable number of arguments, it uses the normal C/C++ calling convention cdecl, and the caller of the function is responsible for removing arguments from the stack.

Because every interface that a COM component supports is inherited from the IUnknown interface, any interface can be used to get to any other interface that a component supports. The QueryInterface method determines whether a component supports an interface, and the AddRef method adds to the reference count of an object (see the following note). The Release method subtracts from the object reference count; when the reference count is 0, the resources used by the component can be released by the system.

Note

> *Reference counting* ensures that a COM object does not release its resources (for example, the memory it is using) until the COM object is no longer being used. Every time an object is obtained, it should be sandwiched between an AddRef call to lock the component's resources and a Release call to free up the resource when it's available. Failure to lock a component's resources could cause them to be freed before your application has finished using them. Failure to release a component when your application is finished with it can cause resources to remain locked and associated memory to be unreleased, even after you have finished with the component.

Table 17.1 describes the parameters used by the QueryInterface method:

```
virtual HRESULT __stdcall QueryInterface(const IID &riid,
➡void **ppvObject) = 0;
```

TABLE 17.1 THE QueryInterface METHOD PARAMETERS

Parameter	Description
riid	The globally unique identifier (GUID) of the interface being queried.
ppvObject	An address that, on return, will contain a pointer to the object whose interface is queried.

You will see the GUIDs of various interfaces throughout the week. These interface identifiers are generally constants. In the case of OLE DB, these constants are defined in the OLE DB library. If you look back at Listing 16.2, you will see where you used an interface definition. Generally, all interface definitions begin with IID. Listing 16.2 references the IID_IDBInitialize interface identifier. I will explain the OLE DB interfaces in detail as you examine the objects that use them.

The QueryInterface method returns an HRESULT, which can be S_OK if an interface is supported or E_NOINTERFACE if not. Because status codes returned in an HRESULT can vary (that is, multiple status codes for success and failure), you can use the SUCCEEDED and FAILED macros to determine whether the QueryInterface method succeeded or failed.

Listing 17.1 defines a function called CheckInterface. You could use the function in
Listing 17.1 in OLE DB consumer applications to discover which interfaces an OLE DB
data provider supports. CheckInterface takes a single parameter that defines the interface ID and returns 1 if the interface is supported or 0 if not.

INPUT   **LISTING 17.1**   THE CheckInterface FUNCTION

```
 1:  int CheckInterface(IUnknown* pInterface, REFIID pIID)
 2:  {
 3:    // Define a pointer to hold the interface being queried
 4:    IUnknown* pChkInterface;
 5:
 6:    // Query for the interface
 7:    HRESULT hr = pInterface->QueryInterface(pIID, pChkInterface);
 8:
 9:  if(SUCCEEDED(hr))
10:  {
11:      pCheckInterface->Release();
12:      return TRUE;
13:  }
14:  else
15:      return FALSE;
```

You can see from line 1 that the CheckInterface function takes an IUnknown pointer and
an interface ID as parameters. The pointer defined in line 4 is used only as a temporary
variable in which to store the pointer to the queried interface. Line 7 calls
QueryInterface to get and stores the HRESULT in a variable named hr. Line 11 causes
the function to return the result of passing hr to the SUCCEEDED macro.

OLE DB Application Flow

Figure 17.5 illustrates the typical flow of an OLE DB application. An Enumerator object
determines which OLE DB data source providers are available. Using the data source
name returned by the ISourcesRowset and IParseDisplayName interfaces, you can create a DataSource object. The DataSource object defines access to the data source and
also defines a security context. Using the IDBCreateSession interface of the DataSource
object, the CreateSession method can create a Session object. The Session object provides a logical scope for transactions and permits access to data source row sets and to
data source schema information.

The CreateCommand method can use the IDBCreateCommand interface of the Session
object to create a Command object that performs provider-specific commands. For
example, if the provider is a database that can interpret SQL statements, these commands

can be SQL commands. Using the `ICommand` interface of the `Command` object, the `Execute`
method can be used to create a `Rowset` object. A `Rowset` object permits access to data
source data in a tabular form.

FIGURE 17.5

*The typical flow of an
OLE DB application*

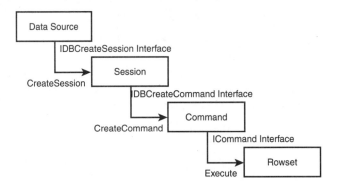

Enumerators

The `Enumerator` object is a good place for you to start exploring the OLE DB classes.
The `Enumerator` object retrieves information regarding the OLE DB providers available
on this system. Much of the information about OLE DB providers is stored in the registry. Using the `Enumerator` object is better than directly accessing the registry, because
in the future this information might be stored elsewhere. The `Enumerator` object
abstracts the source of the data provider information from an application, enabling it to
work even if a new enumeration method is created.

> **Note**
>
> Enumerators and providers are defined in the registry, using the OLE DB
> enumerator or provider subkey, and under the class ID of the enumerator or
> provider. Under the `HKEY_CLASS_ROOT` key in the registry, an enumerator or
> provider requires the following subkeys to be defined:
>
> `EnumOrProvID=DisplayName`
> `EnumOrProvIDID\CLSID=EnumOrProvCLSID`
>
> Under the `HKEY_CLASS_ROOT\CLSID` subkey in the registry, the following
> subkeys are also required:
>
> `EnumOrProvCLSID=DisplayName`
> `EnumOrProvCLSID\PROGID=EnumOrProvProgID`
> `EnumOrProvCLSID\VersionIndependentProgID=VerIndProgID`
> `EnumOrProvCLSID\InProcServer32=EnumOrProvDLL`
> `EnumOrProvCLSID\InProcServer32\ThreadingModel=Apartment¦Free¦`
> `➥Both`
> `EnumOrProvCLSID\OLEDBEnumerator=Description`

The TEnumerator object is defined as supporting the following interfaces:

```
TEnumerator {
        interface IParseDisplayName;          // Required Interface
        interface ISourcesRowset;             // Required Interface
        interface IDBInitialize;
        interface IDBProperties;
        interface ISupportErrorInfo;
};
```

TEnumerator is an OLE DB *CoType*. CoTypes are used to define groups of COM objects that have similar characteristics and that implement certain mandatory interfaces.

An OLE DB Enumerator object is required to define the IParseDisplayName and ISourcesRowset interfaces. The other interfaces are optional. The OLE DB SDK provides a root enumerator, which searches the registry for other data providers and enumerators. The CLASS_ID of this root enumerator is CLSID_OLEDB_ENUMERATOR. Before you look at the implementation details of the Enumerator object, a review of the purpose and methods of the interfaces defined by the Enumerator object is in order.

17

> **Note**
>
> The following presentation of individual OLE DB objects also considers the methods that each object's interfaces provide, as well as the parameters required by each method. For a more complete description of each interface's methods and parameters, refer to the OLE DB documentation.

The IParseDisplayName Interface

The IParseDisplayName interface converts a displayable name string to a moniker. A *moniker* contains the information that uniquely identifies a COM object. In a sample application later today, you will see exactly how the display name and moniker are related. The IParseDisplayName interface defines the standard IUnknown interface methods QueryInterface, AddRef, and Release. The interface provides one additional method, ParseDisplayName, which is defined as follows:

```
HRESULT ParseDisplayName(LPBC pbc, LPOLECHAR lpszDisplayName,
                         unsigned long *pchUsed, LPMONIKER *ppMoniker);
```

When a display name is converted to a moniker, the BindMoniker method can access the object described by the moniker. Figure 17.6 illustrates how a display name is converted to a moniker and how a moniker is bound to an object and an interface.

Note   When an interface method returns an HRESULT, that value can be used to check the success or failure of the method. The SUCCEEDED or FAILED macros should be used to check whether the interface method was successful.

FIGURE 17.6

The process of converting a display name to a moniker and binding it to an object and an interface.

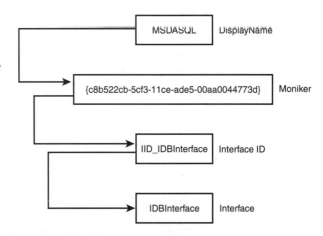

The ISourcesRowset Interface

The ISourcesRowset interface accesses row set data from data sources and enumerators. (See Day 18, "Querying a Data Source," and Day 19, "Navigating the Result of a Query," for more on row sets.) For now you will learn enough about the ISourcesRowset interface to use the Enumerator class. The ISourcesRowset interface defines the standard IUnknown interface methods QueryInterface, AddRef, and Release. The interface provides one additional method, GetSourcesRowset, which is defined as follows:

```
HRESULT GetSourcesRowset(IUnknown pAggInterface, REFIID riid,
            ULONG cPropertySets, DBPROPSET rgPropertySets[],
            IUnknown **ppSourcesRowset);own pAggInterface, REFIID riid,
```

From an Enumerator object, the GetSourcesRowset method returns tabular information about the available data sources. Table 17.2 displays the field names, types, and descriptions of the row set returned by the GetSourcesRowset method. The columns returned in the row set are read-only; they cannot be changed.

TABLE 17.2   THE ROW SET RETURNED BY THE GetSourcesRowset METHOD

Column	Type	Description
SOURCES_NAME	DBTYPE_WSTR	The name of the data source.
SOURCES_PARSENAME	DBTYPE_WSTR	The parse name of the data source, used by the ParseDisplayName method to create a moniker.

Column	Type	Description
SOURCES_DESCRIPTION	DBTYPE_WSTR	The data source description.
SOURCES_TYPE	DBTYPE_UI2	A flag describing the type of the source. If the value is DBSOURCETYPE_DATASOURCE, it describes a data source. If the value is DBSOURCETYPE_ENUMERATOR, it describes an enumerator.
SOURCES_ISPARENT	DBTYPE_BOOL	If the source is an enumerator and the value is TRUE, the enumerator is a parent enumerator. Multiple enumerators can be defined, and a parent enumerator can also be enumerated.

The IDBInitialize Interface

The IDBInitialize interface initializes an enumerator. It is an optional interface for enumerators. The root enumerator provided by the OLE DB SDK doesn't support the IDBInitialize interface. You should use the QueryInterface method to determine whether the Enumerator object you are using supports this interface. The IDBInitialize interface defines the standard IUnknown interface methods QueryInterface, AdddRef, and Release. The interface provides two additional methods: Initialize and Uninitialize. Neither method takes a parameter. Obviously, the Initialize method initializes the enumerator. The Uninitialize method returns the enumerator to an uninitialized state.

The IDBProperties Interface

The IDBProperties interface gets and sets the properties of an Enumerator object. Properties define values that determine the state of an object. Like the IDBInitialize interface, the IDBProperties interface is optional for Enumerator objects. The OLE DB SDK root enumerator doesn't support the IDBProperties interface. Later today in the section on DataSource objects, the IDBProperties interface is discussed briefly and then explained in more detail on Day 20, "Properties, Transactions, and Indexes."

The IDBProperties interface defines the standard IUnknown interface methods QueryInterface, AddRef, and Release. The interface provides three additional methods: GetProperties, GetPropertyInfo, and SetProperties. The GetProperties method retrieves the value of a property. The GetPropertyInfo method returns information about all the properties supported by the enumerator. The SetProperties method sets the value of a property. These methods are defined as follows:

```
HRESULT GetProperties(ULONG cPropIDSets, const DBPROPIDSET rgPropSets[],
                      ULONG *pcPropSets, DBPROPSET **prgPropSets);
```

17

```
HRESULT GetPropertyInfo(ULONG cPropIDSets, const DBPROPIDSET rgPropSets[],
                        ULONG *pcPropInfoSets,
                        ➡DBPROPINFOSET **prgPropInfoSets,
                        OLECHAR **ppDescription);
HRESULT SetProperties(ULONG cPropNum, DBPROPSET rgPropSets[]);
```

The `ISupportErrorInfo` Interface

The `ISupportErrorInfo` interface determines whether an interface supports Automation error objects. OLE DB `Error` objects are returned using the same interface as the Automation error objects. Error handling in OLE DB is discussed in more detail on Day 21, "OLE DB Error Handling." The `ISupportErrorInfo` interface defines the standard `IUnknown` interface methods `QueryInterface`, `AddRef`, and `Release`. This interface provides one additional method: `InterfaceSupportsErrorInfo`. The `InterfaceSupportsErrorInfo` method is defined as follows:

```
HRESULT InterfaceSupportsErrorInfo(REFIID riid);
```

If the interface supports error information, `S_OK` is returned; otherwise, `S_FALSE` is returned. Remember to use the `SUCCEEDED` or `FAILED` macros to check the return value.

Using an Enumerator: A Simple Example

Now that you have a general idea of the interfaces that the `Enumerator` object supports, you need to know how to obtain and use an `Enumerator` object to display the data sources it supports. Listing 17.2 defines the `EnumTest` application. This application accesses an `Enumerator` object and then uses the `ISourcesRowset` interface to loop through the data providers available. The data providers and enumerators are accessed, and the display and parse names are printed to `cout`.

This example also demonstrates the relationship between the display name and parse name (GUID) of a data source provider. The details of how to access a row set are given tomorrow (Day 18). For now, try to get a sense of how the `Enumerator` object and its associated interfaces are accessed.

To build the application, run Visual Studio and select the File New menu choice. Click the Projects tab and specify a Win32 Console Application. Call the application `EnumTest`. Click the OK button and then specify that you want to create an empty project; then click the Finish button. After AppWizard runs, create a new C++ source file as part of the project. You can call it whatever you think is appropriate, for example, main.cpp. Enter the code in Listing 17.2 into the source file. Note that the code in lines 19 and 20 should actually be on one line. In other words, line 20 should be appended onto line 19 in your source file. When you build the project, it should compile and link without errors or warnings.

```
 1:  #define UNICODE
 2:  #define _UNICODE
 3:
 4:  // Standard Application Includes
 5:  #include <windows.h>
 6:  #include <stdio.h>
 7:  #include <iostream.h>
 8:  #include <tchar.h>
 9:  #include <stddef.h>
10:  // OLE DB Header Files
11:  #include <oledb.h>
12:  #include <oledberr.h>
13:
14:  // OLE DB - ODBC Provider Header Files
15:  #include <msdaguid.h>
16:  #include <msdasql.h>
17:
18:  #define NUMELEM(p1) (sizeof(p1) / sizeof(p1[0]))
19:  #define ROUND_TO_NEXT_BYTE( Size, Amount )
20:  ➥(((DWORD)(Size) + ((Amount) - 1)) & ~((Amount) - 1))
21:  #define COLUMN_ALIGNVAL 8
22:
23:  void EnumerateProviders();
24:
25:  int main() {
26:    // Initialize The Component Object Module Library
27:    CoInitialize(NULL);
28:
29:    EnumerateProviders();
30:
31:    // Release The Component Object Module Library
32:    CoUninitialize();
33:
34:    return(0);
35:  };
36:
37:  void EnumerateProviders()
38:  {
39:      ULONG            i,                        // Counter
40:      cRows = 0;                  // Number of rows returned
41:      ISourcesRowset*  pISourceRowset = NULL;  // Source Rowset
                                                 // Interface
42:      IRowset*         pIRowset = NULL;        // Rowset Interface
43:      IAccessor*       pIAccessor = NULL;      // Accessor Interface
44:      BYTE*            pData = NULL;           // Data buffer
45:      DWORD            dwOffset;               // Offset counter
46:      HACCESSOR        hAccessor = NULL;       // Handle to accesspr
                                                 // interface
```

continues

LISTING **17.2**   CONTINUED

```
47:      DBBINDING          rgBind[3];                  // Data bindings
                                                        // buffer
48:      HROW               rghRows[256];               // Row handle array
49:      HROW*              pRows = &rghRows[0];         // Pointer to Row
                                                        // handle array
50:      CHAR               string[256];
51:
52:      // Define A Structure That Represents The
53:      // Data Elements We Wish To Retrieve
54:      struct COLUMNDATA {
55:        DBSTATUS wStatus;      // Column Status
56:        DWORD dwLength;        // Column Length
57:        BYTE bData[1];         // Column Data
58:      };
59:
60:      // Define An Enumerator Type That Defines Each Of The
61:      // Data Columns Returned By The Source Rowset Interface
62:      enum enumSOURCES_COLUMNS {
63:        eid_SOURCES_NAME = 1,
64:        eid_SOURCES_PARSENAME,
65:        eid_SOURCES_DESCRIPTION,
66:        eid_SOURCES_TYPE,
67:        eid_SOURCES_ISPARENT,
68:        eid_SOURCES_CLSID,
69:      };
70:
71:      // Define A Tagged Structure That Identifies The
72:      static struct tagSOURCES
73:      {
74:          ULONG      iOrdinal;
75:          DBTYPE     wType;
76:          ULONG      cbMaxLen;
77:      } s_rgSources[3];
78:
79:      // Initialize the Source Columns to retrieve
80:      s_rgSources[0].iOrdinal = eid_SOURCES_NAME;
81:      s_rgSources[0].wType = DBTYPE_STR;
82:      s_rgSources[0].cbMaxLen = 64;
83:      s_rgSources[1].iOrdinal = eid_SOURCES_PARSENAME;
84:      s_rgSources[1].wType = DBTYPE_WSTR;
85:      s_rgSources[1].cbMaxLen = 64 * sizeof(WCHAR);
86:      s_rgSources[2].iOrdinal = eid_SOURCES_TYPE;
87:      s_rgSources[2].wType = DBTYPE_UI4;
88:      s_rgSources[2].cbMaxLen = sizeof(ULONG);
89:
```

```
90:        cout << "Enumerate The Providers\n" << "------------------\n";
91:
92:        // Allocate the Rows Buffer
93:        memset(rghRows, 0, sizeof(rghRows));
94:
95:        // Initialize the OLE DB Root Enumerator
96:        CoCreateInstance(CLSID_OLEDB_ENUMERATOR, NULL,
97:            CLSCTX_INPROC_SERVER, IID_ISourcesRowset,
               ➡(LPVOID*)&pISourceRowset);
98:
99:        // Retrieve the SourceRowset
100:       pISourceRowset->GetSourcesRowset(NULL, IID_IRowset, 0, NULL,
101:                                   (IUnknown**)&pIRowset);
102:
103:       // Allocate space for row bindings
104:       memset(rgBind, 0, sizeof(rgBind));
105:
106:       // Obtain access to the Accessor Interface
107:       pIRowset->QueryInterface(IID_IAccessor,
                               ➡(LPVOID*)&pIAccessor);
108:
109:       // Initialize the column bindings, from the Source Column array
110:       dwOffset = 0;
111:       for(i=0; i< NUMELEM(s_rgSources); i++)
112:       {
113:            // Bind The Value, Length, And Status
114:            rgBind[i].dwPart = DBPART_VALUE | DBPART_LENGTH |
                             ➡DBPART_STATUS;
115:            // Reminder, This is not a parameter!
116:            rgBind[i].eParamIO = DBPARAMIO_NOTPARAM;
117:            // The ordinal location of the column to retrieve
118:            rgBind[i].iOrdinal = s_rgSources[i].iOrdinal;
119:            // Set the column type
120:            rgBind[i].wType = s_rgSources[i].wType;
121:            // Set the offset length of the column for the value
                // in the buffer
122:            rgBind[i].obValue = dwOffset + offsetof(COLUMNDATA,bData);
123:            // Set the offset length of the column for the length
                // in the buffer
124:            rgBind[i].obLength = dwOffset + offsetof
                   ➡(COLUMNDATA,dwLength);
125:            // Set the offset length of the column for the status
                // in the buffer
126:            rgBind[i].obStatus = dwOffset + offsetof
                   ➡(COLUMNDATA,wStatus);
127:            // Set the maximum column length
128:            rgBind[i].cbMaxLen = s_rgSources[i].cbMaxLen;
129:            // Set the source for the data buffer allocation,
                // in this case the
130:            // Enumerator client
```

continues

LISTING **17.2**   CONTINUED

```
131:                    rgBind[i].dwMemOwner = DBMEMOWNER_CLIENTOWNED;
132:                    // Set to the next column
133:                    dwOffset += rgBind[i].cbMaxLen + offsetof
                          ➥( COLUMNDATA, bData );
134:                    // Round The Offset to the next byte
135:                    dwOffset = ROUND_TO_NEXT_BYTE( dwOffset, COLUMN_ALIGNVAL );
136:            }
137:
138:            // Create The RowSet accessor
139:            pIAccessor->CreateAccessor(DBACCESSOR_ROWDATA,
                                          ➥NUMELEM(s_rgSources),
140:                rgBind, dwOffset, &hAccessor, NULL);
141:
142:            // Retrieve the providers
143:            if( SUCCEEDED(pIRowset->GetNextRows(NULL, 0, 256, &cRows,
                                                   ➥&pRows)) )
144:            {
145:                // Allocate block of memory to retrieve the row data into.
146:                pData = new BYTE[dwOffset];
147:
148:                // Loop over the rows of data, collecting providers
149:                // and discarding enumerators..
150:                for(i=0; (i<cRows) && (i<256); i++)
151:                {
152:                    // Allocate the data buffer
153:                    memset(pData, 0, dwOffset);
154:
155:                    // Get the row set data
156:                    pIRowset->GetData(rghRows[i], hAccessor, pData);
157:                    // Is it a data source? Not an Enumerator!
158:                    if( *((ULONG*)(pData + rgBind[2].obValue)) ==
159:                            DBSOURCETYPE_DATASOURCE )
160:                    {
161:                        // Convert the Parsename from Unicode to
                            // a standard string
162:                        WideCharToMultiByte(CP_ACP, 0,
163:                                            (WCHAR *)(pData + rgBind[1].
                                                            ➥obValue),
164:                                            wcslen((WCHAR *)(pData +
                                            ➥rgBind[1].
                                                            ➥obValue)),
165:                                            string, 256, NULL, FALSE);
166:                        string[wcslen((WCHAR *)(pData + rgBind[1].obValue))]
                            ➥ = '\0';
167:                        cout << "Provider # " << i << "\n\tName: " <<
168:                          (CHAR*)(pData + rgBind[0].obValue) <<
                            ➥"\n\tParse Name: " <<
```

```
169:                    string << "\n";
170:                }
171:            }
172:        };
173:
174:        // Free the Data buffer
175:        if( pData )
176:            delete[] pData;
177:
178:        // Free the Accessor Interface
179:        if( pIAccessor )
180:            pIAccessor->Release();
181:
182:        // Free the Rowset Interface
183:        if( pIRowset )
184:            pIRowset->Release();
185:
186:        // Free the SourceRowset Interface
187:        if( pISourceRowset )
188:            pISourceRowset->Release();
189:    };
```

17

Lines 1 and 2 of Listing 17.2 define this as a Unicode application. Lines 5–16 include the various required headers. Lines 25–35 constitute the main function for the application. Note the calls to CoInitialize and CoUninitialize in the main function. Lines 37–189 constitute the EnumerateProviders function. Lines 39–88 define variables and structures the function will use. Lines 95–101 create an instance of the OLE DB root enumerator and call its GetSourcesRowset function. Lines 103–140 create an Accessor and bind it to variables in the function. Lines 142–172 call the Rowset GetNextRows function to get the providers and display them. Lines 174–188 do the appropriate cleanup.

Note that the error checking in Listing 17.2 is minimized for brevity. The value of the HRESULTs needs to be checked when you are querying for an interface.

Listing 17.3 shows the output of the EnumTest application. The output will vary, based on which OLE DB providers are installed on the system.

OUTPUT **LISTING 17.3** OUTPUT FROM EnumTest

```
1:  Enumerate The Providers
2:  ----------------------
3:  Provider # 0
4:      Name: SampProv
5:      Parse Name: {E8CCCB79-7C36-101B-AC3A-00AA0044773D}
6:  Provider # 1
```

continues

LISTING 17.3 CONTINUED

```
 7:        Name: ADsDSOObject
 8:        Parse Name: {549365d0-ec26-11cf-8310-00aa00b505db}
 9:  Provider # 2
10:        Name: MSDataShape
11:        Parse Name: {3449A1C8-C56C-11D0-AD72-00C04FC29863}
12:  Provider # 3
13:        Name: MSPersist
14:        Parse Name: {7C07E0D0-4418-11D2-9212-00C04FBBBFB3}
15:  Provider # 4
16:        Name: Microsoft.Jet.OLEDB.3.51
17:        Parse Name: {dee35060-506b-11cf-b1aa-00aa00b8de95}
18:  Provider # 5
19:        Name: MSDAOSP
20:        Parse Name: {dfc8bdc0-e378-11d0-9b30-0080c7e9fe95}
21:  Provider # 6
22:        Name: MSDAORA
23:        Parse Name: {e8cc4cbe-fdff-11d0-b865-00a0c9081c1d}
24:  Provider # 7
25:        Name: SQLOLEDB
26:        Parse Name: {0C7FF16C-38E3-11d0-97AB-00C04FC2AD98}
27:  Provider # 8
28:        Name: MSDASQL
29:        Parse Name: {c8b522cb-5cf3-11ce-ade5-00aa0044773d}
```

The DataSource Object

The discussion of OLE DB objects continues with a review of the DataSource object. You create the DataSource object by binding a moniker returned from the Enumerator class or directly calling the CoCreateInstance, using the appropriate CLSID. The DataSource object abstracts the actual data source you want to access. As shown in Figure 17.5, the DataSource object creates a session, which can then create commands and row sets. When a DataSource object is created, if the data provider supports the appropriate interface, it can be *persisted* (that's a fancy object-oriented way of saying that the object is going to be saved) to a file. The OLE DB CoType for the DataSource object is TDataSource. The TDataSource object is defined as supporting the following interfaces:

```
TDataSource {
      interface IDBCreateSession;      // Required Interface
      interface IDBInitialize;         // Required Interface
      interface IDBProperties;         // Required Interface
      interface IPersist;              // Required Interface
      interface IDBDataSourceAdmin;
      interface IDBInfo;
```

```
        interface IPersistFile;
        interface ISupportErrorInfo;
};
```

An OLE DB DataSource object is required to define the IDBCreateSession, IDBInitialize, IDBProperties, and IPersist interfaces. The other interfaces are optionally supported. The OLE DB SDK supplies an ODBC OLE DB provider. If you look at the data providers enumerated in the previous example, you can see this data provider listed as MSDASQL; the class ID constant for the MSDASQL data provider is CLSID_MSDASQL.

This section starts with a survey of interfaces that the DataSource object supports and then shows you how to use the DataSource object to connect to an ODBC data source, including how to specify the ODBC data source name and security context. Earlier today, I discussed the IDBInitialize, IDBProperties, and ISupportErrorInfo interfaces in conjunction with the Enumerator object. (Unlike the Enumerator object though, the DataSource object requires the IDBInitialize and IDBProperties interfaces.)

The IDBCreateSession Interface

The IDBCreateSession interface creates a new session with a data source. A session creates a scope for transactions and provides a mechanism for creating commands and row sets. The IDBCreateSession interface defines the standard IUnknown interface methods QueryInterface, AddRef, and Release. The interface provides one additional method, CreateSession, which is defined as follows:

```
HRESULT CreateSession(IUnknown pAggInterface, REFIID riid,
                      IUnknown **ppDBSession);
```

The CreateSession method creates a Session object, which I cover in more depth tomorrow. An OLE DB DataSource object is required to support the IDBCreateSession interface.

The IDBDataSourceAdmin Interface

The optional IDBDataSourceAdmin interface creates, modifies, and deletes data sources.

 Note
> The IDBDataSourceAdmin interface manipulates the data sources themselves (that is, where the data is actually stored), *not* the DataSource objects.

The IDBDataSourceAdmin interface defines the standard IUnknown interface methods QueryInterface, AddRef, and Release. The interface provides four additional methods:

CreateDataSource, DestroyDataSource, GetCreationProperties, and
ModifyDataSource. These interfaces are defined as follows:

```
HRESULT CreateDataSource(ULONG cPropertySets, DBPROPSET rgPropertySets[],
                         IUnknown* pUnkOuter, REFIID riid,
                         IUnknown** ppSession);
HRESULT DestroyDataSource();
HRESULT GetCreateProperties ( ULONG cPropertyIDSets,
                              const DBPROPIDSET rgPropertyIDSets[],
                            ➥ULONG* pcPropertyInfoSets,
                              DBPROPINFOSET** prgPropertyInfoSets,
                            ➥OLECHAR** ppDescBuffer);
HRESULT ModifyDataSource(ULONG cPropSets, DBPROPSET rgPropSets[]);
```

The CreateDataSource method creates a new data source, and the DataSource object is
initialized to access the new data source. The DestroyDataSource method deletes the
current data source. When a data source is deleted, the DataSource object is returned to
an uninitialized state. The GetCreationProperties accesses the properties that describe
the state of the DataSource object. The ModifyDataSource method modifies the current
data source according to the set of new properties specified.

The IDBInfo Interface

The optional IDBInfo interface determines the keywords and literals that the data source
uses to create data source commands. The IDBInfo interface defines the standard
IUnknown interface methods QueryInterface, AddRef, and Release. The interface provides two additional methods: GetKeyWords and GetLiteralInfo. These methods are
defined as follows:

```
HRESULT GetKeywords(LPOLESTR *pwszKeywords);
HRESULT GetLiteralInfo(ULONG cLiterals,
    const DBLITERAL      rgLiterals[],
    ULONG *              pcLiteralInfo,
    DBLITERALINFO **     prgLiteralInfo,
    OLECHAR **           ppCharBuffer);
```

The GetKeywords method returns a string of comma-separated keywords that the
data source supports. Table 17.3 lists the keywords recognized by OLE DB. The
GetLiteralInfo method determines the additional information about literals supported
in command strings, such as a % used to match zero, or more, characters in a SQL LIKE
clause. Tomorrow, in more depth, I will explain the SQL query language and the process
of creating commands.

TABLE 17.3 THE KEYWORDS RECOGNIZED BY OLE DB

ABSOLUTE	ACTION	ADD
ALL	ALLOCATE	ALTER
AND	ANY	ARE
AS	ASC	ASSERTION
AT	AUTHORIZATION	AVG
BEGIN	BETWEEN	BIT
BIT_LENGTH	BOTH	BY
CASCADE	CASCADED	CASE
CAST	CATALOG	CHAR
CHARACTER	CHAR_LENGTH	CHARACTER_LENGTH
CHECK	CLOSE	COALESCE
COLLATE	COLLATION	COLUMN
COMMIT	CONNECT	CONNECTION
CONSTRAINT	CONSTRAINTS	CONTINUE
CONVERT	CORRESPONDING	COUNT
CREATE	CROSS	CURRENT
CURRENT_DATE	CURRENT_TIME	CURRENT_TIMESTAMP
CURRENT_USER	CURSOR	DATE
DAY	DEALLOCATE	DEC
DECIMAL	DECLARE	DEFAULT
DEFERRABLE	DEFERRED	DELETE
DESC	DESCRIBE	DESCRIPTOR
DIAGNOSTICS	DISCONNECT	DISTINCT
DISTINCTROW	DOMAIN	DOUBLE
DROP	ELSE	END
END-EXEC	ESCAPE	EXCEPT
EXCEPTION	EXEC	EXECUTE
EXISTS	EXTERNAL	EXTRACT
FALSE	FETCH	FIRST
FLOAT	FOR	FOREIGN
FOUND	FROM	FULL
GET	GLOBAL	GO
GOTO	GRANT	GROUP

17

TABLE 17.3 CONTINUED

HAVING	HOUR	IDENTITY
IMMEDIATE	IN	INDICATOR
INITIALLY	INNER	INPUT
INSENSITIVE	INSERT	INT
INTEGER	INTERSECT	INTERVAL
INTO	IS	ISOLATION
JOIN	KEY	LANGUAGE
LAST	LEADING	LEFT
LEVEL	LIKE	LOCAL
LOWER	MATCH	MAX
MIN	MINUTE	MODULE
MONTH	NAMES	NATIONAL
NATURAL	NCHAR	NEXT
NO	NOT	NULL
NULLIF	NUMERIC	OCTET_LENGTH
OF	ON	ONLY
OPEN	OPTION	OR
ORDER	OUTER	OUTPUT
OVERLAPS	PARTIAL	POSITION
PRECISION	PREPARE	PRESERVE
PRIMARY	PRIOR	PRIVILEGES
PROCEDURE	PUBLIC	READ
REAL	REFERENCES	RELATIVE
RESTRICT	REVOKE	RIGHT
ROLLBACK	ROWS	SCHEMA
SCROLL	SECOND	SECTION
SELECT	SESSION	SESSION_USER
SET	SIZE	SMALLINT
SOME	SQL	SQLCODE
SQLERROR	SQLSTATE	SUBSTRING
SUM	SYSTEM_USER	TABLE
TEMPORARY	THEN	TIME
TIMESTAMP	TIMEZONE_HOUR	TIMEZONE_MINUTE

TO	TRAILING	TRANSACTION
TRANSLATE	TRANSLATION	TRIGGER
TRIM	TRUE	UNION
UNIQUE	UNKNOWN	UPDATE
UPPER	USAGE	USER
USING	VALUE	VALUES
VARCHAR	VARYING	VIEW
WHEN	WHENEVER	WHERE
WITH		
YEAR	ZONE	

The `IPersist` Interface

The `IPersist` interface is the base interface for other persist-type interfaces. OLE objects can typically support `IPersistStorage`, `IPersistStream`, and `IPersistFile` interfaces. The `IPersist` interface is like a base class in that it's not usually used directly. The `DataSource` object can optionally support the `IPersistFile` interface described next.

The `IPersistFile` Interface

The `IPersistFile` interface saves and retrieves a `DataSource` object to and from a file. Although the `IPersist` interface is required, the `IPersistFile` interface is optional. The `IPersistFile` interface defines the standard `IUnknown` interface methods `QueryInterface`, `AddRef`, and `Release`. The interface provides five additional methods: `IsDirty`, `Load`, `Save`, `SaveCompleted`, and `GetCurFile`. These methods are defined as follows:

```
HRESULT GetCurFile(LPOLESTR *ppszFileName);
HRESULT IsDirty();
HRESULT Load(LPCOLESTR pszFilename, DWORD dwFileMode);
HRESULT Save(LPCOLESTR pszFileName, BOOL fCurrentFile);
HRESULT SaveCompleted(LPCOLESTR pszFileName);
```

The `GetCurFile` method returns the path of the last file used to `Save` or `Load`. If no current working file exists, the `GetCurFile` method returns the default save filename for the data source. The `IsDirty` method returns `S_OK` if the current `DataSource` object has changed since the last time it was saved to a file; otherwise, `IsDirty` returns `S_FALSE`. Both `S_FALSE` and `S_OK` will resolve to `TRUE` when you use the `SUCCEEDED` macro. You will need to use `SUCCEEDED` and then explicitly check for `S_OK`. If `IsDirty` returns anything other than `S_OK`, you should save the object.

17

The Load method retrieves the DataSource object from a file. The first parameter specifies the full pathname to the file, and the second parameter specifies the mode to use to read the file. Table 17.4 summarizes and describes the mode value constants.

The Save method saves the DataSource object to a file. The first parameter of the Save method specifies the full pathname to the file (if the filename is NULL, the current working file is used), and the second Boolean parameter signals whether the filename specified should now be considered the current working file. The SaveCompleted method determines whether the last Save command has been completed. The SaveCompleted method is not usually used.

TABLE 17.4 A SUMMARY OF MODE VALUE CONSTANTS

Flag	Description
Save Type Flag Group	
STGM_DIRECT	Changes are saved as they occur.
STGM_TRANSACTED	Changes are saved and only written when a commit operation is specified.
STGM_SIMPLE	Provides faster saves when used with compound flags.
Read/Write Flag Group	
STGM_READ	Read-only flag.
STGM_WRITE	Write-enabled flag.
STGM_READWRITE	Read-enabled and write-enabled flag.
Sharing Flag Group	
STGM_SHARE_DENY_NONE	If the file is already opened by another user, access will not be denied.
STGM_SHARE_DENY_READ	Denies other users the ability to read the file while it's opened.
STGM_SHARE_DENY_WRITE	Denies others the ability to write the file if it's opened by another user.
STGM_SHARE_EXCLUSIVE	A combination of the STGM_SHARE_DENY_READ and STGM_SHARE_DENY_WRITE flags.
Priority Flag Group	
STGM_PRIORITY	Open the file for priority access; no one else can commit changes while the file is opened in this mode.
Delete Flag Group	
STGM_DELETEONRELEASE	Used primarily for temporary files. The file is deleted when the associated object is deleted.

Flag	Description
	Creation Flag Group
STGM_CREATE	If there is an existing file, delete it before any changes are saved.
STGM_CONVERT	Create a new data object and preserve any existing data.
STGM_FAILIFTHERE	Don't create the file if an existing file has the same name.
STGM_NOSCRATCH	Don't buffer the file in scratch space (applicable only under Windows 95).

Note File mode constants can be combined, but only one mode constant from each group can be used.

17

Connecting to a `DataSource` Object

The last activity for today is to tie together the new information with the concepts you learned at the end of the day yesterday. You will create another basic OLE DB application, which builds upon the code you wrote in Listing 16.2.

Yesterday's example simply created and released a `DataSource` object. Although you are not yet ready to do anything useful, such as access the data contained in a data source (see Days 18 and 19), you can build on the earlier example. Today's application uses the OLE DB ODBC data provider to access a data source. This time, you use the OLE DB ODBC data source provider object's properties to specify the appropriate connection information: the data source name, username, and password.

Before looking at the code, you need to understand the steps necessary for building an OLE DB–enabled application. The first step, mentioned yesterday, is to initialize the necessary COM-related DLLs. The `CoInitialize` and `CoUninitialize` methods load and release the appropriate COM-related DLLs. You must call these methods at the start and end of any application that uses COM components.

After you initialize the COM environment, the next step is to create access to the `DataSource` object's `IDBInitialize` interface from the OLE DB ODBC data provider. You could use the `Enumerator` object, discussed earlier, to find the OLE DB ODBC data source provider, but if you know which provider you want to access, you can directly access the interface by calling the `CoCreateInstance` method. The definition of the `CoCreateInstance` method is

```
STDAPI CoCreatInstance(REFCLSID rclsid, LPUNKNOWN pAggInterface,
                       DWORD dwClsContext, REFIID riid,
                       ➡LPVOID *ppInterface);
```

The rclsid parameter specifies the class identifier of the COM object you want to use.
To connect to the OLE DB ODBC data provider, you can use the class ID
CLSID_MSDASQL. The pAggInterface parameter specifies whether this object is part of an
aggregate. For this example, the object is not part of an aggregate, so you can specify
NULL. The dwClsContext specifies the context for running the COM object. This application uses the CLSCTX_INPROC_SERVER, which specifies that the COM object runs in the
same process space as the caller. The riid specifies the interface reference ID. You want
to access the IDBInitialize interface, so you should use the IID_IDBInitialize constant. The ppInterface parameter specifies the variable that retrieves the interface.

> **Note**
>
> When you are specifying an interface reference ID, you specify the constants
> by using the prefix IID before the interface name.

The OLE DB ODBC Provider

As I mentioned earlier, the OLE DB ODBC provides access to an ODBC data source.
For your reference, Table 17.5 lists the interfaces that the OLE DB ODBC data source
provider supports. *Only* the OLE DB objects that can use these interfaces (either because
they are mandatory or optional) support them.

TABLE 17.5   INTERFACES SUPPORTED BY THE OLE DB ODBC DATA SOURCE PROVIDER

Interface	
IAccessor	IColumnsInfo
IColumnsRowset	ICommand
ICommandPrepare	ICommandProperties
ICommandText	ICommandWithParameters
IConnectionPoint	IConnectionPointContainer
IConvertType	IDBCreateCommand
IDBCreateSession	IDBInfoIDBInitialize
IDBProperties	IDBSchemaRowset
IErrorLookup	IGetDataSource
IMultipleResults	IOpenRowset
IPersistFile	IRowset

Interface	
IRowsetChange	IRowsetIdentity
IRowsetInfo	IRowsetLocate
IRowsetResynch	IRowsetUpdate
ISessionProperties	ISourcesRowset
ISupportErrorInfo	ITransaction
ITransactionLocal	ITransactionOptions

Note The IPersistFile interface is supported only for the DataSource object.

Initialization Properties Used

The DataSource object of the OLE DB ODBC data source provider must be initialized before it can be used. Table 17.6 lists the properties that the IDBInitialize interface uses to specify the prompt mode, data source name, username, and password needed to access the ODBC data source. The SetProperties method of the IDBProperties interface sets the properties necessary to access the ODBC data source.

TABLE 17.6 THE INITIALIZATION PROPERTIES USED BY THE OLE DB ODBC DATA PROVIDER

Property	Description
DBPROP_AUTH_PASSWORD	The password required to access the ODBC data source
DBPROP_AUTH_USERID	The user ID required to access the ODBC data source
DBPROP_INIT_DATASOURCE	The name of the ODBC data source
DBPROP_INIT_HWND	The HWND argument used by SQLDriverConnect
DBPROP_INIT_LOCATION	The name of the server used by SQLDriverConnect
DBPROP_INIT_MODE	The connection mode, either DB_MODE_READ or DB_MODE_READWRITE
DBPROP_INIT_PROMPT	Specifies the prompting mode used when connecting to the data source
DBPROP_INIT_PROVIDERSTRING	The complete ODBC connection string
DBPROP_INIT_TIMEOUT	Specifies the time-out value for the login

Example: Connecting to an OLE DB ODBC Data Source

Listing 17.4 shows the ODBCTEST.CPP source code. This example extends the example in Listing 16.2 by setting the properties required to access the ODBC data source.

To build the application, run Visual Studio and select the File New menu choice. Click the Projects tab and specify a Win32 Console Application. Call the application ODBCTEST. Click the OK button and then specify that you want to create an empty project; click the Finish button. After AppWizard runs, create a new C++ source file as part of the project. You can call it whatever you think is appropriate, ODBCTEST.CPP, for example. Enter the code shown in Listing 17.4 into the source file.

You need to change the input libraries for the linker to

oledbd.lib kernel32.lib user32.lib gdi32.lib winspool.lib comdlg32.lib advapi32.lib shell32.lib ole32.lib oleaut32.lib uuid.lib

You do this on the Link tab under the Project Settings menu. When you build the project, it should compile and link without errors or warnings.

> **Tip**
>
> You can modify this example to set the properties that specify the connection context for the username, password, and data source name to values that are appropriate for other ODBC data sources set up on your system.

LISTING 17.4 A SAMPLE APPLICATION THAT CONNECTS TO AN ODBC DATA SOURCE

```
 1:  #define DBINITCONSTANTS
 2:
 3:  // Standard Application Includes
 4:  #include <windows.h>
 5:  #include <stdio.h>
 6:  #include <tchar.h>
 7:  #include <stddef.h>
 8:  #include <iostream.h>
 9:
10:  // OLE DB Header Files
11:  #include <oledb.h>
12:  #include <oledberr.h>
13:
14:  // OLE DB - ODBC Provider Header File
15:  #include <msdasql.h>
16:
17:  void main() {
18:     IDBInitialize *pIDBInitialize = NULL;
19:     IDBProperties *pIDBProperties;
20:     DBPROP        InitProperties[4];
```

```
21:     DBPROPSET        rgInitPropSet[1];
22:     int              i;
23:
24:     // Initialize The Component Object Module Library
25:     CoInitialize(NULL);
26:
27:     // Obtain Access To The OLE DB - ODBC Provider
28:     CoCreateInstance(CLSID_MSDASQL, NULL, CLSCTX_INPROC_SERVER,
29:                      IID_IDBInitialize, (void **) &pIDBInitialize);
30:
31:     // Initialize the property values that are the same for each
32:     // property
33:     for (i = 0; i < 4; i++ ) {
34:         VariantInit(&InitProperties[i].vValue);
35:         InitProperties[i].dwOptions = DBPROPOPTIONS_REQUIRED;
36:         InitProperties[i].colid = DB_NULLID;
37:     }
38:
39:     // level of prompting that will be done
        // to complete the connection process
40:     InitProperties[0].dwPropertyID = DBPROP_INIT_PROMPT;
41:     InitProperties[0].vValue.vt = VT_I2;
42:     InitProperties[0].vValue.iVal = DBPROMPT_NOPROMPT;
43:
44:     // Specify the User Name
45:     InitProperties[1].dwPropertyID = DBPROP_AUTH_USERID;
46:     InitProperties[1].vValue.vt = VT_BSTR;
47:     // Note: The L cast directive casts the string into a UNICODE
        // string
48:     InitProperties[1].vValue.bstrVal = SysAllocString((LPOLESTR)L"");
49:
50:     // Specify the appropriate Password
51:     InitProperties[2].dwPropertyID = DBPROP_AUTH_PASSWORD;
52:     InitProperties[2].vValue.vt = VT_BSTR;
53:     InitProperties[2].vValue.bstrVal = SysAllocString((LPOLESTR)L"");
54:
55:     // Specify the Data Source name
56:     InitProperties[3].dwPropertyID = DBPROP_INIT_DATASOURCE;
57:     InitProperties[3].vValue.vt = VT_BSTR;
58:     InitProperties[3].vValue.bstrVal = SysAllocString((LPOLESTR)
                                                    ➥L"OrdersDb");
59:
60:     rgInitPropSet[0].guidPropertySet = DBPROPSET_DBINIT;
61:     rgInitPropSet[0].cProperties = 4;
62:     rgInitPropSet[0].rgProperties = InitProperties;
63:
64:     // set initialization properties
65:     pIDBInitialize->QueryInterface(IID_IDBProperties,
                                    ➥(void **)&pIDBProperties);
66:     pIDBProperties->SetProperties(1,rgInitPropSet);
```

17

continues

LISTING 17.4 A SAMPLE APPLICATION THAT CONNECTS TO AN ODBC DATA SOURCE

```
67:     pIDBProperties->Release();
68:
69:     // Call the Initialize method to establish the connection to
70:     // the ODBC data source specified above
71:     HRESULT hr = pIDBInitialize->Initialize();
72:
73:     if SUCCEEDED(hr)
74:     {
75:       ::MessageBeep(MB_OK);
76:     }
77:
78:     // This Is Where You Would Utilize OLE DB to execute commands and
79:     // access row sets
80:
81:     // Free Up Allocated Memory
82:     pIDBInitialize->Uninitialize();
83:     pIDBInitialize->Release();
84:
85:     // Release The Component Object Module Library
86:     CoUninitialize();
87:   };
```

Lines 20 and 21 in Listing 17.4 define two variables of the type DBPROPSET and DBPROP. The DBPROPSET structure holds the set of properties, and the DBPROP structure holds an individual property. The values of these variables are set in lines 31–62. After the properties are set to the appropriate values, they are used by the IDBProperties interface in lines 64–67. The SetProperties method specifies the appropriate security context for access to the ODBC data source. After the properties are set, the Initialize method of the IDBInitialize interface is called in line 71, and a connection is made to the ODBC data source. Line 75 calls MessageBeep if the connection was made successfully.

Listing 17.4 minimizes the error checking for code brevity. In your code, you should check the return values from CoCreateInstance and QueryInterface to be sure that the interface pointers have been successfully returned.

Tomorrow you learn how to create a session, create commands, and access data source row sets.

Summary

The major components of OLE DB are data consumers and data providers. OLE DB uses COM extensively. You learned about the COM architecture in more detail, the importance of interfaces in the COM architecture, how OLE DB uses these interfaces, that a COM object can support multiple interfaces at different functional levels, and the role of interface factoring in OLE DB. You also learned how the COM architecture uses the QueryInterface method to determine whether an object supports an interface.

You worked on two sample applications: The first uses the Enumerator object to list the available data providers, and the second uses the OLE DB ODBC data provider to connect to an ODBC data source.

The discussion of OLE DB objects continues tomorrow with a look at the Session and Command objects. In addition, Day 18 begins the discussion of how to use OLE DB objects to obtain access to the data contained in a data source.

Q&A

17

This section answers some common questions related to today's topics.

Q How does the COM architecture handle different versions of components?

A The COM architecture is well suited to versioning. As you might realize, when an interface is published using COM, it cannot be changed. Therefore, if a COM component needs to support some added functionality, the current interfaces supported by the COM component are not changed to support this functionality. Instead, a new interface (with a new interface identifier) is added to support these new features. The QueryInterface mechanism determines the exact level of support provided by a COM component. A new interface should be created under the following conditions:

- The number, type, or meanings of a method in an interface change.
- The number, order, return values, or meaning of functions change.

Q What is the best way to access an OLE DB data provider—through enumerators or directly?

A You can use the Enumerator object to determine the data providers supported on the computer on which the application is running. This method is good to use in an application in which the end user can dynamically select the data source. If you know the provider your application is required to use, the CoCreateInstance method is a better method to use. It requires less overhead than the enumeration methodology requires. Remember to check the HRESULT of the CoCreateInstance method to ensure that the computer where the application is currently running actually supports the provider of an interface you have chosen.

Q I know that some of the interfaces provided by OLE DB objects are optional. How do I determine whether the data provider I am using supports a particular interface for a specific object? Can I get this information at runtime?

A The QueryInterface mechanism determines whether a COM object supports a particular interface. If the QueryInterface method doesn't return S_OK, the interface is not supported. The QueryInterface method is used during runtime to establish a "connection" between an application and a particular interface. An application should call the QueryInterface method before it attempts to rely on any methods supported by that interface.

Workshop

The Workshop quiz questions test your understanding of today's material. (The answers appear in Appendix F, "Answers.") The exercises encourage you to apply the information you learned today to real-life situations.

Quiz

1. What is the role of a data provider and a data consumer in the OLE DB architecture?

2. What is an interface? How does the COM architecture use an interface?

3. What is interface factoring?

4. What method is used to determine whether a COM object supports a particular interface?

5. Describe the basic flow of information in an OLE DB application.

6. What is an Enumerator object, and how is it used?

7. What interfaces are supported by an Enumerator object?

8. What is a DataSource object, and how is it used?

9. What interfaces does a DataSource object support?

10. What methods initialize and release the DLLs required by a COM application?

Exercises

1. Review the Visual C++ books online documentation (provided with Visual C++) for more information regarding the specifics of COM programming.

2. The applications developed yesterday and today do not really consider error handling. How would you integrate error handling into the application in Listing 17.4? (*Hint*: Most of the COM related functions return an HRESULT type value.)

WEEK 3

DAY 18

Querying a Data Source with OLE DB

Day 18 continues the examination of OLE DB objects, specifically the Session and Command objects and the interfaces they provide. You learn how to create a Session object by using the IDBCreateSession interface of the DataSource object and how to create a Command object using the IDBCreateCommand interface of the Session object. Although OLE DB data providers don't have to support Command objects, the OLE DB ODBC data provider does support commands on ODBC data sources. The section on Command objects includes a concise summary of Structured Query Language (SQL). Today's examples focus on using the OLE DB ODBC data provider to access a SQL Server data source.

Today you will

- Use Session objects to define a transaction context, create commands, and directly access row sets.
- Work with interfaces supported by the Session object.
- Explore Command objects and how to use them to perform commands supported by the data provider.

- Work with interfaces supported by the Command object.
- Discover the SQL query/command language.
- Understand the differences between SQL data manipulation and data definition commands.
- Use Accessors.
- Use Multiple resultsets

Sessions

The Session object provides a context for transactions and commands. The IDBCreatession interface of the DataSource object creates a Session object. (The CreateSession method of the IDBCreatession interface actually creates the Session object.) You can use the Session object to

- Create a Command object.
- Access a row set directly.
- Create or modify data source tables and indexes.

The Session object is defined as supporting the following interfaces:

```
TSession {
        interface IGetDataSource;            // Required Interface
        interface IOpenRowset;               // Required Interface
        interface ISessionProperties;        // Required Interface
        interface IDBCreateCommand;
        interface IDBSchemaRowset;
        interface IIndexDefinition;
        interface ISupportErrorInfo;
        interface ITableDefinition;
        interface ITransaction;
        interface ITransactionJoin;
        interface ITransactionLocal;
        interface ITransactionObject;
};
```

This is the TSession CoType. A CoType is a way to define a group of COM objects that have similar characteristics. All COM objects that belong to the TSession CoType must expose its mandatory interface. In addition, they can expose the optional interfaces.

The IGetDataSource Interface

The IGetDataSource interface obtains an interface pointer to an interface of the DataSource object that created the Session object. This interface is required by the Session object. It defines the standard IUnknown interface methods QueryInterface,

AddRef, and `Release` and provides one additional method, `GetDataSource`. The GetDataSource method is defined as follows:

```
HRESULT GetDataSource(REFIID riid, IUnknown **ppDataSource);
```

The `riid` parameter specifies the interface of the `DataSource` object you want to access, and the `ppDataSource` parameter returns a pointer to the `DataSource` interface you requested. This method enables your application to access a `DataSource` object directly from a `Session` object (that is, without using a variable to point to the desired object).

The `IOpenRowset` Interface

The `IOpenRowset` interface accesses a row set from a data source that doesn't support commands. You will learn more about commands and the `Command` object later today. The IOpenRowset interface is required by the `Session` object. The `IOpenRowset` interface defines the standard `IUnknown` interface methods `QueryInterface`, `AddRef`, and `Release` and provides one additional method, `OpenRowset`. The `OpenRowset` method is defined as follows:

```
HRESULT OpenRowset(IUnknown *pAggInterface, DBID *pTableID, DBID
*pIndexID,
                   REFIID riid, ULONG cPropSet, DBPROPSET rdPropSet[],
                   IUnknown **ppRowset);
```

The `pAggInterface` parameter is used if the row set is *aggregated* (that is, combined with other row sets). If this parameter is `NULL`, that row set isn't being combined. The pTableID parameter is a `DBID` structure that holds the name of the data source table you want open. The `DBID` structure helps explain how the table name is passed. The `DBID` structure is defined as follows:

```
typedef struct tagDBID {
  union {                          // A union that holds either:
    GUID guid;                     //    An actual GUID, or
    GUID *guid;                    //    A pointer to a GUID
  } uGuid;
  DBKIND eKind;                    // A flag that determines the
                                   // type of ID being held in this
                                   // structure

  union {                          // A union that holds either:
    LPOLESTR pwszName;             //    A string name
    ULONG ulPropid;                //    A numeric ID
  } uName;
} DBID;

enum DBKINDENUM {                  // Values for the eKind flag
                                   // The ID is defined by the
                                   // following structure values:
```

```
  DBKIND_GUID_NAME,                    // A GUID and a Name
  DBKIND_GUID_PROPID,                  // A GUID and a Numeric ID
  DBKIND_NAME,                         // Just the Name
  DBKIND_PGUID_NAME,                   // A pointer to a GUID and a Name
  DBKIND_PGUID_PROPID,                 // A pointer to a GUID and a Numeric
ID
  DBKIND_PROPID,                       // Just a Numeric ID
  DBKIND_GUID                          // Just a GUID
};
```

As you can see, the DBID structure is defined to hold various ID combinations. The eKind flag defines the combination used by the DBID structure to define the ID. The DBKINDENUM enumeration structure defines the flags used by the eKind structure variable. For example, the following specification defines a DBID that holds a table name:

```
DBID      tableID;
LPWSTR    pwszTableName = L"CUSTOMER";

tableID.eKind = DBKIND_NAME;
tableID.uname.pwszName = pwszTableName;
```

Note
The pwszName field of the DBID structure is defined as a LPOLESTR (equivalent to the LPWSTR type), which defines a Unicode string. *Unicode strings* use 16-bit character values to define strings of different languages. The L above tells the compiler that the string literal is of type wchar_t. For more information on Unicode strings, please consult the Visual C++ online documentation.

The pIndexID parameter of the OpenRowset method is a DBID structure that represents the name of the associated index to open. The riid parameter is a reference ID of the row set interface to return. The interface must support row sets. Typically, this ID is IID_Rowset. The cPropSet parameter specifies the number of properties specified in the DBPROPSET array. The rgPropSet parameter is an array of DBPROPSET structures, which contain the row set properties. Finally, the ppRowset parameter returns the row set interface pointer. (A detailed discussion of opening and navigating row sets is part of Day 19, "Navigating the Resultset of a Query.")

The ISessionProperties Interface

The ISessionProperties interface gets and sets the properties of a Session object. *Properties* define values that determine the state of an object. The ISessionProperties interface is required for Session objects. It defines the standard IUnknown interface methods QueryInterface, AddRef, and Release. Also, the interface provides two additional methods: GetProperties and SetProperties. The GetProperties method retrieves the value of a property, and the SetProperties method sets the value of a property. These methods are defined as follows:

```
HRESULT GetProperties(ULONG cPropIDSets, const DBPROPIDSET rgPropSets[],
                      ULONG *pcPropSets, DBPROPSET **prgPropSets);
HRESULT SetProperties(ULONG cPropNum, DBPROPSET rgPropSets[]);
```

The `IDBCreateCommand` Interface

The `IDBCreateCommand` interface creates a new `Command` object and is optional for `Session` objects. This interface defines the standard `IUnknown` interface methods `QueryInterface`, `AddRef`, and `Release` and provides one additional method, `CreateCommand`. The `CreateCommand` method is defined as follows:

```
HRESULT CreateCommand(IUnknown pAggInterface, REFIID riid,
                      IUnknown pCommandInt);
```

The `pAggInterface` parameter is used if the command is part of an aggregate. The `riid` parameter specifies the `Command` interface to create. The `pCommandInt` parameter returns the `Command` interface created.

The `IDBSchemaRowset` Interface

The `IDBSchemaRowset` retrieves data source schema information. *Schema information* describes the data contained in the data source. The `IDBSchemaRowset` interface is optional for `Session` objects. It defines the standard `IUnknown` interface methods `QueryInterface`, `AddRef`, and `Release`. The interface provides two additional methods: `GetRowset` and `GetSchemas`. The `GetRowset` method returns a schema row set. The `GetSchemas` method returns an array of available data source schemas. These methods are defined as follows:

```
HRESULT GetRowset(IUnknown *pAggInterface, REFGUID rguidSchema,
                  ULONG cRestrictions, const VARIANT rgRectricts[],
                  REFIID riid, ULONG cPropSets, DBPROPSET rdPropSet,
                  IUnknown ppRowset);
HRESULT GetSchemas(ULONG *pSchemas, GUID **pgSchemas, ULONG
**pRestrictions);
```

For the `GetRowset` method, the `pAggInterface` parameter is used if the command is part of an aggregate. The `rguidSchema` parameter defines a schema GUID. Table 18.1 defines the schema GUIDs available. Refer to the OLE DB specification documentation for more information regarding the row sets that these schemas return. The `cRestrictions` parameter defines the number of column restrictions. The `rgRestricts` array parameter defines the column restrictions. The `riid` parameter defines the interface ID of the row set interface to return; typically, this value is `IID_Rowset`. The `cPropSet` parameter specifies the number of properties specified in the `DBPROPSET` array. The `rgPropSet` parameter is an array of `DBPROPSET` structures, which contain the row set properties. The `ppRowset` parameter is used to return the row set interface pointer.

For the GetSchemas method, the pSchemas parameter returns the number of schemas supported by the data source. The pgSchemas parameter returns an array of schema GUIDs. The pRestrictions parameter returns an array of schema row set column restrictions.

TABLE 18.1   SCHEMA GUIDs

DBSCHEMA_ASSERTIONS

DBSCHEMA_CATALOGS

DBSCHEMA_CHARACTER_SETS

DBSCHEMA_COLLATIONS

DBSCHEMA_COLUMN_DOMAIN_USAGE

DBSCHEMA_COLUMN_PRIVILEGES

DBSCHEMA_COLUMNS

DBSCHEMA_CONSTRAINT_COLUMN_USAGE

DBSCHEMA_CONSTRAINT_TABLE_USAGE

DBSCHEMA_FOREIGN_KEYS

DBSCHEMA_INDEXES

DBSCHEMA_KEY_COLUMN_USAGE

DBSCHEMA_PRIMARY_KEYS

DBSCHEMA_PROCEDURE_COLUMNS

DBSCHEMA_PROCEDURE_PARAMETERS

DBSCHEMA_PROCEDURES

DBSCHEMA_PROVIDER_TYPES

DBSCHEMA_REFERENTIAL_CONSTRAINTS

DBSCHEMA_SCHEMATA

DBSCHEMA_SQL_LANGUAGES

DBSCHEMA_STATISTICS

DBSCHEMA_TABLE_CONSTRAINTS

DBSCHEMA_TABLE_PRIVILEGES

DBSCHEMA_TABLES

DBSCHEMA_TRANSLATIONS

DBSCHEMA_USAGE_PRIVILEGES

DBSCHEMA_VIEW_COLUMN_USAGE

DBSCHEMA_VIEW_TABLE_USAGE

DBSCHEMA_VIEWS

The ITableDefinition Interface

The ITableDefinition interface creates, deletes, and modifies data source tables. This interface is optional. It defines the standard IUnknown interface methods QueryInterface, AddRef, and Release and provides four additional methods: AddColumn, CreateTable, DropColumn, and DropTable. These methods are defined as follows:

```
HRESULT AddColumn(DBID *pTableID, DBCOLUMNDESC *pColDesc, DBID **ppColId);
HRESULT CreateTable(IUnknown * pUnkOuter,
                        DBID * pTableID,
                        ULONG cColumnDescs,
                        DBCOLUMNDESC rgColumnDescs[],
                        REFIID riid,
                        ULONG cPropertySets,
                        DBPROPSET rgPropertySets[],
                        DBID ** ppTableID,
                        IUnknown ** ppRowset
HRESULT DropColumn(DBID *pTableID, DBID *pColumnID);
HRESULT DropTable(DBID *pTableID);
```

The DropColumn and DropTable methods should be self-explanatory, with both methods taking the name of a table and column (if applicable) to delete. With the AddColumn method, the pTableID parameter takes the name of the table to which the column will be added. The pColDesc parameter describes the column to add. The pColId parameter returns a pointer to the column that was just created. The CreateTable method pAggInterface parameter is used if the command is part of an aggregate, and pTableID specifies the name of the table to create. The cColDescs and pColDescs parameters define the number and description of the columns to create. The riid parameter specifies the row set interface to return for the table you are creating. The cPropSet parameter specifies the number of properties used in the DBPROPSET array. The rgPropSet parameter is an array of DBPROPSET structures, which contain the table properties. Finally the ppTableID and ppRowset parameters return pointers to the table ID and row set for the newly created table. Listing 18.1 demonstrates how the CreateTable and DropTable methods are used.

18

INPUT   **LISTING 18.1**   USING THE ITableDefinition TO CREATE AND DROP A TABLE

```
1:   DBID          cTableID;                 // Holds the table name
2:   DBCOLUMNDESC  cColDescs[2];             // Column definitions
3:   DBID          *pNewTableID = NULL;      // Interface to newly
4:                                           // created table
5:   IRowset       *pRowset = NULL;          // Rowset interface
                                             // pointer
6:
```

continues

LISTING **18.1**   CONTINUED

```
 7:   cTableID.eKind = DBKIND_NAME;                    // Specify the table
 8:                                                    // name to create
 9:   cTableID.uname.pwszName = L"Table1";
10:
11:                                                    // Define Column 1
12:   cColDescs[0].pwszTypeName = L"DBTYPE_CHAR"; // Specify the type of
13:                                                    // column 1
14:   cColDescs[0].pTypeInfo = NULL;                   // No additional type
15:                                                    // information
16:   cColDescs[0].rgPropertySets = NULL;              // No special column
17:                                                    // properties
18:   cColDescs[0].pclsid = IID_NULL;                  // If this is an OLE
19:                                                    // type column, this is
20:                                                    // where the OLE type is
21:                                                    // specified
22:   cColDescs[0].cPropertySets = 0;                  // Number of properties
23:                                                    // specified
24:   cColDescs[0].ulColumnSize = 255;                 // Size of the column,
25:                                                    // in this case 255
                                                       // characters
26:   cColDescs[0].dbcid.eKind = DBKIND_NAME;          // Specify the field name
27:   cColDescs[0].dbcid.pwszName = L"Field1";
28:   cColDescs[0].wType = DBTYPE_STR;
29:   cColDescs[0].bPrecision = 0;                     // Only used for
30:   cColDescs[0].bScale = 0;                         // floating-point types
31:
32:   cColDescs[1].pwszTypeName = L"DBTYPE_I4";  // Define Column 2
33:   cColDescs[1].pTypeInfo = NULL;
34:   cColDescs[1].rgPropertySets = NULL;
35:   cColDescs[1].pclsid = IID_NULL;
36:   cColDescs[1].cPropertySets = 0;
37:   cColDescs[1].ulColumnSize = 0;
38:   cColDescs[1].dbcid.eKind = DBKIND_NAME;
39:   cColDescs[1].dbcid.pwszName = L"Field2";
40:   cColDescs[1].wType = DBTYPE_I4;
41:   cColDescs[1].bPrecision = 0;
42:   cColDescs[1].bScale = 0;
43:
44:   // Create the Table
45:   MySession->CreateTable(NULL, &TableID, 2, &ColDescs, IID_IRowset, 0,
      ➥NULL,
46:                          &NewtableID, &pRowset);
```

```
47:
48:    // --------------------------------------------------------------
49:    // Drop the table named Table2
50:    // --------------------------------------------------------------
51:
52:    cTableID.eKind = DBKIND_NAME;                    // Specify the table name
53:    cTableID.uname.pwszName = L"Table2";
54:    HRESULT DropTable(&cTableID);
```

Line 1 in Listing 18.1 defines a variable to hold the table name. Line 2 defines a column
description array with two elements, specifying that there will be two columns. See the
comments following lines 1–25 to understand what the code is doing. Line 38 makes the
CreateTable call to actually create the table. Lines 45–47 drop a (different) table from
the database.

Note

As you can see from this example, using the ITableDefinition interface to
create a table is time-consuming. If your data provider supports a SQL command interface, you should use that instead when you create a table.

18

The IIndexDefinition Interface

The IIndexDefinition interface enables data source indexes to be created and deleted. It
is optional and defines the standard IUnknown interface methods QueryInterface,
AddRef, and Release. The interface provides two additional methods: CreateIndex and
DropIndex, which are defined as follows:

```
HRESULT CreateIndex(    DBID *              pTableID,
   DBID *                                   pIndexID,
   ULONG                                    cIndexColumnDescs,
   const DBINDEXCOLUMNDESC                  rgIndexColumnDescs[],
   ULONG                                    cPropertySets,
   DBPROPSET                                rgPropertySets[],
   DBID **                                  ppIndexID
HRESULT DropIndex(DBID *pTableID, DBID *pIndexID);
```

The CreateIndex, pTableID, and pIndexID parameters define the table and index identifiers. The cIndexCols parameter defines the number of index columns to use when creating the index. The rdIndexColsDescs parameter defines an array of columns to use when
creating the index. The cPropSet parameter specifies the number of properties used in
the DBPROPSET array. The rgPropSet parameter is an array of DBPROPSET structures,
which contain the index properties. The ppIndexID parameter returns a pointer to the

new index. For the DropIndex method, the pTableID and pIndexID parameters define the table and index identifiers of the index to delete. (This book doesn't delve into the DropIndex method. Refer to the discussion of SQL later today for more information about creating and deleting indexes by using the data definition capabilities of SQL.)

The ITransaction, ITransactionJoin, ITransactionLocal, and ITransactionObject Interfaces

Finally, the ITransaction, ITransactionJoin, ITransactionLocal, and ITransactionObject interfaces create transactions. (See Day 20, "Properties, Transactions, and Indexes.")

Commands

Command objects perform commands that the provider supports. Using the OLE DB ODBC provider and a database such as SQL Server, you can use the Command object to execute SQL commands. OLE DB data providers aren't required to support commands.

> **Tip**
>
> Remember that you can use the QueryInterface method to verify whether a data provider supports commands. Use the IID_IDBCreateCommand interface identifier when calling the QueryInterface method. If the QueryInterface command succeeds, the data provider supports commands!

This section begins with a discussion of the Command object and its associated interfaces and then briefly reviews the SQL command language. After you understand the Command object and SQL, you learn how to utilize these objects when using Visual C++.

> **Note**
>
> If the data provider you're using doesn't support commands, the only way you can obtain data source data is by using the IOpenRowset interface of the Session object.

The TCommand CoType supports the following interfaces:

```
TCommand {
        interface IAccessor;                 // Required Interface
        interface IColumnsInfo;              // Required Interface
        interface ICommand;                  // Required Interface
        interface ICommandProperties;        // Required Interface
        interface ICommandText;              // Required Interface
```

```
        interface IConvertType;           // Required Interface
        interface IColumnsRowset;
        interface ICommandPrepare;
        interface ICommandWithParameters;
        interface ISupportErrorInfo;
};
```

The `ISupportErrorInfo` interface was introduced yesterday and is covered in more detail on Day 21, "OLE DB Error Handling."

The `IAccessor` Interface

Accessors manage the buffer in which retrieved row sets or command parameters are stored. The `CreateAccessor` method creates new `Accessors`. An `Accessor` is identified by its handle (an `HACCESSOR` type), which is returned in an out parameter of the `CreateAccessor` method. An `Accessor` created by a `Command` object is inherited by the row sets that the `Command` object subsequently creates. Whenever the consumer finishes using an `Accessor`, the consumer must call the `ReleaseAccessor` method to release the memory it holds. This section briefly describes the `IAccessor` interface; a more detailed discussion of command parameters and Accessors appears at the end of today. (Row set Accessors are covered in more detail tomorrow.)

The `IAccessor` interface is required by `Command` objects. This interface defines the standard `IUnknown` interface methods `QueryInterface`, `AddRef`, and `Release`. The interface also provides four additional methods: `AddRefAccessor`, `CreateAccessor`, `GetBindings`, and `ReleaseAccessor`. These methods are defined as follows:

```
HRESULT AddRefAccessor(
    DBACCESSORFLAGS        dwAccessorFlags,
    ULONG                  cBindings,
    const DBBINDING          rgBindings[],
    ULONG                  cbRowSize,
    HACCESSOR *            phAccessor,
    DBBINDSTATUS          rgStatus[]);
HRESULT GetBindings(HACCESSOR hAccessor, DBACCESSORFLAGS *pdwFlags,
                ULONG *pNumBindings, DBBINDING *prgBinding);
HRESULT ReleaseAccessor(HACCESSOR hAccessor, ULONG *pRefCount);
```

Reference counts control how many times an `Accessor` is currently in use. If an `Accessor` is being used in a multithreaded environment, each thread should call the `AddRefAccessor` method. This procedure adds to the reference count of the `Accessor`. The `ReleaseAccessor` method frees the memory used by an `Accessor`. Before the memory is actually freed, the reference count is decremented. If the reference count is `0` (which means that the `Accessor` isn't being used anywhere else), the memory is released. The `CreateAccessor` method creates and allocates the memory required by

18

is 0 (which means that the 000 isn't being used anywhere else), the memory is released. The CreateAccessor method creates and allocates the memory required by a new Accessor. The GetBindings method retrieves the data bindings associated with an Accessor. I explain these methods in more detail later today and again tomorrow (Day 19).

The IColumnsInfo Interface

The IColumnsInfo method retrieves schema information for a prepared statement. *Prepared statements* are commands that are precompiled to execute faster. The data provider interprets a command once, when it is defined. Then when the command is executed later, it can be executed quickly. The IColumnsInfo interface can work with a prepared statement to retrieve information regarding the columns that will be returned in the row set when the command is executed. The IColumnsInfo interface is required by the Command object. The IColumnsInfo interface defines the standard IUnknown interface methods QueryInterface, AddRef, and Release. The interface also provides two additional methods: GetColumnInfo and MapColumnIDs. These methods are defined as follows:

```
HRESULT GetColumnInfo(ULONG *pNumColumns, DBCOLUMNINFO **prdColInfo,
                      OLECHAR **ppBuffer);
HRESULT MapColumnIDs(ULONG cNumColIDs, const DBID rgColIDs, ULONG rgCols);
```

The GetColumnInfo method retrieves information about the columns returned by a prepared statement. The pNumColumns parameter returns the number of columns created by the prepared statement. The prdColInfo is a DBCOLUMNINFO structure that contains the schema information regarding the columns returned by the prepared statement. The ppBuffer parameter returns a pointer to a block of memory, which is the memory that the GetColumnInfo method used to store strings for the prdColInfo structure. After you review the prdColInfo structure, you must free the memory through the COM task allocator by getting a pointer to IMalloc and calling its Free function or by calling CoTaskMemFree to release this memory.

The MapColumnIDs method takes an array of column IDs rgColIDs and returns another array, rgCols, which contains the ordinal position of each of these columns in the prepared statement. The rgCols array elements match up with the rgColIDs elements. For example, if element 1 of the rgCols array contains any value other than DB_INVALIDCOLUMN, such as the value 5, element 1 in the rgColIDs structure is the fifth column in the row set that the prepared statement will return. A value of DB_INVALIDCOLUMN identifies a column that isn't contained in the prepared statement. The cNumColIDs parameter specifies the number of columns contained in the rgColIDs array.

The `ICommand` Interface

The `ICommand` interface executes and manages executing commands. It is required by the `Command` object and defines the standard `IUnknown` interface methods `QueryInterface`, `AddRef`, and `Release`. This interface also provides three additional methods: `Cancel`, `Execute`, and `GetDBSession`. These methods are defined as follows:

```
HRESULT Cancel();
HRESULT Execute(IUnknown pAggInterface, REFIID riid, DBPARAMS *pDBParams,
                LONG *pcNumRowsAffected, IUnknown **ppRowset);
HRESULT GetDBSession(REFID riid, IUnknown **ppSessionInterface);
```

Tip

In a multithreaded application, a thread can be spawned that executes the command while a different thread is performing other processing. You can use the `ICommand` interface commands to control execution of the command. This control doesn't have to be performed in the same thread as the executing command.

The `Cancel` method aborts command execution. The `Execute` command actually executes a command. The `pAggInterface` parameter is used if the row set created by the command is part of an aggregate. The `riid` parameter specifies the ID of the row set interface to create for the data returned by the command, typically `IID_IRowset`. The `pDBparams` method specifies command parameters; if the command doesn't use parameters, this value is `NULL`. The `pcNumRowsAffected` parameter returns the number of rows that the command changes, deletes, adds, or returns. The `ppRowset` command returns a pointer to the row set interface. Finally, the `GetDBSesion` method returns a pointer to the `Session` object that creates the current `Command` object. The `riid` interface specifies the `Session` interface to return. The `ppSessionInterface` parameter returns a pointer to the specified `Session` interface.

The `ICommandProperties` Interface

The `ICOmmandProperties` interface gets and sets the properties for the command. You can use this interface to specify the properties that the returned rowset must satisfy. As stated before, properties define values that determine the state of an object. The `ICommandProperties` interface is required for `Command` objects. It defines the standard `IUnknown` interface methods `QueryInterface`, `AddRef`, and `Release` and provides two additional methods: `GetProperties` and `SetProperties`. The `GetProperties` method retrieves the value of a property, and the `SetProperties` method sets the value of a property. These methods are defined as follows:

18

```
HRESULT GetProperties(ULONG cPropIDSets, const DBPROPIDSET rgPropSets[],
                      ULONG *pcPropSets, DBPROPSET **prgPropSets);
HRESULT SetProperties(ULONG cPropNum, DBPROPSET rgPropSets[]);
```

The `ICommandText` Interface

The `ICommandText` interface sets and retrieves the actual command text, which specifies
the data source command to execute. The `ICommandText` interface is required to be
implemented on all `Command` objects. It defines the standard `IUnknown` interface methods
`QueryInterface`, `AddRef`, and `Release` and provides two additional methods:
`GetCommandText` and `SetCommandText`. These methods are defined as follows:

```
HRESULT SetCommandText(REFGUID gCmdDialect, LPCOLESTR *pwszCommand);
HRESULT GetCommandText(GUID *pgCmdDialect, LPCOLESTR *pwszCommand);
```

The `SetCommandText` method specifies the data source command. The `gCmdDialect`
specifies the command dialect GUID, for the dialect used in the command. Typically, for
data sources that support the SQL command syntax, this value is `DBGUID_DBSQL`. The
`pwszCommand` parameter specifies a string that contains the command. The
`GetTextCommand` method retrieves a command text. The `pgCmdDialect` parameter returns
the command dialect GUID, and the `pwszCommand` parameter returns the actual command
text. Listing 18.2 demonstrates how to create and execute a command. Note the comments in the source code for an explanation of what the code is doing. The code in
Listing 18.2 does no error checking, nor does it release the allocated interfaces. This is
for code brevity. Of course, you should check return codes and release interfaces that you
allocate in your code.

LISTING 18.2 HOW TO CREATE AND EXECUTE A COMMAND BY USING THE Command OBJECT

```
 1:  IDBCreateCommand    *pCreateCommand;
 2:  ICommandText        *pCommandText;
 3:  IRowset             *pRowset;
 4:  pwszCommandStr = OLESTR("SELECT * FROM TABLE1");
 5:  LONG                cNumRows;
 6:
 7:  // Use a Session object to create a CreateCommand interface
 8:  Session->CreateSession(NULL, IID_IDBCreateComand,
 9:                      (IUnknown **) &pCreateCommand);
10:
11:  // Create a CommandText interface
12:  pCreateCommand->CreateCommand(NULL, IID_ICommandText,
13:                                (IUnknown **) &pCommandText);
14:
15:  // Free the CreateCommand interface pointer
16:  pCreateCommand->Release();
17:
```

```
18:   // Specify the command, using the SetCommandText method
19:   pCommandText->SetCommandText(DBGUID_DBSQL, pwszCommandStr);
20:
21:   // Execute the command
22:   pCommandText->Execute(NULL, IID_Rowset, NULL, &cNumRows,
23:                         (IUnknown **) &pRowset);
```

The `IConvertType` Interface

The `IConvertType` interface determines whether a command can convert data types. The `IConvertType` interface is required by the `Command` object and defines the standard `IUnknown` interface methods `QueryInterface`, `AddRef`, and `Release`. The interface defines one additional method, `CanConvert`, which is defined as follows:

```
HRESULT CanConvert(DBTYPE wTypeFrom, DBTYPE wTypeTo,
                   DBCONVERTFLAGS wConvertFlag);
```

The `wTypeFrom` parameter specifies the type you want to convert from, and the `wTypeTo` parameter specifies the type you want to convert to. The `wConvertFlag` parameter specifies how this conversion is to be performed by using the constants `DBCONVERTFLAGS COLUMN`, `DBCONVERTFLAGS ISFIXEDLENGTH`, `DBCONVERTFLAGS ISLONG`, `DBCONVERTFLAGS PARAMETER`, and `DBCONVERTFLAGS FROMVARIANT`. If the method returns `S_OK`, the type conversion can be performed; otherwise, it cannot. Listing 18.3 demonstrates how to check whether a type conversion from an integer to a string can be performed on a parameter.

LISTING 18.3 CHECKING WHETHER A TYPE CONVERSION IS POSSIBLE

```
1:   if(SUCCEEDED(pCommand->CanConvert(DBTYPE_I4, DBTYPE_STR,
     ➥DBCONVERTFLAGS_PARAMETER))
2:   {
3:     cout << "Conversion can be performed!!!\n";
4:   }
5:   else
6:   {
7:     cout << "Conversion can NOT be performed!!!!\n");
8:   };
```

The `IColumnsRowset` Interface

The `IColumnsRowset` interface is similar to the `IColumnsInfo` interface in that `IColumnsRowset` also returns a row set containing schema information about the columns created by a command. This interface is optional and is provided only by more advanced data providers. It defines the standard IUnknown interface methods QueryInterface, AddRef, and Release, as well as two additional methods: GetAvailableColumns and GetColumnsRowset. These methods are defined as follows:

```
HRESULT GetAvailableColumns(ULONG *pNumOptCols, DBID **ppOptCols);
HRESULT GetColumnsRowset(IUnknown *pAggInterface, ULONG cNumOptCols,
                         const DBID rgOptCols[], REFIID riid,
                         ULONG cNumPropSets, DBPROPSET rgPropSets[],
                         IUnknown **pColumnRowset);
```

The GetAvailableColumns method determines the optional columns that a command could return. The GetColumnsRowset returns a row set containing information about the columns returned by a command.

Tip

> The IColumnsInfo interface almost the same information as the IColumnsRowset interface provides and is easier to use. Unless you specifically require this schema information to be returned as a row set or need to know what optional columns can be returned, use the IColumnsInfo interface instead of the IColumnsRowset interface.

The ICommandPrepare Interface

The ICommandPrepare interface converts a command to a prepared command. A *prepared command* has been precompiled so that it can execute faster after it is run. If you expect a command to be executed repeatedly, it is useful to transform it into a prepared command. This technique improves application performance. The ICommandPrepare interface defines the standard IUnknown interface methods QueryInterface, AddRef, and Release. It defines two additional methods: Prepare and Unprepare, which are defined as follows:

```
HRESULT Prepare(ULONG cNumUsages);
HRESULT Unprepare();
```

The Prepare method takes a single parameter, cNumUsages, which the command optimizer can use to determine the appropriate way to save the command interpretation. If this value is 0, the default optimization method is used. The higher the value, in theory, the more the data provider will try to optimize the command. The Unprepare command deletes the precompiled command.

The `ICommandWithParameters` Interface

The last interface provided by the Command object is the optional `ICommandWithParameters`. The `ICommandWitParameters` interface defines the standard `IUnknown` interface methods `QueryInterface`, `AddRef`, and `Release`. The interface defines three additional methods: `GetParameterInfo`, `MapParameterNames`, and `SetParameterInfo`, which are defined as follows:

```
HRESULT GetParameterInfo(ULONG *pNumParams, DBPARAMINFO prgParamInfo,
                         OLECHAR **ppBuffer);
HRESULT MapParameterNames(ULONG cNumParams, const OLECHAR *rgParamNames[],
                          LONG rgParamOrds[]);
HRESULT SetParameterInfo(ULONG cNumParams, const ULONG rgParamOrds[],
                         const DBPARAMBINDINFO rgParamBindInfo[]);
```

The `GetParameterInfo` method retrieves parameter information. The `MapParameterNames` method maps parameter names to their ordinal positions. The `SetParameterInfo` method specifies command parameter values. At the end of today's lesson, I'll show you how to create commands that use parameters, and I'll explain the appropriate methods in more detail.

The next section is a brief survey of SQL. Using SQL is the easiest way to retrieve row sets and manage the information contained in the data source. You should use SQL with any data source that supports it.

18

A SQL Compendium

This section provides you with a concise summary. This summary of SQL should be helpful for you when learning and working with OLE DB Command objects.

As you know, SQL is the standard language for manipulating relational database information. The American National Standards Institute (ANSI) is responsible for defining computer industry standards. The ANSI SQL-89 standard was established in 1989. Most relational databases comply to the 1989 standard (although each vendor's implementation of SQL is unique in some respects). In 1992 the ANSI SQL-92 standard was introduced. Level I is the highest of the three levels of compliance to the ANSI standard.

 Tip

> Use the `GetProperties` method of the `IDBProperties` interface to determine the level of SQL supported by a particular data source.

You learned earlier that SQL provides two subsets of commands. One set of commands is used for data manipulation, and the other subset is used for data definition. *Data manipulation language* enables you to select and modify database data. *Data definition language* enables you to change the database schema (tables, fields, and indexes).

SQL Queries—Data Manipulation Language

This overview of the SQL command language begins with the data manipulation command subset. The data manipulation commands are the most frequently used SQL commands. The intent of this brief discussion is to give you enough information to write most of the SQL commands your applications will require.

 Note | In the following discussion, SQL keywords appear in capital letters. This style isn't a requirement of SQL, but it helps to identify the keywords in the SQL statements you will write.

The following discussion assumes that you have a database named `Customer`, which contains Tables 18.2–18.4:

TABLE 18.2 CUSTOMERS

Field	Type
CustomerID	Long integer
CompanyName	50-character string
ContactFirstName	30-character string
ContactLastName	50-character string
CompanyOrDepartment	50-character string
BillingAddress	255-character string
City	50-character string
StateOrProvince	20-character string
PostalCode	20-character string
Country	50-character string
ContactTitle	50-character string
PhoneNumber	30-character string
Extension	30-character string
FaxNumber	30-character string

Field	Type
EmailAddress	50-character string
Notes	Memo

TABLE 18.3   ORDER DETAILS

Field	Type
OrderDetailID	Long integer
OrderID	Long integer
ProductID	Long integer
DateSold	Date
Quantity	Double
UnitPrice	Currency
Discount	Double
SalePrice	Currency
SalesTax	Currency
LineTotal	LineTotal

TABLE 18.4   ORDERS

Field	Type
OrderID	Long integer
CustomerID	Long integer
Required-byDate	Date
Promised-byDate	Date
ShipName	50-character string
ShipAddress	255-character string
ShipCity	50-character string
ShipState	50-character string
ShipStateOrProvince	50-character string
ShipPostalCode	20-character string
ShipCountry	50-character string
ShipPhoneNumber	30-character string
ShipDate	Date

continues

18

TABLE **18.4**   CONTINUED

Field	Type
ShippingMethodID	Long integer
FreightCharge	Currency
SalesTaxRate	Double

SELECT

The SELECT statement retrieves subsets of records in the database. SELECT statements read data from the database; they don't change any data. The results of SELECT statements are row sets; I'll discuss this relationship and how to access and navigate row set data in more detail tomorrow.

The most basic SELECT statement has the following form:

```
SELECT fields FROM table
```

The *fields* parameter represents the fields of the table you want to access and the *table* parameter represents the database table from which you want to access data. The *fields* parameter can be the actual names of each field in your table, separated by commas; if you want all the fields contained in the table, use the asterisk (*) instead. To retrieve only the CustomerID and CompanyName fields from a table named Customer, use the following SELECT statement:

```
SELECT CustomerID, CompanyName FROM Customer
```

To retrieve all the fields from the table named Customer, use the following SELECT statement:

   `SELECT * FROM Customer`

Clauses

You can add various clauses to SQL commands to specify subsets of data to operate on, to change the ordering and grouping of the data, and to specify access to external databases. The following paragraphs explain how these clauses apply to the SELECT statement.

WHERE

The WHERE clause of a SELECT statement limits the set of records selected. The SELECT statement controls which fields are retrieved from a table; the WHERE clause filters which data is selected from a table. You can also use the WHERE clause to join two or more tables.

The next example shows how the WHERE clause filters the records from a table. A SELECT statement with a WHERE clause has the following form:

```
SELECT fields FROM table
WHERE field COMPAREOP value {LOGICALOP field COMPAREOP value}...
```

The field parameter specifies the name of a field, and the value parameter specifies the value of that field. The COMPAREOP parameter is a SQL comparison operator, and the LOG-ICALOP parameter is a SQL logical operator. The portion of the WHERE clause contained in the brackets is an optional expression, which can be repeated up to 40 times to create complex SELECT statements.

Table 18.5 summarizes the SQL comparison operators, and Table 18.6 summarizes the SQL logical operators. For the most part, these logical and comparison operators should be familiar to any programmer who has constructed an IF statement.

> **Tip**
>
> The action of a WHERE clause resembles the action of a classic IF statement. After the SELECT statement retrieves the data from the table, the WHERE clause tests the retrieved data values against the logical WHERE clause statement. If the WHERE clause test passes, the record is included in the SELECT subset; otherwise, it is excluded.

18

TABLE 18.5 THE SQL COMPARISON OPERATORS

Operator	Use
=	Equal to
<	Less than
<=	Less than or equal to
>	Greater than
>=	Greater than or equal to
<>	Not equal to
LIKE	Used to match a pattern
BETWEEN...AND	Used to specify a range of values
IN	Used to specify a set of values

TABLE 18.6 THE SQL LOGICAL OPERATORS

Operator	Use
AND	Both conditions joined by the AND operator must be TRUE for the WHERE clause to be TRUE.
OR	Either condition joined by the OR operator must be TRUE for the WHERE clause to be TRUE.
NOT	Logical NOT.

The following SELECT statement builds on the earlier example. This statement retrieves only the CustomerID and CompanyName fields from a table named Customer where the StateOrProvince is NY.

```
SELECT CustomerID, CompanyName FROM Customer
WHERE StateOrProvince = 'NY'
```

Tip

You may enclose SQL string literals in either single quotes (') or double quotes ("). As you will see later today, SQL commands are passed to OLE DB as strings. Using single quotes is easier than using double quotes because a \ precedes double quotes in C++ strings.

As the preceding example shows, you don't have to include a WHERE clause field in the fields that are retrieved. However, a WHERE clause field *must* be a member of the table or tables from which you are retrieving data. You're probably already familiar with how the =, <=, >=, and <> comparison operators work. The IN, BETWEEN, and LIKE comparison operators are explained next.

The following SELECT statement retrieves all the fields from the Customer table where the StateOrProvince is NY, NJ, or CA.

```
SELECT * FROM Customer
WHERE StateOrProvince IN ('NY', 'NJ', 'CA')
```

The IN operator requires a set of values to be defined. If the field's value is in the specified set, the resulting subset of data will include that record.

The BETWEEN operator specifies a range of values that a field's value must be in. You can use the following SELECT statement to retrieve all the fields from the Customer table where the CustomerID is in the range 1 to 1000 inclusive:

```
SELECT * FROM Customers
WHERE CustomerID BETWEEN 1 AND 1000
```

You can combine the previous two SELECT statements to retrieve all the fields from the Customer table where the CustomerID is between 1 and 1000 *and* the StateOrProvince is NY, NJ, or CA. For example, look at the following code:

```
SELECT * FROM Customers
WHERE StateOrProvince IN ('NY', 'NJ', 'CA')
AND   CustomerID BETWEEN 1 AND 1000
```

This example shows how you can combine the WHERE statement expressions to create complex filters. WHERE expressions are evaluated from left to right; you may use parentheses to control the evaluation order if necessary.

The LIKE operator can be used in pattern matching. To specify a match to a single character, the ? is used. To specify a match to a number of characters, the * is used. This method is similar to wild card matching with the DOS DIR command. Table 18.7 shows which values a sample LIKE statement will match.

TABLE 18.7 SAMPLE LIKE STATEMENTS

Like *Statement*	*Values Matched*	*Values Not Matched*
LIKE('*A*')	CA, PA, CAN, DIANE, MARIE	NY, NY, JOHN, Diane
LIKE('?A')	CA, PA, WA	MARIE, NY, NJ
LIKE('A?')	AL, AK	NY, NJ, WA

You can use the following SELECT statement to retrieve all the fields from the Customer table where the StateOrProvince begins with an N:

```
SELECT * FROM Customers
WHERE StateOrProvince LIKE('N*')
```

You have seen how to use the WHERE clause to filter the data retrieved by the SELECT statement. The WHERE clause can also link two or more tables into a single resulting set of data.

The capability to join multiple tables together is the real power of relational databases. You don't have to worry about the details of how to accomplish this task; SQL handles these details for you. A SELECT statement that joins two or more tables together has the simplest form:

```
SELECT table1.field1, table2.field2 FROM table1, table2
WHERE  table1.field1 = table2.field2
```

This example illustrates two important new concepts. First, the FROM clause of the SELECT statement specifies more than one table. Second, the . operator is introduced in naming

18

fields, for example, *table1.field1*. *Field1* is a member of *table1*. If the fields you are selecting have different names, the . operator isn't required. The . operator makes the name of the field you are selecting unique. Although the . operator isn't required, it does help when you are creating complex queries. You can combine the . operator with the * field specifier to retrieve all the fields from a table. The statement *table1.* would retrieve all the fields from *table1*.

The following SELECT statement retrieves all the customer information, along with an order number for each associated order that the customer has placed from the sample database specified earlier:

```
SELECT Orders.OrderID, Customer.*
WHERE  Orders.CustomerID = Customer.CustomerID
```

You don't have to include the Orders.CustomerID field in the set of fields that you are retrieving. On the other hand, you must use the . operator; without it SQL wouldn't know whether you were talking about the CustomerID field in the Orders table or the CustomerID field in the Customer table.

The capability of the WHERE clause to filter selected data can be combined with the capability to join two or more tables. For example, you can extend the preceding SELECT statement to return only the records where the OrderId is between 1 and 2000:

```
SELECT Orders.OrderID, Customers.* FROM Customers, Orders
WHERE  Orders.CustomerID = Customers.CustomerID
AND    Order.OrderID BETWEEN 1 AND 2000
```

Earlier you saw how the IN comparison operator specifies a set of data for a field value. You can also create this subset of data for the IN operator by using another query. A *subquery* creates a set of data that a WHERE clause can use to match a field value. For example, the following SELECT statement selects all the Customer fields that have an order Promised-byDate greater than 05/25/97:

```
SELECT Customers.* FROM Customers
WHERE CustomerID IN
        (SELECT Orders.CustomerID FROM Orders
         WHERE  Orders.Promised-byDate > #05/25/97#)
```

Note You must enclose date literals with the pound sign (#), as shown in the preceding code. Also, date literals must be in U.S. format, even if a non-U.S. version of the database engine is being used.

This example performs two SELECT statements. One SELECT statement, the subquery, creates the set of CustomerIDs from the Orders table that has a Promised-byDate greater than 05/25/97. The other SELECT statement uses the results for the first SELECT statement with the IN logical operator to filter the Customer records.

The general format for subqueries is

```
[ic:syntax]expression [NOT] IN (subquery)
comparison [ANY ¦ ALL ¦ SOME] (subquery)
[NOT] EXISTS (subquery)
```

You are already familiar with the IN operator. Similarly, you can use the ANY, ALL, or SOME operators to match any, all, or just some of the fields in *subquery*. The EXISTS operator checks to see whether *subquery* returns any records.

Aggregate Functions

Aggregate functions enable SELECT statements to return a result that applies to a group of records. Table 18.5 summarizes the aggregate functions available in SQL.

TABLE 18.8 SQL AGGREGATE FUNCTIONS

Function	Use
AVG	Returns the average value of a field
COUNT	Returns the number of records
MAX	Returns the maximum value of a field
MIN	Returns the minimum value of a field
SUM	Returns the sum of the values of a field

The following SELECT statement determines the total amount of all the orders in the Order Detail table:

```
SELECT SUM([Order Detail].LineTotal) FROM [Order Detail]
```

Note

Brackets [] enclose table or field names that contain a space or punctuation.

GROUP BY

The GROUP BY clause combines records with identical field values into a single record. The GROUP BY clause is useful with SQL aggregate functions. For example, you can retrieve the total amount of all orders for each CustomerID with the following SELECT statement:

18

```
SELECT [Order Detail].CustomerID, SUM([Order Detail].LineTotal)
FROM    [Order Detail]
```

This SELECT statement will work, but it will return duplicate records—one for each order a customer has placed. The GROUP BY clause eliminates these duplicate records. To use the GROUP BY clause, you would rewrite this SELECT statement as

```
SELECT    [Order Detail].CustomerID, SUM([Order Detail].LineTotal)
FROM      [Order Detail]
GROUP BY [Order Detail].CustomerID
```

The rewritten statement will return a single record for each CustomerID. Each record will contain the CustomerID and total of all orders in the Order Detail table for that CustomerID.

Aliasing Field Names

When data is selected from a table, the name of the field in the resulting row set is the same as the name of the field in the table. You can change the name of the field in the resulting row set by using the technique called *field aliasing*. For example, you can retrieve all the CustomerIDs from the Customer table, calling the CustomerID field CustomerNum in the resulting row set, with the following SELECT statement:

```
SELECT CustomerID AS CustomerNum FROM Customers
```

HAVING

The HAVING clause is used with the GROUP BY clause. The HAVING clause filters the grouped data resulting from the GROUP BY clause in the same way that the WHERE clause filters the data of the SELECT statement. HAVING and WHERE expressions are constructed in the same way, and both are limited to 40 expressions. For example, you can retrieve the total amount of all orders for CustomerIDs whose totals are greater than $1,000, with the following SELECT statement:

```
SELECT    [Order Detail].CustomerID,
          SUM([Order Detail].LineTotal) AS TotalAmt
FROM      [Order Detail]
GROUP BY [Order Detail].CustomerID
HAVING    TotalAmt > 1000
```

ORDER BY

The ORDER BY clause sorts the SELECT statement resultant set of records. You may specify multiple sort keys and sort records in ascending or descending order. For example, you can retrieve all the records in the Customer table sorted by CompanyName in ascending order with the following SELECT statement:

```
SELECT * FROM Customers
ORDER BY CompanyName ASC
```

The following SQL statement performs the same selection, sorted in descending order:

```
SELECT * FROM Customers
ORDER BY CompanyName DESC
```

To retrieve all the records in the `Customer` table sorted by `StateOrProvince` in ascending order, and then `CompanyName` in ascending order, use the following:

```
SELECT * FROM Customers
ORDER BY StateOrProvince, CompanyName ASC
```

If the ordering directive (`ASC` or `DESC`) is omitted, the records will be sorted in ascending order by default.

DISTINCT and DISTINCTROW

The `DISTINCT` clause removes duplicate records from the resulting data set. The following `SELECT` statement retrieves the unique customer contact last names from the `Customers` table:

```
SELECT DISTINCT ContactLastName FROM Customers
```

If more than one customer contact has the last name `Jones`, the resulting subset of data will include only one record.

The `DISTINCTROW` clause selects data that is distinct in any of the fields. For example, you can retrieve all the nonduplicate records in the `Customers` table with the following `SELECT` statement:

```
SELECT DISTINCTROW * FROM Customers
```

TOP

The `TOP` clause is used with the `ORDER BY` clause. With the `TOP` clause, you can limit the number of records returned to the `TOP` _n_ number of records, where _n_ is specified in the `SELECT` statement. For example, you can retrieve the top 50 total amount of all orders for each `CustomerID` with the following `SELECT` statement:

```
SELECT    TOP 50 [Order Detail].CustomerID,
                 SUM([Order Detail].LineTotal) AS TotalAmt
FROM      [Order Detail]
GROUP BY [Order Detail].CustomerID
ORDER BY TotalAmt
```

The `TOP` clause can also specify a percentage. The following query returns the top 10% of total amounts:

```
SELECT    TOP 10 PERCENT [Order Detail].CustomerID,
                         SUM([Order Detail].LineTotal) AS TotalAmt
FROM      [Order Detail]
```

18

```
GROUP BY [Order Detail].CustomerID
ORDER BY TotalAmt
```

JOIN

Creating a join is one of the more powerful functions that a relational database can perform. Table 18.6 summarizes the three types of joins that relational databases can create.

TABLE 18.9 RELATIONAL DATABASE TYPES OF JOINS

Join Type	Result
INNER JOIN	Records are included in the resulting data set only when the field specified in the first table matches the field specified in the second table.
RIGHT OUTER JOIN	All the records from the second table are included with the matching records from both tables.
LEFT OUTER JOIN	All the records from the first table are included with the matching records from both tables.

The JOIN clause is used in the following manner:

```
FROM table1 [LEFT ¦ RIGHT ¦ INNER] JOIN table2
ON table1.field1 = table2.field2
```

Creating an INNER JOIN is the same as creating a join by using the WHERE clause. LEFT and RIGHT joins produce additional records, as specified in Table 18.6.

One way to retrieve customer information and an order number for each associated order that a customer has placed (a SELECT statement using the WHERE clause) was shown earlier:

```
SELECT Orders.OrderID, Customers.* FROM Orders, Customers
WHERE  Orders.CustomerID - Customer.CustomerID
```

You can achieve the same result by using the following SELECT statement with an INNER JOIN:

```
SELECT Orders.OrderID, Customers.*
FROM   Orders INNER JOIN Customers
ON     Orders.CustomerID = Customer.CustomerID
```

The preceding information should enable you to use the SQL language to retrieve data from a database. The following sections introduce three SQL commands (INSERT INTO, UPDATE, and DELETE) that enable you to modify records in the database.

INSERT INTO

The INSERT INTO command adds records to a table. You can insert records from the result of another SELECT statement, or you can append single records by specifying their values. If any field is omitted from the target of the table insert, it will become a NULL value. You can use the following SQL statement to append a single record to the Customers table:

```
INSERT INTO Customers(CustomerID, CompanyName, ContactFirstName,
                      ContactLastName, CompanyOrDepartment,
                      BillingAddress, City, StateOrProvince,
                      PostalCode, Country, ContactTitle, PhoneNumber,
                      Extension, FaxNumber, EmailAddress)
VALUES (100, 'ABC Manufacturing', 'Marie', 'McCartan', 'Executive'
        '123 Main Street', 'Buffalo', 'New York', '14225', 'USA',
        'President', '716-555-1212', '123', '716-555-2121',
        'president@abcmfg.com')
```

UPDATE

The UPDATE command modifies records in a table, based on specified criteria. The UPDATE command is useful for changing multiple records or fields in multiple tables. For example, here's how to update the sales tax rate to 6% for all orders in the Orders table that are shipped to CA:

```
UPDATE Orders
SET SalesTaxRate = 0.06
WHERE Orders.ShipState = 'CA'
```

DELETE

The DELETE command removes records from a table that meet specified criteria. When records are deleted, they cannot be recovered. Here's how to delete all the records from the Customers table that represent customers from San Diego, CA:

```
DELETE FROM Customers
WHERE   Customers.City = 'San Diego' AND
        Customers.StateOrProvince = 'CA'
```

SQL—Data Definition Language

In addition to retrieving, adding, and modifying records in database tables, SQL has three commands that can modify the schema of the database:

- CREATE creates tables and indexes.
- DROP deletes tables.
- ALTER modifies table fields and indexes.

18

CREATE

The CREATE command creates new tables and indexes. The following example creates a new table named Products:

```
CREATE TABLE Products (ProductID INTEGER, ProductDesc TEXT(50))
```

The new table contains two fields: the ProductID and the ProductDesc. As you can see, the type of the field is specified after the field name.

The following SQL statement creates a new unique index on the ProductID field for the newly created Products table:

```
CREATE UNIQUE INDEX ProdIndex ON Products (ProductID)
```

ALTER

The ALTER command adds or removes fields and indexes to or from a table. The following SQL statement adds the new field SupplierID and ProductColor to the Products table:

```
ALTER TABLE Products ADD COLUMN SupplierID INTEGER
ALTER TABLE Products ADD COLUMN ProductColor TEXT(30)
```

Here's how to remove the ProductColor field from the Products table:

```
ALTER TABLE Products DROP COLUMN ProductColor
```

Here's how to add a secondary index on the SupplierID field in the Products table:

```
ALTER TABLE Products ADD CONSTRAINT ProdSuppIdx FOREIGN KEY SupplierID
```

And here's how to delete the newly created index from the Products table:

```
ALTER TABLE Products DROP CONSTRAINT ProdSuppIdx
```

DROP

The DROP command deletes tables. The DROP command removes the table and its associated indexes, unlike the DELETE command that deletes the selected records from the table. Even if all the table records are deleted from a table by using the DELETE command, the empty table and its indexes will still be present. You cannot recover a dropped table. The following SQL statement deletes the Products table that you just created and modified:

```
DROP TABLE Products
```

Creating and Executing Commands

Now that you have a better understanding of the `Session` objects, `Command` objects, and SQL, you can begin to apply your knowledge by writing some code. Today's business concludes by discussing several issues related to command processing:

- How to create and execute commands
- How to create commands with parameters and how to use parameter `Accessors`
- How to use command states
- How to create commands that return multiple resultsets

Creating and Executing a Command

The process of creating and executing commands is fairly straightforward (you might want to refer to Listing 18.2 for a review):

1. Create a `Command` object by using the `Session` interface `CreateCommand` method.
2. Obtain access to the `ICommandText` interface of the `Command` object.
3. Specify the command string.
4. Use the `Execute` method of the `Command` object to actually run the command.
5. Navigate the row set created, if applicable (discussed in more detail tomorrow).
6. Release the interfaces accessed.

Listing 18.4 continues with the simple application from Listing 17.4. Listing 18.4 starts by using the `CreateSession` method of the `IDBCreateSession` interface and adds some code to create a `Session` object. The `Session` object is then used to create a `Command` object with the `CreateCommand` method of the `IDBCreateCommand` interface. Finally, the command text is specified, and the command is executed. A simple SQL query retrieves the fields `CUSTID` and `CUSTNAME` from the `CUSTOMERS` table in the `IDCDatabase` and creates a row set that contains the information found in the `CUSTOMERS` table. (I'll explain the process of navigating and accessing row sets in more detail tomorrow.)

To build the application, run Visual Studio and select the File, New menu choice. Click the Projects tab and specify a Win32 Console Application. Call the application COM-MANDTEST. Click OK, specify that you want to create an empty project, and click the Finish button. After AppWizard runs, create a new C++ source file as part of the project. You can call it whatever you think is appropriate, such as `COMMANDTEST.CPP`. Enter the code shown in Listing 18.4 into the source file.

18

You will need to change the input libraries for the linker to the following:

```
oledbd.lib kernel32.lib user32.lib gdi32.lib winspool.lib comdlg32.lib
➥advapi32.lib
shell32.lib ole32.lib oleaut32.lib uuid.lib
```

You do this under the Project, Settings menu on the Link tab. When you build the project, it should compile and link with no errors or warnings. For code brevity, the code in Listing 18.4 does no error checking, nor does it release the allocated interfaces. Of course, you should check return codes and release interfaces that you allocate in your code.

INPUT   **LISTING 18.4**   CREATING AND EXECUTING A SIMPLE COMMAND

```
 1:  #define UNICODE
 2:  #define _UNICODE
 3:  #define DBINITCONSTANTS
 4:  #define INITGUID
 5:
 6:  // Standard Application Includes
 7:  #include <windows.h>
 8:  #include <stdio.h>
 9:  #include <tchar.h>
10:  #include <stddef.h>
11:  #include <iostream.h>
12:
13:  // OLE DB Header Files
14:  #include <oledb.h>
15:  #include <oledberr.h>
16:
17:  // OLE DB - ODBC Provider Header Files
18:  #include <msdaguid.h>
19:  #include <msdasql.h>
20:
21:  void main() {
22:     IDBInitialize*    pIDBInitialize = NULL;
23:     IDBCreateSession* pCreateSession = NULL;
24:     IDBCreateCommand* pCreateCommand = NULL;
25:     IRowset*          pRowset = NULL;
26:     ICommandText*     pCommandText = NULL;
27:     IDBProperties*    pIDBProperties;
28:     DBPROP            InitProperties[4];
29:     DBPROPSET         rgInitPropSet[1];
30:     int               i;
31:     LONG              cNumRows;
32:
33:     // The Command to execute
34:     LPCTSTR           wCmdString =
35:                       OLESTR("SELECT * FROM Customers");
```

```
36:
37:    // Initialize the Component Object Module Library
38:    CoInitialize(NULL);
39:
40:    // Obtain Access to the OLE DB - ODBC Provider
41:    CoCreateInstance(CLSID_MSDASQL, NULL, CLSCTX_INPROC_SERVER,
42:                    IID_IDBInitialize, (void **) &pIDBInitialize);
43:
44:    // Initialize the property values that are the same for each
45:    // property. . .
46:    for (i = 0; i < 4; i++ ) {
47:        VariantInit(&InitProperties[i].vValue);
48:        InitProperties[i].dwOptions = DBPROPOPTIONS_REQUIRED;
49:        InitProperties[i].colid = DB_NULLID;
50:    }
51:
52:    // level of prompting that will be done to complete the connection
       // process
53:    InitProperties[0].dwPropertyID = DBPROP_INIT_PROMPT;
54:    InitProperties[0].vValue.vt = VT_I2;
55:
56:    // Specify the User Name
57:    InitProperties[1].dwPropertyID = DBPROP_AUTH_USERID;
58:    InitProperties[1].vValue.vt = VT_BSTR;
59:    // Note: The L cast directive casts the string into a UNICODE
       // string....
60:    InitProperties[1].vValue.bstrVal = SysAllocString((LPOLESTR)L"");
61:
62:    // Specify the appropriate Password
63:    InitProperties[2].dwPropertyID = DBPROP_AUTH_PASSWORD;
64:    InitProperties[2].vValue.vt = VT_BSTR;
65:    InitProperties[2].vValue.bstrVal = SysAllocString((LPOLESTR)L"");
66:
67:    // Specify the Data Source name
68:    InitProperties[3].dwPropertyID = DBPROP_INIT_DATASOURCE;
69:    InitProperties[3].vValue.vt = VT_BSTR;
70:    InitProperties[3].vValue.bstrVal =
71:        SysAllocString((LPOLESTR)L"OrdersDb");
72:
73:    rgInitPropSet[0].guidPropertySet = DBPROPSET_DBINIT;
74:    rgInitPropSet[0].cProperties = 4;
75:    rgInitPropSet[0].rgProperties = InitProperties;
76:
77:    // set initialization properties
78:    pIDBInitialize->QueryInterface(IID_IDBProperties,
79:                    (void **)&pIDBProperties);
80:    pIDBProperties->SetProperties(1,rgInitPropSet);
81:    pIDBProperties->Release();
82:
```

18

continues

LISTING 18.4 CONTINUED

```
83:    // Call the Initialize method to establish the connection to
84:    // the ODBC data source specified above
85:    pIDBInitialize->Initialize();
86:
87:    // Create a Session object...
88:    pIDBInitialize->QueryInterface(IID_IDBCreateSession,
89:                        (void **) &pCreateSession);
90:
91:    // Create a Command object...
92:    pCreateSession->CreateSession(NULL, IID_IDBCreateCommand,
93:                            (IUnknown **) &pCreateCommand);
94:
95:    // Access the ICommandText interface
96:    pCreateCommand->CreateCommand(NULL, IID_ICommandText,
97:                            (IUnknown **) &pCommandText);
98:
99:    // Specify the command text
100:   pCommandText->SetCommandText(DBGUID_DBSQL, wCmdString);
101:
102:   // Execute the command
103:   HRESULT hr;
104:   hr = pCommandText->Execute(NULL, IID_IRowset, NULL, &cNumRows,
105:                       (IUnknown **) &pRowset);
106:
107:   // This is where we would navigate the rowset returned...
108:   if (SUCCEEDED(hr))
109:   {
110:     ::MessageBeep(MB_OK);
111:   }
112:
113:   // Free Up Allocated Memory
114:   pRowset->Release();
115:   pCommandText->Release();
116:   pCreateCommand->Release();
117:   pCreateSession->Release();
118:   pIDBInitialize->Uninitialize();
119:   pIDBInitialize->Release();
120:
121:   // Release the Component Object Module Library
122:   CoUninitialize();
123: };
```

Read the comments in the Listing 18.4 source code to understand the details of what the code is doing.

Accessors

The last major topic for today is how to create commands that use parameters. Command parameters are just like the parameters of methods or procedures in Visual C++. *Command parameters* accept values that are specified at runtime. *Accessors* specify and store parameter values. You can use parameters to input or retrieve values. The DBPARAMBINDINFO structure specifies parameters with the SetParameterInfo method of the ICommandWithParametrs interface.

In SQL commands, parameters are specified by using the ? specifier. For example, the following SQL statement creates a SQL command that inserts records into the Customers table:

```
INSERT INTO CUSTOMERS (CUSTID, CUSTNAME) VALUES (?, ?)
```

The values of the fields (shown as the two ?) are specified as parameters when the command is executed. Before you examine code that creates a command that uses parameters, the following section considers the DBPARAMBINDINFO structure.

Elements of a Parameter Accessor

The DBPARAMBINDINFO structure specifies parameter bindings. This structure has the following definition:

```
typedef struct tagDBPARAMBINDINFO {
LPOLESTR pwszDataSourceType;
    LPOLESTR pwszName;
    ULONG ulParamSize;
    DBPARAMFLAGS dwFlags;
    BYTE bPrecision;
    BYTE bScale;
    } DBPARAMBINDINFO;
```

The pwszDataSourceType field defines the type of the parameter. The pwszName field specifies the name of the parameter, if applicable; otherwise, it is NULL. The ulParamSize parameter specifies the size of the parameter. The dwFlags parameter specifies the relevant parameter flags. Table 18.10 describes the possible parameter flag values. The bPrecision field specifies the number of digits used by a numeric value, if applicable. Finally, the bScale field specifies the number of digits to the right of the decimal point if the number is positive or the number of digits to the left if the number is negative.

18

TABLE 18.10 THE PARAMETER FLAG VALUES

Flag	Value
DBPARAMFLAGS_ISINPUT	Specifies an input parameter
DBPARAMFLAGS_ISOUTPUT	Specifies an output parameter
DBPARAMFLAGS_ISSIGNED	Specifies a signed numeric parameter
DBPARAMFLAGS_ISLONG	Specifies a long integer parameter
DBPARAMFLAGS_ISNULLABLE	Specifies that the parameter can be NULL

Command Parameters

Listing 18.5 demonstrates how to create and execute the parameterized INSERT command you looked at earlier. Note that the ICommandWithParameters interface specifies the parameter values. Tomorrow, you will learn more about using Accessors to specify field values before executing the parameterized command.

INPUT **LISTING 18.5** HOW TO CREATE A PARAMETERIZED COMMAND

```
 1:  IDBCreateCommand        *pCreateCommand;
 2:  ICommandText            *pCommandText;
 3:  ICommandWithParameters  *pCommandWithParams;
 4:  DBPARAMBINDINFO         ParamBindInfo[2];
 5:  ULONG                   ParamOrdinals[] = {1,2};
 6:  LPCSTR                   pwszCommandStr =
 7:     OLESTR("INSERT INTO Customers (CustNumber, CustLastName)
 8:     [ic:ccc] VALUES (?, ?)");
 9:
10:  // Use a Session object to create a CreateCommand interface
11:  Session->CreateSession(NULL, IID_IDBCreateComand,
12:                         (IUnknown **) &pCreateCommand);
13:
14:  // Create a CommandText interface
15:  pCreateCommand->CreateCommand(NULL, IID_ICommandText,
16:                               (IUnknown **) &pCommandText);
17:
18:  // Free the CreateCommand interface pointer
19:  pCreateCommand->Release();
20:
21:  // Specify the command, using the SetCommandText method
22:  pCommandText->SetCommandText(DBGUID_DBSQL, pwszCommandStr);
23:
24:  // Specify the command parameter information
25:  ParamBindInfo[0].pwszDataSourceType = L"DBTYPE_II4";
26:  ParamBindInfo[0].pwszName = L"CUST_ID";
```

```
27:    ParamBindInfo[0].ulParamSize = sizeof(DWORD);
28:    ParamBindInfo[0].dwFlags = DBPARAMFLAGS_ISINPUT;
29:    ParamBindInfo[0].bPrecision = 0;
30:    ParamBindInfo[0].bScale = 0;
31:
32:    ParamBindInfo[1].pwszDataSourceType = L"DBTYPE_CHAR";
33:    ParamBindInfo[1].pwszName = L"CUST_NAME";
34:    ParamBindInfo[1].ulParamSize = 255;
35:    ParamBindInfo[1].dwFlags = DBPARAMFLAGS_ISINPUT;
36:    ParamBindInfo[1].bPrecision = 0;
37:    ParamBindInfo[1].bScale = 0;
38:
39:    pCommandText->QueryInterface(IID_ICommandWithParameters,
40:                         (void **) &pCommandWithParams);
41:    pCommandWithParams->SetParameterInfo(2, ParamOrdinals,
       ➥ParamBindInfo);
42:
43:    // Release interfaces
44:    pCommandText->Release();
45:    pCommandWithParams->Release();
```

Multiple Resultsets

If you specify a query that returns multiple resultsets, you need to use the
IMultipleResults interface. You can create multiple results by using stored
procedures or by specifying multiple commands in the Command object statement.

> **Tip**
>
> Refer to your data source documentation to determine whether it supports
> stored procedures. *Stored procedures* are pieces of code that reside with the
> database provider and execute directly on the database provider server.
> Stored procedures are powerful and can help improve application perfor-
> mance.

The IMultipleResults interface defines the standard IUnknown interface methods
QueryInterface, AddRef, and Release. The interface defines one additional method,
GetResult. This method is defined as follows:

```
HRESULT GetResult(IUnknown *pAggInterface, LONG lResv, REFID riid,
                  LONG *pNumRows, IUnknown **ppRowset);
```

The discussion of OLE DB objects resumes tomorrow with the Rowset object, which
accesses the results of queries. You will learn how to navigate these resulting query row
sets and how to access the data they contain.

18

Summary

Day 18 opens with discussions of the Session object and the Command object and their associated interfaces. You learned how to create Session and Command objects and how to create and execute commands. You read a compendium of the SQL command language, which is supported by some OLE DB data providers, as well as its data manipulation and data definition aspects. One of today's applications demonstrates how to connect to a data source, create a session, and specify and execute a simple SQL command. You also learned about parameterized commands and the DBBINDPARAMINFO structure. Day 18 ends with an explanation of how to manage commands that can return multiple row sets.

Q&A

This section answers some common questions related to today's topics.

Q How do I determine the types supported by a data source?

A The IDBSchemaRowset interface determines the types a data source supports. Use the GetSchemas method, using the DBSCHEMA_PROVIDER_TYPES GUID. I will discuss how to navigate and retrieve this row set data tomorrow. Also, open the OLEDB.H file or the OLE DB Specification help file and search for the DBTYPE string. You will find an enumeration object that contains the definitions for each type supported by OLE DB.

Q What's the best way to manage a data source: with methods such as CreateTable and CreateIndex or with SQL commands?

A If your data source provider supports SQL language commands, you should definitely use the SQL command language to manage your data source. As you can see from the examples in this lesson, you use far less code to create a table with SQL commands than you use when you create a table with the CreateTable command.

Q How do I know whether my data source supports the SQL command language?

A To determine whether a data source supports the SQL command language, you need to use the GetProperties method of the DataSource object, checking for the DBPROP_SQLSUPPORT property. The use of properties is discussed in greater detail during Day 20. If the data source supports this property, it will also support the ANSI standard SQL.

Workshop

The Workshop quiz questions test your understanding of today's material. (The answers appear in Appendix F, "Answers.") The exercises encourage you to apply the information you learned today to real-life situations.

Quiz Questions

1. What is the role of the Session object?

2. What Session interface method retrieves information about the data source schema?

3. What is the role of the Command object?

4. What Command interface method specifies an actual command?

5. How are parameters specified in commands, and why would you use them?

6. What Command interface method can you use to potentially increase the performance of a query?

Exercises

1. Modify the code in Listing 18.4 to perform a data definition command such as the CREATE TABLE, DROP TABLE, or ALTER TABLE command.

2. Modify the code in Listing 18.5 to perform a parameterized SELECT instead of an INSERT.

18

DAY 19

Navigating the Result of a Query

Now that you know how to access a data source, create a session, and specify commands, you are ready to learn how to navigate and access the data contained in the resulting row sets. Day 19 starts with a discussion of the Rowset object and its associated interfaces. Today you start to bring together the concepts presented in the previous three lessons so that you can begin to make productive use of OLE DB. Many of today's examples focus on using the OLE DB ODBC provider to access a SQL Server data source.

Today we will

- Use Rowset objects.
- Create bindings.
- Use Accessors to retrieve the data contained in a row set.
- Work with column types.
- Explore the issues involved in accessing columns that contain Binary Large Object (BLOB) data.
- Process Unicode strings.

- Learn how to specify and use Static, KeySet, and Dynamic cursors.
- Create and use bookmarks.
- Release memory used by a row set when access is completed.

Rowset Interfaces

So far this week you have learned how to access a data source, create a session, and even create a command that can generate a row set. However, you don't yet know how to retrieve and access the data contained in these row sets. You are about to bridge this gap in your understanding of OLE DB. OLE DB uses Rowset objects to provide access to data source data in a tabular form. The row sets that result from executing a command are only one type of row set that OLE DB can generate. You can use Session objects to create row sets and the IDBSchemaRowset interface of the Session object to retrieve row sets that contain schema information. (Refer to Day 18, "Querying a Data Source.")

The TRowset CoType supports the following interfaces:

```
TRowset {
     interface IAccessor;      // Required Interface
     interface IColumnsInfo;   // Required Interface
     interface IConvertType;   // Required Interface
     interface IRowset;        // Required Interface
     interface IRowsetInfo;    // Required Interface
     interface IColumnsRowset;
     interface IConnectionPointContainer;
     interface IRowsetChange;
     interface IRowsetIdentity;
     interface IRowsetLocate;
     interface IRowsetResynch;
     interface IRowsetScroll;
     interface IRowsetUpdate;
     interface ISupportErrorInfo;
};
```

The following sections explain the interfaces supported by the Rowset object and describe how to retrieve row set data.

Note

> The ISupportErrorInfo interface was described on Day 17, "Accessing a Data Source with OLE DB," and will be considered again on Day 21, "OLE DB Error Handling." The IAccessor, IColumnsInfo, IColumnsRowset, and IConvertType interfaces were presented yesterday (Day 18). Column Accessors are covered in more detail later today.

The **IRowset** Interface

The `IRowset` interface is the primary interface used to access row sets and the data they contain. The `IRowset` interface is required by the `Rowset` object and defines the standard `IUnknown` interface methods `QueryInterface`, `AddRef`, and `Release`. The interface also provides five additional methods: `AddRefRows`, `GetData`, `GetNextRows`, `ReleaseRows`, and `RestartPosition`. These methods are defined as follows:

```
HRESULT AddRefRows(ULONG cNumRowHandles, const HROWS rhRows[],
                   ULONG rgRefCounts[], DBROWSTATUS rRowStatus[]);
HRESULT GetData(HROW hRow, HACCESSOR hRowAccessor, void *pBuffer);
HRESULT GetNextRows(HCHAPTER hChapter, LONG lNumRowsToSkip,
                   LONG lNumRows, ULONG *plNumRows, HROW **phRows);
HRESULT ReleaseRows(ULONG cNumRows, const HROW rhRows[],
                   DBROWOPTIONS rRowOptions[], ULONG rRefCounts[],
                   DBROWSTATUS rRowStatus[]);
HRESULT RestartPosition(HCHAPTER hChapter);
```

After looking at the remaining `Rowset` interfaces, today's presentation focuses on the implementation details of obtaining and navigating row set data. Much of that discussion centers on using the `IRowset` interface. This section explains what these interface methods do and the parameters they use.

The `GetNextRows` method retrieves the next sequential set of rows from a row set. `hChapter` is the chapter handle. For nonchaptered rowsets, `hChapter` is ignored. The `lNumRowsToSkip` specifies the number of rows to skip before retrieving the next set of rows. If this value is 0, no rows are skipped. The `lNumRows` parameter specifies the number of rows to retrieve. The `plNumRows` parameter returns the number of rows actually retrieved. The `phRows` parameter returns an array of row handles, which can be used to retrieve the actual row data.

The `GetData` method actually retrieves the row data. The `hRow` parameter specifies a row handle returned by the `GetNextRows` method. The `hRowAccessor` parameter specifies the row `Accessor` handle that retrieves the data. The `pBuffer` parameter specifies a memory buffer in which the actual row data is stored.

The `ReleaseRows` method releases the set of rows obtained by the `GetNextRows` method. The `cNumRows` parameter specifies the number of rows to release, and the `rHRows` parameter specifies an array of row handles to release. The last three parameters typically will be NULL. The `rRowOptions` parameter specifies additional options to be used when releasing a row, the `rRefCounts` parameter specifies an array of row reference counts, and the `rRowStatus` parameter returns the status of each row that was released.

The `AddRefRows` method increments row reference counts. The `cNumRowHandles` parameter specifies the number of row handles passed. The `rhRows` array specifies the array of

19

row handles to increment the reference count for; the rgRefCounts parameter returns an array of new row reference counts, once for each handle. The rRowStatus parameter returns the status of each row.

Finally, the RestartPosition method returns to the beginning of the row set when the next GetNextRows method is called. RestartPosition takes a single parameter that is reserved for future use.

The IRowsetInfo Interface

The IRowsetInfo retrieves information about a row set, including the maximum number of active rows and how many modifications on a row set can be buffered before they can be committed. The IRowsetInfo interface can also return to a bookmarked row. (I'll discuss bookmarks in more detail later today.) The IRowsetInfo interface is required by the Rowset object and defines the standard IUnknown interface methods QueryInterface, AddRef, and Release. The interface also provides three additional methods: GetProperties, GetReferencedRowset, and GetSpecification. These methods are defined as follows:

```
HRESULT GetProperties(ULONG cPropIDSets, const DBPROPIDSET rgPropSets[],
                      ULONG *pcPropSets, DBPROPSET **prgPropSets);
HRESULT GetReferencedRowset(ULONG iColumnNum, REFIID riid,
                            IUnknown **ppRowsetInterface);
HRESULT GetSpecification(REFIID riid, IUnknown **pSpecInterface);
```

Day 17 covers the GetProperties method in relation to the IDBProperties interface; GetProperties retrieves row set properties. The GetReferencedRowset method returns an interface pointer to a bookmarked rowset. The iColumnNum parameter of the GetReferencedRowset method identifies the ordinal position of the column that contains the bookmark marker. The riid parameter specifies the interface ID of the interface to return in the ppRowsetInterface parameter. The GetSpecification method retrieves an interface pointer to the OLE DB object that created the row set. The riid parameter specifies an interface GUID, and the pSpecInterface parameter returns a pointer to that interface.

The IConnectionPointContainer Interface

The IConnectionPointContainer interface is a standard COM interface and is used when connecting data to other COM or OLE objects. It is an optional interface and defines the standard IUnknown interface methods QueryInterface, AddRef, and Release. The interface also provides two additional methods: EnumConnectionPoints and FindConnectionPoint. These methods are defined as follows:

```
HRESULT EnumConnectionPoints(IEnumConnectionPoints **ppEnum);
HRESULT FindConnectionPoint(REFIID riid, IConnectionPoint
*ppConnectPoint);
```

> **Note** Refer to the Visual C++ documentation for more information regarding the use of this interface with Rowset objects.

The `IRowsetChange` Interface

The `IRowsetChange` interface deletes rows, inserts rows, and modifies the data contained in a row. It is an optional interface that defines the standard `IUnknown` interface methods `QueryInterface`, `AddRef`, and `Release`, as well as three additional methods: `DeleteRows`, `InsertRow`, and `SetData`. As you can probably tell by their names, the `DeleteRows` method deletes row set rows, the `InsertRow` method inserts a new row into a row set, and the `SetData` method changes row set data. These methods are defined as follows:

```
HRESULT DeleteRows(HCHAPTER hChapter, ULONG cNumRows,
                const HROW rhRows[], DBROWSTATUS rRowStatus[]);
HRESULT InsertRow(HCHAPTER hChapter, HACCESSOR hAccesor,
                void *pBuffer, HROW *phRow);
HRESULT SetData(HROW hRow, HACCESSOR hAccessor, void *pBuffer);
```

For the `DeleteRows` method, the first parameter `hChapter` is the chapter handle. The `cNumRows` parameter determines the number of rows to delete. The `rhRows` parameter defines an array of row handles that are to be deleted. On return, the `rRowStatus` array is an array of row `DBROWSTATUS` structures that define the status of each deleted row.

For the `InsertRow` method, the first parameter `hChapter` is the chapter handle. The `hAccessor` parameter defines the `Accessor` for the row to insert. The `pBuffer` parameter defines the data buffer, containing the actual row data, described by the `Accessor`. On return, the `phRow` parameter is the row handle of the newly added row.

For the `SetData` method, the `hRow` parameter defines the handle of the row to modify. The `hAccessor` parameter defines the Accessor for the row, and the `pBuffer` parameter defines the buffer containing the modified row data.

> **Tip** SQL commands provide the same functionality as the `IRowsetChange` interface methods and generally use less code to do so. You can use SQL to delete, insert, and modify data. You should use the SQL commands if the data provider supports them.

The `IRowsetIdentity` Interface

The `IRowsetIdentity` interface determines whether two row set rows are identical. Already, you probably realize that row set rows are identified by handles. A *handle* is

19

just a fancy name for a special address that identifies where a row is stored in memory. You can use this interface to determine whether two row handles actually point to the same row set. The IRowsetIdentify interface is optional. It defines the standard IUnknown interface methods QueryInterface, AddRef, and Release and provides one additional method: IsSameRow. This method is defined as follows:

```
HRESULT IsSameRow(HROW hRow1, HROW hRow2);
```

The IsSameRow method takes two parameters, which are the handles of the rows to compare. If the row handles point to the same row, this method returns S_OK. If not, it returns S_FALSE. Both these values give a TRUE result when the SUCCEEDED macro is used. You will need to test for S_OK explicitly or at least nest an explicit test under a SUCCEEDED macro.

The IRowsetLocate Interface

IRowsetLocate is an optional interface that retrieves rows nonsequentially from a row set. This interface has methods that can use bookmarks to jump around in a row set. The standard IUnknown interface methods QueryInterface, AddRef, and Release are defined by the IRowsetLocate interface, as well as four additional methods: Compare, GetRowsAt, GetRowsByBookmark, and Hash. These methods are defined as follows:

```
HRESULT Compare(HCHAPTER hChapter, ULONG cBookMarkLen1,
                const BYTE *pBookMark1, ULONG cBookMarkLen2,
                const BYTE *pBookMark2, DBCOMPARE *pCompare);
HRESULT GetRowsAt(HWATCHREGION hReservedHandle1, HCHAPTER hChapter,
                ULONG cBookMarkLen, const BYTE *pBookMark,
                LONG lNumRowsOffset, LONG lNumRowsToFetch,
                ULONG *lNumRowsRetrieved, HROW **phRows);
HRESULT GetRowsByBookmark(HCHAPTER hChapter, ULONG lNumRowsToFetch,
                const ULONG rBookmarksLen[],
                const BYTE *rBookmarks[],
                HROW rhRows[], DBROWSTATUS rRowStatus[]);
HRESULT Hash(HCHAPTER hChapter, ULONG lNumBookmarks,
                const ULONG rBookmarksLen[], const BYTE *rBookmarks,
                DWORD rHashedBookmarks[],DBROWSTATUS rRowStatus[]);
```

The Compare method compares two bookmarks to determine whether one is before, after, or points to the same position as the other. The GetRowsAt method retrieves a row set from a bookmarked position, as well as a specified offset. The GetRowsByBookmark method retrieves the rows that match a set of bookmarks. The Hash method retrieves the *hash value* (a quick lookup key for a record) that identifies a bookmarked record. If you would like more information about these methods, refer to the OLE DB Specification help file.

The `IRowsetResynch` Interface

The `IRowsetResynch` interface synchronizes row sets when they are part of a transaction. Transactions, as well as this interface, are covered in more detail on Day 20, "Properties, Transactions, and Indexes." The `IRowsetResynch` interface is optional and defines the standard `IUnknown` interface methods `QueryInterface`, `AddRef`, and `Release`. The interface also provides two additional methods: `GetVisibleData` and `ResynchRows`. These methods are defined as follows:

```
HRESULT GetVisibleData(HROW hRow, HACCESSOR hAccessor, void *pBuffer);
HRESULT ResynchRows(ULONG cNumRowsToResynch, const HROW rhRows[],
                    ULONG *pNumRowsResynched, HROW **phRowsResynched,
                    DBROWSTATUS **pRowStatus);
```

The `GetVisibleData` method retrieves the row set data that is visible in the transaction scope. The `ResynchRows` method synchronizes the data contained in the row set buffer with the actual data source.

The `IRowsetScroll` Interface

The `IRowsetScroll` interface facilitates the integration of row sets with window scroll bars. This interface is optional. A `Rowset` object must implement the `IRowsetLocate` interface to support this interface. The `IRowsetScroll` interface defines the standard `IUnknown` interface methods `QueryInterface`, `AddRef`, and `Release` and provides two additional methods: `GetApproximatePosition` and `GetRowsAtRatio`. These methods are defined as follows:

```
HRESULT GetApproximatePosition(HCHAPTER hChapter, ULONG cLenBookmark,
                               const BYTE *pBookmark, ULONG *plPosition,
                               ULONG *plNumRows);
HRESULT GetRowsAtRatio(HWATCHREGION hChapter,
                       HCHAPTER hReserveredhandle2, ULONG lNumerator,
                       ULONG lDemoninator, LONG lNumRowsToFetch,
                       ULONG *plNumRowsFetched, HROW **phRows);
```

The `GetApproximatePosition` method approximately determines the row position of a bookmarked row. The `cLenBookmark` parameter specifies the size of a bookmark, and the `pBookmark` parameter specifies a pointer to the approximate position of the bookmark. The `plPosition` parameter returns the approximate position, and the `plNumRows` parameter returns the total number of rows.

The `GetRowsAtRatio` method retrieves a number of rows located at a specific percentage location in the row set. The percentage location is determined by dividing the `lNumerator` parameter by the `lDenominator` parameter. The `lNumRowsToFetch` parameter specifies the number of rows to retrieve. The `plNumRowsFetched` parameter returns the number of rows actually retrieved, and the `phRows` parameter returns an array of associated row handles.

19

The `IRowsetUpdate` Interface

The final interface supported by the `Rowset` object is the `IRowsetUpdate` interface, which is optional. This interface buffers changes made with the `IRowsetChange` interface and defines the standard `IUnknown` interface methods `QueryInterface`, `AddRef`, and `Release`. The interface also provides five additional methods: `GetOriginalData`, `GetPendingRows`, `GetRowStatus`, `Undo`, and `Update`. These methods are defined as follows:

```
HRESULT GetOriginalData(HROW hRow, HACCESSOR hAccessor, void *pBuffer);
HRESULT GetPendingRows(HCHAPTER hChapter, DBPENDINGSTATUS dRowStatus,
                    ULONG *plNumPendRows, HROW **phPendRows,
                    DBPENDINGSTATUS **pPendStatus);
HRESULT GetRowStatus(HCHAPTER hChapter, ULONG lNumRows,
                    const HROW rhStatusRows, DBPENDINGSTATUS pStatus[]);
HRESULT Undo(HCHAPTER hChapter, ULONG lNumRows, const HROW rhUndoRows[],
            ULONG *plNumRowsUndone, HROW **phRows,
            DBROWSTATUS **pRowStatus);
HRESULT Update(HCHAPTER hChapter, ULONG lNumRows,
            const HROW rhUpdateRows[], ULONG *plNumRowsUpdated,
            HROW **phRows, DBROWSTATUS **pRowStatus);
```

The `GetOriginalData` method is used to update the data from the data source, ignoring any changes that have not been written back. For example, if you make changes to a row and they aren't written back, you can use this method to return to the state before the changes were made. The `hRow` parameter specifies the row handle to re-retrieve. The `hAccessor` parameter defines the `Accessor` for the row to retrieve. The `pBuffer` parameter defines the data buffer that contains the actual row data described by the `Accessor`.

The `GetPendingRows` method retrieves the rows of a row set that have some operation pending, such as a new, changed, or deleted row. The status you're looking for is defined by the `dRowStatus` parameter, which can be a combination of `DBPENDINGSTATUS_NEW`, `DBPENDINGSTATUS_CHANGED`, or `DBPENDINGSTATUS_DELETED`. These flags can be combined with a logical `OR`. The `plNumPendRows` parameter returns the number of rows with the type of pending operation being searched. The `phPendRows` returns an array of row handles for each of these rows, and the `pPendStatus` parameter returns an array containing the actual status of each of these rows. The `pPendStatus` array is useful when you query more than one status type.

The `GetRowStatus` method is similar to the `GetPendingRows` method. The `GetRowStatus` method doesn't search for a specific status, though; it returns the status of the group of rows specified. The `lNumRows` parameter specifies the number of row handles in the array parameter `rhStatusRows`. The row status will be retrieved for the row handles in this array. The `pStatus` array is returned and contains the status of each row in the `rhStatusRows` array.

The Undo method returns a row to the state it was in before the last time it was written back to a data source. You can use the Undo method on a group of row handles specified by the rhUndoRows parameter that contains an array of row handles. The lNumRows parameter specifies the number of rows in this array. The plNumRowsUndone parameter returns the number of rows that operation attempted to undo. The phRows parameter returns an array of the undone row handles; if this parameter is NULL, this array isn't returned. The pRowStatus parameter can return an array containing the status of each row that was undone; if this parameter is NULL, the row status isn't returned.

Finally, the Update method writes back a set of rows to the data source. You can use the Update method on a group of row handles specified by the rhUpdateRows parameter that contains an array of row handles. The lNumRows parameter specifies the number of rows in this array. The plNumRowsUpdates parameter returns the number of rows that operation attempted to update. The phRows parameter returns an array of the updated row handles; if this parameter is NULL, the array isn't returned. The pRowStatus parameter can return an array containing the status of each row that was updated; if this parameter is NULL, the row status isn't returned.

The Six-Step Plan to Retrieving Data

By now you are probably wondering how you can put the Rowset object and its associated interfaces to work. You already understand how to use OLE DB to connect to a data source, initiate a session, and even execute a command. This section explains a basic six-step plan for accessing the data contained in a row set:

1. Identify the data contained in the row set with the GetColumnInfo method.
2. Obtain the column bindings using column information.
3. Create an Accessor with the CreateAccessor method.
4. Retrieve the row set handles with the GetNextRows method.
5. Retrieve the actual row data with the GetData method.
6. Release the row handles before retrieving the next set of row handles.

Step 1 uses the GetColumnInfo method to determine the data contained in the row set. To understand this step, think back to Listing 18.4, in which you created an OLE DB application that connects to an ODBC data source and performs a simple query. The query SELECT * FROM Customers creates a row set that contains all the columns for all the records in the CUSTOMERS table. After the Rowset object is created by executing the command, you can call the GetColumnInfo method to retrieve the size, type, precision, and scale.

19

Listing 19.1 demonstrates how to obtain the IColumnsInfo interface and call its GetColumnInfo method. In step 6 of this process, you will see how Listing 19.4 integrates all the code from the listings developed in the past two days. Note that the code in Listing 19.1 doesn't check the return value from QueryInterface. Without testing the HRESULT, there's no way to know whether the pColumnsInfo interface pointer is valid. You will need to test for the return value in any production code.

LISTING 19.1 USING THE GetColumnIfo METHOD TO DETERMINE WHAT INFORMATION IS STORED IN A ROW SET

```
 1:    IColumnsInfo*       pColumnsInfo;
 2:    DBCOLUMNINFO*       pDBColumnInfo;
 3:    ULONG              lNumCols;
 4:
 5:    // Obtain access to the IColumnsInfo interface, from the Rowset
 6:    // object
 7:    pRowset->QueryInterface(IID_IColumnsInfo, (void **) &pColumnsInfo);
 8:
 9:    // Retrieve the Column Information
10:    pColumnsInfo->GetColumnInfo(&lNumCols, &pDBColumnInfo, NULL);
11:
12:    // Free the Column Information Interface
13:    pColumnsInfo->Release();
```

This code creates a structure that contains column information. The next step is to create column bindings. Before going on to step 2, you need to know what bindings and Accessors are and how you can use them.

Creating Bindings

When you retrieve a row of data by using the GetData method, you create a buffer that contains the actual data in the data source row. How do you determine what's stored in this buffer? Where is the buffer stored? OLE DB uses the DBBINDING structure to define the columns stored in this buffer. The DBBINDING structure is defined as follows:

```
typedef struct tagDBBINDING {
 ULONG iOrdinal;
 ULONG obValue;
 ULONG obLength;
 ULONG obStatus;
 ITypeInfo * pTypeInfo;
 DBOBJECT * pObject;
 DBBINDEXT * pBindExt;
 DBPART dwPart;
 DBMEMOWNER dwMemOwner;
 DBPARAMIO eParamIO;
 ULONG cbMaxLen;
```

```
    DWORD dwFlags;
    DBTYPE wType;
    BYTE bPrecision;
    BYTE bScale;
} DBBINDING;
```

This binding structure defines how columns are stored in the row buffer. The iOrdinal field defines the ordinal position of the field. The obValue field defines the buffer offset (the number of bytes from the beginning of the row buffer) to where the column's value is stored. The obLength field defines the buffer offset to where the length of the column is stored. The obStatus field defines the buffer offset to where the status of the column is stored. The pObject field is used when accessing OLE objects. The dwPart field describes which parts of the buffer are bound.

The dwPart field is created by logically ORing the DBPART_VALUE, DBPART_LENGTH, and DBPART_STATUS constants. These constants define the parts of the column you want to store in the buffer. The dwMemOwner field describes whether the buffer memory is client or provider owned; typically, this field is DBMEMOWNER_CLIENTOWNED. The eParamIO parameter field defines the type of parameter described. The values for this field can be DBPARAMIO_NOTPARAM for fields, DBPARAMIO_INPUT for an input parameter, or DBPARAMIO_OUTPUT for an output parameter. These constants can be logically ORed together.

The cbMaxLen field defines the maximum length of the column. The wType field defines the data type of the column. The bPrecision field defines the column's precision, and the bScale field defines the column's scale. The dwFlags field determines special field attributes, such as whether the field is a bookmark index, whether it can be deferred, and whether it can hold a null value. The pTypeInfo and pBindExt are reserved for future use. The pTypeInfo and pBindExt fields should be NULL.

How do you know what to store in this binding structure? The binding structure should contain an array of binding structures, with an element for each column in the row set. To fill in the fields of the binding structure, you need to return to step 1, where you obtained the DBCOLUMNINFO structure. The DBCOLUMNINFO structure is defined as follows:

```
typedef tagDBCOLUMNINFO {
    LPOLESTR        pwszName;
    ITypeInfo       *pTypeInfo;
    ULONG           iOrdinal;
    DBCOLUMNFLAGS   dwFlags;
    ULONG           ulColumnSize;
    DBTYPE          wType;
    BYTE            bPrecision;
    BYTE            bScale;
    DBID            columnid;
} DBCOLUMNINFO;
```

19

Many fields in this structure are the same fields required by the binding structure. Therefore, after you obtain the DBCOLUMNINFO structure, you can allocate space for a DBBINDING structure array, one element for each column in the row set. You will step through each column in the DBCOLUMNINFO and fill out the corresponding DBBINDING array element with the appropriate information. Listing 19.2 demonstrates step 2, which obtains the column bindings using column information.

LISTING 19.2 OBTAINING THE COLUMN BINDINGS INFORMATION FROM THE COLUMN INFORMATION STRUCTURE

```
 1:     // Create a DBBINDING array
 2:     pBindings = new DBBINDING[lNumCols];
 3:
 4:     // Using the ColumnInfo Structure, Fill Out the pBindings Array
 5:     for(j = 0; j < lNumCols; j++) {
 6:         // Ordinal Positions Start at 1
 7:         pBindings[j].iOrdinal = j+1;
 8:         // Buffer offset, re-calculated at the end of this loop
 9:         pBindings[j].obValue = cbColOffset;
10:         // You're Not Retrieving the Column Length
11:         pBindings[j].obLength = 0;
12:         // You're Not Retrieving the Column Status
13:         pBindings[j].obStatus = 0;
14:         // These Parameters Are for Future Use...
15:         pBindings[j].pTypeInfo = NULL;
16:         pBindings[j].pObject = NULL;
17:         pBindings[j].pBindExt = NULL;
18:         // We're Just Retrieving the Value Part
19:         pBindings[j].dwPart = DBPART_VALUE;
20:         // The Memory Will Be Client Owned
21:         pBindings[j].dwMemOwner = DBMEMOWNER_CLIENTOWNED;
22:         // This Binding Does Not Define a Parameter
23:         pBindings[j].eParamIO = DBPARAMIO_NOTPARAM;
24:         // Use the ColumnInfo Structure to Get the Column Size
25:         pBindings[j].cbMaxLen = pDBColumnInfo[j].ulColumnSize;
26:         pBindings[j].dwFlags = 0;
27:         // Use the ColumnInfo Structure to Get the Column Type
28:         pBindings[j].wType = pDBColumnInfo[j].wType;
29:         // Use the ColumnInfo Structure to Get the Column Precision
30:         pBindings[j].bPrecision = pDBColumnInfo[j].bPrecision;
31:         // Use the ColumnInfo Structure to Get the Column Scale
32:         pBindings[j].bScale = pDBColumnInfo[j].bScale;
33:
34:         // Re-calulate the Next Buffer Offset by
35:         // Adding the Current Offset to the Maximum Column Length
36:         // Obtained from the ColumnsInfo Structure
37:         cbColOffset = cbColOffset + pDBColumnInfo[j].ulColumnSize;
38:     };
```

Now that you have created the column bindings, you need to create the row set `Accessor`.

Row Set Accessors

Accessors are easy. They are just handles to `DBBINDING` binding structures. These handles are easier and faster to pass as parameters than passing around the whole `DBBINDING` binding structure.

> **Tip**
>
> You can create an `Accessor` by combining multiple `DBBINDING` structure arrays. A row set can use more than one `Accessor` (for different views of the row set data, depending on requirements). Today's focus is on using a single binding structure and single `Accessor` to access row sets.

The `CreateAccessor` method of the `IAccessor` interface creates an `Accessor` handle from a binding structure. After you have finished using an `Accessor` handle, you must release it with the `ReleaseAccessor` method. Failure to release the `Accessor` handle when you have finished using it will cause a memory leak. Listing 19.3 displays step 3 in the six-step process of retrieving data from a row—creating an `Accessor` from the binding information array. Note that the code in Listing 19.3 doesn't check the return value from `QueryInterface`. You will need to test for the return value in your production code.

19

LISTING 19.3 CREATING AN ACCESSOR WITH THE PREVIOUSLY CREATED BINDING ARRAY

```
 1:     // Obtain Access to the IAccessor Interface
 2:     pRowset->QueryInterface(IID_IAccessor, (void **) &pAccessor);
 3:
 4:     // Create an Accessor Handle, Using the CreateAccessor Method
 5:     pAccessor->CreateAccessor(DBACCESSOR_ROWDATA,    // We Are
 6:                                                      // Retrieving Row
                                                         // Data
 7:                             lNumCols,                // The Number of
                                                         // Columns
 8:                                                      //   We Are
                                                         // Binding
 9:                             pBindings,               // The Bindings
                                                         // Structure
10:                             0,                       // Not Used
11:                             &hAccessor,              // The Returned
                                                         // Accessor
```

continues

LISTING 19.3 CREATING AN ACCESSOR WITH THE PREVIOUSLY CREATED BINDING ARRAY

```
12:                                                    //    Handle
13:                          NULL);                    // We're Not
                                                       // Returning
14:                                                    //    Status
                                                       // Information
15:
16:    // Use The Accessor To Access The Row Data... Steps 4 Through 6
17:
18:    // Free Up Allocated Memory
19:    pAccessor->ReleaseAccessor(hAccessor, NULL);
20:    pAccessor->Release();
```

You are now halfway through the process of accessing the previously defined row set data. The next two steps retrieve a row from a row set and then retrieve the actual data described by the `Accessor` you just created. Step 6 is a required housekeeping step that frees up any memory allocated for the retrieved row data.

Retrieving Rows and Columns

Two `Rowset` object methods are instrumental to the process of getting the data: `GetNextRows` and `GetData`. The `GetNextRows` method retrieves a set of rows from a row set. To improve performance, more than one row can be read at a time. The `GetData` method creates a buffer, which you can read using the binding information. You need to create two loops to read all the rows generated by your query: an outer loop that retrieves a set of rows until all the sets have been returned and an inner loop that loops through these row subsets and prints out the column information they contain. After you use the row subset, you must call the `ReleaseRows` method to release the memory allocated to the subset.

The `GetData` method fills a character buffer, and the binding structure determines where each field begins in that buffer. The binding structure contains the `obValue` field, which defines the offset from the beginning of the buffer to the location of the column's value. This offset value is an index into the buffer returned by the `GetData` method. Depending on how you use these row values, you might have to do some typecasting.

Note The application is responsible for allocating and freeing the buffer used by the `GetData` method. The size of this buffer is determined as you calculate the current offset when defining the bindings. When that loop is complete, the `cbColOffset` variable contains the length of the buffer. You allocate a character string of that length. After you have finished using the `GetData` method, you can free this buffer.

Now that you understand what's involved in these last three steps, you should be able to assemble all the steps to access and display the row set data. Listing 19.4 presents the complete simple OLE DB application. This application accesses the OrdersDb ODBC data source, creates a session, and executes the SQL command SELECT CustNumber, CustFirstName FROM CUSTOMERS. The application also displays the title of each column and the data contained in each row. The output of this application appears in Listing 19.5.

To build the application, run Visual Studio and select File, New. Click the Projects tab and specify a Win32 Console Application. Call the application ROWACCESS. Click OK, specify that you want to create an empty project, and click Finish. After AppWizard runs, create a new C++ source file as part of the project. You can call it whatever you think is appropriate, such as ROWACCESS.CPP. Enter the code shown in Listing 19.4 into the source file.

You will need to change the input libraries for the linker to the following:

```
oledbd.lib kernel32.lib user32.lib gdi32.lib winspool.lib comdlg32.lib
➥advapi32.lib
shell32.lib ole32.lib oleaut32.lib uuid.lib
```

You do this under Project, Settings on the Link tab. When you build the project, it should compile and link with no errors or warnings. Note that the code in Listing 19.4 doesn't check the return value from QueryInterface. You will need to test for the return value in your production code.

INPUT   **LISTING 19.4**   THE COMPLETED RowAccess APPLICATION, DEMONSTRATING HOW TO ACCESS AND DISPLAY QUERY RESULT ROW DATA

19

```
 1: #define UNICODE
 2: #define _UNICODE
 3: #define DBINITCONSTANTS
 4: #define INITGUID
 5:
 6: // Standard Application Includes
 7: #include <windows.h>
 8: #include <stdio.h>
 9: #include <tchar.h>
10: #include <stddef.h>
11: #include <iostream.h>
12:
13: // OLE DB Header Files
14: #include <oledb.h>
15: #include <oledberr.h>
16:
17: // OLE DB - ODBC Provider Header Files
```

continues

LISTING 19.4   CONTINUED

```
18: #include <msdaguid.h>
19: #include <msdasql.h>
20:
21: void main() {
22:    IDBInitialize*     pIDBInitialize = NULL;
23:    IDBCreateSession*  pCreateSession = NULL;
24:    IDBCreateCommand*  pCreateCommand = NULL;
25:    IRowset*           pRowset = NULL;
26:    ICommandText*      pCommandText = NULL;
27:    IDBProperties*     pIDBProperties;
28:    IColumnsInfo*      pColumnsInfo;
29:    IAccessor*         pAccessor;
30:    HACCESSOR          hAccessor;
31:    DBCOLUMNINFO*      pDBColumnInfo;
32:    DBPROP             InitProperties[4];
33:    DBPROPSET          rgInitPropSet[1];
34:    int                i;
35:    ULONG              j,
36:                       lNumCols,
37:                       cbColOffset = 0;
38:    ULONG              lNumRowsRetrieved;
39:    HROW               hRows[5];
40:    HROW*              pRows = &hRows[0];
41:    LONG               cNumRows;
42:    DBBINDING*         pBindings;
43:    char               *pBuffer;
44:    WCHAR*             pStringsBuffer;
45:
46:    // The Command to execute
47:    LPCOLESTR wCmdString =
48:      OLESTR("SELECT CustNumber, CustFirstName FROM CUSTOMERS");
49:
50:    // Initialize the Component Object Module Library
51:    CoInitialize(NULL);
52:
53:    // Obtain Access to the OLE DB - ODBC Provider
54:    CoCreateInstance(CLSID_MSDASQL, NULL, CLSCTX_INPROC_SERVER,
55:                     IID_IDBInitialize, (void **) &pIDBInitialize);
56:
57:    // Initialize the property values that are the same for each
58:    // property...
59:    for (i = 0; i < 4; i++ ) {
60:        VariantInit(&InitProperties[i].vValue);
61:      InitProperties[i].dwOptions = DBPROPOPTIONS_REQUIRED;
62:      InitProperties[i].colid = DB_NULLID;
63:    }
64:
65:    // level of prompting that will be done to complete the
```

```
66:    // connection process
67:    InitProperties[0].dwPropertyID = DBPROP_INIT_PROMPT;
68:    InitProperties[0].vValue.vt = VT_I2;
69:    InitProperties[0].vValue.iVal = DBPROMPT_NOPROMPT;
70:
71:    // Specify the Username
72:    InitProperties[1].dwPropertyID = DBPROP_AUTH_USERID;
73:    InitProperties[1].vValue.vt = VT_BSTR;
74:    // Note: The L cast directive casts the string into a UNICODE
       // string....
75:    InitProperties[1].vValue.bstrVal = SysAllocString((LPOLESTR)L"");
76:
77:    // Specify the appropriate Password
78:    InitProperties[2].dwPropertyID = DBPROP_AUTH_PASSWORD;
79:    InitProperties[2].vValue.vt = VT_BSTR;
80:    InitProperties[2].vValue.bstrVal = SysAllocString((LPOLESTR)L"");
81:
82:    // Specify the Data Source name
83:    InitProperties[3].dwPropertyID = DBPROP_INIT_DATASOURCE;
84:    InitProperties[3].vValue.vt = VT_BSTR;
85:    InitProperties[3].vValue.bstrVal =
86: ➥SysAllocString((LPOLESTR)L"OrdersDb");
87:
88:
89:    rgInitPropSet[0].guidPropertySet = DBPROPSET_DBINIT;
90:    rgInitPropSet[0].cProperties = 4;
91:    rgInitPropSet[0].rgProperties = InitProperties;
92:
93:    // set initialization properties
94:    pIDBInitialize->QueryInterface(IID_IDBProperties,
95: ➥(void **)&pIDBProperties);
96:    pIDBProperties->SetProperties(1,rgInitPropSet);
97:    pIDBProperties->Release();
98:
99:    // Call the Initialize method to establish the connection to
100:   // the ODBC data source specified above
101:   pIDBInitialize->Initialize();
102:
103:   // Create a Session object...
104:   pIDBInitialize->QueryInterface(IID_IDBCreateSession, (void **)
105: ➥&pCreateSession);
106:
107:   // Create a Command object...
108:   pCreateSession->CreateSession(NULL, IID_IDBCreateCommand,
109: ➥(IUnknown **) &pCreateCommand);
110:
111:   // Access the ICommandText interface
112:   pCreateCommand->CreateCommand(NULL, IID_ICommandText, (IUnknown **)
113: ➥&pCommandText);
114:
115:   // Specify the command text
```

continues

19

LISTING **19.4**   CONTINUED

```
116:    pCommandText->SetCommandText(DBGUID_DBSQL, wCmdString);
117:
118:    // Execute the command
119:    pCommandText->Execute(NULL, IID_IRowset, NULL, &cNumRows,
120:    ➥(IUnknown **) &pRowset);
121:
122:    //
*********************************************************************
123:    // Step 1: Determine the data contained in the row set, using the
124:    //         GetColumnInfo method.
125:    //
*********************************************************************
126:
127:    // Obtain access to the IColumnsInfo interface, from the Rowset
        // object
128:    pRowset->QueryInterface(IID_IColumnsInfo, (void **) &pColumnsInfo);
129:
130:    // Retrieve the Column Information
131:    pColumnsInfo->GetColumnInfo(&lNumCols, &pDBColumnInfo,
        ➥&pStringsBuffer);
132:
133:    // Free the Column Information Interface
134:    pColumnsInfo->Release();
135:
136:    //
*********************************************************************
137:    // Step 2: Obtain the column bindings, using column information.
138:    //
*********************************************************************
139:
140:    // Create a DBBINDING array
141:    pBindings = new DBBINDING[lNumCols];
142:
143:    // Using the ColumnInfo Structure, Fill Out the pBindings Array
144:    for(j = 0; j < lNumCols; j++) {
145:        // Ordinal Positions Start at 1
146:        pBindings[j].iOrdinal = j+1;
147:        // Buffer offset, re-calculated at the end of this loop
148:        pBindings[j].obValue = cbColOffset;
149:        // We're Not Retrieving the Column Length
150:        pBindings[j].obLength = 0;
151:        // We're Not Retrieving the Column Status
152:        pBindings[j].obStatus = 0;
153:        // These Parameters Are for Future Use...
154:        pBindings[j].pTypeInfo = NULL;
155:        pBindings[j].pObject = NULL;
156:        pBindings[j].pBindExt = NULL;
157:        // We're Just Retrieving the Value Part
158:        pBindings[j].dwPart = DBPART_VALUE;
```

```
159:        // The Memory Will Be Client Owned
160:        pBindings[j].dwMemOwner = DBMEMOWNER_CLIENTOWNED;
161:        // This Binding Does Not Define a Parameter
162:        pBindings[j].eParamIO = DBPARAMIO_NOTPARAM;
163:        // Use the ColumnInfo Structure to Get the Column Size
164:        pBindings[j].cbMaxLen = pDBColumnInfo[j].ulColumnSize;
165:        pBindings[j].dwFlags = 0;
166:        // Use the ColumnInfo Structure to Get the Column Type
167:        pBindings[j].wType = pDBColumnInfo[j].wType;
168:        // Use the ColumnInfo Structure to Get the Column Precision
169:        pBindings[j].bPrecision = pDBColumnInfo[j].bPrecision;
170:        // Use the ColumnInfo Structure to Get the Column Scale
171:        pBindings[j].bScale = pDBColumnInfo[j].bScale;
172:
173:        // Re-calulate the Next Buffer Offset by
174:        // Adding the Current Offset to the Maximum Column Length
175:        // Obtained from the ColumnsInfo Structure
176:        // Note: When Done with This Loop, This Value Will Be the
177:        // Length Of the Record Buffer
178:        cbColOffset = cbColOffset + pDBColumnInfo[j].ulColumnSize;
179:    };
180:
181:    //
     *****************************************************************
182:    // Step 3: Create an Accessor, using the binding information and
the
183:    //         CreateAccessor method.
184:    //
     *****************************************************************
185:
186:    // Obtain Access to the IAccessor Interface
187:    pRowset->QueryInterface(IID_IAccessor, (void **) &pAccessor);
188:
189:    // Create an Accessor Handle, Using the CreateAccessor Method
190:    pAccessor->CreateAccessor(DBACCESSOR_ROWDATA,  // We Are Retrieving
191:                                                   // Row Data
192:                                lNumCols,          // The Number of
                                                      // Columns
193:                                                   //   We Are Binding
194:                                pBindings,         // The Bindings
                                                      // Structure
195:                                0,                 // Not used
196:                                &hAccessor,        // The Returned
                                                      // Accessor
197:                                                   //   Handle
198:                                NULL);             // We're Not
                                                      // Returning
```

continues

19

LISTING 19.4   CONTINUED

```
199:                                          //    Status
                                              // Information
200:
201:    // Loop through the ColumnInfo Structure and Display
202:    // Each Column Name...
203:    for(j = 0; j < lNumCols; j++) {
204:       // Note: the %S Let's Us Print Out UNICODE Strings from printf
205:       printf("%S\t",pDBColumnInfo[j].pwszName);
206:    };
207:    printf("\n----------------------------------------------------
    ➥\n");
208:
209:    //
****************************************************************
210:    // Step 4: Retrieve the row set handles, using the GetNextRows
        // method.
211:    //
****************************************************************
212:
213:    // Get a Set of 5 Rows...
214:    pRowset->GetNextRows(0,                     // For future use
215:                         0,                     // Number of Rows to
                                                   // Skip
216:                         5,                     // Number of Rows to
217:                                                //   Retrieve
218:                         &lNumRowsRetrieved,    // Number of Rows
219:                                                //   Returned
220:                         &pRows);               // The Row Buffer
221:
222:    // Allocate Space for the Row Buffer
223:    pBuffer = new char[cbColOffset];
224:
225:    // While We Have Retrieved Some Rows...Display Them
226:    while(lNumRowsRetrieved > 0) {
227:       // For Each Row in the Set We Retrieved, Print Out the
228:       // Fields We Retrieved...
229:       for(j = 0; j < lNumRowsRetrieved; j++) {
230:          // Clear the Buffer
231:          memset(pBuffer, 0, cbColOffset);
232:
233:    //
****************************************************************
234:    // Step 5: Retrieve the actual row data using the GetData method.
235:    //
****************************************************************
236:
237:             // Get the Row Data Values
238:             pRowset->GetData(hRows[j], hAccessor, pBuffer);
239:             // Print Out The Field Values
```

```
240:               // Note Our Typecast of the First Column to a Long, Because
241:               // It's a Numeric Field...Also We Will Print Only the First
242:               // 40 Characters of the Second Column
243:               // Also, We Use the obvalue Value to Index The Buffer
244:               printf("%ld\t%.40s\n", (ULONG)
                   ➥pBuffer[pBindings[0].obValue],
245:                       &pBuffer[pBindings[1].obValue]);
246:          };
247:
248:     //
*******************************************************************
249:     // Step 6: Release the row handles before retrieving the next set
of
250:     //          row handles.
251:     //
*******************************************************************
252:
253:          // Release the Rows Retrieved...
254:          pRowset->ReleaseRows(lNumRowsRetrieved, hRows, NULL, NULL,
                  ➥NULL);
255:          // Get a Set of 5 Rows...
256:          pRowset->GetNextRows(0,                  // For future use
257:                               0,                  // Number of Rows to
                                                       // Skip
258:                               5,                  // Number of Rows to
259:                                                   //    Retrieve
260:                               &lNumRowsRetrieved, // Number of Rows
261:                                                   //    Returned
262:                               &pRows);            // The Row Buffer
263:
264:     };
265:
266:     // Free Up All Allocated Memory
267:     delete [] pBuffer;
268:     pAccessor->ReleaseAccessor(hAccessor, NULL);
269:     pAccessor->Release();
270:     delete [] pBindings;
271:     pRowset->Release();
272:     pCommandText->Release();
273:     pCreateCommand->Release();
274:     pCreateSession->Release();
275:     pIDBInitialize->Uninitialize();
276:     pIDBInitialize->Release();
277:
278:     // Release the Component Object Module Library
279:     CoUninitialize();
280:
281: };
```

19

The code in Listing 19.5 should produce this output:

```
1:   CustNumber      CustFirstName
2:   - - - - - - - - - - - - - - - - - - - - - - - - - - - -
3:   1     Bruce
4:   2     Homer
5:   3     Clark
6:   4     John
7:   5     Bill
```

The key feature of this simple application is that it isn't tied to any particular query result. You can modify the SQL command to access a different number of rows or for different tables, and the application will still work!

Today's discussion of how to access row set information continues by examining the more advanced aspects of data access and navigation: column types supported, handling these various types, defining and using cursors, using bookmarks, and making changes to row data.

Navigation

Listing 19.4 shows you how to navigate a row set sequentially, using the GetNextRows method of the IRowset interface. As you know, a *cursor* is a type of pointer that points to the current row you are accessing. With the GetNextRows method, the cursor starts at the beginning of the row set and moves sequentially through the row set as you call the GetNextRows method.

As demonstrated in the example, you can use the GetNextRows method to move the cursor a number of rows at a time. The GetNextRows method functions until the end of the row set; then the RestartPosition method of the IRowset interface repositions the cursor to the beginning of the row set.

Bookmarks

If a data provider supports nonsequential access, it can access rows based on a key value, called a *bookmark* in OLE DB terminology. OLE DB supports two types of bookmarks: numeric and key value bookmarks.

> **Tip**
>
> Check the DBPROP_BOOKMARKTYPE of the DataSource object to determine whether a data provider supports bookmarks.

As you may recall from the discussion of bindings earlier today, you can use the dwFlags field of the binding structure to indicate whether a field can be used as a bookmark. This is done by setting the dwFlags field to the DBCOLUMNSINFO_ISBOOKMARK flag. If a field is a bookmark, it can be used as a search key. OLE DB also defines a set of standard bookmarks, which are outlined in Table 19.1.

TABLE 19.1 THE STANDARD PREDEFINED BOOKMARKS

Constant	Description
DBBMK_INVALID	An undefined bookmark
DBBMK_FIRST	A bookmark to the first row
DBBMK_LAST	A bookmark to the last row

Bookmarks are valid only while a row set is opened. After the row set is closed, all bookmarks on that row set become invalid. The IRowsetLocate interface uses bookmarks to reposition the row set cursor to access records nonsequentially. Listing 19.5 demonstrates how the GetRowsAt method retrieves a specific row. This example assumes that the same query that was executed in Listing 19.4 and assumes that the CustomerID field has been defined as a bookmark type field. Note that the code in Listing 19.5 doesn't check the return value from QueryInterface. You will need to test for the return value in your production code.

LISTING 19.5 USING THE GetRowsAt METHOD TO JUMP TO A PARTICULAR RECORD

```
 1:   // Lookup CustomerID 3!
 2:   lLookup = 3;
 3:
 4:   // Obtain Access to the IRowsetLocate Interface
 5:   pRowset->QueryInterface(IID_IAccessor, (void **) &pRowsetLocate);
 6:   pRowsetLocate->GetRowsAt(0,                  // Reserved for Future
                                                   // Use
 7:                            NULL,               // Reserved for Future
                                                   // Use
 8:                            sizeof(lLookup),    // Size of the
                                                   // Bookmark
 9:                            (BYTE *) &lLookup,  // The Bookmark
10:                            0,                  // Number of Rows to
                                                   // Skip
11:                            1,                  // Number of Rows to
                                                   // Retrieve
12:                            &lNumRowsRetrieved, // Number of Rows
                                                   // Retrieved
13:                            &pRows);            // Row Handles
```

continues

19

LISTING 19.5 CONTINUED

```
14:
15:     // Clear the Buffer and Retrieve the Data
16:     memset(pBuffer, 0, cbColOffset);
17:     pRowset->GetData(hRows[0], hAccessor, pBuffer);
18:     // Print Out The Field Values
19:     printf("%ld\t%.40s\n", (ULONG) pBuffer[pBindings[0].obValue],
20:             &pBuffer[pBindings[1].obValue]);
21:     pRowset->ReleaseRows(lNumRowsRetrieved, hRows, NULL, NULL, NULL);
```

Deferred Access

One way to improve application performance is to set up columns to be deferred, that is, retrieved only when the GetData method is called. If a column isn't deferred, its value is read when it is retrieved from the data source. Deferring the column read can improve performance, especially if you retrieve large columns or a large number of columns. To specify reading a column only when the GetData method is called, you must set the DBPROP_DEFERRED property for the column. If a column contains an OLE object, it is set to be a deferred column by default.

Column Types

OLE DB supports all the standard Windows data types. You can use these types to describe database columns. A column's type is found in the wType field of both of the DBCOLUMNINFO and DBBINDING structures. Table 19.2 lists all the column type constants and the associated descriptions that OLE DB supports.

TABLE 19.2 OLE DB—SUPPORTED DATA TYPES FOR COLUMNS AND PARAMETERS

Type Constant	Description
DBTYPE_EMPTY	A type was not specified. Used when defining variant type fields.
DBTYPE_NULL	A NULL value. Used when defining variant type fields.
DBTYPE_RESERVED	Reserved for future use.
DBTYPE_I1	A single-byte integer, signed.
DBTYPE_I2	A 2-byte integer, signed.
DBTYPE_I4	A 4-byte integer, signed
DBTYPE_I8	An 8-byte integer, signed.
DBTYPE_UI1	A single-byte integer, unsigned.
DBTYPE_UI2	A 2-byte integer, unsigned.
DBTYPE_UI4	A 4-byte integer, unsigned.

DBTYPE_UI8	An 8-byte integer, unsigned.
DBTYPE_R4	A single-precision floating point.
DBTYPE_R8	A double-precision floating point.
DBTYPE_CY	A currency value.
DBTYPE_DECIMAL	An exact numeric decimal value, stored in OLE form.
DBTYPE_NUMERIC	An exact numeric decimal value, stored in standard form.
DBTYPE_DATE	A date stored in OLE form.
DBTYPE_BOOL	A Boolean value, stored in OLE form.
DBTYPE_BYTES	An array of bytes. The length is specified by the cbMaxLen field.
DBTYPE_BSTR	A Unicode character string. The length of the string is stored in the first two bytes.
DBTYPE_STR	An ANSI NULL-terminated character string.
DBTYPE_WSTR	A Unicode NULL-terminated character string.
DBTYPE_VARIANT	A variant in OLE form.
DBTYPE_IDISPATCH	A pointer to an OLE object.
DBTYPE_IUNKNOWN	A pointer to an OLE interface.
DBTYPE_GUID	A GUID (Globally Unique Identifier).
DBTYPE_ERROR	An error code.
DBTYPE_BYREF	A pointer to a type. Used in combination with the other data types listed here. For example, to specify a pointer to a single-byte signed integer, use DBTYPE_I1 ¦ DBTYPE_BYREF. (Note: The ¦ specifies a logical OR operation.)
DBTYPE_ARRAY	A pointer to a SAFEARRAY.
DBTYPE_VECTOR	A DBVECTOR structure used to define an array of another type; used in conjunction with another type. For example, to specify a vector of single-byte signed integers, use DBTYPE_I1 ¦ DBTYPE_VECTOR.
DBTYPE_UDT	A user-defined data type.
DBTYPE_DBDATE	A DBDATE structure.
DBTYPE_DBTIME	A DBTIME structure.
DBTYPE_DBTIMESTAMP	A DBTIMESTAMP structure.

19

BLOBs

Binary Large Objects (BLOBs) can hold images, long text fields, or other large binary field types. OLE DB supports BLOB fields if your data provider also supports them. Consult your data source documentation to determine how to create a BLOB type field. BLOB columns can be retrieved as one large chunk and stored in memory, or they can be retrieved one piece at a time. When you are accessing a BLOB column or one chunk of data, the process of retrieving the field data is the same as for any other column. The only difference is that you need to allocate a large buffer. Listing 19.6 demonstrates how to retrieve a 7,500-byte BLOB column from a data source. This example assumes that this column will never be bigger than 7,500 bytes. Typically, a BLOB field has the type DBTYPE_BYTES, DBTYPE_WSTR, or DBTYPE_STR.

INPUT   **LISTING 19.6** HOW TO RETRIEVE A BLOB COLUMN AS A SINGLE MEMORY OBJECT

```
1:    #define BLOB_LENGTH 7500
2:
3:    HACCESSOR     hAccessor;
4:    DBBINDING     pBinding[1];
5:    IRowset       *pRowset;
6:    IAccessor     *pAccessor;
7:    void          *pData;
8:    HROW          *phRow;
9:    ULONG         lNumRows;
10:
11:     // The First Column
12:     pBindings[0].iOrdinal = 1;
13:     // Buffer offset, Just one column in our row set
14:     pBindings[0].obValue = 0;
15:     // We're Not Retrieving the Column Length
16:     pBindings[0].obLength = 0;
17:     // We're Not Retrieving the Column Status
18:     pBindings[0].obStatus = 0;
19:     // These Parameters Are for Future Use...
20:     pBindings[0].pTypeInfo = NULL;
21:     pBindings[0].pObject = NULL;
22:     pBindings[0].pBindExt = NULL;
23:     // We're Just Retrieving the Value Part
24:     pBindings[0].dwPart = DBPART_VALUE;
25:     // The Memory Will Be Client Owned
26:     pBindings[0].dwMemOwner = DBMEMOWNER_CLIENTOWNED;
27:     // This Binding Does Not Define a Parameter
28:     pBindings[0].eParamIO = DBPARAMIO_NOTPARAM;
29:     // A 7500 Byte Wide Column
30:     pBindings[0].cbMaxLen = BLOB_LENGTH;
31:     pBindings[0].dwFlags = 0;
32:     // Use the ColumnInfo Structure to Get the Column Type
33:     pBindings[0].wType = DBTYPE_BYTES;
34:     // Use the ColumnInfo Structure to Get the Column Precision
35:     pBindings[0].bPrecision = pDBColumnInfo[j].bPrecision;
36:     // Use the ColumnInfo Structure to Get the Column Scale
37:     pBindings[0].bScale = pDBColumnInfo[j].bScale;
38:
```

```
39:       // Obtain Accessor Interface
40:       pRowset->QueryInterface(IID_Accessor, (void **) &pAccessor);
41:
42:       // Create an Accessor, Using the Binding Information
43:       pAccessor->CreateAccessor(DBACCESSOR_ROWDATA,    // A Row
44:                                 1,                     // 1 Column
45:                                 pBinding,              // The Bindings
46:                                 BLOB_LENGTH,           // 7500 bytes
47:                                 &hAccessor,            // The Accessor
48:                                 NULL);                 // No Status
49:                                                        // Returned
50:  Data = new char[BLOB_LENGTH]; // Cast it to the appropriate type
                                   // later
51:
52:       pRowset->GetNextRows(NULL, 0, 1, &lNumRows, &phRow);
53:       pRowset->GetData(phRow[0], hAccessor, pData);
54:       // Remember to release pAccessor;
```

As this example shows, the process of accessing a BLOB column as a single in-memory object isn't very difficult. You can also access a BLOB column by using the OLE streaming interfaces. Day 20 covers these interfaces in more detail, including how to use them to access BLOB columns.

Unicode String Processing

Unicode strings are used to support international character sets. Many strings defined by OLE DB are defined as Unicode character strings. Each Unicode character is 16-bits, twice the size of an ANSI character string. For the most part, NULL-terminated Unicode strings can be manipulated like NULL-terminated ANSI strings. The following special considerations apply to Unicode strings:

- When using the printf function, use the %S format directive to print Unicode strings.

- You can use the functions MultiByteToWideChar and WideCharToMultiByte to convert ANSI strings to Unicode strings, and vice versa.

- Many functions defined for ANSI character strings are also defined for Unicode character strings, for example, lstrcat and lstrlen.

- To use the generic string functions for Unicode characters in Visual C++, you must use the #define _UNICODE directive and include the <wchar.h> header files.

19

Cursors

The final topic for today is cursors. Cursors are used to navigate a row set. If you have used Data Access Objects (DAO), Remote Data Objects (RDO), or Open Database Connectivity (ODBC) you are probably already familiar with different types of cursors that facilitate record navigation and locking. This discussion concentrates on the various types of cursors, why they are used, and the Rowset object properties that must be set to invoke them. Tomorrow's topics (Day 20) include OLE DB object properties and the implementation of cursors in more detail.

Static Cursors

When using a Static cursor, the order of the rows is in the natural data source order, and if the row set is changed in any way while it is opened, those changes aren't reflected. Changes are recognized only when the row set is closed and reopened. To specify that a row set uses a static type of cursor, the DBPROP_CANSCROLLBACKWARDS property is set to VARIANT_TRUE and the DBPROP_OTHERINSERT and DBPROP_OTHERUPDATEDELETE properties are set to VARIANT_FALSE.

KeySet Cursors

When you use a KeySet cursor, the order of the rows is in some sorted order based on a key. As with a Static cursor, if the row set is changed in any way while it is opened, those changes aren't reflected immediately. If a row is updated, the changes will be reflected the next time the row is retrieved, but if a row is deleted or inserted, the change is recognized only when the row set is closed and reopened. To specify that a row set uses a KeySet type of cursor, the DBPROP_CANSCROLLBACKWARDS and DBPROP_OTHERUPDATEDELETE properties are set to VARIANT_TRUE, and the DBPROP_OTHERINSERT is set to VARIANT_FALSE.

Dynamic Cursors

When you use a Dynamic cursor, the currently open row set actively reflects all changes to the row set. Changes are reflected the next time the row is retrieved. To specify that a row set should use a Dynamic type of cursor, the DBPROP_CANSCROLLBACKWARDS, DBPROP_OTHERUPDATEDELETE, and DBPROP_OTHERINSERT properties are set to VARIANT_TRUE.

Summary

Day 19 opens with a survey of the Rowset object and its interfaces, then sets out a six-step plan for retrieving data, and finally explains how to handle BLOB columns and specify various cursor types.

Today you learned how to access row set data sequentially, how to use bookmarks to access row set data in a random fashion, and how to use deferred access to improve application performance. Day 19 ends with a discussion of different types of cursors, how they affect row set access, and the `Rowset` properties that must be set to invoke these cursor types. The discussion of OLE DB continues tomorrow with a more detailed look at properties, transactions, and OLE DB streaming mechanisms.

Q&A

This section answers some common questions related to today's topics.

Q Does OLE DB provide any way for me to search for a particular value in a row set?

A OLE DB provides the `IRowsetIndex` interface, which I didn't discuss in this lesson. You can use this interface with an associated data source index to search for specific rows in a row set, based on key values. A data provider must support indexing to use this interface.

Q Are queries the only way to create row sets?

A No, row sets can be generated directly from the `Session` object if a data provider doesn't support the `Rowset` object. Row sets generated in this manner will contain the complete contents of a data provider object in a tabular form. (In the case of a database, a data provider object would typically be the contents of a table.) The `IDBSchemaRowset` interface can also be used to generate row sets that contain data source schema information.

Q How does OLE DB handle multiuser row set access?

A OLE DB provides a `Transaction` object for managing record locking and sharing in a multiuser environment. Day 20 covers the `Transaction` object in more detail.

19

Workshop

The Workshop quiz questions test your understanding of today's material. (The answers appear in Appendix F, "Answers.") The exercises encourage you to apply the information you learned today to real-life situations.

Quiz Questions

1. What is the OLE DB `Rowset` object, and what is it used for?
2. What `Rowset` interface is used to perform basic column data retrieval and navigation?

3. List the six steps used to retrieve column data.

4. What information is stored in the DBCOLUMNINFO structure?

5. What structure stores column bindings? How do column bindings relate to the row buffer?

6. What are BLOB columns? What are the two ways OLE DB provides for accessing their contents?

7. List and describe the different cursor types that OLE DB supports.

Exercises

1. Modify the application in Listing 19.4 to display schema information for the result of the query. Include the column name, type, length, and so on. *Hint:* Look at what's stored in the DBCOLUMNINFO structure and at the IDBSchemaRowset interface.

   Lines 156–164 use the DBCOLUMNINFO structure to discover the columns and their types. Lines 194 through 199 show the column names. You can simply add code here that uses the information from lines 156–164.

DAY **20**

Properties, Transactions, and Indexes

Today's lesson covers three important topics in OLE DB application development: properties, transactions, and the Index object. You have already learned about OLE DB objects and have used their methods, but you haven't yet discovered how to change the state of an object. Today you will learn how to use properties to control the state of an object, or in other words, how to set and retrieve property values of OLE DB objects by using special interfaces. The other major topics for today are the Transaction object and the Index object.

Today you will

- Learn how to use properties and groups to set the state of various OLE DB objects by using the interfaces they provide.

- Retrieve and set property values.

- Explore the major properties supported by OLE DB objects.

- Create, commit, and abort Transaction objects by using the supported interfaces.

- Use transactions to ensure data security and integrity.
- Use the interfaces supported by the Index object.
- Use the Index object to search for a row in the row set by using a key value.

Properties and Groups

Properties specify the attributes of an OLE DB object and can determine how the object behaves. Some properties can only be read, whereas others can be read and written. Properties are identified by globally unique identifier (GUID) constants and grouped according to the object on which they function. The following objects have special properties: Columns, DataSource, DataSource initialization objects, Index, Rowset, Session, and Table. Today's explanation of properties begins by discussing how to retrieve a property value.

Getting Properties

Most OLE DB objects use the GetProperties method to retrieve property values. Table 20.1 summarizes the methods used by each OLE DB object to access its properties. Because most objects use the GetProperties method, this section focuses on that mechanism for retrieving property values.

TABLE 20.1 THE METHODS USED BY OLE DB OBJECTS TO RETRIEVE PROPERTY VALUES

OLE DB Object	Interface	Method
Columns	IColumnsRowset	GetColumnsRowset
DataSource	IDBProperties	GetProperties
Index	IRowsetIndex	GetIndexInfo
Rowset	IRowsetInfo	GetProperties
	ICommandInfo	GetProperties
	ICommandProperties	GetProperties
Session	ISessionProperties	GetProperties
Table	ITableDefinition	CreateTable

The GetProperties method is defined as follows:

```
GetProperties(ULONG lNumPropIDs, DBPROPIDSET rPropIDs[],
              ULONG lNumPropSets, DBPROPSET **prPropSets);
```

The lNumPropIDs parameter specifies the number of elements in the rPropIDs array. The rPropIDs array contains a collection of DBPROPIDSET structures that specify the collection of properties for which you want to see values. The DBPROPIDSET structure is defined as follows:

```
typedef struct tagDBPROPIDSET {
    DBPROPID *rgPropertyIDs;
    ULONG    cPropertyIDs;
    GUID     guidPropertySet;
} DBPROPIDSET;
```

The rgPropertyIDs field defines an array of Property IDs. That is, the DBPROPIDSET holds a collection of property IDs, and the GetProperties method actually takes a collection of DBPROPIDSET structures, which in themselves contain a collection of property IDs. You will typically define a single DBPROPIDSET structure, which contains a collection of the property IDs you want to retrieve. The cPropertyIDs field defines the number of elements in the rgPropertyIDs array. The guidPropertySet field holds a GUID that defines the property group to which the properties in the rgPropertyIDs array belong. Table 20.2 defines the group GUID constants and the OLE DB object they define.

TABLE 20.2 THE OLE DB PROPERTY GROUPS

OLE DB Object	Group GUID Constant
Column	DBPROPSET_COLUMN
DataSource	DBPROPSET_DATASOURCE
DataSource (information)	DBPROPSET_DATASOURCEINFO
DataSource (initialization)	DBPROPSET_DBINIT
Index	DBPROPSET_INDEX
Rowset	DBPROPSET_ROWSET
Session	DBPROPSET_SESSION
Table	DBPROPSET_TABLE

To retrieve a property value, you must create the DBPROPIDSET structure that contains the properties you want to retrieve. On return, the prPropSet parameter contains a pointer to an array of DBPROPSET structures, and each array element contains a collection of property values. The DBPROPSET structure is defined as the following:

```
typedef struct tagDBPROPSET {
    DBPROP *rgProperties;
    ULONG   cProperties;
    GUID    guidPropertySet;
} DBPROPSET;
```

20

Note

> The memory used by the prPropSet parameter is allocated by the call to the GetProperties method. The Free method of the IMalloc interface should be used to deallocate this memory when it is no longer required. You can also use the CoTaskMemFree API call if you don't have a pointer to the IMalloc interface available. It saves several lines of code, and it's functionally equivalent.

The rgProperties field defines an array of DBPROP structures. The DBPROP structures hold the actual property values. The cProperties field defines the number of elements in the rgProperties array. The guidProperties defines the property group to which the properties in the rgProperties array belong. The DBPROP structure, which holds the actual property values, is defined as follows:

```
typedef struct tagDBPROP {
    DBPROPID        dwPropertyID;
    DBPROPOPTIONS   dwOptions;
    DBPROPSTATUS    dwStatus;
    DBID            colid;
    VARIANT         vValue;
} DBPROP;
```

The dwPropertyID field defines the property ID; it is defined as a simple DWORD type. The dwOptions field determines whether the property is optional or required and what to do if much of processing is required to set the value. The dwOptions field is a combination of the constants: DBPROPOPTIONS_REQUIRED if the value is required and DBPROPOP-TION3_9CTIГOIICAГ to determine whether it should be set if it takes much processing. The dwStatus determines the status of the property. Table 20.3 defines the possible values of the dwStatus field and their meanings. The colid field defines the column for which this property is defined. The colid is a DBID type structure, as you might recall from Day 18, "Querying a Data Source." Finally the vValue field defines the value of the property; it's defined as a standard C++ VARIANT type.

TABLE 20.3 THE PROPERTY STATUS VALUES

Status Value	Description
DBPROPSTATUS_OK	The property's value has been successfully set.
DBPROPSTATUS_BADCOLUMN	The colid field doesn't define a valid field.
DBPROPSTATUS_BADOPTION	The dwOptions field contained an illegal value.
DBPROPSTATUS_BADVALUE	The vValue field contained an illegal value.
DBPROPSTATUS_CONFLICTING	Changing the value of this property would result in a conflicting state; the operation was performed.

Status Value	Description
DBPROPSTATUS_NOTALLSETTABLE	When trying to set a property that applies to a set of columns, the operation was denied because it couldn't be set for all columns.
DBPROPSTATUS_NOTSET	The DBPROPOPTIONS_SETIFCHEAP option prevented the property from being set.
DBPROPSTATUS_NOTSETTABLE	You can't set the value of a read-only property.
DBPROPSTATUS_NOTSUPPORTED	The data provider doesn't support the specified property.

Now that you have the background information you need in order to use the GetProperties method, you can construct the appropriate structures to retrieve a property's value and interpret the results. You need to define one structure to define the property ID you want to retrieve, and you need to define one structure to return the actual property values. (A listing and descriptions of OLE DB object property IDs appear later in this lesson.)

In the Day 18 compendium of the SQL command language, I discussed the use of the GetProperties method of the IDBProperties interface to determine whether the data provider supported the SQL command language. The property ID to check for SQL support is DPROP_SQLSUPPORT. This property is represented as a long integer, which determines the level of SQL support provided by the data provider. Listing 20.1 demonstrates how to retrieve the DBPROP_SQLSUPPORT property of the DataSource object to determine the level of SQL support provided by the data provider. Note that for brevity, the code in Listing 20.1 doesn't check the return value from GetProperties. Without testing the HRESULT, you have no way of knowing whether the properties were actually returned. In your production code, you will need to test for the return value.

LISTING 20.1 DETERMINING THE LEVEL OF SQL SUPPORT PROVIDED BY A DATA PROVIDER, USING THE DBSQL_SUPPORT PROPERTY

20

```
 1:    PropID = DBPROP_SQLSUPPORT;              // SQL Support
 2:                                             // Interface
 3:    PropIDSet.rgPropertyIDs = &PropID;       // Specify the
 4:                                             // property ID
 5:    PropIDSet.cPropertyIDs = 1;              // Only one Property ID
 6:    PropIDSet.guidPropertySet = DBPROPSET_DATASOURCEINFO;
                                                // It's a DataSource
 7:                                             // object Property
 8:
 9:    // Retrieve the Properties
10:    pIDBProperties->GetProperties(1, &PropIDSet, &lNumProps,
                            ➥&pPropSet);
```

continues

LISTING 20.1 CONTINUED

```
11:
12:        // Interpret the property value
13:        if(pPropSet->rgProperties->vValue.lVal & DBPROPVAL_SQL_NONE) {
14:            cout << "SQL Commands are not supported\n";
15:        };
16:
17:        if(pPropSet->rgProperties->vValue.lVal &
              ➥DBPROPVAL_SQL_ODBC_MINIMUM) {
18:            cout << "ODBC Minimum SQL Commands supported\n";
19:        };
20:
21:        if(pPropSet->rgProperties->vValue.lVal &
              ➥DBPROPVAL_SQL_ODBC_CORE) {
22:            cout << "ODBC Core SQL Commands supported\n";
23:        };
24:
25:        if(pPropSet->rgProperties->vValue.lVal &
              ➥DBPROPVAL_SQL_ODBC_EXTENDED) {
26:            cout << "ODBC Extended SQL Commands supported\n";
27:        };
28:
29:        if(pPropSet->rgProperties->vValue.lVal &
              ➥DBPROPVAL_SQL_ANSI92_ENTRY) {
30:            cout << "ANSI 92 Entry SQL Commands supported\n";
31:        };
32:
33:        if(pPropSet->rgProperties->vValue.lVal &
              ➥DBPROPVAL_SQL_FIPS_TRANSITIONAL) {
34:            cout << "FIPS Transitional SQL Commands supported\n";
35:        };
36:
37:        if(pPropSet->rgProperties->vValue.lVal &
              ➥DBPROPVAL_SQL_ANSI92_INTERMEDIATE) {
38:            cout << "ANSI 92 Intermediate SQL Commands supported\n";
39:        };
40:
41:        if(pPropSet->rgProperties->vValue.lVal &
              ➥DBPROPVAL_SQL_ANSI92_FULL) {
42:            cout << "ANSI 92 Full SQL Commands supported\n";
43:        };
44:
45:        if(pPropSet->rgProperties->vValue.lVal &
              ➥DBPROPVAL_SQL_ANSI89_IEF) {
46:            cout << "ANSI 89 Integrity Enhancement Facility
                  ➥SQL Commands supported\n";
47:        };
```

Note

OLE DB also provides the `GetPropertyInfo` and `GetCreationProperties` methods to retrieve additional information about the properties that each object makes available.

Setting Properties

To establish a connection to the `DataSource` object by using the OLE DB ODBC provider, you used the `SetProperties` method (refer to Day 18) to specify the required ODBC connection parameters. The primary method that OLE DB objects use to specify property values is the `SetProperties` method. The `SetProperties` method is defined as follows:

```
SetProperties(ULONG cPropertySets, DBPROPSET rgPropertySets[]);
```

The `cPropertySets` parameter specifies the number of elements in the `rgPropertySets` array. This array contains a collection of property values. The `rgPropertySets` parameter is a `DBPROPSET` type, discussed earlier today. To set the value of a property, you need to create the `rgPropertySets` array and call the `SetProperties` method.

Tip

On return from the `SetProperties` method, check the status of each property to determine whether it was set properly.

Property status values are listed in Table 20.3. Table 20.4 lists the methods that each OLE DB object uses in order to specify property values.

TABLE 20.4 THE METHODS USED BY OLE DB OBJECTS TO SPECIFY PROPERTY VALUES

OLE DB Object	Interface	Method
Columns	IColumnsRowset	AddColumn
DataSource	IDBProperties	SetProperties
Index	IRowsetIndex	GetIndexInfo
Rowset	IRowsetInfo	GetProperties
	ICommandProperties	SetProperties
Session	ISessionProperties	SetProperties
Table	ITableDefinition	CreateTable

20

Now that you understand the structures involved in specifying a property, you can specify a property value and check the status of the property set operation. Listing 20.2 demonstrates how to use the DBPROP_INIT_TIMEOUT property. (The complete source code is on the CD-ROM.) This property is part of the DBPROPSET_DBINIT group and is used to specify the number of seconds to wait while a connection to the data source is established. Note that for brevity, the code in Listing 20.2 doesn't check the return values. In your production code, you will need to test for the return values.

INPUT

LISTING 20.2 HOW TO USE THE SetProperties METHOD TO SET THE DBPROP_INIT_TIMEOUT PROPERTY

```
 1:   // Obtain Access To The OLE DB - ODBC Provider
 2:   CoCreateInstance(CLSID_MSDASQL, NULL, CLSCTX_INPROC_SERVER,
 3:                    IID_IDBInitialize, (void **) &pIDBInitialize);
 4:
 5:   // Initialize the property values
 6:   VariantInit(&InitProperties[0].vValue);
 7:   InitProperties[0].dwOptions = DBPROPOPTIONS_REQUIRED;
 8:   InitProperties[0].colid = DB_NULLID;
 9:   InitProperties[0].dwPropertyID = DBPROP_INIT_TIMEOUT;
10:   InitProperties[0].vValue.vt = VT_I4;
11:
12:   // Set the timeout value to 90 seconds
13:   InitProperties[0].vValue.lVal = 90;
14:
15:   // Specify the Property Set
16:   rgInitPropSet[0].guidPropertySet = DBPROPSET_DBINIT;
17:   rgInitPropSet[0].cProperties = 1;
18:   rgInitPropSet[0].rgProperties = InitProperties;
19:
20:   // set initialization properties
21:   pIDBInitialize->QueryInterface(IID_IDBProperties,
                                 ➥(void **)&pIDBProperties);
22:   pIDBProperties->SetProperties(1,rgInitPropSet);
23:   // Remember to release pIDBInitialize and pIDBProperties.
```

A Review of OLE DB Object Properties

Table 20.5 lists all the properties that OLE DB objects support. This table lists each property ID and its variant type. An asterisk (*) after a property name signifies that it is a read-only property.

Note | Certain data providers might provide their own set of properties, so check the data provider documentation for more information. For example, the OLE DB ODBC data provider supports its own set of properties. These properties are part of two OLE DB ODBC provider-specific groups: DBPROPSET_PROVDERDATASOURCEINFO and DBPROPSET_PROVIDERROWSET.

TABLE 20.5 THE PROPERTIES SUPPORTED BY OLE DB OBJECTS

Property	Description
Column Object Properties	
DBPROP_COL_AUTOINCREMENT	A VT_BOOL type property. If it's true, the column will automatically increment.
DBPROP_COL_DEFAULT	A property of any type. It specifies the default value of a column.
DBPROP_COL_DESCRIPTION	A VT_STR type property. It specifies a column description.
DBPROP_COL_FIXEDLENGTH	A VT_BOOL type property. If it's true, the column has a fixed length.
DBPROP_COL_NULLABLE	A VT_BOOL type property. If it's true, the column can contain NULL values.
DBPROP_COL_PRIMARYKEY	A VT_BOOL type property. If it's true, this column is part of the primary key.
DBPROP_COL_UNIQUE	A VT_BOOL type property. If it's true, this column must be unique.
DataSource Object Properties	
DBPROP_CURRENTCATALOG	A VT_BSTR type property. It names the current data source catalog.
DataSource Object Properties (Information)	
DBPROP_ACTIVESESSIONS *	A VT_I4 type property. It specifies the maximum number of sessions; if 0, sessions are unlimited.
DBPROP_ASYNCTXNABORT *	A VT_BOOL type property. If it's true, transactions can be aborted asynchronously.
DBPROP_ASYNCTXNCOMMIT *	A VT_BOOL type. If it's true, transactions can be committed asynchronously.

continues

20

TABLE 20.5 CONTINUED

Property	Description
DataSource Object Properties (Information)	
DBPROP_BYREFACCESSORS *	A VT_BOOL type property. If it's true, the data source can accept parameters passed by reference (as pointers).
DBPROP_CATALOGLOCATION *	A VT_I4 type property. It returns DBPROP-VAL_CL_START if the catalog name is at the beginning or DBPROPVAL_CL_END if it's at the end.
DBPROP_CATALOGTERM *	A VT_BSTR type property. It specifies the name that a data source uses for a catalog.
DBPROP_CATALOGUSAGE *	A VT_I4 type property. It's used to determine where catalog names are supported.
DBPROP_COLUMNDEFINITION *	A VT_I4 type property. It's used to determine valid column states.
DBPROP_CONCATNULLBEHAVIOR	A VT_I4 type property. It determines how NULL strings are handled when added to other character strings.
DBPROP_DATASOURCENAME *	A VT_BSTR type property. It specifies the name of the data source.
DBPROP_DATASOURCEREADONLY *	A VT_BOOL type property. If it's true, the data source is read-only.
DBPROP_DBMSNAME *	A VT_BSTR type property. It specifies the name of the data provider.
DBPROP_DBMSVER *	A VT_BSTR type property. It specifies the version of the data provider.
DBPROP_DSOTHREADMODEL *	A VT_I4 type property. It specifies the threading model supported by the data provider.
DBPROP_GROUPBY *	A VT_I4 type property. It specifies how the GROUP BY clause functions.
DBPROP_HETEROGENEOUSTABLES *	A VT_I4 type property. It specifies whether joins can be performed across providers or catalogs.
DBPROP_IDENTIFIERCASE *	A VT_I4 type parameter. It specifies whether the case of identifiers is significant.
DBPROP_MAXINDEXSIZE *	A VT_I4 type parameter. It specifies the maximum size of a key; if 0, there is no limit.

Property	Description
DataSource Object Properties (Information)	
DBPROP_MAXROWSIZE *	A VT_I4 type parameter. It specifies the maximum length of a row; if 0, there is no limit.
DBPROP_MAXROWSIZEINCLUDESBLOB *	A VT_BOOL type parameter. If it's true, the DBPROP_MAXROWSIZE property includes BLOB fields.
DBPROP_MAXTABLESINSELECT *	A VT_I4 type parameter. It specifies the maximum number of tables that can be used in a SELECT statement.
DBPROP_MULTIPLEPARAMSETS *	A VT_BOOL type parameter. If it's true, the data source supports multiple parameter sets.
DBPROP_MULTIPLERESULTS *	A VT_I4 type parameter. It specifies whether the data source can support multiple resultsets.
DBPROP_MULTIPLESTORAGEOBJECTS *	A VT_BOOL type parameter. If it's true, the data source can open multiple objects at the same time.
DBPROP_MULTITABLEUPDATE *	A VT_BOOL type parameter. If it's true, the data source can update row sets that contain multiple tables.
DBPROP_NULLCOLLATION *	A VT_I4 type parameter. It specifies how NULL values are handled when sorting.
DBPROP_OLEOBJECTS *	A VT_I4 type parameter. It specifies whether BLOB and OLE objects can be accessed through streaming or storage objects.
DBPROP_ORDERBYCOLUMNSINSELECT *	A VT_BOOL type parameter. If it's true, the columns specified in an ORDER BY clause must be part of the SELECT statement.
DBPROP_OUTPUTPARAMETERAVAILABILITY *	A VT_I4 type parameter. It specifies when output parameters can be accessed.
DBPROP_PERSISTENTIDTYPE *	A VT_I4 type parameter. It specifies the type of persistent DBID supported by a data source.
DBPROP_PREPAREABORTBEHAVIOR *	A VT_I4 type parameter. It specifies what happens to a prepared statement when it's aborted in a transaction.

continues

20

TABLE 20.5   CONTINUED

Property	Description
DataSource Object Properties (Information)	
DBPROP_PREPARECOMMITBEHAVIOR *	A VT_I4 type parameter. It specifies what happens to a prepared statement when it's committed in a transaction.
DBPROP_PROCEDURETERM *	A VT_BSTR type parameter. It specifies what the data source calls a procedure.
DBPROP_PROVIDERNAME *	A VT_BSTR type parameter. It specifies the executable filename of the provider.
DBPROP_PROVIDEROLEDBVER *	A VT_BSTR type parameter. It specifies the OLE DB specification version supported by the provider.
DBPROP_PROVIDERVER *	A VT_BSTR type parameter. It specifies the version of the data provider.
DBPROP_QUOTEDIDENTIFIERCASE *	A VT_I4 type parameter. It specifies how case is handled for quoted identifiers.
DBPROP_ROWSETCONVERSIONSONCOMMAND *	A VT_BOOL type parameter. If it's true, an inquiry can be made about conversions on the row sets of a command.
DBPROP_SCHEMATERM *	A VT_BSTR type parameter. It specifies the term used by the data source for a schema.
DBPROP_SCHEMAUSAGE *	A VT_I4 type parameter. It specifies how schema names can be used in commands.
DBPROP_SQLSUPPORT *	A VT_I4 type parameter. It specifies the level of SQL supported by the data source.
DBPROP_STRUCTUREDSTORAGE *	A VT_I4 type parameter. It specifies streaming interfaces supported for row sets.
DBPROP_SUBQUERIES *	A VT_I4 type parameter. It specifies whether subqueries are supported in commands.
DBPROP_SUPPORTEDTXNDDL *	A VT_I4 type parameter. It specifies whether data definition commands are supported in transactions.
DBPROP_SUPPORTEDTXNISOLEVELS *	A VT_I4 type parameter. It specifies the transaction isolation levels supported by the data source.

Property	Description
DataSource Object Properties (Information)	
DBPROP_SUPPORTEDTXNISORETAIN *	A VT_I4 type parameter. It specifies the retention levels supported by transaction isolation.
DBPROP_TABLETERM *	A VT_BSTR type parameter. It specifies the term used by the data source for tables.
DBPROP_USERNAME *	A VT_BSTR type parameter. It specifies the name of the user attached to the data source.
DataSource Object Properties (Initialization)	
DBPROP_AUTH_CACHE_AUTHINFO	A VT_BOOL type parameter. If it's true, the data source can store password and user information in a local cache.
DBPROP_AUTH_ENCRYPTPASSWORD	A VT_BOOL type parameter. If it's true, the data source requires the password to be sent in an encrypted form.
DBPROP_AUTH_INTEGRATED	A VT_BSTR type parameter. It specifies the name of the authentication service to be used.
DBPROP_AUTH_MASK_PASSWORD	A VT_BOOL type parameter. If it's true, the password must be masked before it's sent to the data source.
DBPROP_AUTH_PASSWORD	A VT_BSTR type parameter. This is the password used for authentication (can be masked).
DBPROP_AUTH_PERSISTENCRYPTED	A VT_BOOL type parameter. If it's true, the data source must save authentication information.
DBPROP_AUTH_PERSIST_SENSITIVEAUTHINFO	A VT_BOOL type parameter. If it's true, the data source is allowed to persist authentication information.
DBPROP_AUTH_USERID	A VT_BSTR type parameter. It specifies the username used to connect to the data source.
DBPROP_INIT_DATASOURCE	A VT_BSTR type parameter. This is the name of the data source to connect to.
DBPROP_INIT_HWND	A VT_I4 type parameter. This is the window handle used if a prompt window must be displayed when accessing the data source.

continues

20

TABLE 20.5 CONTINUED

Property	Description
DataSource Object Properties (Initialization)	
DBPROP_INIT_IMPERSONATIONLEVEL	A VT_I4 type parameter. It specifies the impersonation level used for remote procedure calls.
DBPROP_INIT_LCID	A VT_I4 type parameter. It specifies the location identifier.
DBPROP_INIT_LOCATION	A VT_BSTR type parameter. It specifies the location of the data source (that is, the name of the server).
DBPROP_INIT_MODE	A VT_I4 type parameter. It specifies the read, write, share access level to the data source.
DBPROP_INIT_PROMPT	A VT_I4 type parameter. It specifies whether a prompt should be displayed for user/data source information if it's required when connecting to a data source.
DBPROP_INIT_PROTECTION_LEVEL	A VT_I4 type parameter. It specifies the remote procedure call connection level used.
DBPROP_INIT_PROVIDERSTRING	A VT_BSTR type parameter. It specifies provider-specific connection parameters.
DBPROP_INIT_TIMEOUT	A VT_I4 type parameter. It specifies the amount of time to wait for a connection to complete.
Index Object Properties	
DBPROP_INDEX_AUTOUPDATE	A VT_BOOL type parameter. If it's true, the index is automatically updated whenever a change is made.
DBPROP_INDEX_CLUSTERED	A VT_BOOL type parameter. If it's true, the index uses clustering.
DBPROP_INDEX_FILLFACTOR	A VT_I4 type parameter. It specifies the B+tree fill factor for the index.
DBPROP_INDEX_INITIALSIZE	A VT_I4 type parameter. It specifies the initial size to allocate for the index.
DBPROP_INDEX_NULLCOLLATION	A VT_I4 type parameter. It specifies how NULL values are treated in the sorting order.

Property	Description
Index Object Properties	
DBPROP_INDEX_NULLS	A VT_I4 type parameter. It specifies whether an index can use NULL values.
DBPROP_INDEX_PRIMARYKEY	A VT_BOOL type parameter. If it's true, this index is based on the primary key.
DBPROP_INDEX_SORTBOOKMARKS	A VT_BOOL type parameter. If it's true, the index sorts bookmarks.
DBPROP_INDEX_TEMPINDEX	A VT_BOOL type parameter. If it's true, the index is temporary.
DBPROP_INDEX_TYPE	A VT_I4 type parameter. It specifies the type of index mechanisms used by the data source.
DBPROP_INDEX_UNIQUE	A VT_BOOL type parameter. If it's true, the index keys must be unique.
RowSet Object Properties	
DBPROP_ABORTPRESERV	A VT_BOOL type parameter. If it's true, the row set is preserved even after an aborted transaction.
DBPROP_APPENDONLY	A VT_BOOL type parameter. If it's true, rows can only be added to the row set. You use this when creating new tables.
DBPROP_BLOCKINGSTORAGEOBJECTS	A VT_BOOL type parameter. If it's true, storage objects could prevent other operations.
DBPROP_BOOKMARKS	A VT_BOOL type parameter. If it's true, bookmarks can be used by the row set.
DBPROP_BOOKMARKSKIPPED	A VT_BOOL type parameter. If it's true, the GetRowsAt method can skip deleted bookmark rows.
DBPROP_BOOKMARKTYPE	A VT_I4 type parameter. It specifies the type of bookmarks used: numeric or key.
DBPROP_CACHEDEFERRED	A VT_BOOL type parameter. If it's true, deferred columns can be cached.
DBPROP_CANFETCHBACKWARDS	A VT_BOOL type parameter. If it's true, methods used to get rows can retrieve rows before the current row.

20

continues

TABLE 20.5 CONTINUED

Property	Description
RowSet Object Properties	
DBPROP_CANHOLDROWS	A VT_BOOL type parameter. If it's true, additional rows can be fetched when changes are pending.
DBPROP_CANSCROLLBACKWARDS	A VT_BOOL type parameter. If it's true, you can retrieve rows before the current row.
DBPROP_CHANGEINSERTEDROWS	A VT_BOOL type parameter. If it's true, you can make modifications to rows that have been added to the row set.
DBPROP_COLUMNRESTRICT *	A VT_BOOL type parameter. If it's true, access can be restricted at the column level.
DBPROP_COMMANDTIMEOUT	A VT_I4 type parameter. It specifies the amount of time before a command times out.
DBPROP_COMMITPRESERVE	A VT_BOOL type parameter. If it's true, the row set is preserved after the transaction has been committed.
DBPROP_DEFERRED	A VT_BOOL type parameter. If it's true, the column data is retrieved only when the GetData method is called.
DBPROP_DELAYSTORAGEOBJECTS	A VT_BOOL type parameter. If it's true, updates to storage objects are delayed.
DBPROP_IAccessor	A VT_BOOL type parameter. If it's true, the row set supports the IAccessor interface.
DBPROP_IColumnsInfo	A VT_BOOL type parameter. If it's true, the row set supports the IColumnsInfo interface.
DBPROP_IColumnsRowset	A VT_BOOL type parameter. If it's true, the row set supports the IColumnsRowset interface.
DBPROP_IConnectionPointContainer	A VT_BOOL type parameter. If it's true, the row set supports the IConnectionPointContainer interface.
DBPROP_IConvertType	A VT_BOOL type parameter. If it's true, the row set supports the IConvertType interface.
DBPROP_IRowset	A VT_BOOL type parameter. If it's true, the row set supports the IRowset interface.
DBPROP_IRowsetChange	A VT_BOOL type parameter. If it's true, the row set supports the IRowsetChAnge interface.

DBPROP_IRowsetIdentity	A VT_BOOL type parameter. If it's true, the row set supports the IRowsetIdentity interface.
DBPROP_IRowsetInfo	A VT_BOOL type parameter. If it's true, the row set supports the IRowsetInfo interface.
DBPROP_IRowsetLocate	A VT_BOOL type parameter. If it's true, the row set supports the IRowsetLocate interface.
DBPROP_IRowsetResynch	A VT_BOOL type parameter. If it's true, the row set supports the IRowsetResynch interface.
DBPROP_IRowsetScroll	A VT_BOOL type parameter. If it's true, the row set supports the IRowsetScroll interface.
DBPROP_IRowsetUpdate	A VT_BOOL type parameter. If it's true, the row set supports the IRowseUpdate interface.
DBPROP_ISupportErrorInfo	A VT_BOOL type parameter. If it's true, the row set supports the ISupportErrorInfo interface.
DBPROP_ILockBytes	A VT_BOOL type parameter. If it's true, the row set supports the ILockBytes storage interface.
DBPROP_ISequentialStream	A VT_BOOL type parameter. If it's true, the row set supports the ISequentialStream storage interface.
DBPROP_IStorage	A VT_BOOL type parameter. If it's true, the row set supports the IStorage storage interface.
DBPROP_IStream	A VT_BOOL type parameter. If it's true, the row set supports the IStream storage interface.
DBPROP_IMMOBILEROWS	A VT_BOOL type parameter. If it's true, updated rows will not be reordered.
DBPROP_LITERALBOOKMARKS	A VT_BOOL type parameter. If it's true, bookmarks can be compared in an ordinal fashion.
DBPROP_LITERALIDENTITY *	A VT_BOOL type parameter. If it's true, row handles can be compared to see whether they are the same.

continues

20

TABLE 20.5 CONTINUED

Property	Description
RowSet Object Properties	
DBPROP_MAXOPENROWS *	A VT_I4 type parameter. It specifies the maximum number of rows that can be opened at once; if 0, there is no limit.
DBPROP_MAXPENDINGROWS *	A VT_I4 type parameter. It specifies the maximum number of rows that can simultaneously have pending updates.
DBPROP_MAXROWS *	A VT_I4 type parameter. It specifies the maximum number of rows that can be in a row set, and if 0, there is no limit.
DBPROP_MAYWRITECOLUMN	A VT_BOOL type parameter. If it's true, a column is writable.
DBPROP_MEMORYUSAGE	A VT_I4 type parameter. It specifies the percentage of memory that a row set can use. If it's 0, there is no limit.
DBPROP_NOTIFICATIONGRANULARITY	A VT_I4 type parameter. It specifies when notification occurs.
DBPROP_NOTIFICATIONPHASES *	A VT_I4 type parameter. It specifies when notifications are supported by the data provider.
DBPROP_NOTIFYCOLUMNSET *	A VT_I4 type parameter. It specifies when notifications are generated by a column set.
DBPROP_NOTIFYROWDELETE *	A VT_I4 type parameter. It specifies when notifications are generated by a row delete.
DBPROP_NOTIFYROWFIRSTCHANGE *	A VT_I4 type parameter. It specifies when notifications are generated by a first row change.
DBPROP_NOTIFYROWINSERT *	A VT_I4 type parameter. It specifies when notifications are generated by an insert.
DBPROP_NOTIFYROWRESYNCH *	A VT_I4 type parameter. It specifies when notifications are generated by a row set resynchronization.
DBPROP_NOTIFYROWSETRELEASE *	A VT_I4 type parameter. It specifies when notifications are generated by a row set release.
DBPROP_NOTIFYROWSETFETCHPOSITIONCHANGE*	A VT_I4 type parameter. It specifies when notifications are generated by a position change.

Property	Description
RowSet Object Properties	
DBPROP_NOTIFYROWUNDOCHANGE *	A VT_I4 type parameter. It specifies when notifications are generated by an undo of a change.
DBPROP_NOTIFYROWUNDODELETE *	A VT_I4 type parameter. It specifies when notifications are generated by an undo of a delete.
DBPROP_NOTIFYROWUNDOINSERT *	A VT_I4 type parameter. It specifies when notifications are generated by an undo of an insert.
DBPROP_NOTIFYROWUPDATE *	A VT_I4 type parameter. It specifies when notifications are generated by a row update.
DBPROP_ORDEREDBOOKMARKS	A VT_BOOL type parameter. If it's true, bookmarks can be compared in an ordinal fashion.
DBPROP_OTHERINSERT	A VT_BOOL type parameter. If it's true, rows inserted by others into a row set can be seen when they are inserted.
DBPROP_OTHERUPDATEDELETE	A VT_BOOL type parameter. If it's true, changes by other users are visible.
DBPROP_OWNINSERT	A VT_BOOL type parameter. If it's true, rows inserted by this user into the row set can be seen when they are inserted.
DBPROP_OWNUPDATEDELETE	A VT_BOOL type parameter. If it's true, rows updated or deleted by this user are visible.
DBPROP_QUICKRESTART	A VT_BOOL type parameter. If it's true, the command that generated the row set is not re-executed when restarting.
DBPROP_REENTRANTEVENTS *	A VT_BOOL type parameter. If it's true, reentrant events (events that can happen at the same time) are supported.
DBPROP_REMOVEDELETED	A VT_BOOL type parameter. If it's true, rows that have been marked for deletion are not included in the row set.
DBPROP_REPORTMULTIPLECHANGES *	A VT_BOOL type parameter. If it's true, updates and deletes on row sets that affect multiple rows can be handled.

20

continues

TABLE 20.5 CONTINUED

Property	Description
RowSet Object Properties	
DBPROP_RETURNPENDINGINSERTS *	A VT_BOOL type parameter. If it's true, rows with pending changes are included in the row set.
DBPROP_ROWRESTRICT *	A VT_BOOL type parameter. If it's true, access to rows can be specified on a row basis.
DBPROP_ROWTHREADMODEL	A VT_I4 type parameter. It specifies the threading model used by row sets.
DBPROP_SERVERCURSOR	A VT_BOOL type parameter. If it's true, the data source supports server-side cursors.
DBPROP_STRONGIDENTITY *	A VT_BOOL type parameter. If it's true, row handles to newly inserted rows can be compared with existing rows in an ordinal fashion.
DBPROP_TRANSACTEDOBJECT	A VT_BOOL type parameter. If it's true, data changes for a column must be made through transactions.
DBPROP_UPDATABILITY	A VT_I4 type parameter. It specifies the change methods supported by the row set.
Session Object Properties	
DBPROP_SESS_AUTOCOMMITISOLEVELS	A VT_I4 type parameter. It specifies the isolation level of transactions while the Autocommit mode is active.
Table Object Properties	
DBPROP_TBL_TEMPTABLE	A VT_BOOL type parameter. If it's true, this is a temporary table.

Now that you understand how to set and retrieve properties, and you know all the properties supported by OLE DB objects, you can begin to manipulate OLE DB objects at a higher level of detail. You will use these properties in the examples presented during the remainder of the book.

Transactions

Transactions control operations on a data source and encapsulate data source operations. A transaction starts before an operation begins and can commit the operation or abort the changes an operation makes. Transactions can coordinate multiuser operations on a data source. Typically, transactions enable a user to start some data source operation and to abort this operation at a later point. The use of transactions can also significantly improve application performance. The OLE DB TTransaction CoType is defined as follows:

```
TTransaction {
    interface IConnectionPointContainer;    // Required Interface
    interface ITransaction;                 // Required Interface
    interface ISupportErrorInfo;
};
```

The IConnectionPointContainer and ISupportErrorInfo are discussed in previous lessons (Day 19, "Navigating the Result of a Query," and Day 17, "Accessing a Data Source with OLE DB"), and error handling is discussed in more detail on Day 21, "OLE DB Error Handling." On Day 17 you learned that the Session object supports the following Transaction-related interfaces: ITransaction, ITransactionJoin, ITransactionLocal, and ITransactionObject. I'll discuss these interfaces in detail before examining the actual mechanics of using them.

The ITransaction Interface

The ITransaction interface controls a transaction; it commits transactions, aborts transactions, and obtains the current transaction status. The ITransaction interface is required by the Transaction object but optional for the Session object. The ITransaction interface defines the standard IUnknown interface methods QueryInterface, AddRef, and Release. The interface also provides three additional methods: Abort, Commit, and GetTransactionInfo. These methods are defined as follows:

```
HRESULT Abort(BOID *pboidReason, BOOL fRetaining, BOOL fAsync);
HRESULT Commit(BOOL fRetaining, DWORD grfCommitType, DWORD grfReserved);
HRESULT GetTransactionInfo(XACTTRANSINFO *pTransInfo);
```

20

The Abort method aborts a series of operations performed on a data source. For logging purposes, the pboidReason parameter specifies a reason that the transaction is being aborted. This parameter is a BOID type, which is defined as follows:

```
typedef struct BOID {
    BYTE rgb[16];
};
```

This simply defines a 16-byte buffer. If no reason is required, the BOID_NULL constant is used. The fRetaining parameter defines the retain behavior of the abort operation, which is sometimes referred to as *Autocommit mode*. If true, when the abort operation is carried out and subsequent transactions are created, the abort is performed in a separate (server-side) process thread. If false, a new thread is not created to carry out the abort. The fAsync flag determines whether the operation is carried out in the background. If true, the abort command returns immediately, and the abort processing happens in the background.

> **Caution**
>
> You must use the ITransactionOutcomeEvents interface to retrieve the results of the abort operation. If the abort is not asynchronous, you get the abort result in the return value from the Abort method call.

The Commit method commits a series of operations performed on a data source. The fRetaining parameter functions in the same way as it does in the Abort method, controlling the Autocommit mode. The grfCommitType parameter specifies the type of commit to be performed. Table 20.6 defines and describes the various types of commit parameters. The grfReserved parameter is reserved for future use and should always be 0.

TABLE 20.6 COMMIT PARAMETERS

Commit Type	Description
XACTTC_ASYNC	The commit is performed in an asynchronous mode. The Commit method returns immediately, and commit processing is carried out in the background.
XACTTC_SYNC_PHASEONE	The Commit method returns after the first phase of the commit operation is performed. Commit methods are usually performed in two phases.
XACTTC_SYNC_PHASETWO	The Commit method returns after the second phase of the commit operation is performed; that is, it returns when the entire operation is complete.
XACTTC_SYNC	The commit is performed in a synchronous mode, the same as the XACTTC_SYNC_PHASETWO commit type.

The last method of the ITransation interface, GetTransactionInfo, retrieves information about a transaction. It returns a single parameter, pTransInfo, which is a pointer to an XACTTRANSINFO structure. This structure holds information about the transaction and is defined as follows:

```
typedef struct tagXACTTRANSINFO {
    XACTUOW    uow;
    ISOLEVEL   isoLevel;
    ULONG      isoFlags;
    DWORD      grfTCSupported;
    DWORD      grfRMSupported;
    DWORD      grfTCSupportedRetaining;
    DWORD      grfRMSupportedRetaining;
} XACTRANSINFO;
```

The uow field defines the level at which the transaction works, typically row. The XAC-TUOW type is defined as the BOID type that was defined earlier. The isoLevel field specifies the isolation level (discussed in more detail shortly) of this transaction. The isoFlags field is reserved for future use and will always be 0. The grfTCSupported field specifies special transactional-level flags. The grfRMSupported, grfTCSupportedRetaining, and grfRMSupportedRetaining are reserved for future use and will currently return 0. Unless you need to determine the isolation level of a previously started transaction, the GetTransactionInfo method currently does not return much more useful information.

The ITransactionLocal Interface

Just as you can use the ITransaction interface to end a transaction by committing or aborting it, you can use the ITransactionLocal interface of the Session object to begin a transaction. The ITransactionLocal interface is optional for the Session object and is supported only if the data provider supports transactions. The ITransactionLocal interface defines the standard IUnknown interface methods QueryInterface, AddRef, and Release. The interface also provides two additional methods: GetOptionsObject and StartTransaction. These methods are defined as follows:

```
HRESULT GetOptionsObject(ITransactionOptions **pOptionsInt);
HRESULT StartTransaction(ISOLEVEL isoLevel, ULONG isoFlagsResv,
                         ITransactionOptions *pIOptions,
                         ULONG *lNewTransLevel);
```

The StartTransaction method begins a set of operations that will be enveloped by a transaction. The isoLevel parameter specifies the isolation level of the transaction. The lisoFlagResv parameter is reserved for future isolation level flags, but for now it should be 0. The pIOptions parameter specifies a pointer to the ITransactionsOption interface. If options aren't required, you can pass a NULL value. Next I will discuss how to obtain and use the ITransactionsOption interface. The lNewTransLevel parameter returns the new transaction level.

The GetOptionsObject obtains access to the ITransactionOptions interface. A pointer to this interface is returned in the pOptionsInt parameter. What options, then, can be specified for a transaction?

20

The `ITransactionOptions` Interface

As I stated earlier, the `ITransactionOptions` interface specifies transaction-level options. This interface is accessed through the `GetOptionsObject` method. The `ITransactionOptions` interface defines the standard `IUnknown` interface methods `QueryInterface`, `AddRef`, and `Release`. Also, the interface provides two additional methods: `SetOptions` and `GetOptions`. These methods are defined as follows:

```
HRESULT SetOptions(XACTOPT *pOptions);
HRESULT GetOptions(XACTOPT *pOptions);
```

The names tell us that these methods set and retrieve option values. Both methods take a single parameter, a pointer to an `XACTOPT` structure, which defines the transaction options. This structure is defined as follows:

```
typedef struct tagXACTOPT {
    ULONG ulTImeout;
    unsigned char szDescription[MAX_TRANS_DESC];
} XACTOPT;
```

The `ulTimeout` field defines the number of milliseconds that the transaction can remain open before it's automatically aborted. If this value is `0`, there will be no time limit. The `szDescription` field defines the transaction's description.

The `ITransactionObject` Interface

The `ITransactionObject` interface obtains access to a `Transaction` object by specifying its level. This interface is especially useful when using nested transactions (which are discussed shortly). This interface is provided through the `Session` object and is available only if transactions are supported. The `ITransactionObject` interface defines the standard `IUnknown` interface methods `QueryInterface`, `AddRef`, and `Release`. The interface provides one more method: `GetTransactionObject`. This method is defined as follows:

```
HRESULT GetTransactionObject(ULONG lTransLevel, ITransaction **ppITrans);
```

The `lTransLevel` specifies the transaction level for which you are searching. The `pITrans` parameter returns the level's corresponding `Transaction` object.

The `ITransactionJoin` Interface

The final transaction interface discussed today is the `ITransactionJoin` interface, which supports distributed transactions. This interface is provided through the `Session` object and is available only if transactions are supported. The `ITransactionJoin` interface defines the standard `IUnknown` interface methods `QueryInterface`, `AddRef`, and `Release`. The interface provides two additional methods: `GetOptionsObject` and `JoinTransaction`. These methods are defined as follows:

```
HRESULT GetOptionsObject(ITransactionOptions **ppITransOptions);
HRESULT JoinTransaction(IUnknown *punkDistTrans, ISOLEVEL isoLevel,
                        ULONG isoFlags, ITransactionOptions
                     ➥*pITransOptions);
```

The `GetOptionsObject` retrieves distributed transaction options. The `JoinTransaction` method joins a distributed transaction, a transaction in which multiple clients can take part. Currently, the OLE DB ODBC data provider doesn't support distributed transactions.

Creating Transactions

To create a transaction that encapsulates a series of operations, you must first obtain access to the `ITransactionLocal` interface and then use the `StartTransaction` method to open the transaction. The transaction remains opened until it's committed or aborted. Listing 20.3 demonstrates how to use the `StartTransaction` method to open a database transaction. Note that for brevity, the code in Listing 20.3 doesn't check the return values. In your production code, be sure you test for the return values.

INPUT   **LISTING 20.3**   How to Start a Transaction

```
 1:     // Create a Session object...
 2:     pIDBInitialize->QueryInterface(IID_IDBCreateSession,
 3:                                     (void **) &pCreateSession);
 4:
 5:     // Create a Command object...
 6:     pCreateSession->CreateSession(NULL, IID_IDBCreateCommand,
 7:                                    (IUnknown **) &pCreateCommand);
 8:
 9:     // Access the ICommandText interface
10:     pCreateCommand->CreateCommand(NULL, IID_ICommandText,
11:                                    (IUnknown **) &pCommandText);
12:
13:     // Specify the command text
14:     pCommandText->SetCommandText(DBGUID_DBSQL, wCmdString);
15:
16:     // Access the Transaction Interface
17:     pCreateCommand->QueryInterface(IID_ITransactionLocal,
18:                                     (void **) &pTransLocal);
19:
20:     // Start the Transaction
21:     pTransLocal->StartTransaction(ISOLATIONLEVEL_SERIALIZABLE, 0,
22:                                    NULL, &lTransLevel);
23:     cout << "Transaction Level = " << lTransLevel << "\n";
24:
25:     // Execute the command
26:     pCommandText->Execute(NULL, IID_IRowset, NULL, &cNumRows,
27:                            (IUnknown **) &pRowset);
28:     // Remember to release the interface pointers.
```

20

Committing and Aborting Transactions

When the StartTransaction method is called, all database operations are saved until they are committed or aborted. When a transaction is committed, all the operations that have been saved are actually carried out on the data source. As you saw earlier, the commit operation enables you to specify whether it is carried out asynchronously, semi-synchronously, or synchronously and whether Autocommit mode is used. The state of any open row sets depends on the DBPROP_COMMITPRESERVE property (a Rowset object group property). If DBPROP_COMMITPRESERVE is true, the row set remains valid and is automatically synchronized when the transaction is committed or aborted; otherwise, the row set becomes invalid. This property is set on the basis of row set by row set. The Commit method is provided through the ITransaction interface, so you must access this interface to access the Commit method. The Commit method will commit the transaction at the current level. Listing 20.4 demonstrates how to commit the transaction started in Listing 20.3. Note that you should check the return value of QueryInterface in your production code.

INPUT   **LISTING 20.4**   HOW TO COMMIT THE CURRENT TRANSACTION

```
1:    // Commit The Transaction
2:    pCreateCommand->QueryInterface(IID_ITransaction,
                                  ➥(void **) &pTrans);
3:    pTrans->Commit(FALSE,XATTC_SYNC,0);
```

Aborting a transaction is just as easy. Listing 20.5 demonstrates how to use the Abort method to abort a transaction at the current level. Again, note that you should check the return value of QueryInterface in your production code.

INPUT   **LISTING 20.5**   HOW TO ABORT THE CURRENT TRANSACTION

```
1:    // Abort The Transaction
2:    pCreateCommand->QueryInterface(IID_ITransactionLocal,
                                  ➥(void **) &pTrans);
3:    pTrans->Abort(NULL, FALSE, TRUE);
```

Nesting Transactions

If the data provider supports it, transactions can be nested. A *nested transaction* is created by starting a transaction while another transaction is already open. The inner transaction must be released before outer transactions can be committed or aborted.

Isolation Levels and Locking

OLE DB supports four levels of transaction isolation, which ensures coherent access to a data source. The transaction levels are Read Uncommitted, Read Committed, Repeatable Read, and Serializable.

With Read Committed isolation, any row sets that are created will view only rows that have been changed after those changes have been committed. Operations in this type of isolation level will see any rows that have been added or deleted. With Repeatable Read isolation, any changes to rows already read will not be seen, and any operation that deletes a row will not be seen. Any new rows that have been added will be visible. With Read Uncommitted, no attempt is made to isolate any types of changes. Rows that are retrieved will reflect the current database state. Finally, with Serializable isolation, the rows retrieved are guaranteed to be in the consistent state, reflecting only the changes of the current transaction.

Provider-specific, user-defined locking mechanisms implement these isolation levels. Table 20.7 defines the constants related to each isolation level. The isolation level is determined when the StartTransaction method starts a transaction.

TABLE 20.7 THE OLE DB ISOLATION LEVELS

Isolation Constant	Description
ISOLATIONLEVEL_UNSPECIFIED	Used only with the JoinTransaction method
ISOLATIONLEVEL_CHAOS	Preserves changes made by higher-level transactions
ISOLATIONLEVEL_READUNCOMMITTED	Read Uncommitted isolation
ISOLATIONLEVEL_BROWSE	Read Uncommitted isolation
ISOLATIONLEVEL_READCOMMITTED	Read Committed isolation
ISOLATIONLEVEL_CURSORSTABILITY	Read Committed isolation
ISOLATIONLEVEL_REPEATABLEREAD	Repeatable Read isolation
ISOLATIONLEVEL_SERIALIZABLE	Serializable isolation
ISOLATIONLEVEL_ISOLATED	Serializable isolation

20

The Index Object

The final OLE DB object today is the Index object. The Index object can directly access a data source index through a row set mechanism. Index objects access data source tables in a sorted manner and search for records, based on a key value. The TIndex CoType is defined as follows:

```
TIndex {
     interface IAccessor;            // Required Interface
     interface IColumnsInfo;         // Required Interface
     interface IConvertType;         // Required Interface
     interface IRowset;              // Required Interface
     interface IRowsetIndex;         // Required Interface
     interface IRowsetInfo;          // Required Interface
     interface IRowsetChange;
     interface ISupportErrorInfo;
};
```

You have already seen all these interfaces—except for the IRowsetIndex interface—in the context of the Rowset object. The next section describes the IRowsetIndex interface and explains how to implement the Index object.

The IRowsetIndex Interface

The IRowsetIndex interface is required by the Index object. It retrieves index information, searches for specific key values, and limits the set of visible rows to a range of key values. The IRowsetIndex interface defines the standard IUnknown interface methods QueryInterface, AddRef, and Release. The interface also provides three more methods: GetIndexInfo, Seek, and SetRange. These methods are defined as follows:

```
HRESULT GetIndexInfo(ULONG *plNumKeyCols, DBINDEXCOLUMNDESC
                     **pprdIdxColDesc, ULONG *plNumIdxProps,
                     DBPROPSET **prgIdxProps);
HRESULT Seek(HACCESSOR hAccessor, ULONG lNumKeys, void *pSeekData,
             DBSEEK dwSeekOpt);
HRESULT SetRange(HACCESSOR hAccessor, ULONG lNumStartKeyCols,
                 void *pStartKeyData, ULONG lNumEndKeyCols,
                 void *pEndKeyData, DBRANGE dwRangeOpt);
```

The GetIndexInfo method retrieves information about the index. The plNumKeyCols parameter returns the number of key columns in this index. The prdIdxColDesc parameter returns an array that describes each column. The plNumIdxProps parameter returns the number of elements in the prgIdxProps array. The prgIdxProps parameter returns an array that holds a collection of index properties.

> **Tip**
>
> Partial key searches are possible with the Seek method. You must supply the complete key set binding and then include only the partial key value for the key value.

The Seek method searches for a specific record in the index row set. The hAccessor parameter holds an Accessor to a set of bindings that describe the key structure. The lNumKeys parameter specifies the number of keys in the search criteria. The pSeekData parameter specifies the key set data for which you are searching. The `dwSeekOpt` parameter specifies the seek options. Seek options are outlined in Table 20.8.

TABLE 20.8   THE OLE DB SEEK OPTIONS

Seek Constant	Description
DBSEEK_FIRSTEQ	Searches for the first value that matches the key specified.
DBSEEK_LASTEQ	Searches for the last value that matches the key specified.
DBSEEK_GE	Searches for the first value that is greater than or equal to the key specified.
DBSEEK_GT	Searches for the first value that is greater than the key specified.
DBSEEK_LE	Searches for the first value that is less than or equal to the key specified.
DBSEEK_LT	Searches for the first value that is less than the key specified.

The `SetRange` method restricts the rows visible in the index row set to a range of key values. The `hAccessor` parameter holds an Accessor to a set of bindings that describe the key structure. The `lNumStartKeyCols` defines the number of key columns in the start range key. The `pStartKeyData` parameter specifies the start key data. The `lNumEndKeyCols` defines the number of key columns in the end range key. The `pEndKeyData` parameter specifies the end key data. The `dwRangeOpt` parameter specifies how the start and end keys will be used to limit the rows that will be visible. Table 20.9 defines the range options. These options can be combined with a logical `OR` operation.

TABLE 20.9   THE OLE DB RANGE OPTIONS

Range Option	Description
DBRANGE_INCLUSIVESTART	Includes all keys greater than or equal to the start key.
DBRANGE_EXCLUSIVESTART	Includes all keys greater than the start key.
DBRANGE_INCLUSIVEEND	Includes all keys less than or equal to the end key.
DBRANGE_EXCLUSIVEEND	Includes all keys less than the end key.
DBRANGE_EXCLUDENULLS	Excludes NULL values from the range.
DBRANGE_PREFIX	Uses the start key as a prefix, which enables faster searches on some data sources.
DBRANGE_MATCH	Includes only keys that are equal to the start key. The end key must be NULL if this flag is set.

20

Using the `Index` Object

Here's how to open and use an `Index` object:

1. Open an index row set, using the `IOpenRowset->OpenRowset` method of the `Session` object.

2. Retrieve the columns information, using the `IColumnsInfo->GetColumnInfo` method of the `Index` object.

3. Create a binding structure that includes the rows that are part of the index. The `dwFlags` field of the column information structure will contain the flag value `DBCOLUMNFLAGS_ISBOOKMARK` if the column is a key field.

4. Use the binding structure to create an Accessor, using the `IAccessor->CreateAccessor` method of the `Index` object.

5. Use the `IRowsetIndex` interface methods to manipulate the index.

 Note

> Rather than rely on your OLE DB provider's support for the `IRowsetIndex` interface, you might need to use the appropriate SQL commands to retrieve specific rows or to retrieve rows in a specific order.

Summary

Day 20 focuses on three main topics: OLE DB properties and groups, the `Transaction` object, and the `Index` object. Today you learned how to retrieve and set property values and how to use the different types associated with properties. You reviewed the set of properties that OLE DB objects support and how to use these properties to determine whether a data source supports use of the SQL command language. You learned how to use the `Transaction` object to encapsulate your data source operations and to commit and abort transactions. Other transaction-related topics discussed today are nesting transaction, transaction isolation levels, and how to control locking. Today's final topic is the `Index` object, its associated interfaces, and how to use the `Index` object to search for specific rows in a row set that contain specific key values. Tomorrow's theme is how to integrate error handling into your OLE DB applications.

Q&A

This section answers some common questions related to today's topics.

Q How can you use transactions to improve application performance?

A When a transaction is opened, all operations that are performed are buffered until they are committed or aborted. In a client/server environment, using transactions can cut down on the network traffic. Only transactions that actually commit are transmitted to the server data source. This performance improvement doesn't come without a cost, however. In this case, the cost can be higher memory requirements (physical or disk space) on the client side. In a multiuser environment, though, this tradeoff can be worthwhile because it can yield significant performance improvements under the right conditions.

Q How do isolation levels relate to specific locking schemes?

A OLE DB doesn't specify the locking mechanisms used by a provider. The OLE DB specification leaves it to the data provider to implement its own appropriate locking methods that support the defined isolation levels. When using OLE DB, you should focus on isolation levels rather than on specific locking mechanisms, and you must use transactions to invoke these locking methodologies.

Q How can you determine whether a data provider supports its own set of properties?

A You can use the `GetPropertyInfo` method of the `IDBProperties` interface to return information about all properties supported by the data provider. This method returns a `DBPROPINFOSET` structure that contains information about each property supported by a data provider. You must navigate through this structure to determine the provider-specific properties it supports.

Workshop

The Workshop quiz questions test your understanding of today's material. (The answers appear in Appendix F, "Answers.") The exercises encourage you to apply the information you learned today to real-life situations.

20

Quiz

1. List the major property groups.

2. What structure returns the collection of property values?

3. Name the property that determines the level of SQL command support provided by an OLE DB data provider?

4. What method opens a transaction?

5. What isolation level maintains the most consistent access to a row set in a multi-user environment?

6. What property ensures that a row set is retained in a valid state after a transaction is closed?

7. What Index object method searches for a specific key value in an index?

Exercises

1. Review the properties supported by the OLE DB objects.

2. Open the OLE DB ODBC provider Help file and review the provider-specific properties it supports.

DAY 21

OLE DB Error Handling

The focus this week has been OLE DB objects, their interfaces, and some simple OLE DB applications. OLE DB also provides a means for you to build robust applications by using mechanisms to integrate error handling into your applications. The first step in error handling is to examine the value returned by a method, which is where today's discussion of OLE DB error handling begins. OLE DB uses the basic error-handling techniques of Automation, the technology formerly known as OLE Automation, and adds another layer of error handling that can return multiple provider-specific errors. The goal of Day 21 is to show you how to integrate these techniques into your own applications.

Today you will

- Integrate basic error handling into your OLE DB applications.
- Check the result of a call to an OLE DB method with the SUCCEEDED and FAILED macros.
- Look at OLE DB interface extensions to Automation error handling.
- Work with advanced error-handling issues, including multithreading.
- Understand OLE DB HRESULT error codes.

Basic Error Handling

Although all the OLE DB interface methods discussed this week return an HRESULT type value, the OLE DB code you have written so far assumes that all method calls always execute successfully. Obviously, this approach isn't the way to build a robust application that can handle unexpected situations. Therefore, the first step in adding robustness to OLE DB applications is to check the method's result value.

 Note   A *robust application* can handle all error conditions without crashing. As an application developer, you have the responsibility of handling all errors that your application might generate.

Checking Error Results

As you know, the HRESULT type return value indicates the success or failure of a method. (Later today you will explore the status codes that a method can return.) Visual C++ provides two macros that you can use to determine generally whether a method was successful. These macros are aptly named SUCCEEDED and FAILED. The SUCCEEDED macro returns true if the call to the method was successful, and the FAILED macro returns true if the call to the method was unsuccessful. If a call to a method is successful, it returns the constant value S_OK. A method can return other success and error values as well. Typically, the success value constants begin with an S_ or DB_S_, and the error value constants begin with an E or DB_E. You will learn about these status value constants later today, also. Listing 21.1 demonstrates how to check the HRESULT value of a method to determine whether it executed successfully.

Note   The standard error and success return codes are defined in the Visual C++ documentation.

INPUT   **LISTING 21.1**   CHECKING THE HRESULT VALUE OF A METHOD

```
1:    // Create a Command object...
2:    if(FAILED(pCreateSession->CreateSession(NULL, IID_IDBCreateCommand,
3:                                            (IUnknown **)
                                             ↪&pCreateCommand))) {
4:        printf("The Create Session Method Failed!\n");
5:    };
```

As you can see, checking the status of a call to an OLE DB method is fairly simple. That information enables your application to take the necessary steps to prevent a failure. In addition, OLE DB and Automation support interfaces that can help you retrieve more-detailed information regarding the failure of a method. The following section explains how to integrate these interfaces to retrieve additional error information. The immediate goal here is to build a procedure you can use in your application to display this additional error information.

Automation Error Objects

The OLE DB specification is an extension of the Automation interface. Automation defines two interfaces that assist in the error-handling process. These interfaces are not required by OLE DB data providers. The first interface, ISupportErrorInfo, determines whether the additional support is provided. The second interface, IErrorInfo, assists in retrieving additional specific error information, including a more complete description of the error and whether any further information is available in an associated help file.

The ISupportErrorInfo Interface

The ISupportErrorInfo interface determines whether an object supports the necessary interfaces to retrieve additional error information. The ISupportErrorInfo defines a single method, InterfaceSupportsErrorInfo, which is defined as follows:

```
HRESULT InterfaceSupportsErrorInfo(REFIID riid);
```

This method takes a single parameter, riid, which represents the interface you are checking to determine whether it supports additional error information. If the interface supports additional error information, the InterfaceSupportsErrorInfo method returns S_OK.

Listing 21.2 demonstrates the first step in creating a procedure that retrieves and displays the additional error information if it's supported. The procedure DispErrorInfo takes two parameters: a pointer to the interface that generated the error and the globally unique identifier (GUID) of that interface. Because this procedure should function for any type of OLE DB object, it will pass the pointer to the interface that generated the error as a pointer to the generic IUnknown type.

 Caution   You must always call the InterfaceSupportsErrorInfo method before attempting to retrieve additional error information. If the interface doesn't support additional error information and you call any of the additional error-information methods, you will generate yet another error! Never create error-handling routines that generate more errors themselves.

21

LISTING 21.2 THE FIRST STEP IN BUILDING A PROCEDURE TO HANDLE AND DISPLAY OLE DB ERRORS

```
1:  HRESULT DispErrorInfo(IUnknown *pErrorInt, GUID ErrorIID) {
2:    ISupportErrorInfo *pSupportErrorInfo;
3:
4:    // Obtain Access to the ISupportErrorInfo Interface
5:    if(SUCCEEDED(pErrorInt->QueryInterface(IID_ISupportErrorInfo,
6:                                  (void **) &pSupportErrorInfo))) {
7:      // Check if Extended Error Information is Available
8:      if(pSupportErrorInfo->InterfaceSupportsErrorInfo(ErrorIID) ==
       ➥S_OK) {
9:          // Process the Error Information Available Here!...
10:       } else {
11:         cerr << "Extended Error Information Unavailable!\n";
12:       };
13:       pSupportErrorInfo->Release();
14:     } else {
15:       cerr << "Could Not Obtain Access To The ISupportErrorInfo
         ➥Interface\n";
16:       cerr << "Additional Error Information Unavailable!\n";
17:     };
18:     return S_OK;
      ➥};
```

As Listing 21.2 demonstrates, after the `ISupportErrorInfo` interface is successfully obtained, you can use the `InterfaceSupportsErrorInfo` method to determine whether the object supports the `IErrorInfo` interface. The next section explains the `IErrorInfo` interface.

The `IErrorInfo` Interface

The `IErrorInfo` interface is the generic Automation interface that retrieves extended error information about a single error. However, OLE DB objects don't use this interface directly. As you already know, the `ISupportErrorInfo` interface determines whether the application supports the `IErrorInfo` interface. The `IErrorInfo` interface defines five methods: `GetDescription`, `GetGUID`, `GetHelpContext`, `GetHelpFile`, and `GetSource`. These methods are defined as follows:

```
HRESULT GetDescription(BSTR *pbstrDesc);
HRESULT GetGUID(GUID *pGUID);
HRESULT GetHelpContext(DWORD *pwHelpContext);
HRESULT GetHelpFile(BSTR *pbstrHelpFile);
HRESULT GetSource(BSTR *pbstrSource);
```

The `GetDescription` method returns a string that contains a natural-language description of the error that occurred. This description is suitable to display to an end user.

The GetGUID method returns the interface ID of the interface that generated the error. If the error isn't attributable to a specific interface, the value of the GUID is set to DBGUID_NULL.

The GetHelpContext and GetHelpFile methods retrieve the name of the help file and help file lookup. This information can launch the help viewer and place the user in a context that displays additional error information. These values are returned only if the data provider supports a help file. The GetHelpContext method returns a context value, and the GetHelpFile method returns a string that contains the name of the help file, including the path.

The GetSource method returns the name of the source operating-system object that generated the error. The source name is generally the name of the dynamic link library (DLL) that encapsulates the data provider interfaces.

Note   The consumer must use the SysFreeString method to deallocate any string values that the IErrorInfo interfaces return.

OLE DB Error Objects

The IErrorInfo interface works quite well for standard COM objects. However, the OLE DB has two requirements that the standard IErrorInfo interface can't meet:

- OLE DB needs to return provider-error information.
- OLE DB needs to return multiple error values simultaneously. (The IErrorInfo interface returns information regarding only one error at a time.)

Therefore, OLE DB defines three additional interfaces to overcome these limitations. These interfaces are IErrorRecords, IErrorLookup, and ISQLErrorInfo. The IErrorRecords interface returns multiple errors simultaneously. The IErrorLookup interface provides extended error-description information. Finally, the ISQLErrorInfo interface returns custom SQL error information.

A detailed explanation of these interfaces and the methods they provide follows. When you understand how to use these interfaces, you can integrate them into the completed DispErrorInfo procedure started in Listing 21.1.

The IErrorRecords Interface

Rather than return one record as defined by the IErrorInfo interface, OLE DB methods can return multiple errors. The IErrorRecords interface navigates and manages this

21

collection of error records. The reason OLE DB needs to return multiple errors is that an error can have a cascading effect. This record structure enables these multiple cascading errors to be captured and returned. Each error record contains the following information:

- An ERRORINFO structure
- Parameters defined in the error message
- A pointer to a custom error object (for example, ISQLErrorInfo)
- A dynamic error ID
- A lookup ID

I explain each of the preceding components in the following discussion of the specific OLE DB error interfaces. The IErrorRecords interface defines the following methods: AddErrorRecord, GetBasicErrorInfo, GetCustomErrorObject, GetErrorInfo, GetErrorParameters, and GetRecordCount. These methods are defined as follows:

```
HRESULT GetBasicErrorInfo(ULONG lRecNum, ERRORINFO *pErrorInfo);
HRESULT GetCustomErrorObject(ULONG lRecNum, REFIID riid,
                             IUnknown **ppCustomErrorInt);
HRESULT GetErrorInfo(ULONG lRecNum, LCID LocaleID,
                     IErrorInfo **ppErrorInfoInt);
HRESULT GetErrorParameters(ULONG lRecNum, DISPPARAMS *pDispParam);
HRESULT GetRecordCount(ULONG *plNumRecs);
HRESULT AddErrorRecord(ERRORINFO *pErrorInfo, DWORD dwLookupID,
                       DISPPARAMS *pDispParam, IUnknown *pCustomErrorInt,
                       DWORD dwDynamicID);
```

The GetBasicErrorInfo method retrieves the basic ERRORINFO structure for the record number specified in the lRecNum parameter. The ERRORINFO structure holds basic information about an error. The structure is defined as follows:

```
typedef struct tagERRORINFO
     HRESULT    hrError;
     DWORD      dwMinor;
     CLSID      clsid;
     IID        iid;
     DISPID     dispid;
} ERRORINFO;
```

The hrError field contains the HRESULT error value for the record specified. Each record can have an HRESULT value different from the one that the method initially returned. The dwMinor field contains a provider-specific error value. You must consult the documentation for the data provider for more information about the meanings of this value. The clsid field contains the class ID of the OLE DB object that generated this error. The iid parameter contains the interface ID of the interface that generated this error. If the method belongs to multiple interfaces, the interface ID where the method is defined first is returned. The `dispid` field contains the method that generated the error. This method ID may or may not be defined, depending on the data provider.

The `GetCustomErrorObject` method retrieves a provider-specific customer error. OLE DB provides one custom error interface, `ISQLErrorInfo` (discussed shortly), for providers that support the SQL command language. The `GetCustomErrorObject` method parameter `lRecNum` specifies the error record number to access. The `riid` parameter specifies the interface ID of the custom error object you want to retrieve. The `ppCustomErrorInt` parameter returns a pointer to the interface requested. If the requested custom error interface isn't available, `ppCustomErrorInt` will be `NULL` on return. If this method succeeds, `ppCustomErrorInt` returns `S_OK`.

The `GetErrorInfo` method retrieves an `IErrorInfo` interface for the specified record number. The `lRecNum` parameter specifies the record number to retrieve. The `LocalID` parameter specifies the locale ID. The locale ID specifies the current location and selects the appropriate language version of the error descriptions. The `ppErrorInfoInt` parameter returns a pointer to `IErrorInfo` interface for the selected record number.

> **Tip**
>
> To retrieve the default system locale ID, use the standard Visual C++ method `GetSystemDefaultLCID()`.

The `GetErrorParameters` method retrieves error message parameters. Some error messages might use parameters, as in the following example: Access to table *<table1>* denied. In this case, *<table1>* is a parameter. If the parameter *<table1>* had the value CUSTOMERS, the error message would be automatically reformatted as follows: Access to table CUSTOMERS denied. A consumer usually won't use a parameter structure without knowing which values are available in that structure. The `lRecNum` parameter specifies the record number. The `pDispParams` parameter retrieves the error message parameters.

The `GetRecordCount` method returns the number of error records available. The parameter `plNumRecs` returns the number of error records available. Error records have the index values 0 to `plNumRecs` −1.

The `AddErrorRecord` method is used only by data providers. It adds a new error record to the error records collection. The `pErrorInfo` structure holds a pointer to a filled-in `ERRORINFO` structure, specifying information about the error. The `dwLookupID` specifies the error's lookup ID. The `pDispParam` parameter specifies the error's message parameters. The `pCustomErrorInt` parameter specifies the custom error object, if applicable. The `dwDynamicID` parameter specifies the error ID if the provider uses dynamic errors; otherwise, it has a value of 0. You will generally not use this method.

21

You will use the IErrorRecords interface extensively to complete the DispErrorInfo procedure from Listing 21.2. In its final form, the procedure loops through and retrieves the information in each error record. First, though, you need to look at the IErrorLookup and ISQLErrorInfo interfaces.

The IErrorLookup Interface

Data providers use the IErrorLookup interface to retrieve help file information, combine the error parameters with the error message to create a completed error message, and release dynamic error information. The IErrorLookup interface defines three methods: GetErrorDescription, GetHelpInfo, and ReleaseErrors. These methods are defined as follows:

```
HRESULT GetErrorDescription(HRESULT hError, DWORD dwLookupID,
                            DISPPARAMS *pDispParam, LCID lcid,
                            BSTR *pErrorObject, BSTR *pDesc);
HRESULT GetHelpInfo(HRESULT hError, dwLookupID, LCID lcid,
                    BSTR *pHeloFileName, DWORD *pContext);
HRESULT ReleaseErrors(const DWORD dwDynErrorID);
```

The GetDescription method retrieves the source error object string, specified in the pErrorObject parameter, and the error description, specified in the pDesc parameter. The GetHelpInfo method retrieves an error's associated help file information, if applicable. The GetErrorDescription and GetHelpInfo functions return BSTRs that must be freed by the caller, using SysFreeString.

The ISQLErrorInfo Interface

The final error-related interface covered today is the ISQLErrorInfo interface. This interface is used in the custom error object pointer of an error record. You access the ISQLErrorInfo interface by using the GetCustomErrorObject method of the IErrorRecord interface. The ISQLErrorInfo interface defines a single method: GetSQLInfo. This method is defined as follows:

```
HRESULT GetSQLInfo(BSTR *pSQLStateStr, LONG *plSQLErrorNum);
```

The pSQLStateStr parameter returns a string containing the current SQL state. The plSQLErrorNum returns the provider-specific SQL error number. The pSqlStateStr is an [out] bstr, so the caller must free it by using SysFreeString.

The Completed DispErrorInfo Source Code

Armed with the information provided by these error interfaces, you are ready to return to the DispErrorInfo procedure in Listing 21.2. The final procedure accesses the IErrorRecord interface and loops through each available error record, one at a time.

DispErrorInfo retrieves an IErrorInfo interface for each error record and uses that IErrorInfo interface to access the error description, source, and GUID. The GetCustomErrorObject is accessed for each record. If a ISQLErrorInfo interface is available, the current SQL state and error number are also displayed. The complete DispErrorInfo procedure appears in Listing 21.3.

Note Remember to use the SysFreeString method to release the returned string memory. The BSTR type is a Unicode type string. (Refer to Day 19, "Navigating the Result of a Query," for more information about the methods available to process Unicode strings.)

INPUT **LISTING 21.3** THE COMPLETED DispErrorInfo PROCEDURE

```
 1:    HRESULT DispErrorInfo(IUnknown *pErrorInt, GUID ErrorIID) {
 2:    ISupportErrorInfo *pSupportErrorInfo;
 3:    IErrorInfo        *pErrorInfo,
 4:                      *pErrorInfoRecord;
 5:    IErrorRecords     *pErrorRecords;
 6:    ISQLErrorInfo     *pSQLErrorInfo;
 7:    BSTR               pDescription = NULL;
 8:    BSTR               pSource = NULL;
 9:    BSTR               pSQLState = NULL;
10:    GUID               ErrorGUID;
11:    ULONG              i,
12:                       lNumRecs;
13:    LONG               lSQLErrorNum;
14:    HRESULT            retcode = S_OK;
15:
16:    // Obtain Access to the ISupportErrorInfo Interface
17:    if(SUCCEEDED(pErrorInt->QueryInterface(IID_ISupportErrorInfo,
18:                                   (void **) &pSupportErrorInfo))) {
19:      // Check if Extended Error Information is Available
20:      if(SUCCEEDED(pSupportErrorInfo->InterfaceSupportsErrorInfo
             ➥(ErrorIID))) {
21:        // Access the Error Info interface
22:        if(SUCCEEDED(GetErrorInfo(0,&pErrorInfo))) {
23:          // Retrieve the Error Records Interface
24:          if(SUCCEEDED(pErrorInfo->QueryInterface(IID_IErrorRecords,
25:                                   (void **) &pErrorRecords))) {
26:            // Retrieve the Number of Error Records
27:            if(SUCCEEDED(pErrorRecords->GetRecordCount(&lNumRecs))) {
28:              for(i=0; i < lNumRecs; i++) {
29:                // Get the Error Info Interface
30:                pErrorRecords-
                   ➥>GetErrorInfo(i,GetSystemDefaultLCID(),
```

continues

21

LISTING 21.3 CONTINUED

```
31:                                              &pErrorInfoRecord);
32:                 // Get the Error Description
33:                 pErrorInfoRecord->GetDescription(&pDescription);
34:                 // Get the Error Source
35:                 pErrorInfoRecord->GetSource(&pSource);
36:                 // Get the Error GUID
37:                 pErrorInfoRecord->GetGUID(&ErrorGUID);
38:                 // Print the Error Record Interface
39:                 fprintf(stderr,"Error GUID: %lx\n",ErrorGUID);
40:                 fprintf(stderr,"Source: %S\n",pDescription);
41:                 fprintf(stderr,"Description: %S\n\n",pDescription);
42:                 // Free the Strings
43:                 SysFreeString(pDescription);
44:                 SysFreeString(pSource);
45:                 // Get SQL State if Available
46:                 if(SUCCEEDED(pErrorRecords->GetCustomErrorObject(i,
47:                                  IID_ISQLErrorInfo,
48:                                  (IUnknown **) &pSQLErrorInfo))) {
49:                     pSQLErrorInfo->GetSQLInfo(&pSQLState,
                                                    ➥&lSQLErrorNum);
50:                     fprintf(stderr,"SQL State: %S\n",pSQLState);
51:                     fprintf(stderr,"SQL Error Number:
                                 ➥%ld",lSQLErrorNum);
52:                     SysFreeString(pSQLState);
53:                     pSQLErrorInfo->Release();
54:                 };
55:                 // Release the Interface
56:                 pErrorInfoRecord->Release();
57:                 };
58:             } else {
59:               fprintf(stderr,"Can't retrieve the number
                           ➥of error records!\n");
60:               retcode = E_FAIL;
61:             };
62:             pErrorRecords->Release();
63:           } else {
64:             fprintf(stderr,"Can't retrieve the ErrorRecords
                         ➥interface\n");
65:             retcode = E_FAIL;
66:           };
67:           pErrorInfo->Release();
68:         } else {
69:           fprintf(stderr,"Can't retrieve the ErrorInfo
                       ➥interface.\n");
70:           retcode = E_FAIL;
71:         };
72:         pSupportErrorInfo->Release();
73:       } else {
```

```
74:          fprintf(stderr,"Extended Error Information Unavailable!\n");
75:          retcode = E_FAIL;
76:        };
77:      } else {
78:        fprintf(stderr,
79:                "Could Not Obtain Access To
              ➡The ISupportErrorInfo Interface\n");
80:        fprintf(stderr,"Additional Error Information Unavailable!\n");
81:          retcode = E_FAIL;
82:        };
83:      return(retcode);
84:    };
```

How to Integrate the `DispErrorInfo` Procedure

When you call an OLE DB method, you should check the HRESULT return value, as I mentioned at the beginning of the day. If the method fails, you can call the DispErrorInfo procedure to display any additional error information that's available. Listing 21.4 demonstrates how to integrate the DispErrorInfo method into an OLE DB method call.

INPUT   **LISTING 21.4**   HOW TO INTEGRATE THE DispErrorInfo PROCEDURE INTO AN OLE DB METHOD CALL

```
1:    if(FAILED(pCommandText->Execute(NULL, IID_Rowset, NULL, &cNumRows,
2:                                    (IUnknown **) &pRowset))) {
3:        // The Execute method Failed! Display Error!
4:        DispErrorInfo(pCommandText,IID_ICommandText);
5:        // Exit and call free pCommandText and CoUninitialize?...
6:        exit(0);
7:    };
```

Error-Handling Considerations

So far, you have learned about Automation and OLE DB error-handling interfaces, created a procedure to assist in the interpretation of errors that occurred, and integrated the error-handling interfaces into your applications. Here is a review of the basic steps in error handling:

1. Check the HRESULT value of a method when it is called.

2. If the method didn't succeed, possibly print some error information.

21

3. If the error is critical to the execution of the application, gracefully end the application. Be sure to release any allocated memory and close any open data sources and files.

4. If the error isn't critical (perhaps the data provider doesn't support a specific method), dynamically change the functionality of the application. For example, an application feature might not be available with lower-level data providers.

Returning Error Objects

Now that you know what a data consumer expects from a data provider, the data provider implementation requirements should be easy to understand. The final part of today's discussion of error handling explains how to implement error handling from the data provider side, including how a multithreaded environment affects data provider error handling.

Listing 21.5 demonstrates how an error is created and returned by a data provider method. The following survey of the basic steps involved in returning an error from a provider will help you understand that listing:

1. Call the SetErrorInfo method to clear out any current errors.

2. If the current operation fails, begin by using the GetErrorInfo method to access the IErrorInfo interface. If the interface isn't available, use the CreateInstance method of the IClassFactory interface to create a new IErrorInfo interface.

3. Fill in the ERRORINFO structure with the appropriate information.

4. Obtain access to the IErrrorRecords interface and use the AddErrorRecord method to add the newly created error record.

5. Call the SetErrorInfo method to pass the error to the Automation interface, signaling an error occurred.

The SetErrorInfo method sets the current ErrorInfo object, and the GetErrorInfo method retrieves the current ErrorInfo object.

LISTING 21.5 HOW AN OLE DB DATA PROVIDER RETURNS AN ERROR

```
1:      IErrorInfo       pErrorInfoObj = NULL;
2:      IErrorRecords    pErrorRecs;
3:      ERRORINFO        ErrorInf;
4:
5:      // Clear any current errors
6:      SetErrorInfo(0, NULL);
7:
```

```
 8:        // Perform whatever is necessary to implement the method
 9:        // Save error result in hrError and set Error flag
10:
11:        // Check if an Error Occurred?
12:        if(Error) {
13:          if(FAILED(GetErrorInfo(0, &pErrorInfoObj)) ||
             ➥(!pErrorInfoObj)) {
14:            pClassFactoryObject->CreateInstance(NULL,
15:            ➥CLSID_EXTENDEDERRORINFO, (void *) &pErrorInfoObj);
16:          };
17:          if (pErrorInfoObj) {
18:            // Create the ERRORINFO record
19:            pErrorInfoObj->QueryInterface(IID_IErrorRecords,
                                      ➥(void *) &pErrorRecs);
20:            ErrorInf.hrError = hrError;         // Set error result
21:            ErrorInf.dwMinor = INTERNAL_ERROR;  // Set Internal Error
                                                   // Number
22:            ErrorInf.clsid = CURRENT_CLSID;     // Set the Current CLSID
23:            ErrorInf.iid = IID_CURRENT;         // Set current IID
24:            ErrorInf.dispid = DISPID_CURRENT;   // Set current DISPID
25:
26:            // Add the Error Record
27:            pErrorRecs->AddErrorRecord(&ErrorInf,  ErrorInf.dwMinor,
28:                                    NULL, NULL, 0);
29:
30:            // Set the Error
31:            SetErrorInfo(0,pErrorInfo);
32:
33:            // Release Error Interfaces
34:            pErrorRecs->Release();
35:            pErrorInfo->Release();
36:            pErrorInfoObj->Release();
37:          }
38:        };
```

Threads

When operating in a multithreaded application, an error message generated by a previously called method might be sitting in the message queue when another message is called. (Recall that in the OLE DB environment, each application thread has only one error object.) To clear out the error message queue, the OLE data provider must call the SetErrorInfo method when a method is called. This step ensures that only the most current errors are in the queue on return.

21

A Summary of OLE DB HRESULT Error Codes

The first thing you did today was to check the HRESULT of a method to determine whether it succeeded. Table 21.1 lists the HRESULT values specifically defined by OLE DB. Refer also to the Visual C++ documentation for information about generic HRESULT constants.

TABLE 21.1   THE HRESULT VALUES DEFINED BY OLE DB

HRESULT *Constant*	*Description*
	Warning Results
DB_S_BADROWHANDLE	A row handle is invalid.
DB_S_BOOKMARKSKIPPED	A bookmark was skipped for a row that was deleted or filtered.
DB_S_BUFFERFULL	The buffer that holds fields or parameters is full.
DB_S_CANTRELEASE	A lock could not be released until the transaction is complete.
DB_S_COLUMNSCHANGED	While re-executing a query during a cursor reposition operation, the order or number of columns changed.
DB_S_COLUMNTYPEMISMATCH	Some columns cannot be converted during the copy operation because of type-conversion incompatibilities.
DB_S_COMMANDREEXECUTED	The command was re-executed.
DB_S_DELETEDROW	A row handle refers to a previously deleted row.
DB_S_DIALECTIGNORED	The language of the command was ignored; translated command returned.
DB_S_ENDOFROWSET	The end of the current row set was encountered.
DB_S_ERRORSINTREE	An error occurred in the validation tree.
DB_S_ERRORSOCCURRED	An unspecified error occurred.
DB_S_ERRORSRETURNED	Errors were encountered and returned.
DB_S_GOALCHANGED	The current goal was changed to an unsupported value.
DB_S_LOCKUPGRADED	A record lock was upgraded.
DB_S_MULTIPLECHANGES	The requested change affects multiple data source rows.
DB_S_NONEXTROWSET	End of multiple return row sets reached.
DB_S_NORESULT	End of results reached.
DB_S_PARAMUNAVAILABLE	The specified parameter is invalid.
DB_S_PROPERTIESCHANGED	The properties of the object were changed successfully.

HRESULT *Constant*	*Description*
	Warning Results
DB_S_ROWLIMITEXCEEDED	The number of requested rows is greater than the number of active rows that the Rowset object supports.
DB_S_STOPLIMITREACHED	Execution of a command was halted because of a resource limit; the results returned are incomplete.
DB_S_TOOMANYCHANGES	Too many changes were encountered; data must be refreshed.
DB_S_TYPEINFOOVERRIDDEN	The type of the parameter was overridden.
DB_S_UNWANTEDPHASE	Notifications for this phase are no longer desired.
DB_S_UNWANTEDREASON	Notifications for this phase are no longer desired for a specific reason.
	Error Results
DB_E_ABORTLIMITREACHED	The command was aborted because of resource limitations; no results returned.
DB_E_ALREADYINITIALIZED	The data source was previously initialized.
DB_E_BADACCESSORFLAGS	The Accessor flag is not valid.
DB_E_BADACCESSORHANDLE	The Accessor handle is not valid.
DB_E_BADACCESSORTYPE	The Accessor specified is invalid.
DB_E_BADBINDINFO	The binding information is not valid.
DB_E_BADBOOKMARK	The bookmark is not valid.
DB_E_BADCHAPTER	The chapter specified is not valid.
DB_E_BADCOLUMNID	The column ID specified is not valid.
DB_E_BADCONVERTFLAG	The conversion flag specified is not valid.
DB_E_BADCOPY	An error was encountered while copying.
DB_E_BADDYNAMICERRORID	The DynamicError ID specified is not valid.
DB_E_BADHRESULT	The HRESULT value specified is not valid.
DB_E_BADID	The table ID value specified is not valid.
DB_E_BADLOCKMODE	The lock mode specified is not valid.
DB_E_BADLOOKUPID	The lookup ID specified is not valid.
DB_E_BADORDINAL	The column specified is not valid.
DB_E_BADPARAMETERNAME	The specified parameter name is not valid.
DB_E_BADPRECISION	The precision value specified is not valid.
DB_E_BADPROPERTYVALUE	The property value is not valid.

21

continues

TABLE 21.1 CONTINUED

HRESULT *Constant*	*Description*
	Error Results
DB_E_BADRATIO	The ratio specified is not valid (greater than 1 or undefined).
DB_E_BADRECORDNUM	The record number specified is not valid.
DB_E_BADREGIONHANDLE	The region handle specified is not valid.
DB_E_BADROWHANDLE	The row handle is not valid.
DB_E_BADSCALE	The scale value specified is not valid.
DB_E_BADSOURCEHANDLE	The source handle specified is not valid.
DB_E_BADSTARTPOSITION	The offset position specified is past the end or before the beginning of the row set; rows not retrieved.
DB_E_BADSTATUSVALUE	The status flag specified is not valid.
DB_E_BADSTORAGEFLAG	The storage flag specified is not valid.
DB_E_BADSTORAGEFLAGS	The storage flags specified are not valid.
DB_E_BADTYPE	The type specified is not valid.
DB_E_BADTYPENAME	The type name specified is not valid.
DB_E_BADVALUES	The value specified is not valid.
DB_E_BOOKMARKSKIPPED	No row was found that matched the bookmark.
DB_E_BYREFACCESSORNOTSUPPORTED	Cannot pass Accessor by reference for this data provider.
DB_E_CANCELED	The command was canceled; changes not saved.
DB_E_CANNOTFREE	Cannot deallocate this memory.
DB_E_CANNOTRESTART	Cannot restart the new row set.
DB_E_CANTCANCEL	Cannot stop the current command.
DB_E_CANTCONVERTVALUE	Cannot convert the specified value correctly.
DB_E_CANTFETCHBACKWARDS	Cannot retrieve the row set rows backwards.
DB_E_CANTSCROLLBACKWARDS	The row set cannot scroll backwards.
DB_E_CANTTRANSLATE	Cannot translate the current command tree.
DB_E_CHAPTERNOTRELEASED	The chapter was not released.
DB_E_CONCURRENCYVIOLATION	A concurrency violation was encountered.
DB_E_COSTLIMIT	When attempting to optimize the query, the cost constraints could not be met.
DB_E_DATAOVERFLOW	A command value caused an overflow.
DB_E_DELETEDROW	The row handle points to a deleted row.

HRESULT *Constant*	*Description*
	Error Results
DB_E_DIALECTNOTSUPPORTED	The language of the command is not supported.
DB_E_DUPLICATECOLUMNID	A column was duplicated.
DB_E_DUPLICATEDATASOURCE	The data source name is already in use.
DB_E_DUPLICATEINDEXID	The index specified is already in use.
DB_E_DUPLICATETABLEID	The table specified already exists.
DB_E_ERRORSINCOMMAND	Errors were encountered in the command.
DB_E_ERRORSOCCURRED	An unspecified error occurred.
DB_E_GOALREJECTED	The goal specified was not valid; current goal unchanged.
DB_E_INDEXINUSE	The index specified is already opened.
DB_E_INTEGRITYVIOLATION	A column value violated integrity constraints for that object.
DB_E_INVALID	Cannot use bookmarks on this row set.
DB_E_INVALIDTRANSITION	The transition specified is not valid.
DB_E_LIMITREJECTED	Cost limits specified were not valid.
DB_E_MAXPENDCHANGESEXCEEDED	The maximum number of pending changes has been exceeded.
DB_E_MULTIPLESTATEMENTS	Multiple statement commands are not supported.
DB_E_MULTIPLESTORAGE	More than one storage object opened concurrently.
DB_E_NEWLYINSERTED	Cannot establish the identity of the new rows.
DB_E_NOAGGREGATION	This object does not support aggregation.
DB_E_NOCOMMAND	The command has not been specified.
DB_E_NOINDEX	The specified index is not valid.
DB_E_NOLOCALE	The locale ID specified is not valid.
DB_E_NONCONTIGUOUSRANGE	The set of rows specified are not contiguous.
DB_E_NOQUERY	The query was not defined.
DB_E_NOTABLE	The table specified does not exist.
DB_E_NOTAREFERENCECOLUMN	The column does not contain a bookmark or chapter identifier.
DB_E_NOTASUBREGION	The region specified is not a valid subregion.
DB_E_NOTFOUND	Cannot find the specified key value.
DB_E_NOTPREPARED	Cannot prepare the specified command.
DB_E_NOTREENTRANT	A method was called while another was still executing.

21

continues

TABLE 21.1   CONTINUED

HRESULT *Constant*	*Description*
	Error Results
DB_E_NOTSUPPORTED	The method specified is not supported.
DB_E_NULLACCESSORNOTSUPPORTED	Cannot pass NULL value Accessor to this data provider.
DB_E_OBJECTOPEN	Operation performed on an object that was not opened.
DB_E_PARAMNOTOPTIONAL	A value was not specified for a required parameter.
DB_E_PARAMUNAVAILABLE	The parameter specified is not available.
DB_E_PENDINGCHANGES	Changes are pending on an unreferenced row.
DB_E_PENDINGINSERT	Cannot perform the pending insert.
DB_E_READONLYACCESSOR	Accessor is read-only; write invalid.
DB_E_ROWLIMITEXCEEDED	Adding this row exceeds the number of active rows for this row set.
DB_E_ROWSETINCOMMAND	Cannot copy a command that contains row sets.
DB_E_ROWSNOTRELEASED new rows.	The current row handles were not released before retrieving
DB_E_SCHEMAVIOLATION	The values supplied are inconsistent with the data source schema.
DB_E_TABLEINUSE	The table specified is already opened.
DB_E_UNSUPPORTEDCONVERSION	Cannot perform the requested type conversion.
DB_E_WRITEONLYACCESSOR	The specified Accessor can only be written.
DB_SEC_E_AUTH_FAILED	Security error; data source access authorization was not successful.
DB_SEC_E_PERMISSIONDENIED	Permission denied because of a security violation.

> **Tip**
>
> If you attempt to check for any of these return values explicitly and receive an identifier unknown error when compiling, be sure that you have included the oledberr.h header file.

Summary

Day 21 explains how to integrate error handling into OLE DB applications. You learned how to implement basic error-handling techniques and how to check the HRESULT of a method with the SUCCEEDED and FAILED macros to determine whether the method executed correctly. Then you learned how to use the ISupportErrorInfo interface to determine whether an OLE DB object supports extended error information.

You used the `IErrorRecords` and `ISQLErrorInfo` methods to create the `DispErrorInfo` procedure, which can display extended error information for any OLE DB object.

Q&A

This section answers some common questions related to today's topics.

Q Should my application look for and try to interpret specific HRESULT values?

A If you look at the OLE DB error information, you will see that as each method is defined, the most common HRESULT values that the method can return are listed. A useful exercise is to try to interpret certain warning result values. You can be assured only that an OLE DB provider supports the methods and interfaces that are required. If you attempt to access an optional interface, you will need to be sure that your application can still function if the data provider doesn't support that interface.

Q Is there any way other than checking the HRESULT value of each method call to add error handling to my OLE DB application?

A Unfortunately, no. To ensure the highest degree of error checking in your applications, you must check each method's HRESULT value. You must realize that one failed method can cause a cascading error effect. Again, the best technique is to design your applications to be robust so that they offer only the functionality provided by the OLE DB data provider. A robust application is one that can handle all error conditions without crashing for the end user. As an application developer, you are responsible for handling all errors that your application might generate.

Workshop

The Workshop quiz questions test your understanding of today's material. (The answers appear in Appendix F, "Answers.") The exercises encourage you to apply the information you learned today to real-life situations.

Quiz

1. Name the two macros used to check the result of an OLE DB method call.
2. Which interface checks whether an OLE DB object supports extended error information?
3. What are the special requirements of OLE DB error handling that aren't resolved by Automation error-handling objects?

21

4. What information does the GetBasicErrorInfo method return? Describe the elements of this structure.

5. How do you retrieve a custom error object? What custom error objects does OLE DB provide?

6. List the basic techniques for OLE DB error handling.

7. Which method does a data provider use to add a new error?

8. Explain the difference between HRESULT constants with the prefix DB_S and those with the prefix DB_E.

Exercises

1. Review the generic HRESULT return values. They can be found in the Visual C++ documentation.

   A sample called DECODE is available in the Microsoft Software Library. The DECODE application enables you to enter an HRESULT in a dialog and have it decoded to its text description.

2. Integrate the DispErrorInfo procedure and error checking into one of the data consumer examples created in an earlier lesson.

   Listing 21.4 shows how to call the DispErrorInfo procedure from within another program.

Week 3

In Review

In Day 15, to start your final week of study, you learned to view ODBC and DAO API applications and understand the mechanisms used to process databases. You took a look at using the MFC wrapper classes. Also, you saw that data binding is automatically performed and the RFX mechanism is configured.

In Day 16's lesson, you saw how OLE DB builds on and expands the capabilities of ODBC. Because OLE DB providers can be written for nonrelational data sources, OLE DB provides an interface to relational, as well as nonrelational, data sources. OLE DB takes an object-oriented approach to database client development, whereas ODBC takes a function-based API approach. The OLE DB object hierarchy consists of just a few objects, which expose COM interfaces to perform well-defined sets of functions.

You learned on Day 17 the process of integrating OLE DB into applications by examining the relationship between COM and OLE DB and seeing how COM technology influences the OLE DB programming model.

On Day 18, you examined OLE DB objects, specifically the Session and Command objects, and the interfaces they provide. You learned how to create a Session object by using the IDBCreateSession interface of the DataSource object and how to create a Command object by using the IDBCreateCommand interface of the Session object. The section on Command objects includes a brief review of Structured Query Language (SQL). Examples also focus on using the OLE DB ODBC data provider to access a SQL Server data source.

In Day 19's lesson, you started with a discussion of the Rowset object and its associated interfaces. You brought together the concepts presented in the previous three lessons so that you could begin to make productive use of OLE DB.

You learned, on Day 20, three important topics in OLE DB application development: properties, transactions, and the Index object. Other topics covered include how to use properties to control the state of an object, the Transaction object, and the Index object.

In your final lesson in this book, you learned the mechanisms that OLE DB provides at multiple levels to integrate error handling into your applications. OLE DB uses the basic error-handling techniques of OLE Automation and adds another layer of error handling that can return multiple provider-specific errors. You learned how to integrate these techniques into your own applications.

APPENDIX A

What's on the CD?

On the back of this book, you'll find a CD-ROM containing the code that you work on as you go through the lessons. The following is an explanation of the directories and files you will find on the CD.

AddressBookDB.mdb: A Microsoft Access database that is used on Days 14 and 15.

AddressBookODBC: A Visual C++ project that uses ODBC. It is covered on Days 14 and 15.

AddressBookDAO: A Visual C++ project that uses DAO. It is covered on Days 14 and 15.

ADOMFC1: A Visual C++ project that uses MFC and ADO. It is a database client application that you begin working on in Day 4.

ATLTest1: A simple ATL COM application that you build in Day 9.

ADOSDK: An ADO application that uses ADO without the `#import` directive. It is mentioned in Day 4.

COMMANDTEST: A Win32 console application that uses the OLE DB `Command` object. It is covered in Day 18.

DataProject1: A Visual Studio project that uses ODBC to access a database inside the Visual Studio environment. You create a project similar to this on Day 2.

EnumTest: A Win32 console application that enumerates the OLE DB providers installed on your machine. You create this application on Day 17.

MTSComp1: An ATL COM application that builds a COM component that runs under MTS and returns a disconnected ADO Recordset. You create this application on Day 12.

ODBCTest: A Win32 console application that uses the OLE DB ODBC provider to attach to an ODBC data source. You create this application in Day 17.

Polymorph: A Win32 console application that demonstrates polymorphism with virtual functions in C++. You create this application on Day 9.

ClientTier.asp: An Active Server Page that presents a database client UI, using an ActiveX grid control and RDS. You create this on Day 11.

ClientTierAsync.asp: An Active Server Page that presents a database client UI, using an ActiveX grid control and RDS. It can retrieve data from a database asynchronously. You create this on Day 11.

ClientTierForMTSADORs.asp: An Active Server Page that uses MTSComp1, the MTS component you created on Day 12. You create this ASP on Day 12.

DataInHtml.htm: A simple HTML page that demonstrates the difficulty of building a database interface in straight HTML. You create this on Day 11.

Sample.xml: A simple XML sample that demonstrates how a database recordset can be represented in XML. You create this on Day 11.

VCDb.mdb: A Microsoft Access database for which you write SQL code. You begin using it on Day 2.

VCDbNormalized.mdb: Similar to VCDb.mdb, except that VCDbNormalized.mdb contains the changes you made to the database when you learned about database design on Day 7.

Appendix B

Additional Resources

One of the best sources of information on modern database technology and C++ programming is the World Wide Web. There are several Web sites where you can find valuable technical information. The topics of information and the sites include

- XML information, at `http://www.microsoft.com/XML`
- Microsoft Internet Client SDK, at `http://msdn.microsoft.com/developer/sdk/inetsdk`
- Microsoft's Universal Data Access (MDAC) strategy, at `http://www.microsoft.com/data/`
- OLE DB information, at `http://www.microsoft.com/data/oledb/`
- The ADO Web site, at `http://www.microsoft.com/data/ado/`
- Persistence Software, for object-oriented software and relational database tools, at `http://www.persistence.com`
- Searchable Internet newsgroup archives, at `http://www.dejanews.com`
- My first C++ ADO article, at `http://www.vcdj.com/vcdj/jan98/ado.htm`

APPENDIX C

Installing the Microsoft Data Access Components

The latest version of the Microsoft Data Access Components (MDAC) can always be found on the MDAC Web site.

1. Go to the Microsoft Universal Data Access Web site at `http://www.microsoft.com/data`.

2. Navigate to the page that lists the free downloads.

3. Click the link for the Microsoft Data Access Components. Read through the information on this page pertaining to system and software requirements.

4. Click the link for registering and downloading the MDAC.

5. After you have registered, you will get the download page. Select the appropriate download to begin the download process, which will result in an .EXE file being downloaded to your system.

6. Run the .EXE file to start the installation of the MDAC.

APPENDIX D

Interpreting HRESULTS

When you use the #import directive with ADO, as in this book, ADO will usually throw an exception rather than return an HRESULT for runtime errors. Because exceptions provide detailed information on the error and its cause(s), it is generally easy to figure out what went wrong.

HRESULTs, on the other hand, are just numbers. HRESULTs by themselves provide very little information to enable you to figure out what went wrong. For those times when you are forced to decipher an HRESULT, it is sometimes very helpful to know the meaning of HRESULT return codes.

There are several resources to which you can turn to discover the meaning of HRESULT return codes. The Microsoft Knowledge Base has several articles that deal with HRESULTs. The best way to find these articles is to search the Knowledge Base for HRESULT ADO. You can also search for adovc to find ADO C++ articles, some of which deal with decoding HRESULTs.

One Knowledge Base article, "Q168354," contains a list of the frequently encountered HRESULTs and their meanings. Specifically, the article explains the HRESULTs that you could receive from the underlying OLE DB providers when using ADO.

Other Knowledge Base articles show sample code for decoding, or cracking, HRESULTs. The Knowledge Base article "Q169498" illustrates a method you can use to interpret an HRESULT with a function and display the text description.

Two code samples from Microsoft contain code that shows how to crack HRESULTs. These are the ADOVC sample and the DECODE sample. You can obtain these from the Microsoft Software Library or from MSDN.

APPENDIX E

Using ADO via the OLE DB SDK

To use ADO in your C++ applications, you can use the ADO header files and import library from the OLE DB SDK. You include the ADO header files (adoid.h and adoint.h) in your source, and add the ADO import library adoid.lib to your linker input. This enables you to create instances of the ADO objects and access their member functions. The code listings that follow show the changes you would need to make to a typical MFC application to use ADO via the OLE DB SDK. A sample MFC application called ADOSDK is on the CD.

LISTING E.1 ADDITIONS TO STDAFX.H

```
1:  #include <adoid.h>
2:  #include <adoint.h>
3:  #include <comdef.h>
```

LISTING E.2   ADDITIONS TO THE DOCUMENT HEADER FILE

```
 1:   class CADOSDKDoc : public CDocument
 2:   {
 3:   protected: // create from serialization only
 4:     CADOSDKDoc();
 5:     DECLARE_DYNCREATE(CADOSDKDoc)
 6:
 7:   // Attributes
 8:   public:
 9:     ADOConnection* m_piConnection;
10:     BOOL m_ConnectionOpen;
```

Lines 9 and 10 are the new lines you need to add. The other lines should be there already.

LISTING E.3   ADDITIONS TO THE DOCUMENT CONSTRUCTOR

```
 1:   CADOSDKDoc::CADOSDKDoc()
 2:   {
 3:     m_piConnection = NULL;
 4:     m_ConnectionOpen = FALSE;
 5:   }
```

Lines 4 and 5 are the new lines you need to add. The other lines should be there already.

LISTING E.4   ADDITIONS TO THE OnNewDocument FUNCTION

```
 1:   BOOL CADOSDKDoc::OnNewDocument()
 2:   {
 3:     if (!CDocument::OnNewDocument())
 4:       return FALSE;
 5:
 6:     HRESULT hr;
 7:
 8:     hr = CoCreateInstance(CLSID_CADOConnection, NULL,
 9:       CLSCTX_INPROC_SERVER, IID_IADOConnection,
10:       (LPVOID *)&m_piConnection);
11:     if (!FAILED(hr))
12:     {
13:       hr = m_piConnection->Open(bstr_t(
14:         _ L"Provider=Microsoft.Jet.OLEDB.3.51;Data
                       ➥Source=c:\\tysdbvc\\vcdb.mdb;"),
15:         NULL, NULL);
16:       if (!FAILED(hr))
17:       {
```

```
18:        m_ConnectionOpen = TRUE;
19:      }
21:    }
22:
23:    return TRUE;
24:  }
```

Lines 6–21 are the new lines you need to add. The other lines should be there already. Line 14 will change, depending on the location of the file.

LISTING E.5 ADDITIONS TO THE `OnCloseDocument` FUNCTION

```
1:  void CADOSDKDoc::OnCloseDocument()
2:  {
3:    if (m_ConnectionOpen)
4:    {
5:      m_piConnection->Close();
6:      m_ConnectionOpen = FALSE;
7:    }
8:    if (m_piConnection)
9:    {
10:      m_piConnection->Release();
11:    }
12:
13:    CDocument::OnCloseDocument();
14:  }
```

Lines 3–11 are the new lines you need to add. The other lines should be there already from ClassWizard.

LISTING E.6 ADDITIONS TO THE `OnRButtonDown` FUNCTION

```
1:  void CADOSDKView::OnRButtonDown(UINT nFlags, CPoint point)
2:  {
3:    CADOSDKDoc * pDoc = GetDocument();
4:    HRESULT hr;
5:    ADORecordset * pRs = NULL;
6:    short sEOF;
7:    _variant_t vLastName;
8:
9:    if (pDoc->m_ConnectionOpen)
10:    {
11:      hr = pDoc->m_piConnection->Execute(
12:        _bstr_t(L"SELECT * FROM Customers"),
13:        &(_variant_t(0L)),
14:        adCmdText,
```

continues

E

```
15:        &pRs);
16:
17:     if (SUCCEEDED(hr))
18:     {
19:       pRs->get_EOF(&sEOF);
20:       while (!sEOF)
21:       {
22:         hr = pRs->get_Collect(_variant_t(L"CustLastName"),
              ➥&vLastName);
23:         if (SUCCEEDED(hr))
24:         {
25:           TRACE("Last Name:%s.\n", (LPCTSTR) (_bstr_t) vLastName);
26:         }
27:         pRs->MoveNext();
28:         pRs->get_EOF(&sEOF);
29:       }
30:       pRs->Close();
31:       pRs->Release();
32:     }
33:
34:   }
35:
36:   CView::OnRButtonDown(nFlags, point);
37: }
```

Lines 3–34 are the new lines you need to add. The other lines should be there already from ClassWizard.

APPENDIX F

Answers

Day 1, "Choosing the Right Database Technology"

Quiz

1. What are the primary benefits of using a record manager (such as Btrieve) rather than inventing your own database routines?

   If you use a record manager (such as Btrieve), you don't have to build the code for navigation, searching, indexing, and locking for multiple users.

2. What do the desktop databases provide that record managers do not?

   Desktop databases provide data files that contain metadata, so the data files are self-describing. Record managers do not.

3. What are the benefits of using a database technology that provides open, accessible data stores?

   If you use a database technology that provides open, accessible data stores, your application will live longer. Also, in the future, you will not be derided by your customers and other developers for your lack of vision in building an inaccessible database with your application.

4. Which database technologies provide open, accessible data stores?

The database technologies that provide open, accessible databases are desktop databases and relational database servers.

5. What is the significance of server-side processing of set-based operations in a client/server architecture?

Server side processing of set-based operations means less network traffic and greater scalability of your application.

Exercises

1. The code in Listing 1.1 creates a data file that contains order information. Write a program that reads the order data from that file.

The code below opens the data.dat file and reads the date and product. It then sends the product name to the display.

```
ifstream is( "data.dat", ios::binary | ios::nocreate );
   if( is )
   {
      is.read( (char *) &dt, sizeof( dt ) );
      is.read( (char *) &prod, sizeof( prod ) );
      cout << prod.szName  << endl;
   }
   else
   {
      cout << "ERROR: Cannot open file 'data.dat'." << endl;
   }
)
```

2. Decide which database technology would be most appropriate for the sample application described earlier. Create a list of capabilities that the database for this application needs to provide. Justify your decision by comparing the database requirements with the capabilities of the database technology that you have chosen.

The database for this application needs to work well in a LAN environment, provide multiple users with simultaneous access to the data, give good performance so that people don't have to wait long when placing their orders, and use an open database format so that the data can be analyzed by managers. Also, of course, you don't want to spend a long time just building the database. A desktop database such as Access fills most requirements, except perhaps in the area of performance. If the number of users (the sales reps who take the phone calls) is fewer than five or six, Access's performance will probably be adequate. If the number of users is more than five or six, a relational database server is the technology that will fill all the requirements.

Day 2, "Tools for Database Development in Visual C++ Developer Studio"

Quiz

1. Which editions of Visual C++ enable viewing and editing data from relational databases inside Visual Studio?

   The Visual C++ Professional and Enterprise Editions.

2. What is a DSN?

   A DSN is a data source name. The term *DSN* refers to an ODBC data source created on a computer, which points to some database and specifies some ODBC driver that can read from and write to that database.

3. What gives a database its value and why?

   A database's value is derived from its structure. The better, the more complete, the more descriptive, the more widely accepted the structure of a database, the more valuable its data can be.

4. What is the fundamental requirement for records in relational database?

   Each record must be unique. There must not be any duplicate records in a relational database.

5. What mechanism is used to relate records in different tables to one another?

   Records in different tables are related to each other through primary and foreign keys. A record's primary key uniquely identifies it in the database. That primary key can appear in other tables to indicate a relationship between that record and the records in other tables. A primary key that appears in another table is called a *foreign key*.

Exercises

1. Open the Orders table in the database project you created today. Note the foreign keys that appear in the table. Open the Customers and Products tables and see primary keys for customers and products. Try to change one of the foreign key values, such as a customer number, to a number that doesn't exist as a primary key. What happens? Does the database help enforce the integrity of the data?

   When you try to change one of the foreign key values in the Orders table, such as a customer number, to a number that does not exist as a primary key, the database will not accept the change, and you will get an error message saying that this change would violate referential integrity rules.

F

2. Open the Orders table in the database project you created today. Try to change one of the order numbers in the table by typing in letters for the contents of the field. When you move the cursor off that record, what happens? Does the database validate the data type you tried to enter? (You can press Esc to abort the edit.)

Day 3, "Retrieving Data Through Structured Query Language (SQL)

Quiz

1. What is SQL?

   SQL is an acronym for *Structured Query Language*. SQL is a data manipulation and definition language designed specifically for relational databases.

2. What is an SQL join?

   An SQL join is a SELECT statement that produces a resultset by using data from two or more tables in a relational database.

3. What is wrong with this SQL query?

   ```
   SELECT customers.*
   WHERE customers.custnumber = 3
   ```

   The query is missing the FROM clause. It needs to say the following:

   ```
   SELECT customers.*
   FROM customers
   WHERE customers.custnumber = 3
   ```

4. What is an aggregate function?

   An aggregate function operates on multiple records and returns a single value.

5. What does a cursor make possible?

   A cursor defines a position in a resultset and makes it possible to move through the resultset one record at a time.

Exercises

1. Discover what happens when you add a table name to the FROM clause without mentioning that table in the WHERE class of an SQL SELECT statement, like this:

   ```
   SELECT customers.*
   FROM customer, orders
   WHERE customers.custnumber = 3
   ```

The resultset contains a Cartesian product of the two tables, meaning that if one table has 3 records and the other has 5 records, the resultset will contain 15 records. In the case of the database you've been using today, the resultset will contain 4 records.

2. Add a join to the SQL query shown in Figure 3.22 to retrieve the name of the customer who placed the most recent order.

You must nest the subquery that finds the last order date in the subquery that finds the customer number, which subquery you must nest in the query to obtain the customer information.

```
SELECT 'Customers'.*
FROM 'Customers'
WHERE custnumber IN
(
        SELECT 'Orders'.customernumber
        FROM 'Orders'
        WHERE orderdate =
        (
                SELECT MAX(orderdate)
                FROM Orders
        )
)
```

Day 4, "Retrieving SQL Data Through a C++ API"

Quiz

1. What does a database API do?

A database API translates between the type system of C++ and the type system of the database. It also provides a means for passing SQL code to the database's interpreter for execution and a means for retrieving data queried from the database.

2. What database APIs work with nonrelational data sources?

OLE DB and ADO.

3. What does an ADO Connection object do?

ADO Connection object encapsulates the functionality of logging in to and out of a database, making queries, and retrieving resultsets.

4. What does the *current* record mean?

The current record is the record at which the cursor in the recordset is positioned.

F

Exercises

1. Change the code in Listing 4.12 so that the customers are sorted by last name.

   You need to change line 7 in Listing 4.12 to include an ORDER BY clause on the last-name field.

2. Change the code in Listing 4.12 to display the customer number as well as the customer first and last name.

   You need to add a column to the list control for the customer number. You must also add a call to the Recordset GetCollect function to retrieve the customer number field and store it in a _variant_t. After the GetCollect call, you can simply cast this _variant_t to a _bstr_t, even though the original data type is numeric. _variant_t and _bstr_t handle the conversion for you.

Day 5, "Adding, Modifying, and Deleting Data"

Quiz

1. What is a forward-only cursor?

   A forward-only cursor is a cursor that moves only forward through the resultset.

2. What function do you use to place a value in a field of the current record in an ADO Recordset?

   The PutCollect function places a value in a field in the current record of an ADO Recordset.

3. What is wrong with this SQL statement?

   ```
   DELETE FROM customers
   ```

   Perhaps nothing is wrong with it. However, it's crucial to note that this statement will delete every record in the Customers table because it has no WHERE clause.

4. What are the two arguments that you must pass to the ADO Recordset AddNew function?

   You must pass two arrays of VARIANTs, the first containing the list of fields and the second containing the list of data values to be placed in those fields.

5. What happens if you specify only one field/value pair in the SET clause of the SQL UPDATE function?

   Only the data in that one field is updated. The other fields are unchanged.

Exercises

1. Discover what happens in the Price field when you specify only the PartNumber and ProductName fields in a SQL INSERT statement for the Products table, like this:

```
INSERT INTO Products(PartNumber, ProductName)
VALUES ('xxx', 'yyy')
```

The database will place a default value in the field. In this case, zero is the default value for the Price field, so zero will appear in the Price field of the new record.

2. Modify the code in Listing 5.1 so that it doesn't specify a price for the new record.

You need to change the CreateOneDim function call so that the arrays have two elements instead of three. Then you delete the code that defined the third elements (the Price field name and data) in each array.

```
// Create an array for the list of fields in
// the Products table.
COleSafeArray vaFieldlist;
vaFieldlist.CreateOneDim(VT_VARIANT,2);
// Fill in the field names now.
long lArrayIndex[1];
lArrayIndex[0] = 0;
vaFieldlist.PutElement(lArrayIndex,
  &(_variant_t("PartNumber")));
lArrayIndex[0] = 1;
vaFieldlist.PutElement(lArrayIndex,
  &(_variant_t("ProductName")));
// Create an array for the list of values to go in
// the Products table.
COleSafeArray vaValuelist;
vaValuelist.CreateOneDim(VT_VARIANT,2);
// Fill in the values for each field.
lArrayIndex[0] = 0;
vaValuelist.PutElement(lArrayIndex,
  &(_variant_t("8TRACK-003")));
lArrayIndex[0] = 1;
vaValuelist.PutElement(lArrayIndex,
  &(_variant_t("Bell Bottom Hits")));
```

Day 6, "Harnessing the Power of Relational Database Servers"

F

Quiz

1. What is a single-tier application?

A single-tier application consists of a single program that contains all the code and logic, which runs in one process and tries to accomplish all the work of the application.

2. How do you make the SQL INSERT statement insert multiple records?

   You make the SQL INSERT statement insert multiple records by replacing the VALUES clause with a SELECT statement that returns multiple rows.

3. What databases help you preserve the referential integrity of your data?

   The databases that help you preserve the referential integrity of your data are relational database servers and Microsoft Access.

4. How is a stored procedure in a relational database different from a Query in Microsoft Access?

   A Query in Microsoft Access is not compiled like a stored procedure. A Query in Microsoft Access doesn't execute at the server like a stored procedure. Also, a Query in Microsoft Access is treated as a View in Visual Studio.

5. Where can you find the data types available for use in ADO Parameter objects?

   You can find the data types available for use in ADO Parameter objects in the ParameterDirectionEnum in msado15.tlh.

Exercises

1. Modify the SELECT statement in Listing 6.2 so that the customer number is not hard-coded. Make it so that the customer number is retrieved based on the customer's last name.

   To retrieve the customer number based on the customers last name, the SELECT statement needs to use a subquery. It would look like this:

   ```
   SELECT 4, { d '1998-11-16' },
          (SELECT custnumber
           FROM customers
           WHERE custlastname = 'clinton'),
          PartNumber, Price,
          4, 'MC 1223 9873 2028 8374 9/99'
   FROM Products
   WHERE (PartNumber LIKE '8TRACK%')
   ```

2. Add code to the OrderedSinceDate handler shown in Listing 6.8 to change the value of the parameter after it has been appended to the command but before the Command has been executed.

   The code to change the value of a parameter attached to an ADO Command object could look like this:

   ```
   (pCommand->Parameters->GetItem(_variant_t("ParamDate")))
   ->PutValue(_variant_t(COleDateTime(1998, 11, 15, 0, 0, 0)));
   ```

Day 7, "Database Design"

Quiz

1. What is the highest normal form in the relational database model?

   The highest normal form in the relational model is the domain/key normal form.

2. What are entity relationships?

   Entity relationships are the relationships between records in various tables in a relational database.

3. How can you guarantee that a table conforms to the second normal form?

   The second normal form requires that no fields apply to only part of the primary key. If a table has a single key field, the table is guaranteed of conforming to 2NF.

4. What is the proper term for the structure (the tables, indexes, constraints, and so on) of a relational database?

   The structure of a relational database is called its *schema*.

5. What does a referential integrity constraint do?

   A referential integrity constraint ensures that the records related through primary and foreign keys are not deleted independently of each other. The constraint keeps the records in related tables in synch with each other.

Exercises

1. Write a SELECT statement that shows all the products purchased on each order. Hint: The SELECT statement should perform a join between the NewOrders, ProductsPurchased, and Products tables.

   This SELECT statement shows all the products purchased on each order:

   ```
   SELECT neworders.ordernumber, products.productname
   FROM neworders, productspurchased, products
   WHERE neworders.ordernumber = productspurchased.ordernumber
   AND productspurchased.partnumber = products.partnumber
   ```

2. Write a SELECT statement showing the products purchased by each customer.

   This SELECT statement shows the products purchased by each customer:

   ```
   SELECT customers.custfirstname, customers.custlastname,
   products.productname
   FROM neworders, productspurchased, products, customers
   WHERE neworders.ordernumber = productspurchased.ordernumber
   AND productspurchased.partnumber = products.partnumber
   AND neworders.customernumber = customers.custnumber
   ```

F

Day 8, "Utilizing the Capabilities of Database Servers"

Quiz

1. What are the ACID properties of a transaction?

   The ACID properties of a transaction are atomicity, consistency, isolation, and durability.

2. What is the isolation level of a transaction?

   The isolation level of a transaction is a setting in the database that specifies how zealous it should be in protecting a user's work from interaction with the work of other concurrent users.

3. How does the GROUP BY clause interact with the SQL aggregate functions?

   Placing a GROUP BY clause with an aggregate function in a SELECT statement causes the aggregate function to perform its calculation on sets of records that are determined by the GROUP BY clause.

4. How many triggers can be attached to a table in Microsoft SQL Server?

   Three triggers can be attached to a table in Microsoft SQL Server: an insert trigger, an update trigger, and a delete trigger.

5. Does a view on a large table occupy much room in the database? Why or why not?

   A view on a large table doesn't occupy much room in the database because the view stores no records. Only the SQL SELECT statement that defines the view is stored in the database (and a SELECT statement is relatively small).

Exercises

1. Modify the SELECT statement in Listing 8.7 so that the resultset is sorted by the total sales volume, from the highest volume to the least.

   The code to sort the resultset in order to total sales, the highest first, would look like this:

   ```
   SELECT neworders.ordernumber,
   SUM(price + shippingandhandling)
   FROM neworders, productspurchased
   WHERE neworders.ordernumber = productspurchased.ordernumber
   GROUP BY neworders.ordernumber
   ORDER BY SUM(price + shippingandhandling) DESC
   ```

2. Modify the SELECT statement in Listing 8.7 so that the query returns the average product price, from the highest to the least.

The code to return the average product price, from the highest to the least, would look like this:

```
SELECT neworders.ordernumber,
AVG(price)
FROM neworders, productspurchased
WHERE neworders.ordernumber = productspurchased.ordernumber
GROUP BY neworders.ordernumber
ORDER BY AVG(price) DESC
```

Day 9, "Understanding COM"

Quiz

1. Why can't you load a DLL into memory and send messages to it from your app?

   When your application loads a DLL into memory, the DLL becomes part of your app. Your app cannot send messages (window messages or otherwise) to the DLL and have the DLL act independent of your application. The DLL code is mapped into your app's address space, and any objects the DLL creates, your app owns.

2. What makes a C++ class an abstract base class?

   An abstract base class must have at least one pure virtual function as a member. A pure virtual function is a function with =0 after its declaration.

3. What is a class factory?

   A class factory is a class that knows how to create instances of a class that is a COM server. A class factory must be implemented in every COM DLL and EXE. The class factory exposes a function named CreateInstance, which the OS can call to get pointers to instances of the COM servers whose code resides in that file.

4. Why is it necessary for a COM client to call Release on a COM server after it's finished with it?

   The Release function decrements the usage count for that COM object (the server). When the usage count reaches zero, the server object is deleted or is told to delete itself. If no clients are using a server object, it can and should be deleted to free its resources.

5. What is a CLSID, and why must all CLSIDs be unique?

   A CLSID uniquely identifies a COM server. The CLSID is used in the registry to store information on the location of the DLL or EXE file that contains the COM server code. If there were duplicate CLSIDs, there would be a chance that one CLSID could be overwritten by another in the registry, preventing the first one from ever being launched. Also, COM clients expect certain behavior and support for certain interfaces from COM servers, based on the CLSID. The uniqueness of the CLSID makes that expectation possible.

F

Exercises

1. Add another method to the IDbComponent interface. Make this method take, as a parameter, an address to a variable of some sort. Modify this variable in the server code and make sure it gets back okay to the client.

   The important thing for a parameter that is passed in to the server to be modified and returned is that it be marked as [out] in the Parameters edit box in the Add Method to Interface dialog.

2. Use the ATL COM AppWizard to create a COM server in an EXE. Expose a function in its interface that is similar to one in the DLL COM server. Compare the performance of the EXE-based COM server (the out-of-proc server) versus the DLL-based COM server (the inproc server).

   You should find that the out-of-proc server is much slower—has much more function call overhead—than the inproc server.

Day 10, "Database Client Technologies and the Secrets of ADO"

Quiz

1. What is the goal or purpose of ODBC?

   The goal or purpose of ODBC is to provide a uniform API for communicating with relational databases from different vendors.

2. How is ODBC's call-level interface different from embedded SQL?

   ODBC's call-level interface differs from embedded SQL in that the SQL code in an ODBC application is not compiled by a precompiler and translated to native database calls. Rather, the SQL code in an ODBC application is interpreted at run-time by the database (or by the database's ODBC driver).

3. Where does the ADO type library reside and how can you view it?

   The ADO type library resides in the ADO DLL, which is called MSADO15.DLL and is typically installed in the C:\Program Files\Common Files\System\ADO directory. You can view the ADO type library by using the OLE-COM Object Viewer included with Microsoft Visual Studio.

4. Why does ADO throw exceptions when errors occur?

   ADO throws exceptions when errors occur because that is how the high-level ADO functions produced by #import are implemented. The code for the high-level ADO functions can be found in the MSADO15.TLI file.

5. What function that you use with `#import` does not throw exceptions but returns a failed HRESULT instead?

   The smart pointer `CreateInstance` function doesn't throw exceptions but returns a failed HRESULT in the case of an error.

Exercises

1. Set break points in the inline functions in MSADO15.TLI, such as the `_Connection::Open` function, and run ADOMFC1 in debug mode to develop a feel for how code in MSADO15.TLH and MSADO15.TLI is executed. Debug step into all the functions to discern when you are executing code in your ADOMFC1 project and when you are executing code in the ADO DLL.

   When you set breakpoints in the MSADO15.TLI file, you will find that the functions with the `raw_` prefix directly call into the ADO library.

2. Modify the code in Listing 10.7 so that the call to the ADO `Command Execute` function in line 24 directly calls the low-level `Execute` function.

   The code for the `Execute` call should look like this:
   ```
   22:        _RecordsetPtr pRS;
   23:
   24:        hr = pCommand->Raw_Execute( &vNull, &vNull, adCmdUnknown,
           ➥&pRS );
   ```

Day 11, "Multitier Architectures"

Quiz

1. Interfaces and abstractions are the two pillars on which multitier applications rest. Each tier that provides an effective level of abstraction has interfaces that are understandable and distinct. Distinct interfaces between the tiers enable the tiers to be updated independently of each other.

2. Thin client programs are often more desirable than fat clients, because they do not require updates as often as fat client programs.

3. HTML specifies how information will be displayed. XML specifies what the data is and what it means.

4. In a typical RDS application, the RDS `DataControl` object is instantiated on the client machine in the browser's process space. Often COM server(s) such as ActiveX controls are also instantiated in the browser to enable a feature-rich UI. The RDS `DataControl` object causes a `DataFactory` object to be instantiated on the middle tier (Web server) machine.

F

5. The security risk posed by the RDS COM servers is caused by the fact that the DataFactory object can be instantiated on a Web server machine. This can provide access to the database to anyone on the Web who knows a valid data source, username, and password for that database.

Day 12, "Using Microsoft Transaction Server to Build Scalable Applications"

Quiz

1. DCOM alone is insufficient for building multitier applications because DCOM by itself provides no support for transactions, thread pooling, or database connection pooling. You would have to write those features yourself to develop a multitier application with just DCOM and without MTS.

2. [out, retval] is the specification in IDL for a parameter that is the return value of the method.

3. Yes, MTS will run on Windows 98, if the machine has at least 32MB of RAM.

4. Each MTS package specifies a process in which MTS components are to run. This enables process isolation, as well as common security settings for the collection of components that reside in the package.

5. A disconnected Recordset is an ADO Recordset that contains data but currently has no a connection to a database. Disconnected Recordsets can be sent between COM servers and clients as a flexible and powerful data structure.

Exercises

1. The linker will produce an error because it cannot open the DLL file for writing. This is because the DLL is loaded. To fix the problem, you need to click the Refresh button on IE4 or exit IE4 completely. Sometimes even this does not work. At those times, you need to shut down the server processes using the Transaction Server Explorer by right-clicking My Computer and selecting Shutdown Server Process.

2. Run the Transaction Server Explorer and navigate to the package that contains MTSComp1.Component1. Select MTSComp1.Component1 and press the Delete key to remove the component from MTS. To register the DLL so that you can use it as a normal COM server, enter regsvr32 MTSComp1.DLL from the DOS prompt in the directory where the DLL resides. You might need to mark it safe for scripting and initialization again.

Day 13, "Melding Object-Oriented Programming with Relational Databases"

Quiz

1. You can't store C++ objects in relational database fields because the only things that the database lets you store in fields are instances of the data types that exist in the database's type system.

2. You can't use SQL for object-oriented programming because the language has no object constructs or mechanisms. Its sole purpose is to manipulate data in two-dimensional tables inside relational databases.

3. C++ object databases directly support the C++ type system, including types (classes) that programmers create themselves. Data in C++ object databases is accessible only to C++ programs that understand the types (the classes) that are stored therein. A relational database supports only the data types that it defines. The data in relational databases is accessible to any application that can understand the relational model and that can map between its type system and the database's type system.

4. When you are designing an application that will use object and relational technology, it is generally best to start by designing the relational database schema. You can then use the schema as the basis for the object schema.

5. The benefits of a live object cache include greatly improved application performance because of reduced database access, and reduced network traffic, again because of reduced database access.

Exercises

1. This SELECT statement retrieves the shoe type based on the shoe ID from the Shoes table.

```
SELECT ShoeType
FROM Shoes
WHERE ShoeID = 1
```

F

2. This SELECT statement shows the products purchased by each customer.

```
SELECT Shoes.*, BasketballShoes.*
FROM Shoes, BasketballShoes
WHERE Shoes.ShoeID = BasketballShoes.ShoeID
```

Day 14, "Legacy Database APIs"

Quiz

1. CDatabase

2. The environment handle saves information necessary for the application to connect to a data source. The Driver Manager will construct the handle and then give the connected driver a copy.

3. dbDBEngine. No

4. CRecordSet::dynaset

Exercises

1. You can find the DAO classes in the OLE/COM Object Viewer by expanding the All Objects element in the tree control in the left window pane. The DAO classes all start with DAO. To view the type information, double-click one of the classes to instantiate the object, double-click one of the non-IUnknown interfaces, and click the View Type Info button.

Chapter 15, "The ODBC API and the MFC ODBC Classes"

Quiz

1. The Record Field Exchange (RFX) implemented by DoFieldExchange().

2. The document class contains the recordset. The Document in the MFC Document/View architecture represents the application's data store, whereas the View is a window to that data.

3. OnInitialUpdate

4. CRecordSet::dynaset

Exercises

1. The edit boxes should match the field declarations in the AddressBook database. Yes, the fields are updated whenever the cursor is moved. This is accomplished via the Record Field Exchange (RFX) implemented by DoFieldExchange(). The ODBC wrappers implement the cursor as part of the recordset, and the View automatically creates a message interface from the cursor buttons to the recordset's cursors.

2. Identical to answer 1.

3. The code should look something like this:

```
rs.AddNew();
rs.m_Last_Name = "Smith";
rs.m_First_Name = "Jennifer";
rs.Street = "234 WayWay St.";
rs.m_City = "Columbus";
rs.m_State = "OH";
rs.m_Zip = 45400;
rs.m_Phone = "614-5550101";
rs.Update();
```

Day 16, "The Ultimate Database API: OLE DB"

Quiz

1. What are the two basic OLE DB components?

   A data provider and a data consumer. A data provider is an application that responds to queries and returns data in a usable form. A data consumer is an application, or other COM component, that uses the OLE DB API to access a data source.

2. How does OLE DB currently enable access to ODBC data sources for which no OLE DB provider is yet available?

   The OLE DB SDK contains an OLE DB provider for ODBC data, called MSDASQL, which allows you to access ODBC data sources from OLE DB consumer applications. The OLE DB provider for ODBC resides in MSDASQL.DLL.

3. What are the major OLE DB objects?

   The OLE DB. The major OLE DB components are called CoTypes. The OLE DB CoTypes are TDataSource, TDBSession, TCommand, TRowset, TIndex, TErrorObject, and TTransaction.

4. Which header files must be included to access OLE DB objects?

   The header files OLEDB.H and OLEDBERR.H must be included for OLE DB applications. These header files are used to include the OLE DB classes and OLE DB error-handling classes, respectively.

5. What is the URL for the OLE DB home page?

   The URL of the OLE DB Web site is http://www.microsoft.com/data/oledb/.

F

Day 17, "Accessing a Data Source with OLE DB"

Quiz

1. What is the role of a data provider and a data consumer in the OLE DB architecture?

   A data provider is a COM component that provides an OLE DB–compliant interface. A data consumer is an application or component that uses an OLE DB interface to access a data source.

2. What is an interface? How does the COM architecture use an interface?

   Interfaces describe the functionality provided by the component and also provide the structured mechanism that these components use to talk with each other. A COM component is an object that uses the rules in the COM specification to provide access to the interfaces provided by a component.

3. What is interface factoring?

   Interface factoring is the capability of COM objects to support multiple interfaces, which can provide different levels of functionality, depending on the consumer. A consumer uses the interface appropriate to its needs.

4. What method is used to determine whether a COM object supports a particular interface?

   The interfaces supported by a COM component can be determined by calling the `QueryInterface` method. When an application determines whether a component supports a specific interface, it is guaranteed the functionality of that interface.

5. Describe the basic flow of information in an OLE DB application.

   The consumer application uses the `Enumerator` object to determine which OLE DB data source providers are available. It then creates a `DataSource` object and uses the `DataSource` object to create a `Session` object. Then the application uses the `Session` object to create a `Command` object. The application uses the `Command` object's `Execute` function to create a `Rowset` object. Next, the application navigates through the `Rowset` containing the data. Finally, the application releases the objects.

6. What is an `Enumerator` object, and how is it used?

   The `Enumerator` class retrieves information regarding all the OLE DB providers available on the system.

7. What interfaces are supported by an `Enumerator` object?

   The `Enumerator` object supports the following interfaces: `IparseDisplayName`, `IsourcesRowset`, `IDBInitialize`, `IDBProperties`, and `IsupportErrorInfo`.

8. What is a `DataSource` object, and how is it created?

The `DataSource` object abstracts the actual data source. It is created by binding a moniker returned from the `Enumerator` class or by directly calling `CoCreateInstance`, using the appropriate `CLSID`.

9. What interfaces does a `DataSource` object support?

The `DataSource` object supports the following interfaces: `IDBCreateSession`, `IDBInitialize`, `IDBProperties`, `Ipersist`, `IDBDataSourceAdmin`, `IDBInfo`, `IpersistFile`, and `IsupportErrorInfo`.

10. What methods initialize and release the DLLs required by a COM application?

The `CoInitialize` and `CoUninitialize` functions load and release the appropriate COM-related DLLs. You must call these functions at the start and end of any application that uses COM.

Exercises

1. Review the Visual C++ books online documentation (provided with Visual C++) for more information regarding the specifics of COM programming.

Several places in the online documentation deal with COM. The best way to find them is to search for terms such as *COM*, *QueryInterface*, and *OLE DB*. When you find a useful article (or document), press the Locate button to find that article in the table of contents. Often you will find other useful information in the neighboring documents.

2. The applications developed yesterday and today do not really consider error handling. How would you integrate error handling into the application in Listing 17.4? (*Hint*: Most of the COM related functions return an `HRESULT` type value.)

You should always check the value of the `HRESULT`s returned by COM functions.

Chapter 18, "Querying a Data Source with OLE DB"

F

Quiz

1. The `Session` object provides a context for transactions and commands. A `Session` object is created by using the `IDBCreateSession` interface of the `DataSource` object. The `CreateSession` method of this interface actually creates a session. You can use the `Session` object to create a `Command` object, to access a row set directly, and to create or modify data source tables and indexes.

2. The IDBSchemaRowset retrieves data source schema information. Schema information describes the data contained in the data source. The IDBSchemaRowset interface is optional for Session objects.

3. The Command object performs commands that the provider supports. Using the SQL Server data provider (or even the OLE DB ODBC provider) and a database such as SQL Server, you can use the Command object to execute SQL commands. OLE DB data providers aren't required to support commands.

4. The ICommandText interface sets and retrieves the actual command text, which specifies the data source command to execute. The Command object requires the ICommandText interface.

5. In SQL, parameters in commands are usually specified with the ? placeholder. The actual parameter value replaces the ?. Parameterized statements are similar to procedures in any programming language; they are useful for executing a particular statement repeatedly. A parameterized statement can execute a command whose parameters are specified while an application is running.

6. The ICommandPrepare interface converts a command to a prepared command. A prepared command is a command that has been precompiled so that it can execute faster. If you expect a command to be executed repeatedly, transforming it into a prepared command can improve application performance.

Day 20, "Properties, Transactions, and Indexes"

Quiz

1. List the major property groups.

   The major property groups are DBPROPSET_COLUMN_DATASOURCE, DBPROPSET_DATASOURCEINFO, DBPROPSET_DATAINIT, DBPROPSET_INDEX, DBPROPSET_ROWSET, DBPROPSET_SESSION, and DBPROPSET_TABLE. These groups are used to group properties in the DBPROPIDSET and DBPROPSET structures.

2. What structure returns the collection of property values?

   The DBPROPSET structure holds the collection of property values when retrieving and setting properties.

3. Name the property that determines the level of SQL command support provided by an OLE DB data provider?

   The DBPROP_SQLSUPPORT property determines the level of SQL command support provided by an OLE DB data provider.

4. What method opens a transaction?

    The StartTransaction method opens a transaction.

5. What isolation level maintains the most consistent access to a row set in a multi-user environment?

    The ISOLATIONLEVEL_SERIALIZABLE flag specifies the serializable isolation level, which offers the highest level of data integrity inside a transaction.

6. What property ensures that a row set is retained in a valid state after a transaction is closed?

    The Rowset property DBPROP_COMMITPRESERVE determines the state of a row set when a transaction is committed or aborted. If true, the row set is resynchronized to reflect the results of the transaction; otherwise, the row set becomes invalid.

7. What Index object method searches for a specific key value in an index?

    The Seek method of the Index object searches for a specific key value.

Day 21, "OLE DB Error Handling"

Quiz

1. Name the two macros used to check the result of an OLE DB method call.

    Visual C++ provides two macros that can determine generally whether a method was successful. These macros are SUCCEEDED and FAILED. As you can tell by their names, the SUCCEEDED macro returns true if the call to the method is successful, and the FAILED macro returns true if the call to the method is not successful.

2. Which interface checks whether an OLE DB object supports extended error information?

    The IsupportErrorInfo interface determines whether an object supports the necessary interfaces to retrieve additional error information. The IsupportErrorInfo defines a single method, InterfaceSupportsErrorInfo, that returns S_OK if additional error information is supported.

3. What are the special requirements of OLE DB error handling that aren't resolved by Automation error-handling objects?

    The OLE DB has two requirements that the standard IerrorInfo interface does not meet:

    - OLE DB must return provider-specific error information.
    - OLE DB must return multiple error values at the same time, but the IerrorInfo interface can return information regarding one error only.

F

4. What information does the `GetBasicErrorInfo` method return? Describe the elements of this structure.

   The `GetBasicErrorInfo` method retrieves the basic `ERRORINFO` structure for the record number specified in the `lRecNum` parameter. The `ERRORINFO` structure holds basic information about an error.

5. How do you retrieve a custom error object? What custom error objects does OLE DB provide?

   The `GetCustomErrorObject` method retrieves a provider-specific custom error. OLE DB provides one custom error interface for providers that support the SQL command language: `ISQLErrorInfo`. The `ISQLErrorInfo` method returns the current SQL status and error value. The `dwMinor` field contains a provider-specific error value. The `clsid` field contains the class ID of the OLE DB object that generated this error. The `iid` parameter contains the interface ID of the interface that generated this error. The `dispid` field contains the method that generated the error.

6. List the basic techniques for OLE DB error handling.

   The basic error-handling techniques are the following:

   - Check the `HRESULT` value of a method when it is called.
   - If the method did not succeed, possibly print some error information.
   - If the error is critical to the execution of the application, gracefully end the application. Be sure to release any allocated memory and close any open data sources and files.
   - If the error is not critical (perhaps the data provider doesn't support a specific method), dynamically change the functionality of the application. For example, an application feature might not be available with lower-level data providers.

7. Which method does a data provider use to add a new error?

   Data providers use the `AddErrorRecord` method to add new error records.

8. Explain the difference between `HRESULT` constants with the prefix `DB_S` and those with the prefix `DB_E`.

   `HRESULT` constants that begin with `S` or `DB_S` are values that indicate success, and `HRESULT` constants that begin with `E` or `DB_E` are error value constants.

INDEX

D

Other Related Titles

What's on the CD-ROM

The companion CD-ROM contains Chapters 3–5 and 8–9 of the book, all the authors' source code, samples from the book, and some third-party software products.

Windows NT 3.5.1 Installation Instructions

1. Insert the CD-ROM disc into your CD-ROM drive.

2. From File Manager or Program Manager, choose Run from the File menu.

3. Type `<drive>\START.EXE` and press Enter, where `<drive>` corresponds to the drive letter of your CD-ROM. For example, if your CD-ROM is drive D:, type `D:\START.EXE` and press Enter.

4. Follow the onscreen instructions to finish the installation.

Windows 95, Windows 98, and Windows NT 4 Installation Instructions

1. Insert the CD-ROM disc into your CD-ROM drive.

2. From the desktop, double-click the My Computer icon.

3. Double-click the icon representing your CD-ROM drive.

4. Double-click the icon titled `START.EXE` to run the installation program.

5. Follow the onscreen instructions to finish the installation.

> **NOTE**
>
> If Windows 95, Windows 98, or Windows NT 4 is installed on your computer and you have the AutoPlay feature enabled, the `START.EXE` program starts automatically whenever you insert the disc into your CD-ROM drive.

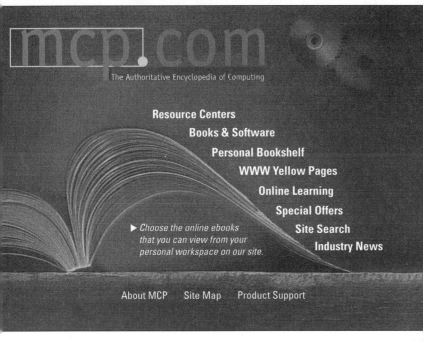

Which Database Technology Is Right for Your Visual C++ Application?

As a Visual C++ programmer, several database technologies are available to you. This book will teach you about the database technologies available to you and how to use them with Visual C++.

The table on the inside back cover illustrates the relative strengths and weaknesses of the various database technologies. In this table, a plus sign (+) indicates a strength of the technology, a minus sign (–) indicates a weakness, a blank indicates no particular strength or weakness, and a question mark (?) indicates that it varies between vendors or implementations of the technology.

- *Openness of the data* refers to the capability of other routines or applications to make sense of the data file without access to your source code.

- *Complex data models* refers to the technology's capability to handle applications that have complex data entities and relationships.

- *Multiuser* refers to the capability of multiple threads, applications, and users to access the data simultaneously.

- *Performance* refers to the speed with which data can be read from and written to the database.

- *Scalability and capacity* refers to the database's capability to sustain good performance as the amount of data increases.

- *Set-based operations in code* indicates whether the technology offers set-based operations in its programming model.

- *Set-based operations at the server* refers to the capability of the technology to process data at the server without having to send it all to the client machine to be processed.

- *Embeddable with your application* indicates how easy or difficult it would be to ship this technology with a commercial application.

- *Data validation/integrity* refers to the database's capability to validate the data to ensure the integrity of the data.

- *Code-to-functionality ratio* refers to how much code you have to write compared to the database functionality you get from that code.